A Century United

A Century United

The Centenary History of Southend United

Peter Miles & Dave Goody

Shrimper Publishing Limited

First published in Great Britain by Shrimper Publishing Limited 2007

ISBN 978-0-9555976-0-2

Printed by HSW Print, Cambrian Industrial Park, Tonypandy, Rhondda CF40 2XX

Published by Shrimper Publishing Limited, PO Box 1025, Hockley, Essex SS5 5WS

Contents

Acknowledgements

There have been many people who have helped the authors with the complex task of compiling this book; some to a greater extent than others, but all have played their part, for which we are eternally grateful. Those that deserve a large "pat on the back" are:-

Mr. Geoffrey King, Dave Scriven and all those at Southend United Football Club, who have been patient and supportive whilst we have done our best to produce a book that maintains the high standards set by the club itself.

Chris Phillips, Luan Marshall and all at the Evening Echo (echo-news.co.uk) for their help and support, and for providing us with many of the photos used to illustrate the chapters relating to the last twenty years.

Peter Flower for providing comprehensive information on the otherwise elusive Southend Invicta Rugby League club.

Vince Taylor at Groundtastic Magazine for sourcing some hitherto unseen photos of both The Kursaal and The Stadium.

Phil Cox, Keith Roe and Paul Yeomanson for supplying numerous instances of additional material.

Dave "Nobbler "Brabbing, Jeff Shillingford and Terry Jeffreys for carrying out proofreading duties, and also providing moral support throughout what has been a long, hard project.

Gary Bray (unicomsystems.co.uk) for allowing us to use many of the pictures he took when he was the official photographer of Southend United in the 1980's.

Julian Flanders for his encouragement when we felt the whole project would be beyond our capabilities.

Ben Shingleton (onrec.com) and George Crockford (maniike.com) for their help in getting our InDesign skills above zero.

Jeff Della Mura (fuse.uk.net) for his help and advice on the design and layout of the book.

Katey J (kateyj.com) for spending more hours than could be reasonably expected designing the cover.

Phil Hitchman (hitchman.co.uk) for his help with our fantastic website (shrimperpublishing.co.uk).

All at HSW Print (hswprint.co.uk) for their advice, help and professionalism in the production of this book.

The authors would also like to thank the invaluable assistance given at Southend Library over a period of several years.

Shrimper Publishing Limited

Shrimper Publishing are always interested in hearing from our readers, whether it is with comments about our books, updates or corrections to one of our existing books, or with ideas for future titles. If you'd like to contact us, you can email us at comments@shrimperpublishing.co.uk, or you can write to us at the following address:-

Shrimper Publishing Limited
PO Box 1025
Hockley
Essex
SS5 5WS

If you have a book burning inside you (preferably football or sporting-based) or you have already written one and are looking to get it published, why not contact us; we may be able to help.

Introduction

The history of Southend United Football Club is not just the story of how eleven men have kicked a ball around in the name of the town; it is much more than that. From the first meeting in 1906, many great men (and women) have been involved in the creation, development and, ultimately, the success of a club that many thousands have followed over its one hundred year history.

From humble beginnings at a Roots Hall ground unrecognisable from that of today, through the famous Kursaal, with its fairground and watershute, onto The Stadium with its dog track and giant tote board, and finally back to a new and improved Roots Hall, there are hundreds of fascinating stories that go to make up the history of our club.

Whether you are an old supporter who has followed the club for many years or a new supporter who is just beginning to get captivated by the sound, feel and smell of football at Southend United, there will be something in this book to make you smile, grimace, laugh and cheer. Memories that have long been pushed to the back of the mind will come tumbling forth, some good, some painful. Last-minute winners, long fruitless trips away from home, stunning goals, terrible players, cup giant-killings, favourite players being sold, packed stadiums on a Friday night, dodgy kits, journeys to Cardiff, open-top bus parades, flirtations with non-league status; it's all here, plus lots more. Whether you read it from cover to cover, or flick through at your leisure, moments you witnessed, heard about, read about or just imagined from looking at the scores on Teletext will be brought vividly back to life.

We hope we have managed to capture much of what has made the history of Southend United Football Club great in these pages; we are sure that many of you will have events etched in your mind that we may not have included, and for that we are sorry. But there is only a finite amount that a book can contain, and we have done our best to include everything that we believe has had a major effect on the history of this club; we hope you agree, and that you enjoy the book.

Peter Miles and Dave Goody

Dedications

Peter Miles would like to dedicate this book to his Dad, Len. Words escape me when I try to adequately describe your support, dedication and selflessness. *Grazie per tutto il mio padre.*

Dave Goody would like to dedicate this book to the memory of his late Dad, Jim. If I turn out to be half the person you were, I will be a very great man. I love you Dad.

Illustrations

Many of the photographs and illustrations used in this book have been taken from original programmes, newspapers and magazines. To source high quality items that would reproduce well from the club's early years has proved to be very difficult, so we have been forced to use some photographs and illustrations that were not of the standard we would ideally have liked to use. We took the decision that it was better to use items of a slightly lower quality than not to use them at all, thus enabling you, the reader, the see how the club has progressed and grown through these first one hundred years. Some of those lower quality items are very rare and have not seen the light of day since they were first published, so we hope you will agree that their inclusion has been worthwhile.

FOOTBALL IN SOUTHEND BEFORE THE SHRIMPERS

Southend and Its Development

The name of Southend dates back to the early fourteenth century, although the first documentary evidence to "Southende" is recorded in 1481. The term refers to the path leading down from Prittlewell village to the seashore; villagers used the path to gather gravel from the shore for building work. Eventually, in the early eighteenth century, the shore from Shoebury in the east to Hadleigh in the west was used for oyster cultivation. Indeed fishermen's cottages were the first dwellings built around the area currently occupied by The Kursaal.

Ironically, it was the rapid expansion of "South End" that eventually killed the oyster industry in Victorian times due to pollution of the Thames estuary. By the 1790's, bathing resorts such as Scarborough and Margate were in vogue and Southend soon became popular due to the apparent restorative qualities of the sea water. The burgeoning town was initially called New Southend.

The resort boomed and enjoyed royal patronage, with numerous coach companies beating a path to the town. The original incarnation of the world famous pleasure pier was opened in 1830 and steamboats could dock easily without risking getting stuck in tidal mud. By 1856, Southend Central train station had opened, connecting London to the coastal towns of Tilbury and Southend. This had a massive impact on the numbers of visitors and migrants to the town; the local population exploded.

The Southend Local Board of Health, the precursor to the town council, was established in 1866 and eventually took over the running of Prittlewell parish. Between 1871 and 1901 the census records the town's population rising from just under 5,000 to in excess of 27,000. The townsfolk had the need for entertainment and it was during Victorian times that football came to the area.

Football in the town of Southend

Football had begun to rise to prominence when Southend Athletic won the South Essex League in the 1904/05 season. In the same season, Leigh Ramblers celebrated victory in the Essex Junior Cup, soundly defeating Braintree Manor Works 4-1 in the final. The 1905/06 season was less successful for the Athletic, as they relinquished

Southend Athletic Football Club
Champions of the South-Eastern League 1904-05

their South Essex League title to South Weald. The 1905/06 Southend Charity Shield was contested between Shoebury Garrison and Leigh Rectory Yard, with the soldiers victorious by two goals to one; the chosen charity to benefit in this year was the Leigh Nursing Fund. Another prestigious local tournament was the Shoebury Junior Cup, and in 1905/06 Shoebury Town defeated Shamrocks 3-1 in a hotly contested final. It was Town's second win in a row as they had defeated Southend Victoria by a single goal in the previous year's final. Interestingly as it turned out, the Essex Senior Cup was contested by two South Essex League clubs, South Weald and Wanstead, the latter won by two goals to nil, with their prolific marksman Harold Halse scoring twice. The South Essex League had a Second Division which was split into two geographical sections, East and West. Leigh Ramblers won the Eastern Section while Barking Victoria headed the Western Division. A play-off final for the overall Second Division was held but even after extra time the two clubs could not raise a goal between them. Bigger clubs came to the Borough looking for talent and in early 1905, Andrew Ducat, a Southend Athletic player, signed professional forms with the Woolwich Arsenal club. More locally there were two further competitions, the Southend and District League, which had two divisions, and the Mara League. In the Mara League for 1905/06, a dead heat was the outcome between Leigh Ramblers and "The Zebras" of Southend Corinthians. Strangely, Corinthians drew level on goal difference by winning their final game 6-0 against Southend Ramblers, despite fielding only ten men.

Corinthians played at West Street and were none too popular with other local clubs. This was due to a tie-in with the Selection Committee of the Southend Schools League, whereby Corinthians would be boosted each year by the best five boys selected by the committee on the grounds that they were now too old to compete in the Schools League. Something of a campaign was waged against the Corinthians club but the local schoolmasters agreed that selection of the boys by the committee would give the youngsters something to strive for.

The Southend Corinthians club was run by Charles Stein and their first season had been the 1904/05 campaign. They had lost only four of their 28 matches and therefore decided to apply for membership of the South Essex League for the 1905/06 season. The club had a strict code of conduct which was derived from the great Corinthian club itself. Their overwhelming ethos was

to promote young local talent at all costs and the playing membership was strictly limited to 27 individuals per season. The regular members of the first eleven were always presented with a pierced silver badge to be worn on a watch chain. The medal had the Borough coat of arms in relief with the club name in raised letters, set off by enamel bands of dark and light blue. Loyalty and distinguished service to the Corinthian club would be marked by the presentation of a gold centre badge and in cases of extreme merit the entire silver medal would be replaced by a solid gold version.

There was a slight amendment to schools football in 1906, when the age limit was abolished and a Schools representative side would be entered into a local League playing home matches on the lower field at Chalkwell Hall Park; a reserve team would contest a schedule of friendly matches.

The 1906 Annual General Meetings of local Leagues and clubs provide some interesting information. The AGM of the Southend and District League was slightly inconclusive, final accounts not being available due to "certain circumstances" and the formation of the First Division was dependent on the membership of Southend Athletic, which at the time of the meeting (May 14th 1906) was undecided pending their contesting of membership for the Southern League. The AGM decided that the First Division would remain one with a six team membership while Division Two would be split into two Leagues of six members. In the 1905/06 season, a Second Division of twelve teams resulted in only four clubs complet-

South Essex League Division 1							
Final Table 1905/06							
	P	W	D	L	F	A	Pts
South Weald	12	9	1	2	30	10	19
Wanstead	12	7	2	3	38	10	16
Southend Athletic	12	7	2	3	17	11	16
Barking	12	5	3	4	17	16	13
Romford	12	3	2	7	12	22	8
Chelmsford	12	3	1	8	22	44	7
Woodford	12	2	1	9	15	33	5

South Essex League Division 2 (Eastern)							
Final Table 1905/06							
	P	W	D	L	F	A	Pts
Leigh Ramblers	14	10	2	2	28	15	22
Shoebury Garrison*	14	10	1	3	35	13	19
Leigh Rectory Yard	14	6	3	5	31	33	15
Southend Victoria	14	5	4	5	28	10	14
Shoebury Town	14	6	2	6	27	34	14
Southend Athletic "A"	14	4	4	6	21	28	12
Southend Corinthians	14	3	4	7	22	29	10
Southend Wesleyans	14	1	2	11	15	36	4
* Two points deducted for breach of registration rules							

Southend & District League Division 1				
Last Published Table 1905/06				
	P	W	D	L	Pts
Shoebury Garrison	8	6	1	1	13
Southend Victoria	9	6	1	2	13
Southend Athletic	8	2	5	1	9
Leigh Ramblers	9	3	3	3	9
Leigh Rectory Yard	10	2	1	7	5
Shoebury Town	10	1	3	6	5

on May 23rd, the AGM of the Southend Victoria club announced a modest profit of £4 18s, sufficient to continue running teams in both the South Essex League and the Southend and District League. The AGM of the Southend Athletic club, held the same month, was the most revealing of all. The club had failed to win any of the competitions they entered for, relinquishing their grip on the South Essex League Championship and the Chelmsford Charity Cup. The club announced a trading loss of 12s 5d for the season; significantly, receipts had dropped from £524 17s 4d in 1904/05 to £315 6s 3d, a deficit of £209 in a single season. The major factor in this was a significant loss in revenue from gate receipts, dropping from £427 to £240.

There was a motion to move back to the ground in Prittlewell (Roots Hall) but the motion failed when the best season at Prittlewell compared less favourably to the worst at Marine Park, their current ground. Mr R.A. Jones suggested that either turning fully professional or even semi-pro-

Southend & District League Division 2				
Last Published Table 1905/06				
	P	W	D	L	Pts
Southend Shamrock	22	19	2	1	40
Rochford Congregational	21	16	2	3	34
Shoebury Garrison II	20	15	2	3	32
Rayleigh United	19	11	0	8	22
Leigh Ramblers II	20	9	4	7	22
Hadleigh United	22	10	1	11	21
Southchurch Rovers	21	8	4	9	20
Leigh Park Rangers	22	9	1	12	19
Stambridge United	21	5	1	15	11
Southend Wesleyans	21	5	1	15	11
Benfleet United	21	3	0	18	6

ing all their fixtures. The only other matter attended to was the application for membership to the Southend and District League of two clubs, Southend Borough Officials and Wickford. Therefore a re-election ballot was contested between the two new applicants and the bottom two in Division Two from the previous campaign, Southend Wesleyans and Benfleet United. Benfleet had performed poorly in the League and there were doubts as to whether Wesleyans would continue at all for the coming season, so the two new clubs were successful in their application. Meanwhile,

fessional would ensure bigger gates at Marine Park and attract better talent, bemoaning the fact that "The A's" forward line had not been the same since the departure of Ducat to Woolwich Arsenal. Jones proposed the motion for professionalism and stated that he was prepared to finance a professional outfit in conjunction with like minded gentlemen of the Borough. However, the motion was deferred and the committee decided to carry on as normal despite the rumblings of a proposed professional club being formed for the coming season. In fact, the only significant matter decided at Athletic's AGM was the changing of the colour of the club from an all red kit to blue shirts and white shorts!

Andy Ducat

The town's first prominent player, Andrew Ducat was born in Brixton on February 16th 1886, but was brought up locally as his father ran a builders firm in the Borough; he was educated at the Brewery Road School and later Compton House School. Ducat's playing career began with the Westcliff Athletic club before stepping up a level with Southend Athletic. He signed for Woolwich Arsenal on January 10th 1905, initially on amateur forms but turned professional a month later. In total he played 199 first team games for Arsenal, scoring 23 goals from his wing half position; he won the Southern Charity Cup in 1906 and in the 1906/07 season helped Arsenal become London League and South Eastern League champions. Ducat made his full England debut against Scotland in 1910 and won six caps in total. In June 1912 he moved to Aston Villa for a fee of £1,000 and with them won an F.A.Cup winners medal in 1920 when Huddersfield Town were defeated 1-0 in the final. He played 74 times for Villa scoring four goals before moving in May 1921 to Fulham for £2,000. He retired from playing professional football in 1924 having played 64 times for the Cottagers, becoming their manager for two years before being reinstated as an amateur player with The Casuals. An all round sportsman, he played county cricket for Surrey and played one England Test match in 1921; he was also made one of Wisden's "Cricketers of the Year" in 1920. Although he only scored 5 runs in his solitary test appearance, his highest first class score was 306 not out. After his playing days were over, he held a variety of jobs including cricket master at Eton, journalist, publican, a sports outfitter and he also tried his hand at hotel management. Ducat died on July 27th 1942, playing cricket at Lord's for the Home Guard.

BIRTH OF THE SHRIMPERS

Birth of the Shrimpers - A Meeting of Extraordinary Gentlemen

Southend's footballing landscape changed forever on the evening of May 19th 1906 in the humble surroundings of the Blue Boar public house in Victoria Avenue, Prittlewell. Just three days earlier, Southend Athletic's annual general meeting had proved to be an embarrassment, where the sole decision taken on the club's future was to change the colour of their playing kit. The major problems of dwindling gate receipts, issues with their Marine Park ground and a very poor showing in defending their title in the modest South Essex League were not addressed. Athletic's governing body decided to bury its head in the sand, despite a growing move towards the formation of a professional football club for the town surfacing as early as the previous month.

On April 19th, a meeting had been held in the same public house which resulted in the securing of a seven year lease on the adjacent Roots Hall field. At first, the formation of a rival amateur or semi-professional club "Prittlewell United" was suggested but rejected as it was rightly stated that Athletic would "fight tooth and nail" to keep the new club out of their league. Opposition was also encountered from other local amateur sides Leigh Ramblers and Leigh Rectory Yard. By the May 19th meeting, the packed public house would soon learn that the town would have a fully professional club, come what may.

The meeting duly elected a five man board of directors, these being:

Charles Albert Stein, a member of the Stock Exchange and residing at Manor Road, Westcliff.

Oliver Trigg, licensed victualler and landlord of The Blue Boar Public House.

George Hatton Hogflesh, described as an agent and also secretary of the Southend Harriers Athletics club, residing at Finchley Road, Westcliff.

Frederick England, licensed victualler and landlord of the nearby Nelson Hotel.

Thomas Stuart Tidy, a cigar merchant, residing in Hamlet Court Road, Westcliff.

Charles Anderson was also elected as club secretary on the basis of his expertise in local sporting circles. A further addition to the board came in the shape of local businessman Mr. Arthur Brown.

Oliver Trigg

The new board was charged with engaging professional players of a suitable standard and ensuring the new club's application to the Southern League Second Division was successful. It was, the club well and truly stealing Southend Athletic's thunder, as the amateur outfit made a hasty but abortive attempt just four days later.

The fledgling club took shape very quickly; registered offices were found at 15 West Street and Coopers of the High Street, Southend were appointed as the clubs' solicitors. John Holtom, a chartered accountant with premises also in the High Street, was engaged as auditor. The club opened a bank account with the London Provincial Bank, Oliver Trigg parting with a personal contribution of £861. The Roots Hall field was described in the clubs' share prospectus as a commodious 6,000 capacity enclosure with dressing rooms and a grandstand seating 500. The club soon issued shares, planning to realise a working capital of £2,000, eight thousand shares being sold at five shillings each. However, the share issue was under subscribed and the shortfall was underwritten by the new board. It was decided that the new club would adopt the "uniform" of royal blue jerseys with black collars and cuffs and white knickers.

Within weeks, the former Plymouth Argyle manager Robert Jack had been hired as manager and secretary, whilst Arthur Norris, a renowned distance runner and formerly of the Tottenham Hotspur club, was engaged as trainer. Jack duly raided the shell-shocked Athletic club and offered professional terms to William "Jerry" Thomson,

Manager and Secretary Robert Jack

Samuel Blott and Harry Owen, as well as taking Cantor, Finn and Cotgrove as back up players. Bloodied and beaten, Athletic threw in the towel and were forced into a merger with Southend Victoria in order to field any sort of a team. Bob Jack very quickly secured the signatures of more players with professional pedigrees. Former England international, George Molyneux, arrived from Portsmouth and was handed the captaincy; Arthur Holden also moved to Southend from Fratton Park. Goalkeeper Charlie Cotton was poached from West Ham United and Welsh cap Fred Watkins came from Millwall. Jack also scoured the local sides, with Arthur Johnson, Ben Freeman and Jimmy Axcell all arriving from Grays United. However, Jack's most astute signing came in the diminutive figure of Harold Halse, a prolific scorer for amateur sides such as Newportonians, Barking Town and Wanstead.

In late May 1906, the AGM of the Southern League contested the applications for membership of the 2nd Division; the thirteen team division had five vacancies. Champions from the 1905/06 season, Crystal Palace and runners up Leyton were promoted to Division One while Watford Reserves and Grays United had resigned from the League. However, a late change of heart meant that Grays were one of seven clubs applying for a place in the League. Also contesting the election were Wycombe Wanderers and Swindon Town Reserves who were applying for re-election having finished in the bottom two places in the previous campaign. The four new applicants were Southend United, Royal Engineers (Aldershot), Hastings and Tunbridge Wells Rangers; the application of Southend Athletic was not considered as it had arrived four days after the allotted deadline. The vote was very encouraging

Arthur Norris, Southend United's first trainer

Three stalwarts of Southend United's first season (left to right): goalkeeper Charlie Cotton, George Molyneux and Albert Frost.

with Southend United gaining the most votes with 33. Also elected for membership were Swindon Town Reserves (re-elected with 30 votes), Royal Engineers (27 votes), Wycombe Wanderers (re-elected with 18 votes) and Tunbridge Wells Rangers (16 votes). Grays United and Hastings were not elected, although the latter would effectively gain a place in the division by merging with existing members St.Leonards United. Much to Grays United's undoubted chagrin, the Southern League later decided to level up the division to fourteen members, with Salisbury City becoming the latest member club. However, the plans for an evenly distributed division were taken asunder when Southern United folded halfway through the 1906/07 season, leaving an odd number of clubs once again.

The telegram containing the result of the ballot was received with great excitement at Southend United, with members and interested well wishers tossing their hats into the air amid raucous scenes. A further meeting was held at the Masonic Hall on July 5th and a message of support was read out from Mr. Frederic Wall, the secretary of the Football Association.

1906/07 - A New Beginning

There was grave concern that the new field would not be ready in time for the first match on September 1st, but despite having only three months to complete preparations and, with funds running short, the ground was successfully enclosed and some rudimentary spectator facilities provided. The work was completed in time to stage an "A Team" versus "B Team" practice match, 800 people watching the B team win 4-0 on August 25th. The game was notable for the club inadvertently fielding a banned player, Billy Leslie, after he told the club his name was Dark. Meanwhile, Bob Jack had continued to scour the local scene for talent and had bolstered his squad by the signings of Ernest Emery from Leigh Ramblers, Albert Frost from the Southend Corinthians club and Peter Wilson, who joined from Tilbury.

The first official 1st team game was against the reserves of Swindon Town and a healthy crowd

Southend United's complete record for their first season.

1906/07	Home						Away						Total					
	P	W	D	L	F	A	P	W	D	L	F	A	P	W	D	L	F	A
Southern League	11	9	1	1	39	9	11	5	4	2	19	14	22	14	5	3	58	23
South-Eastern League	9	9	0	0	44	1	9	8	0	1	41	5	18	17	0	1	85	6
Friendlies	22	17	3	2	67	22	1	0	0	1	0	2	23	17	3	3	67	24
Expunged Matches	1	1	0	0	5	1	1	1	0	0	7	0	2	2	0	0	12	1
Totals	43	36	4	3	155	33	22	14	4	4	67	21	65	50	8	7	222	54

of around 4,000, paying an entry fee of sixpence each, gathered expectantly. The game was played in sweltering heat and despite dominating possession and having the majority of chances, the new side slipped to a narrow single goal defeat. Fortunately this was to prove the only competitive defeat on home soil in the whole campaign.

The first ever Southend United team to line up in a competitive game was:

Charlie Cotton; Jerry Thomson; George Molyneux; Arthur Johnson; Harry Owen; Ben Freeman; Arthur Holden; Harry Mitchell; Harold Halse; Fred Watkins and Bob Jack.

Visiting Southern League Secretary, Nat Whittaker, declared the proceedings a triumph.

In addition to the Southern League Second Division, the club had also decided to join the Second Division of the South Eastern League, to provide extra income and opportunities for matches on midweek afternoons.

The inaugural season could not have been more successful on the field, with the primary aim of winning the championship of the Southern League Second Division achieved by a margin of two points from West Ham United Reserves, despite having a 7-0 victory against Southern United wiped out when the Nunhead based club folded mid-season. The championship of the

The local papers soon made Harold Halse the doyen of Roots Hall. Here he is shown scoring in fine fashion.

South Eastern League Second Division was also claimed with the club winning seventeen of their 18 fixtures, with only a 0-1 reversal at Tunbridge Wells Rangers preventing a clean sweep of victories.

The club played a total of 65 matches during their inaugural season, including friendlies, suffering only seven defeats.

The remarkable total of 222 goals in the first season was helped by the new club winning three matches with double figure goal tallies. The first arrived on September 15th in the club's third Southern League fixture. The Aldershot based Royal Engineers club were the visitors to Roots Hall; a disappointing crowd of 2,000 saw the new club run riot, winning by twelve goals to nil. Harold Halse helped himself to five, while Bombardier Newlands scored a hat-trick on his debut appearance. On October 24th, Halse's old club Wanstead paid a visit to Southend for a friendly encounter and the homesters were ruthless on their amateur opponents, scoring eleven times without repost. The third instance of a double figure goal tally came in a South Eastern League encounter with Chesham Generals at Roots Hall on December 15th. Despite the absence of leading marksmen, Harold Halse, United rattled in thirteen goals without reply, which remains the club's highest tally in one match. Jimmy Axcell scored five of the goals and Halse's deputy, Albert Frost, claimed four against the hapless visitors. Over the complete season, Harold Halse scored 91 of the 222 goals and was by far the club's leading marksmen. Jimmy Axcell trailed in his wake with a mere 30 goals. Even goalkeeper Charlie Cotton made his mark on the goalscorers chart when he was given responsibility for two penalty kicks in matches towards the end of the campaign.

Off the field, however, the picture was distinctly gloomy, with the 43 home games mustering an aggregate attendance of 47,768 and gate receipts totalling £875 4s 8d. The wage bill totalled £1,443 and with other expenditure, a concerning loss on the campaign of £1,142 10s was reported at the Annual General Meeting. To help balance the books, Arthur Holden was sold to Plymouth Argyle and Arthur Johnson went to Sheffield United.

A further body blow was dealt to the club at the AGM of the Southern League. The expected election to the First Division as champions was not forthcoming and instead, the members of the First Division elected a newly formed club, Brad-

HAROLD HALSE.

J. AXCELL.

Harold Halse and Jimmy Axcell, who joined Manchester United together for a total of £700.

ford Park Avenue, in their place. The club were rightly outraged, accusing the League of bowing to commercial interests at the expense of a proven and *bona fide* southern club. The Park Avenue club had been born out of the Bradford rugby club and had no playing pedigree at all. The club however was heavily backed by wealthy textile merchants and, the club effectively bypassing the Second Division for financial reasons, was viewed dimly by the sporting press and public and was one of many decisions that would see the Southern League's perceived parity with the Football League crumble. The fact that a northern club had usurped Southend's rightful elevation really grated with the board of directors and their anger was compounded during the summer of 1907 when tricky local born forward Samuel "Prince" Blott defected to the Park Avenue club under the lure of a large pay increase.

1907/08 - Champions Again

Despite the setbacks of the summer, the club started the second season with vigour, winning nine games on the bounce before a 1-3 reversal against the powerful reserves of Portsmouth. Finances stabilised, with the club selling season tickets for the first time, the stand costing £1 1s for the season while ground tickets were available for 10s 6d. Crowds grew steadily and the club made money by allowing betting kiosks into the ground, although this met with vocal disapproval in some quarters.

Despite the loss of players in the summer, Bob Jack again utilised his knowledge of local talent to bolster the ranks. Dot Cantor arrived from Southend Athletic and a highly regarded youngster, George Harrod, signed on from the local Corinthians club. The talented Bombardier Newlands, since elevated to Inspector, again made himself available to assist when possible from his duties at the Shoeburyness Garrison.

The club entered the English Cup (the FA Cup) for the first time and enjoyed some success, including a feisty encounter with Clapton at the Old Spotted Dog Ground, a venue still in use today, in East London. A replay was needed in the third qualifying round against Clapton Orient from the Second Division of the Football League and a big midweek crowd at Roots Hall generated gate receipts of £84; the team eventually bowed out at the 5th qualifying round stage away to Carlisle United.

The exceptional form of Harold Halse attracted the attention of many clubs. In March, Halse scored five against Southampton Reserves and repeated the feat a week later against Swindon Town Reserves. Despite rising crowds, debts were mounting and the board agreed to listen to offers for the diminutive front man. Speculation gathered surrounding his impending departure and after a lacklustre display against Maidstone United on March 21st, it was clear Halse had made his mind up to leave. Later that night, Halse joined Manchester United for the maximum allowable fee of £350. They also offered to buy

Jimmy Axcell and Ernest Emery to "keep Halse company in the north" and after some deliberation Axcell agreed although Emery decided to remain at Roots Hall. United also paid £350 for Axcell; although a decent player he would never figure in the first team, and the fee was seen as a way of circumventing the maximum fee rule. The transfer wiped out the clubs debts and despite protests from the supporters, his departure was seen as inevitable. To assuage the discontent among the club's supporters, Manchester United agreed to a friendly fixture for the following season with the proceeds remaining entirely at Roots Hall.

With the squad weakened by the loss of two pivotal players at a vital time of the season, the board acted quickly, securing the services of Alex "Nutty" King and Frank Cotterill from the Maidstone United club.

During the season, the gate receipts record was again beaten, when £93 swelled the coffers for the Easter Monday visit to Roots Hall of Woolwich Arsenal Reserves.

The club were riding high and, as the season drew to a close, the contest for the title went back and forth between United and Portsmouth Reserves. Despite a home defeat to Tunbridge Wells Rang-

Alex "Nutty" King

ers, a draw between Portsmouth and Hastings meant that Southend retained the championship and the trophy was brought down from the display cabinet at the Blue Boar and filled with ale to celebrate, amid raucous scenes at Roots Hall. The press had made much of the crowd's behaviour at home games, being variously described

as "uncouth" and "ill-mannered", although this actually amounted to little more than the occasional booing of opponents.

By the end of the season, in all matches, Southend again had a notable record:

P: 74   W: 44   D: 12   L: 18   F: 167   A: 102

Aggregate crowds had risen to a far more respectable 68,571. Gate receipts had increased by £600 to £1,434 1s 1d. The club reported a healthy profit of £305 11s 8d, although this was due to the Halse and Axcell transfer fees and Oliver Trigg waving his personal debt of £877.

If Southend had feared a repeat of the previous season's election fiasco, they were proved to be unfounded. Both Tottenham Hotspur and Bradford Park Avenue, the latter despite finishing 13th in the Southern League, were elected to the Football League Second Division. The League, having already agreed to increase the size of the top division anyway, elected three clubs: Southend United (26 votes), Exeter City (a newly formed club) (33 votes) and Coventry City from the Birmingham League (25 votes). Leyton (32 votes) and New Brompton (31 votes) retained their membership. Croydon Common were not elected and remained in the Second Division. The manager of West Ham United, Sid King, telegraphed the club to pass on his congratulations on the election results.

1908/09 - In With The Big Boys

In order to compete at an elevated status, Southend desperately needed more funding. The board immediately pledged £150 to cover the increased cost of travelling. A public meeting was held at the Masonic Hall and was chaired by the town mayor Alderman Ingram. At its close the meeting had raised pledges of £400; the funds were very welcome but should be put into perspective against the £500 fine imposed by the Southern League against Bradford Park Avenue who had clearly used the league as a stepping stone to the Football League; the club paid the fine with almost cursory ambivalence.

Southend re-engaged virtually all the successful championship winning team and Bob Jack sought out more players to cope with the expected standard. Prince Blott returned from a season at Bradford Park Avenue, although he would subsequently be sold to Manchester United to join up with former colleague Harold Halse.

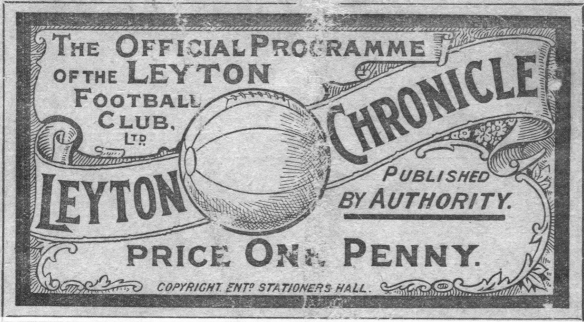

Leyton were disposed of in the FA Cup. This is the cover of the programme for the match.

Alec Birnie, an impressive outside right was signed from Sittingbourne, although he too would depart before the season's end to Bury; the fee would again go to help balance the club's books. Duncan Ronaldson, a free scoring forward, was engaged from Brighton and fellow Scot "Jocky" Wright arrived from Watford. Tommy Caldwell signed from Clapton Orient, having previously seen service at West Ham. Billy Leslie joined from Finchley, although bizarrely his true identity was investigated and was found to be Billy Askew! Unfortunately Southend were found guilty of deliberately fielding a banned player under a pseudonym and were fined £10. Askew had played under a false identity for several clubs as he had been handed a lengthy ban from football which did not expire until 1910. Bob Jack continued his penchant for developing local talent by signing Charlie Axcell from Leigh Ramblers, Ernie Fincke from Walthamstow Grange and Tommy Little from Ilford, although he soon departed for Bradford Park Avenue. During the season, Little's departure and an injury to the stalwart back Jerry Thomson saw Wally Smith sign from Liverpool and Andy Clark from Brentford; he had also served Plymouth Argyle. Both players would perform admirably.

The first home game of the season saw the visit to Roots Hall of Millwall Athletic from the East Ferry Road. A new record crowd of 6,000 gathered, although a greater fig-ure was suspected due to interlopers scaling the perimeter fences in large numbers to gain free access to the spectacle. The club issued a commemorative match programme for the first time and against all expectation, the youthful United bested their esteemed visitors by three goals to nil, Jocky Wright and a second half brace from Alec Birnie earning the headlines which bought United to national attention for the first time.

The magnificent result against Millwall was a catalyst for a tremendous run of form at Roots Hall which saw the team fail to lose or concede a goal at home until the Christmas Day visit of Portsmouth. Both records were spectacularly shattered when the visitors triumphed 2-6.

The club enjoyed another exciting FA Cup run, although again they were forced to compete in the qualifying round phases. Tricky away ties at London Caledonians, Leyton and Ilford were overcome and Shoeburyness Garrison and Cromer were dispatched by 4-0 and 2-0 respectively at Roots Hall. However, the tie at Leyton hit the headlines for the wrong reason when a large scale fight broke out between rival supporters at the Osborne Road ground. A 5th qualifying round tie pitched United against Luton Town, where a magnificent display from Charlie Cotton in the United goal secured a 1-1 draw at The Hatters' Kenilworth Road. In the replay at Roots Hall, Southend led until

LEYTON v. SOUTHEND UNITED.
ENGLISH CUP TIE, OCTOBER 3rd, 1908.

LEYTON. 3

Goal.
1. WHITBOURNE

Backs.
2. MEREDITH   ASTON
                                      3. BUSBY

Half-backs.
4. BUCHANAN   5. JONES   6. GRAY

Forwards.
7. KINGABY   8. DISS   9. AYWARD   10. RYDER   11. MAIR
RIGHT WING   BUSBY   LEFT WING

Referee: MR. H. A. MOSELEY.

LEFT WING   RIGHT WING.
12. JACK   13. WRIGHT   14. RONALDSON   15. FROST   16. BIRNIE

Forwards.
                          OWEN
17. BLOTT   18. LESLIE   19. EMERY

Half-backs.
20. MOLYNEUX   21. THOMSON

Backs.
22. COTTON

Goal.

SOUTHEND UNITED. 1

---

the final minute when the visitors equalised, United eventually going down 2-4 in extra time.

The first home game of 1909, against New Brompton, saw remarkable scenes at the end of the game. An irate visiting supporter encroached onto the pitch, kicking the linesman and attempting to strike the referee. The interloper was escorted away by local police but was subjected to a hail of missiles such as stones and potatoes hurled by the home contingent. The incident did not end there, as when the villain of the piece was found to be waiting for his bus connection at the terminus by the Middleton Hotel, a large crowd gathered baying for retribution. The police locked the man in a waiting room at the terminus for his own safety.

The 1908/09 season saw the club finish 12th from the 21 clubs, a respectable return for the newcomers. The only real concern was the team's form away from home, thirteen defeats from the twenty played. The only victories secured on the road came at Crystal Palace (3-1), a surprising result on their notoriously sloping Sydenham pitch, at Norwich City (3-0) and at fellow new boys Coventry City (5-2). It was, however, worthy of note that

How the teams lined up for the FA Cup tie at Leyton. Although the supporter who purchased this programme noted the score as 3-1 to Leyton, that must have been wishful thinking on their part, as Southend actually ran out winners by one Ronaldson goal to nil.

Southend finished higher than five of the six London clubs in the division. Only Millwall finished higher, in 11th and this only due to a superior goal average. The club also fielded a team in the short lived United League but due to player availability, the strength of the side selected would vary wildly. Wins against Brentford (4-3) and Croydon (5-0) would be contradicted with defeats such as a 0-7 thrashing at New Brompton.

The campaign closed with the Football League attempting to poach 18 clubs from the Southern League to form a new Third Division of their own competition. The Football League were keen to divest the rival League of its clubs as previously Football League players could join Southern League clubs without a transfer fee being owed. Sixteen clubs were sounded out and agreed in principle. The remaining five clubs and Second Division champions Croydon Common were put to a vote for the remaining two places. The voting went as follows:

Coventry City	11 votes
Brentford	9 votes

Croydon Common	6 votes
New Brompton	4 votes
Watford	2 votes
Southend United	No votes

This meant that Coventry and Brentford would join the other 16 teams in the new division. The remaining four clubs convened an emergency meeting at the Holborn Restaurant in London. The leading light in the meeting was the Southend contingent, led by the fiercely opposed Robert Jack. The meeting proposed to fight the proposal in the strongest manner possible. The Southend United representation was completed by Chairman Alderman Prevost, and Messrs Davies, Cooper and Burrows. The interest of the Supporters Club was led by Tom Byford.

The club held a campaign meeting at the Hotel Victoria on April 24th and the drafting of the circular below was unanimously passed:

"That this meeting of supporters of Southend United expresses its deepest dissatis-

faction at the very unfair and unsportsman-like action which has been taken by sixteen Southern League clubs in meeting in secret and endeavouring to control the nomination of the eighteen clubs to form part of the proposed Third Division of the English League. This meeting, believing that the directors will take every possible step to vindicate the claims of Southend United Football Club, assures the directors that it will do everything in any action they may take to support Southend's just cause."

Much subsequent canvassing and lobbying took place until the election meeting was held at the Midland Hotel in Manchester. Southend United's interests were represented by Chairman Alderman Prevost and Messrs Davies, Robert Jones, Robert Jack and Oliver Trigg. There was undoubted and respected opposition to the proposal; Mr Houghton of the Preston North End club paid tribute to the stature of the sportsmen of the south and Sir Henry Norris of Fulham proclaimed outline support for the proposal of Football League expansion, but cited the southern bias to the division to be unfair on all sides. Captain

---

10

WHAT THE OLD HANDS CAN DO
In Brief.

COTTON is a steady goal-saver with a sure pair of hands, brainy head, and a gift of intelligent anticipation of events.

THOMPSON is a fearless, dashing back, who takes risks, frightens opposing forwards, and kicks with power and accuracy.

MOLYNEAUX is the slow but sure man of the defence. He plays as well as ever and is expected to surprise many of the old opponents he will meet.

HARROD is a tackler, dribbler, and placer very little removed from the highest class.

OWEN is a centre-half who will prove equal to the best in the competition. He is as fearless as he is clever, and as judicious as he is dashing.

Manager JACK is still fast and he dribbles and centres with all his old precision.

FROST is a moody player; clever enough at inside right, but dreadfully disappointing as a centre forward.

ANDERSON is a goal-getter and very useful centre forward.

CHILD is a useful man, possessing plenty of shooting power, which he can generally direct on the target with some accuracy.

ABOUT THE NEW BOYS.
(SPECIAL BY J. H.)

Amongst the new boys who hope to delight Southend enthusiasts, BLOTT is the best known, for he was one of Southend's best before he migrated to Bradford for a season. BIRNIE, RONALDSON, and WRIGHT will all be treading on new ground, while COTTERILL is practically a recruit, for he did not wear Southend's colours until last Eastertide.

12

There is no best about the new boys. They are all good, and all of them should be happy and comfortable with Southend.

IRRESISTIBLE BIRNIE.

BIRNIE is a right winger of distinct class. On his day he is irresistible. With West Ham, Norwich City, and Maidstone, Birnie accomplished many remarkable achievements. He is fast. He can dribble. He can centre, and when opportunity offers he can shoot. Birnie's rushes down the right wing will create plenty of excitement at Prittlewell during the rapidly approaching season.

SPEEDY COTTERILL.

COTTERILL many of you know. He has all the pace and cleverness of Birnie, and he knows how to shoot. He will be a great favourite on the Southend ground if he plays up to his best form.

TRICKY BLOTT.

BLOTT is a local star, who will get one of the biggest welcomes home any player ever enjoyed. He is tricky with the ball, parts with it advantageously, and shoots where the goalkeeper very often is not. In this respect he is, at his best, a living example of how goals are scored.

GIANT RONALDSON.

RONALDSON has weight. He knows how to use it. He is fast for his size, and can play in any forward position with distinction. He dribbles well, passes neatly and shoots with excellent judgment. He has enjoyed experience with Grimsby, Queens Park Rangers, Norwich City and Brighton.

STEADY WRIGHT.

WRIGHT is just the partner to make Manager Jack shine. He was Watford's best forward last season. The old Bolton Wanderer and Plymouth Argyle man is a clever dribbler, brainy passer and consistent goal getter. It is to be hoped he, Birnie, Ronaldson and Blott have brought there shooting boots to Southend.

How the 1908/09 Southend United handbook saw the players.

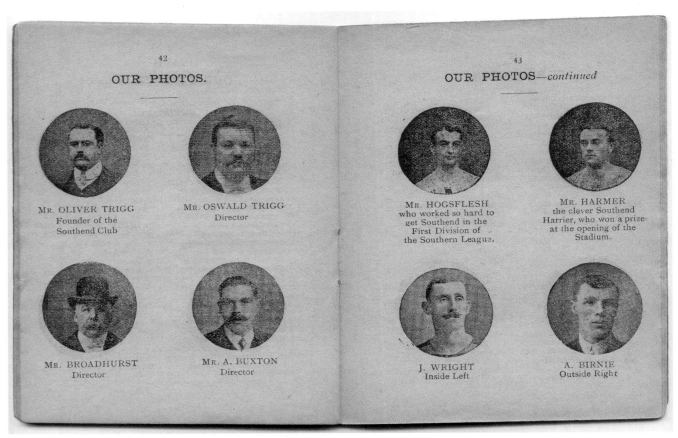

OUR PHOTOS.

MR. OLIVER TRIGG
Founder of the
Southend Club

MR. OSWALD TRIGG
Director

MR. BROADHURST
Director

MR. A. BUXTON
Director

OUR PHOTOS—*continued*

MR. HOGSFLESH
who worked so hard to
get Southend in the
First Division of
the Southern League.

MR. HARMER
the clever Southend
Harrier, who won a prize
at the opening of the
Stadium.

J. WRIGHT
Inside Left

A. BIRNIE
Outside Right

Some of the men who made United, from the 1908/09 handbook.

Henry Wells-Holland of the Clapton Orient club suggested the proposal be deferred for twelve months. It would seem that the support gained from all quarters would be sufficient to defeat the expansionist's plans. Indeed, as the meeting proceeded, the matter would appear to be dead in the water. The only eventual question tabled was whether the existing Football League clubs wanted a Third Division at all, aside from any plans the rebel clubs cherished. The proposal was denied as those in favour numbered 25 to those against 13, two short of the three quarters majority required to pass the motion. The defeat of the threat against the club was widely reported in the Southend Standard and the journal stated that the contemptible actions of the sixteen Southern League clubs had weakened the competition as a whole and would delay the expansion of the Football League for a number of years, such was the bitter taste garnered by the whole sorry episode. Robert Jack earned widespread praise for his oratory skills and this only enhanced his reputation among the nation's sporting cognoscenti.

In the summer of 1909, the supporters created the first formal Supporters' Club, with the express object of fundraising for the club. Mr Tom Byford was elected chairman, O.M. Howard was Honorary Secretary with Mr John Burrows, Honorary

Treasurer. Within no time, £200 was raised to cover the player's summer wages and sufficient capital raised to erect a cover on the western side of the ground. Byford and Howard with a third member of the Supporters club committee, J.A. Faers, were subsequently elected to the expanded board of club directors. The reserve team manager, George Radford, was also elected to the board. A further change saw Mr R.A. Jones replace Alderman Prevost as club chairman.

The first season in Division One was regarded as a success, with a total of 105,334 spectators attending Southern League matches at Roots Hall. This was an increase of 36,000 on the previous campaign. A record attendance had been set for the Northampton game, a crowd of 7,200 generating gate receipts of £191 14s 3d. The board suggested a campaign for the club to be exempted from the preliminary qualifying round matches of the FA Cup, as this had meant four Southern League matches had to be staged on less financially rewarding midweek dates the previous season, something the club wanted to avoid. Indeed, the visit of Reading in February attracted only 1,200 spectators and receipts of £29 5s. An estimated £200 of gate receipts had been lost and

A CENTURY UNITED

compensation to Brentford and Brighton had to be found for late changes to dates for Southern League matches. This, and an increase in squad size, lead to a nett annual loss of £746 being reported at the Annual General Meeting.

1909/10 - Goodbye Charlie

Player/Secretary Robert Jack re-engaged the majority of the players who had done such a sterling job in the first season at the elevated status. Cotton, Molyneux, Thomson, Cairns, Emery, Owen, Frost and Wright were all signed up for the new campaign. There were many newcomers to the squad as well, and several Scottish players moved to the Essex coast. Tommy Murray arrived from Partick Thistle whilst Sandy McLellan and James Harrower arrived from the King's Park club in Stirling. Norman Brown signed from Luton Town, James Bigden arrived from Bury and Alex King returned to the fold after a brief spell with Woolwich Arsenal. Louis Parke, an amateur winger from Tunbridge Wells Rangers, T. Crews of Everton Reserves, Sid Sugden of Brentford and E.W. Meare of the Woolwich Polytechnic club were also engaged by the club. George Lavers, a local centre half, also performed well despite being profoundly deaf and often caused amusement by playing on after a whistle had been blown until being called to a halt by a team mate.

There had been several rule changes during the close season. The maximum transfer fee was abolished and players could now be tempted with a slice of any proposed fee. There was also automatic promotion and relegation implemented between Divisions One and Two of the Southern League, with the bottom two clubs being replaced by the champions of the new two sections of Division Two (North and West, and South and East). In the FA Cup, Southern League clubs, including Southend United, would now be exempted to the fourth qualifying round, having previously being required to enter at the first qualifying round stage.

The season never really got going for the club with some heavy defeats sustained. The club would finish 20th from 22

Charlie Cotton takes it easy, as seen by the local papers of the time.

COTTON HAS A QUIET TIME IN GOAL.

with only relegated Reading and Croydon Common below them in the final table. However, the disappointment of the 20th place finish was overshadowed by the death on January 3rd 1910 of popular Southend custodian Charlie Cotton. Only 30 years of age, Cotton had become ill in November and was diagnosed with the rare kidney condition Bright's disease. The Southend Standard reporter wrote in Cotton's appreciation: "When the history of the Southend United Club comes to be inscribed – and I sincerely hope it will – those who remember the early inception of it will always have a kindly remembrance for the name of Charles Cotton, and it will be cherished by the youths and sportsmen of our town for years to come." The difficult task of replacing Cotton was undertaken, and initially Haggar took over in goal but he had originally been engaged by the club as a full back. His lack of experience as a goalkeeper was cruelly exposed and fourteen goals were conceded in his first five outings. Percy Toone was signed from Woolwich Arsenal but fared scarcely any better. He was in goal on December 30th for the match at Northampton Town when the club went down to its all time record defeat, 1-11 at the hands of the Cobblers.

Moderate success was achieved by the club in reaching the second round proper of the FA Cup for the first time, before bowing out in a hotly contested replay to Queens Park Rangers by the odd goal in five at Park Royal. At one point, the match descended into a fist fight as the referee struggled to maintain order, a player from each side being dismissed from the field. The competition was also memorable for a January trip to Gainsborough Trinity. The match occurred during the General Election and the team stayed on the Friday night in the Saracen's Head in Lincoln. This was also the campaign headquarters for the Conservative Party, and a large crowd had gathered outside for a final speech from the local candidate. His arrival, however, had been delayed and Southend's half back Dot Cantor gave a twenty minute oration from the balcony to an enthusiastic response from the locals. However his efforts came to nothing when the Liberals retained the seat the following day.

The season also saw the long awaited visit to Roots Hall of Manchester United as part of the agreement that took Harold Halse to Bank Street. The full FA Cup winning team, including Halse, took part in an entertaining 2-2 draw. The visitors opened the scoring after eight minutes when Dick Duckworth's shot eluded Cotton. Albert Frost levelled after thirty minutes only for Manchester United to restore their advantage through Sandy Turnbull. Southend equalised after 68 minutes when a Crews' corner was headed goalwards by Jocky Wright before Frost crashed the ball into

The team line-ups for the match between Millwall and Southend United, played in January 1909. The Shrimpers lost 1-3.

the net for his second goal. Disappointingly only 2,500 watched the match on a bitterly cold and damp day. However, the crowd were appreciative of a capital match and Ernie Emery in particular was singled out for an excellent individual performance.

The season has to be looked on as very disappointing; the crowd, used to a free scoring team, saw only 26 goals scored at Roots Hall in 21 Southern League matches. Seven homes games were lost and four drawn. In away games, only 25 goals were scored while a shocking 73 were conceded. However, the team suffered from a horrendous injury list throughout the campaign; Bigden was injured in pre-season training and only featured twice, veteran back Jerry Thomson missed half the season and Molyneux was injured at his old club Portsmouth in February and was absent from the last dozen outings of the season. "Nutty" King missed two months after contracting rheumatic fever and Norman Brown was never a regular due to a persistent groin injury and a dislocated shoulder sustained against Queens Park Rangers. Of course Cotton's illness and subsequent death was a savage blow.

The club's annual general meeting reported a loss of £450 3s 9d. A bigger loss however was that of secretary/manager Robert Jack, who had accepted an offer to return to Plymouth Argyle. The meeting raised £300 from the directors towards the debt and a bazaar was also arranged to raise funds. Popular team captain George Molyneux was appointed as team manager and O.M. Howard accepted the position of Honorary Secretary. The final decision taken was to change the clubs blue jerseys to "a more imposing" red and gold hooped shirt for the new season.

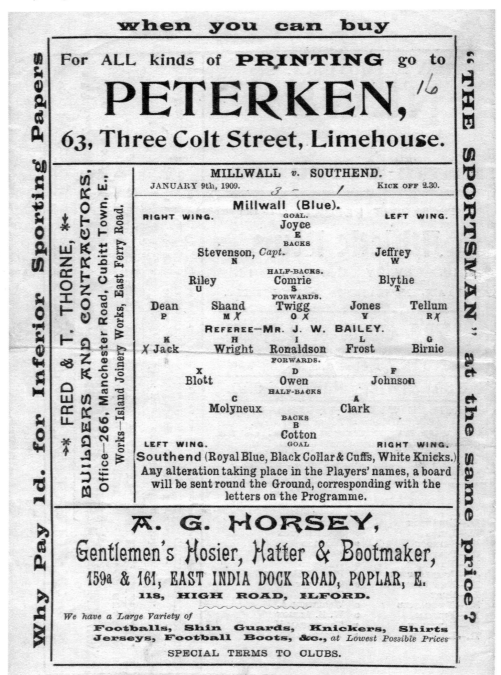

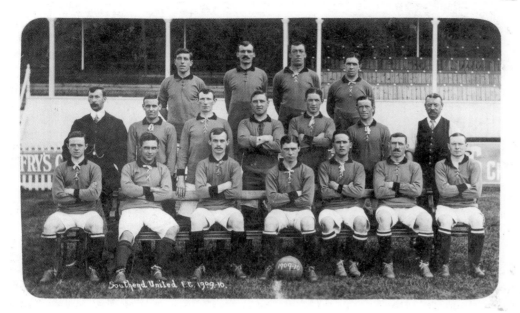

Southend United 1909/10. The royal blue shirts with black collars and cuffs can clearly be seen.

1910/11 - The "Beef and Mustards" Come A Cropper

Much jocularity was levelled at the new choice of shirts, being variously compared to beer barrels and beef and mustard sandwiches. However, the new season was looked forward to with no little degree of optimism. Jack Harwood, a centre-half, joined from Tooting Town, becoming Bob Jack's final signing for the club. A new goalkeeper, Da-vid Clark, arrived from West Ham United and two players, McKenna and Dunn, arrived from Newcastle United. Charlie Craig also moved to Roots Hall, having previously served Reading and Norwich City.

The season, however, was a struggle from the start with goalscoring proving a major problem. This was not assist-ed by the departure in February of Albert Frost to West Ham United. Also in February, the board acquiesced to the supporters request to return to the traditional blue jersey with black trim. Despite a 7-0 thrashing of Millwall at Roots Hall on Boxing Day, the board scoured the country for new forwards. Archie Wilson was tempted from Tottenham Hotspur, Joe Bradshaw came from Queens Park Rangers and Albert Hodgkinson joined, having previously served Southampton and Croydon Common. Curtis joined from Chelsea Reserves and Holman, a postman and ama-

1910 German Tour

The season came to a close with a two week tour to Germany. The first game was against Hertha Berlin and Alex King scored the only goal for Southend in a 1-3 reversal. Union Berlin were the next opponents and a hat-trick for King and another for George Harrod saw a comfortable 4-0 triumph. The tourists moved on to Magdeburg and defeated Victoria 1896 Sportplaz by eight goals to two; there was another hat-trick for "Nutty" King, two for Harrod with Ernie Emery, Billy Sutherland and Albert Frost completing the scorecard. Halle Hohenzollern hosted the next match and the tourists again emerged triumphant by 3-1 with King, Sutherland and Dits Anderson finding the target. Returning to Berlin, Southend then defeated fellow tourists Oxford City by 10-1 with King this time scoring a double hat-trick, Billy Sutherland (2), Murray and Emery completing the rout. The final tour match took place in Hamburg where Combine were defeated by four goals to one.

Southend United goalkeeper Toone (right) poses with German goalkeeper Eichelman before one of Southend's 1910 German Tour matches.

teur with Somerstown, also signed up. Holman proved a useful acquisition, scoring six goals in eight games late in the season as the club tried manfully to claw their way out of the relegation zone.

The rot had set in between January and March, when no matches were won at all and six consecutive games saw the team fail to even register a single goal. April bought five victories but two defeats over Easter to Norwich and Queens Park Rangers saw the threat of relegation looming large. The final day of the season came with Portsmouth already doomed. The remaining relegation place rested between Southend and Bristol Rovers. The Rovers had the upper hand, only needing to avoid defeat at Brighton and Hove Albion, while United had to secure a win in Gillingham at New Brompton, a feat they had never managed before. Goals for Holman and Hodgkinson helped Southend to a 2-1 victory over the Kent side, but news filtered through that Rovers had held Brighton to a goalless draw to save themselves from the drop and condemn Southend to relegation.

The Cup saw the club again reach the competition proper, having dispatched Enfield (after a replay) and Tunbridge Wells Rangers in the qualifying rounds. Southend were drawn at home to the mighty Blackburn Rovers of Division One but in a controversial move, accepted a £400 offer to switch the tie to Ewood Park. Rovers triumphed by five goals to one.

The reserve team had been moved from the South-Eastern League to the South Essex League in a bid to cut costs and had been expected to win the competition with ease. However, to compound a miserable season, this was not the case and the club finished third behind South Weald and champions Custom House.

The experiment of Molyneux as player/manager was a failure and, indeed, his own playing form suffered greatly; recognising his advancing age, he dropped himself from the team in favour of a fit again Jerry Thomson. Injuries again hindered the team, with McKenna and Dunn (broken jaw) spending substantial periods on the sidelines. The only real success stories of the season were Clark, who played every game in goal and Joe Bradshaw, whose skill and experience were clearly evident in a struggling team. At the season's end, George Molyneux tendered his resignation and departed for the more sedate surroundings of Colchester Town.

1911/12 - Welsh Adventures

The board announced that Joe Bradshaw would be placed in charge of the team in succession to Molyneux. Three of the directors, including Tom Byford, took a walking holiday to south Wales during the summer to view the opponent's grounds for the coming campaign. They returned from the principality with horror stories regarding the standards provided, being variously regarded as cinder pitches and slag heaps. The ground of Cwm Albion held the greatest concern. The pitch was heavily rutted and had little grass, there were no

SOUTHEND UNITED FOOTBALL TEAM. - SEASON 1910/1911.

Southend United 1910/11

facilities for spectators or press and indeed the only building on the ground was a shed with a leaky roof that provided a changing room for visiting teams. Treharris' ground was scarcely any better, with players having barely enough room to take corner kicks and throw-ins on one side of the ground. The trip to Mardy was also unusual, as the edge of the pitch was next to a deep drop to the railway station below. The team was often kept waiting while a posse of boys were employed in ball retrieving from the tracks.

The perilous financial position of the club following relegation meant Bradshaw was only able to re-engage a handful of the previous team. Murray, Thomson, Emery, Harwood, Wilson and Holman remained at the club and notable losses included David Clark to Bristol Rovers, Hodgkinson to Ilkeston United and Sutherland to Plymouth Argyle. Bradshaw set about bolstering his squad, which would be facing 82 matches this season, as the board had decided to rejoin the South-Eastern League while remaining in the South Essex League. Early acquisitions included George Arnold, McNaught, Heneage Wileman (from

Southend United made their first appearance at White Hart Lane when they played Reading in the semi-finals of the Southern Counties Charity Cup in April 1912. Southend were triumphant by one goal to nil, and went on to lift the trophy by beating Coventry City by the same scoreline. Although the final was also played at White Hart Lane, a paltry crowd of only 586 witnessed the match.

Chelsea) and two new goalkeepers, Griffiths and Nurthen.

The season went well, although the goal of an instant return to Division One was not achieved. The promotion places went to champions Merthyr Town and Portsmouth whilst The Shrimpers finished fourth behind Cardiff City. The lower standard of competition was clearly evident and indeed Cwm Albion were unable to complete their remaining four fixtures due to the coal strike and the Southend Standard writer was asked to run the line at Aberdare when an official failed to arrive. Heavy travelling expenses were incurred, with games in Wales fixed for a Saturday afternoon followed by another on the Monday. Expenditure was not helped by the team arriving at Portsmouth on Boxing Day only to be confronted with a flooded pitch. Successes of the season were Nurthen in goal, who had quickly displaced the abject Griffiths between the posts, Wileman, who scored 21 goals and Holman, who followed his promise from the previous campaign by scoring 16 goals in as many games.

A trophy found its way to Roots Hall in April when the club won the Southern Counties Charity Cup at the third attempt, having previously only made the quarter-final stages. The competition had begun with a comfortable 3-0 win at New Brompton. The quarter-final again paired Southend with Queens Park Rangers, who had accounted for the club at the same stage in the previous two seasons. However, in an astonishing game at Roots Hall, Southend emerged triumphant by five goals to four. The semi-final was staged at White Hart Lane with Reading providing the opposition. A tight encounter was won by a single first half strike from Louis Parke. The final was again held at White Hart Lane with Southend defeating Coventry City by a goal to nil, the goal coming five minutes from time from Joe Bradshaw; sadly a crowd of only 586 witnessed the game. It was a notable success, with Southend having defeated four opponents from the First Division of the Southern League on their way to lifting the trophy.

Some substantial victories were obtained during the Southern League campaign. The clubs' record victory on opposition territory was achieved when McNaught and Bradshaw helped themselves to hat-tricks in a 9-0 demolition of Chesham Town; the same opponents were beaten by 7-0 at Roots Hall. Cwm Albion also had fifteen goals put past them without reply, with eight being scored in Wales and another seven in the return match.

The Southend United team pose for a photograph outside their hotel in Cardiff, before the league match against Cardiff City. Due to the distances involved in travelling to matches in Wales, the team were occasionally given a "treat", and allowed to stay in a hotel, but it was rare.

However, promotion was lost when defeats were suffered against key rivals, Merthyr winning both league encounters, including a 0-5 drubbing at Penydarren Park. Portsmouth took three points off the Shrimpers and Cardiff won at Roots Hall late in the campaign. Costly defeats against Kettering, Ton Pentre, Mardy and Pontypridd also weighed heavily in the final analysis. The F.A.Cup was a disappointment, with the club bowing out at the fifth qualifying round stage to Brentford. In the previous round, a 3-1 victory had been secured against London Caledonians at Tufnell Park after the match had to be rearranged following a flooded pitch on the original date.

Injuries again affected the team at vital times; Bradshaw himself had no choice but to play in goal in a South Eastern League encounter at Norwich City. Wilson suffered from knee trouble, Murray tore a thigh muscle and the veteran Thomson also missed the last few matches with injury.

The club's finances remained a grave concern and in February the extinction of the club became a distinct possibility when a writ was served by a creditor for the sum of £90. Excluding debts to directors, liabilities had reached the sum of £456. An emergency fund raising meeting was held and the Mayor, Charlton Hubbard JP, announced he would open a fund to wipe out the debts. Dona-

tions would be sought from all areas of the town and Hubbard spoke glowingly of the clubs' value to the town. The initial Mayor's Fund list was published in the Standard on March 7th and in one week £263 16s and 6d had been raised, and included contributions from all of the directors and a £30 pledge from the Supporters club. A £10 donation was forthcoming from West Ham supporter George Webb, who had organised a collection at the Hammers home game with Millwall. The progress of the fund was portrayed on a large donations clock sited at Victoria Circus. Within three weeks, the Mayor's Fund stood at £614 7s 2d. It was a remarkable effort and without doubt proved to be the club's salvation.

1912/13 - Promotion Achieved

The Southern League had promised to strengthen its Second Division for the new campaign, but the quest suffered a major set back when Walsall, Kettering and Chesham Town all announced their withdrawal from the league. Leyton, relegated from Division One, announced they were folding rather than face the trips to Wales. To soften the blow, the Southern League decreed that the three English clubs in the thirteen team division, Southend, Luton Town and Croydon Common would be paid a £100 one off payment and then £15 a month to assist with the crippling travelling costs incurred in partaking in what was essentially a Welsh League.

Many of the players from the previous season were offered new contracts and the stalwart Jerry Thomson was handed the captaincy. New signings included Billy Kebbell, who kept goal for the local Garons club, Tommy Clarke arrived from the disbanded Cwm Albion club and full back Spencer arrived from Blackpool. New forwards A.J. Chapman, Jack Bradshaw and Tommy Stott were also offered terms. Notable were three old players returning to the fold, these being Jimmy Axcell, Arthur Holden and Albert Frost, the latter after a disappointing spell at West Ham.

An administrative oversight saw the club fail to submit the correct paperwork to gain exemption to the fourth qualifying round of the F.A.Cup. Indeed the club would even have to start in the competitions preliminary round; local team Southend Amateurs were beaten 5-0 thanks to a Tommy Stott hat-trick. The club negotiated all six rounds

Football League Expansion – Third Division Proposed and Dropped

A meeting was held in Sheffield on October 26th 1911. Fifteen clubs were in attendance with the meeting overseen by the Management Committee of the Football League. Southend United were one of the fifteen clubs keen for elevation to the League. The other clubs represented were Burslem Port Vale, Cardiff City, Chesterfield, Crewe Alexandra, Croydon Common, Hartlepool United, Lincoln City, Portsmouth, Rochdale, Rotherham Town, Southport Central, South Shields Adelaide, St. Helen's Town and Walsall. Darlington sent apologies for their absence but tabled their interest in the proposal. Postal applications were received from Merthyr Town, Burton Town, Macclesfield and South Liverpool and Newcastle City announced verbal interest although did not formally apply.

The criteria of sixteen applicants would have been met from these teams but the notoriously ponderous Football League management committee decided not to proceed with the plans. However, ambitious Lincoln City continued to exert pressure on the Football League and in December of the same year the committee reconvened and the matter put to a vote. Those in favour numbered eleven with 26 against. The expansion plans were shelved for the second time in two years. In 1909, 16 of the 18 Southern League First Division clubs had unsuccessfully applied for League membership.

The Cardiff Leek: "Indeed to goodness, don't forget, I've warned you."
(Cardiff City were defeated by Southend, at Cardiff, in the Fifth Qualifying Round.)

Southend United suffered a 2-5 defeat at First Division Chelsea in the 1912/13 FA Cup, although Chelsea were worried enough to take a warning from Cardiff City about "The Southend Bruiser"; Southend had beaten Cardiff in the previous round.

before making the first round proper. A visit to mighty Chelsea, then of the First Division, at Stamford Bridge was the reward and Frost scored twice in a 2-5 defeat which truly did not reflect the closeness of the contest, the homesters being awarded two hotly disputed penalties. Disappointingly inclement weather restricted the visitors to a £240 share of a low crowd of 14,000.

The amount of cup ties meant League progress was slow up to Christmas and then a disastrous reversal at Llanelly in January made promotion prospects seem a distant horizon. The 1-4 defeat at Llanelly came in strange circumstances. United were winning one goal to nil in rain sodden conditions thanks to a Joe Bradshaw strike when a blunder allowed the Welsh side to equalize. The advantage seemed to fall to Southend when the home goalkeeper was dismissed for a serious foul on Louis Parke. However, the local crowd rallied their team by singing hymns and "Land of my Fathers" at deafening volume. The support had the desired effect as the visitors crumbled and Llanelly ran in three late goals to take the points.

The treacherous nature of the Welsh pitches came to the fore again in February when the match against Newport was abandoned just prior to kick off when the referee decided that the clinkers on the cinder pitch represented a significant danger to the players. At Ton Pentre, the players had to change in a nearby hall and walk across a bridge in mackintoshes to beat the atrocious weather. The pitch was described as quite unfit for play, consisting of coal dust and liquid mud. Even the coin toss was a farce when the coin disappeared in a pool of slushy mud. The match was played and the players were reported as being so mud-caked that they "looked more like niggers than white men". Despite the appalling conditions, United triumphed 2-0 with goals from Wilson and Wileman, the United players being revived with hot whisky at the end of the game. The clubs' home form remained good and promotion rivals Swansea Town were beaten 3-1 at Roots Hall in February. This triumph started a run of eleven matches unbeaten and even a last day reversal at Swansea failed to stop Southend gaining promotion as runners-up to Cardiff City. Promotion had been confirmed with a brave 3-1 triumph at the appalling Mardy ground, when

Southend finished with ten men after Batchelor could not continue following a rough challenge. The news was posted in the window of the Southend Standard office and a large crowd greeted promotion with wild cheering.

Despite loss making FA Cup ties (the club were drawn "away" in six consecutive rounds), the club concluded a most satisfying campaign by announcing only a modest loss of £73 2s, £60 of which had been incurred on players' promotion bonuses.

1913/14 - A New Dawn

Southend United's first season back in the top flight saw manager Joe Bradshaw spend the summer trying to strengthen his team. Fred Robson, a young full back from the North East, was a shrewd acquisition. Amateur international Lionel Louch joined from Portsmouth and Billy Barnes signed up from Queens Park Rangers; Alec Steel was also to prove a valuable addition to the team.

An early blow was sustained in November when the veteran Jerry Thomson was injured at Cardiff and never regained sufficient fitness to return to the first team. Robson was promoted to the

Southend United 1913/14

first team and this gave Southend the youngest back line in the division. Goalkeeper Billy Kebbell and Billy Probert were only 20 while Robson was a year younger. The board strengthened the defence by securing the services of Clapton Orient's Ned Liddell in November.

Despite an awful home record (six teams won at Roots Hall), the club had a moderately successful first season back in the First Division. A final position of 16th from twenty clubs was viewed as a reasonable return. The club again qualified for the first round proper of the F.A.Cup, where for the eleventh tie running, they were drawn away from home, this time to the mighty Birmingham City. The club had beaten Tunbridge Wells Rangers (in a match switched to Roots Hall) and Brentford after a replay to earn the plum tie. A crowd of more than 20,000 at St. Andrews gathered in atrocious conditions to witness a plucky fight from the underdogs, City being victorious by 1-2 with Heneage Wileman netting a penalty for United.

Wileman was quite the star player for Southend and in November 1913, his wedding to local woman Gwendoline Rehm was a high profile event in the town. Best man duties on the big day were undertaken by his team mate Archie Wilson.

The main problem in the Southern League campaign was Bradshaw's inability to find a successful forward line on a consistent basis. Indeed thirteen players were used in those positions, with Albert Frost being the most prolific with eleven in the League and another three in F.A.Cup ties. During the entire campaign, 25 players were used in first team matches.

The reserve team had been placed in the Kent League for this season but after some disappointing performances, crowds dwindled so badly that the reserve team accrued a financial loss for the season.

The season had been one of turmoil among the board of directors. Chairman George Radford had purchased the ground from his own funds to protect the club's interests, however, his relationships with the rest of the board had deteriorated to such a degree that he tendered his resignation at a board meeting in April. At the same time, the remaining board members accepted an undisclosed fee from Middlesbrough for Archie Wilson. Although the exact figure was never revealed, it was described as the highest fee ever received for a Southend player. Wilson had signed for Middlesbrough in April although his new employ-

ers kindly allowed the player to remain at Roots Hall until the end of the campaign, as relegation remained a possibility.

The fee doubtless helped to balance the books and the club announced a season's profit of £12 10s 8d.

1914/15 - A Season Of Struggle As War Engulfs Britain

As the 1914/15 season started, the Great War had already got underway, but both the Football League and Football Association passed the motion to continue with footballing activities. It was a controversial decision, as many young men had already signed up for duty and crowds would be small, scarcely covering player's wages. The close season saw only Wileman, Steel, Robson, Emery and Frost retained from the previous season's squad as manager Joe Bradshaw undertook a massive recruitment drive in the summer months. Goalkeepers Ted Leahy and Tommy Lonsdale arrived from Leicester Fosse and Grimsby Town respectively, new backs included Bassett from Swansea, Hamilton from Portsmouth, Marshall from Shankhouse, Neil from the Bradford City club and Woodward followed Leahy from Leicester Fosse. New names for the forward line were Frank Burrill from West Ham, Bennett and Burton from Cardiff, Jack Young from South Shields and Ted Rogerson from Huddersfield Town. Regular goalkeeper Billy Kebbell left for North-Eastern League side South Shields on the promise of a weekly wage of £4.

After a bright start, with home victories against Southampton and Bristol Rovers, the team's home form suffered and crowds began to dwindle. The club fell into arrears with player's wages, not helped by the abandonment of the Swindon game in November due to a waterlogged pitch. The board had hoped to assist the players and their families by a sizeable donation from the bumper crowd expected for the Christmas morning clash with Croydon Common, however, the game could not take place due to fog. The gathered board and crowd had an impromptu collection for the players' benefit, although the gesture of seasonal cheer was spoilt by the sighting of a German Taube aeroplane flying low over the pier heading towards Purfleet.

Worse financial news was felt in January when the F.A.Cup tie at Bristol Rovers was called off due to a waterlogged pitch at Stapleton Road, with the board having no income to cover a Friday night hotel stay in Bristol. Rovers were overcome after a replay and Southend received some cheer with the Second Round pitching them against Cup holders Burnley at Turf Moor. Although the side were outclassed to the tune of 0-6, a share of a 12,500 crowd gave welcome respite from the austerity. However, only a portion of wage arrears could be settled as other creditors, including all the directors, were deemed a priority. Manager Joe Bradshaw had been taken ill at the Burnley game and was sufficiently incapacitated as to be unable to take the team to Watford for a rearranged Southern League fixture. The team were accompanied by local benefactor Percy Garon, who also personally footed the team's expenses for the fixture.

The whole club had descended into depression and players and directors alike were loath to carry on. After the home defeat to Northampton in February, the board passed the motion to tender their resignation from the Southern League with immediate effect and thus terminate the existence of the Southend United Football Club. However, with an extraordinary act of sporting and civil generosity, ousted chairman George Radford stepped in to conduct an eleventh hour rescue act. He agreed to personally bankroll the team to the end of the season including salary arrears, with any incoming revenue offsetting what would be an undoubted loss making venture. It is interesting to note that without George Radford's late intervention, Southend United could have followed in the footsteps of Croydon Common, who folded at the end of the season never to re-emerge after the War.

The team dug in and the run-in saw one of the greatest Southend victories when Millwall were beaten 4-1 at The Den. The Standard described the win as "a triumph the brilliancy of which was unexampled in its history". The club finished 18th in the table, just ahead of relegated Croydon Common and Gillingham.

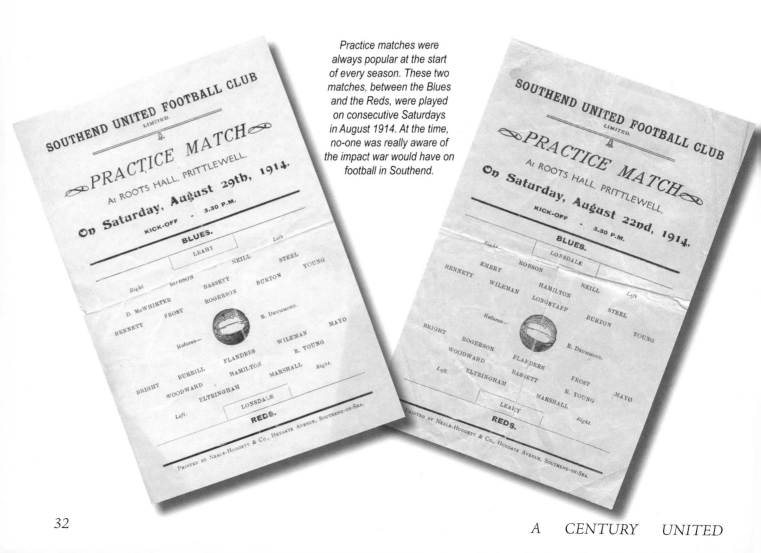

Practice matches were always popular at the start of every season. These two matches, between the Blues and the Reds, were played on consecutive Saturdays in August 1914. At the time, no-one was really aware of the impact war would have on football in Southend.

Paying The Ultimate Sacrifice

The euphoria of the 1914/15 Millwall victory was tempered the following week when news reached the club that one of its former players had fallen in combat.

Billy Sutherland had been called up by the Argyll and Sutherland Highlanders; he was killed in action in Flanders. Sadly a further three former Southend players failed to return from the conflict.

Harry Owen had enlisted at Hornchurch and joined the 23rd Battalion of the Royal Fusiliers (City of London Regiment). Private Owen was killed in action on March 13th 1916 in Flanders.

Archibald Wilson, then of the Middlesbrough Football Club, had enlisted in London and joined the 14th County of London Battalion (London Scottish). Private Wilson was killed in action on July 1st 1916 in Flanders.

Edward Anderson, universally known by the nickname "Dits", had enlisted at Stratford in East London and been assigned to the 4th Battalion of the Royal Fusiliers (City of London Regiment). Private Anderson was killed in action on August 16th 1916 in Flanders.

Arthur Wileman never played for the first team at Southend United but was also killed during World War One.

Other Southend players and former players that served their country included Lionel Louch, who joined the Civil Service Rifles and the manager Joe Bradshaw, who signed up with the Kensington Rifles. Reserve team player Longstaff became a Private with the RFA, Maurice Woodward was a Lance Corporal while Tommy Lonsdale and Fred Robson joined the Footballer's Battalion.

Harry Owen

Edward "Dits" Anderson

ASSOCIATION FOOTBALL.

Shaftesbury Athletic v. Southend United Reserves, played at Earlsfield with a 2—2 result.

1. The Shaftesbury Athletic team which consisted of Guy Watson (goal), R. Jessop and R. Garrett (backs), A. Howlett, J. Harwood and T. Burns (half-backs), C. S. Garrett, A. Sentance, E. Holmes, C. Jeacocke and A. Hodson (forwards). The referee of the game, Mr. A. J. Davies, is in the centre of the top row.
2. Section of the crowd with a "marked man" qualified to receive a guinea from us.

3. A heading bout in mid-field.
4. The Shaftesbury goalkeeper fists away a well placed "centre."
5. The Southend United Reserves:—Clark (goalkeeper), C. Watson and J. Donneley (backs), A. Layzell, Owen and Chalkley (half-backs), S. J. Carter, Parke, Prior, McKenna, Childs (forwards).

The October 29th 1910 edition of Lotinga's Weekly magazine carried this full page article on the match between Shaftesbury Athletic and Southend United Reserves. The Southend United Reserves team is pictured in the striped kit at the bottom of the page, along with a fearsome-looking lady.

INTO THE FOOTBALL LEAGUE

1919/20 – Starting Over

The reconstruction of the club was undertaken in the early months of 1919, although this was done without the parochial guidance of Oliver Trigg, who had passed away in February. The club faced a bleak future. Their home ground at Roots Hall was no longer available or indeed a viable proposition and the burden of debt weighed heavily. Some £3,028 had been carried throughout the period of operational abeyance. W.J. Kirby had been elected as club chairman and he approached the town council with the task of finding a new home for the club. A meeting on March 18th adopted a proposal by Councillor John Mitchell that the Entertainments and Park Committee be tasked with allocating a pitch gratuitously to the club in either Chalkwell or Southchurch Parks. However, a month of prolonged negotiations by all interested parties meant Kirby and vice chairman E.J. Grant negotiated the rental of The Kursaal ground with its' owner Clifton Jay Morehouse. The directors' had to advance the £200 rental for the first season.

Gestures of goodwill saw the debts soon shrink to £1,789 and then West Ham waived the transfer fee still owing for Albert Frost. The players themselves were owed a total of £468 but agreed for the debt to be deferred until funds allowed. The Kursaal ground needed to be kitted out for first class

Welsh International Lot Jones

football, boasting only a pavilion at the south end of the ground. A joint meeting with the council and public was held and it was stated that a fighting fund of £5,000 was needed to provide a grandstand, banking and turnstiles. The Supporters Club launched a "100,000 shilling fund" but the response for once was disappointing, raising only just over £300. The appeal for funds must have been very disheartening but the directors loaned the money needed to ready the ground for its official opening on August 9th, conducted by the Mayor and Mayoress Senier.

Virtually all of the pre-War directors regained their position on the board with the notable exception of George Radford, whose humanitarian gesture from the 1914/15 season was strangely overlooked. Also forgotten was the pre-War manager Joe Bradshaw, who had performed admirably in a difficult time. He was not offered the managerial

Southend United Football Team, Season 1919 - 1920.

Southend United 1919/20

reins and subsequently joined Swansea Town as manager. The board decided that former centre half Ned Liddell would be engaged as first team manager.

Liddell re-engaged several pre-War players including Ted Leahy, George Marshall, Heneage Wileman, Maurice Woodward, Richard and Jack Young, Frank Burrill and the veteran Ernie Emery. New signings included the new club captain, Bob Reid, joining from Burnley. George Nicholls and Billy Bridgeman both came from Chelsea while Percy Sands moved from Arsenal. Dick Upex signed from the disbanded Croydon Common club, John Bollington had previously served Walsall but was unattached when he was demobilised from the Army, young full back Jimmy Evans arrived from Ton Pentre. Star signing was undoubtedly that of William "Lot" Jones from Manchester City, who had already been capped at international level by Wales. Fred Robson had initially re-signed for the club but was moved on to Swansea before the campaign started.

The season was modestly successful, the club finishing 11th in the table of 22 clubs. An early highlight included a 3-1 win over Brentford at home. The visitors were leading by the only goal when George Nicholls broke his leg in a heavy challenge. Down to ten men the home side were fortified by an equaliser from Frank Burrill and eventually ran out comfortable winners against the odds. Home form was generally sound but away matches often resulted in heavy defeats. Before Christmas Exeter City (0-3), Bristol Rovers (1-4) and Southampton (0-4) were instantly forgettable trips on the road.

The F.A.Cup provided an interesting story; the club had been drawn at home to reigning FA Cup-holders Sheffield United, having dispatched Watford in the 6th qualifying round. However, The Kursaal was ill equipped at that stage to host such a big match, having only shallow terracing, no banking and a modest grandstand, so the board approached their opponents with a view to staging the game at Bramall Lane. The Sheffield club initially refused to move the fixture although strangely after Southend's unexpected 1-0 win at Portsmouth, the eventual Southern League champions, a deal was hastily arranged. It proved a wise move, despite a 0-3 defeat, the gate of nearly 40,000 generating a share of the gate of £841, all but wiping out the club's debts. During the season, Jack Emblem wrestled the goalkeeping jersey from Ted Leahy and made a name for himself by saving five consecutive pen-

alty kicks. In the 2-2 draw at Queens Park Rangers, Emblem had excelled himself by saving two penalties from the home side.

In March 1920, manager Ned Liddell was offered a substantial pay increase to become manager of Queens Park Rangers; his sudden defection left the club rudderless for a full month before the board appointed Tom Mather as the new man in charge. As the season wound down, the club were offered a substantial fee for three players from Wolverhampton Wanderers. George Marshall, Frank Burrill and Maurice Woodward all moved to Molineux, Woodward costing £700 while £800 each was received for Marshall and Burrill, who were both allowed to finish the campaign at Southend. All three would play in the 1921 FA Cup Final although they would have to

Southend United erased nearly all their debt by switching their FA Cup match against Sheffield United to Bramall Lane. A gate of nearly 40,000 earned Southend £841 in gate receipts.

Shenanigans Thwart The Shrimpers...

Coming out of the horrors of The Great War, football was struggling, with money scarce and many grounds in need of repair. In particular, the Southern League was floundering and in January 1919 the Southern League petitioned to have its leading clubs elected en bloc to a proposed new division of the Football League. The meeting, held at the Grand Hotel in Manchester, produced the same result as a similar attempt back in April 1909. The Football League president, John McKenna, moved that the proposals of the Southern League, often at loggerheads with the northern dominated Football League, "should not be entertained". The member clubs of the Football League sided with McKenna unanimously.

To fully understand the northern bias of the Football League, it is prudent to look at the final tables of the two divisions at the end of the 1914-15 season. Of the forty club membership there were only six clubs south of Birmingham. Bristol City were the sole team outside the capital. Of the five London clubs Chelsea and Tottenham Hotspur finished in the bottom two places in the First Division while Clapton Orient and Fulham were mid-table Second Division also-rans. The remaining club, Arsenal, were massively in debt to the tune of £60,000 following Sir Henry Norris' controversial relocation of the club from Woolwich to North London. The club initially suffered from poor support and spent twelve of their first 22 seasons in the Football League in Division Two.

However, at the same meeting, the Football League did vote to expand their membership to 44 clubs meaning Spurs, based on previous precedence, should have remained in Division One despite finishing next to bottom. However, using his not inconsiderable financial clout and influence, Norris forced sufficient members to allow the "promotion" of his club Arsenal at Tottenham's expense, despite their modest fifth place finish in 1914-15. The reshuffle meant there were four vacancies in the Second Division and, for once, the election process provided an even geographical split. Coventry City arrived from the Southern League, having been co-opted in the Football League emergency war leagues. South Shields gained election from the North Eastern League and Port Vale came from the Central League. The final electee was West Ham United, who gained enough votes despite only finishing fourth in the Southern League during the 1914-15 campaign. The rejection of the Southern League's proposals saw relations between the two bodies deteriorate to an all-time low and the Southern League made a futile attempt to reverse West Ham's election, stating the East London club had never officially resigned from the Southern League.

...But Then A Change In Fortune

By March 1920, past animosity had been set aside and in a meeting at the same Manchester hotel, among several momentous decisions, the Southern League's 21 leading clubs, including Southend United, were elected to the new Third Division of the Football League. Cardiff City had already been voted in alongside the newly formed Leeds United. The latter had come about following the sudden collapse of Leeds City in October 1919. Cardiff and Leeds had been elected in place of the bottom two clubs in Division Two, Lincoln City and Grimsby Town. This left an odd number of clubs in the new Third Division, therefore it was decided that the remaining place would go to Grimsby Town, as they had gained many more votes than Lincoln on the re-election voting for the Second Division. Lincoln City were unceremoniously booted out to the Midland League. It was also decided that because of doubts about playing strength, the election of a new division of northern clubs would be deferred for a year when the new Third Division would be split into two regionalised sections of equal numbers.

So it came to pass that in the inaugural season of Football League membership, Southend United would compete against many familiar teams, with only Grimsby Town being new adversaries.

Left to right: Jimmy Evans, Ernie Emery and Frank Burrill

settle for loser's medals as Tottenham triumphed 1-0 at Stamford Bridge.

The club's final position would have been more greatly rewarded if goalscoring had proved to be an easier task. Only 46 goals were registered in 42 League games, resulting in 17 of the matches ending in draws. The departing Frank Burrill led the way with 16 goals, Heneage Wileman ending the campaign with a modest eight. The reserves had a season to forget, finishing bottom of the South-Eastern League with only two wins and two draws from the 28 games played.

Some big crowds, notably the tie at Sheffield United, and the home match with Millwall on Christmas Day, in addition to the transfer fees for Woodward, Marshall, Burrill and Jack Young (£500 to West Ham United) led to the end of season accounts showing a modest profit.

1920/21 – Modest Beginnings

Despite effectively playing the same opposition, Tom Mather spent the summer looking for a new team as many of the previous squad had moved on. The veterans Ernie Emery and Billy Bridgeman had retired and Albert Frost, Percy Sands and Dick Upex had been released; goalkeeper Ted Leahy and full back Lot Jones both opted to join Aberdare Athletic. Only Jimmy Evans, Heneage Wileman, Bob Reid, George Nicholls and Jack Bollington had been re-engaged by the club, although the latter would scarcely feature in the first team.

Interestingly, Mather relied on players from outside the Football League for the nucleus of his

squad. The only player signed with extensive League experience was Arthur Whalley of Manchester United, who had previously served Blackpool. Another five new faces had some limited League experience, Albert Fairclough and the Scot Jim Henderson had seen action for Manchester City, Blakey Martin arrived from Derby County and also played Football League matches for Glossop. Colin Myers (Bradford City) and Andrew Newton (Port Vale and Manchester City) had also turned out in Football League matches. The new goalkeeper would be Tommy Capper, formerly of Dundee, recruited from Southport Central, Joe Dorsett arrived from Colne, Tommy Nuttall was previously with St.Mirren but signed from Northwich Victoria and Joe Walters joined from Accrington Stanley. The northern recruitment drive continued with Mather employing his knowledge of the local leagues in Bolton to take a chance on Ted Baldwin, Edward and Stan Mather. All three would figure in the first team during the campaign. The only southern based recruit was Henry Allen, who signed from Gnome Athletic of the London League.

The campaign started brightly, with Albert Fairclough netting twice in a 2-0 win at The Kursaal against Brighton and Hove Albion in the clubs' inaugural Football League match. The interest generated in the town over the election to the Football League attracted a new record gate of 10,000. Home form remained steady throughout the campaign, assisted by crowds often in excess of 6,000 in the compact Kursaal ground; the undoubted partisanship of the gathered locals would invariably intimidate visiting teams.

The real problem was away form; only one win was secured on their travels in the entire campaign and fourteen of the 21 away matches would result in defeat. The solitary success came in November when eventual champions Crystal Palace were defeated 3-2 at The Nest. This was a hotly contested game and the home crowd invaded the pitch on several occasions and jostled the United players at the end of the game. Bob Reid was punched to the ground and the referee was left incapacitated on the ground having been kicked several times. The crowd trouble was deemed so severe that The Nest was closed by League order for a fortnight, forcing the club to stage their next home game against Exeter City at The Dell in Southampton. It seemed to be a prolific month for unpleasant matches, the home game with Merthyr Town resulted in Albert Fairclough being dismissed from the field for reacting to an umpteenth hefty challenge. The home crowd burst into open hostility and the referee and visitors were blockaded in the dressing rooms after the game. The Football Association officially warned the club over its control of supporters. Earlier in the month, the game at Fratton Park descended into lawlessness with Southend players seemingly bent on extracting revenge on their hosts after Fred Sergeant had been left with a broken wrist at the home game the previous week. Portsmouth were already renowned for employing roughhouse tactics and both clubs were subsequently warned about their conduct following an enquiry by the Football League commissioner.

A decent F.A.Cup run was enjoyed by the home fans, with the club having seen off Hednesford Town and Eccles United at The Kursaal before being drawn at home to Second Division Blackpool in Round Two.

In previous years, the board were all too keen to take the financial view when it came to attractive opposition and often agreed settlements to stage the game at their opponent's grounds. Blackpool offered financial recompense to move the tie to Bloomfield Road, but this time the board held firm and insisted the tie be staged at Southend. Despite hiking admission prices to two shillings, a huge gate of 9,250 watched Southend defeat their supposedly superior opponents by a Joe Dorsett goal to nil.

The reward for this victory was an even more attractive home tie in the Third Round. First Division Tottenham Hotspur were paired with Southend and a new record gate of 11,661 packed into the seafront ground. Some bad publicity in the London papers about the limitations of The Kursaal prevented the gate from being even higher. Still, the board must have been delighted with record gate receipts of £2,963. Spurs won the tie by 4-1 and would eventually win the cup itself, beating Wolverhampton Wanderers (with their three ex-Shrimpers) by a goal to nil at Stamford Bridge.

Away support had grown as well, with 2,000 Southend supporters attending the 1-1 draw at Gillingham in March. The majority of supporters arrived in Kent from a small armada of boats departing from the pier head.

Southend players skipping with ropes during a training session at The Kursaal.

39

Sadly, League results tailed off as the season progressed and the club had to settle for a modest 17th place out of 22 clubs. Albert Fairclough, as expected, topped the scorers chart with a healthy total of 15. The clubs goalscoring problems were highlighted by the fact that Tommy Nuttall, with 11, was the only other player managing a double figure tally.

1921/22 – Re-election Woes For A Wretched Blues Team

If the inaugural Football League campaign had been somewhat of a disappointment, the second would be an unmitigated disaster. Only eight of the 42 League matches would be won, and the total of 34 goals for and 74 against was by far the worst in the division. It was no surprise, therefore, that the club propped up the rest at the end of a dismal campaign.

The main problem seemed to be that Mather could not get a team of consistent performers together. He bolstered his squad in the summer with a host of signings. Billy Evans and Fred Harris both arrived from Swansea Town while Blackpool were also relieved of two players, Fred Halstead and Stephen Howard. Billy Kettle also came from South Wales, leaving Ebbw Vale and the Scot David Reid came from Aston Villa. Northern recruits again proliferated with Stan Dellow (Bradford City), Bill Ruddock (The Wednesday), Alex

Elliott (Wigan Borough) and George Lawrence (Darlington) all heading to the Essex coast.

The season started poorly and got progressively worse. The club had to wait until their twelfth match, at the end of October, before securing their first victory, a 2-0 win over Gillingham at The Kursaal. Mather tried manfully to stop the rot in November by securing the services of Harry Buddery from Portsmouth, Harry Pidgeon (QPR) and yet another from the Bolton local leagues, Andrew Hawarden. Narrow wins were secured against Aberdare, Plymouth and Merthyr, but the writing was already on the wall. Following a 1-4 reversal against Watford at Cassio Road, the board decided to relieve Mather of his duties. His successor had been watching the latest debacle from the stands.

Ted Birnie acted quickly to bolster the beleaguered squad, immediately signing Harry Dobson from Newport, Bert Gibbons from Dartford and a back up goalkeeper, Joe Hall, from Backworth Percy. However, the existing squad was so poor that only three more victories, against Northampton Town, Reading and Bristol Rovers were forthcoming. But for the dead eyed Jimmy Evans and his spectacular penalty kicks, the season would have been even more abysmal. Evans converted all ten penalty kicks awarded to the club in the campaign, the Welsh international full back's swooping run in and shot becoming something of

Southend United 1921/22. This team group photograph included a very unusual member of the squad - a lucky black cat!

A CENTURY UNITED

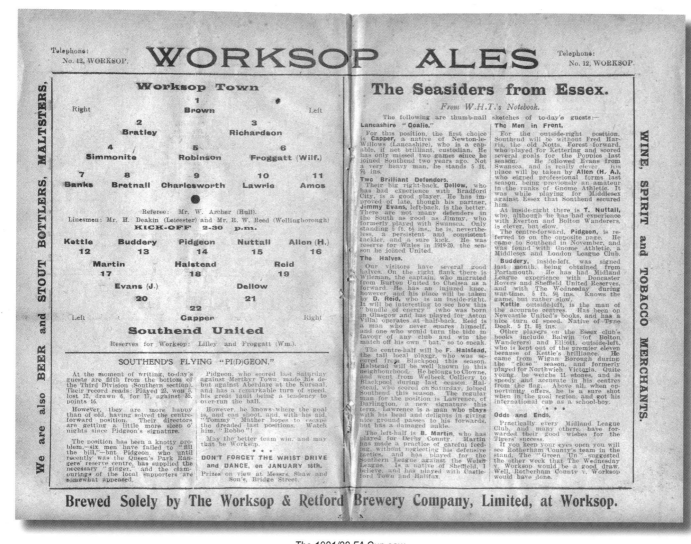

a trademark; he is still the only full-back to finish a season as United's top scorer.

The newly reconstituted reserve team (Southend Corinthian had played the 1920/21 season at The Kursaal instead of having a reserve team) were equally abject, finishing bottom of the Southern League (English Section), five points adrift of Norwich City Reserves.

So the board were faced with having to drum up support for the clubs re-election campaign. A slogan was adopted for the publicity drive:

"Southend without its football would be as the sea without its salt".

The opposition in the ballot were old rivals Exeter City who had finished next to bottom, Bath City from the Southern League (English Section), Pontypridd (Southern League Welsh Section) and Llanelly (Welsh League). The result of the ballot was:

The 1921/22 FA Cup saw Southend United travel north, with a visit to Worksop Town in the first round. A 2-1 victory was followed by a poor performance, as Southend were eliminated in the second round at home to Swansea Town.

Southend United	36 votes
Exeter City	32 votes
Pontypridd	21 votes
Bath City	1 vote
Llanelly	0 votes

The vote of confidence must have been a great encouragement to the board to rebuild the team. The town mayor, John Francis, a great campaigner for sport in the borough, launched a public appeal to raise £1,500 to assist the club, citing that the team had "become an advertising medium for the town".

1922/23 - Birnie Rebuilds Shrimpers

Within weeks the Mayor's Fund stood at £600, allowing the capture of Billy Goodwin from Man-

Pinnace Cards

In 1923, Godfrey Phillips Ltd. introduced a new brand of cigarettes named "Pinnace". Along with the cigarettes, they began issuing what would become the largest set of football cigarette cards ever produced.

Altogether, over a two year period, 2462 miniature photographs of football players were issued, although due to the errors and varieties available, the total number of different cards total nearly 5000.

When players were transferred, which was very common in those days, a new card would be issued, thus meaning that at least 188 players are shown with two different clubs, and 15 players have three different cards. There were also many different printers used, some of whom used different abbreviations for club names; thus, some players have their team name as "Southend United", "Southend U." or just "Southend".

Shown here are the majority of Southend United Pinnace cards available, although not in all their variations!

chester United. A pivotal signing, the new centre forward would rattle in 23 goals in his first campaign at The Kursaal. Ted Birnie scoured the country in his rebuilding programme; the rich vein of talent coming out of South Wales continuing with Jimmy Bissett signing from Ebbw Vale and both Jackie Slater and goalkeeper Walter Jennings decamping from Swansea Town. George Davies arrived from West Midlands League Wellington Town and the Midlands also provided Robert Booth (Birmingham City), Joe Humphreys (Aston Villa), Arthur Woodland (Notts County) and Robert Firth (Port Vale). Strangely, in an antithesis of the previous two campaigns, northern based players were ignored with the exception of George Halley who would sign from Burnley in November. Charlie Dorey was recruited from local football and performed well when called upon.

The campaign started well, with four of the opening eight League matches ending in victories. However, a decline set in during October and November, when the sole points accrued were through draws with Bristol Rovers and Plymouth Argyle. Goalkeeper Walter Jennings bore the brunt of criticism and after conceding five at Bristol City and five more at Northampton Town, he was replaced between the sticks by Joe Hall.

A 5-0 thrashing of Exeter City at The Kursaal in mid-December signalled a change of fortune and in late February, a notable 4-0 victory was secured against Millwall Athletic, Billy Goodwin scoring all the goals.

There was disappointment in the F.A.Cup, with the club failing to reach the competition proper, exiting in the fifth qualifying round in a narrow 1-2 replay defeat at Norwich City. Kent League Sittingbourne had put up stern opposition in the previous round, holding The Shrimpers to a goalless draw at The Bull Ground. In the replay The Shrimpers were three to the good by half time, but survived a second half scare to hold out for a 4-2 triumph.

Although the large influx of new players meant the season would have been regarded as a period of transition, the eventual placing of 15th must have been regarded as something of a disappointment. However, from what was generally accepted as being the poorest Southend team ever, Birnie had achieved his goal of building a happy and talented squad of players. Notably, the average home crowd had almost doubled on the dismal re-election season.

1923/24 - Savage Injury Blow Sustained In Another Season Of Struggle

It was another close season of frenetic activity at The Kursaal. Bob Firth had announced his retirement at the end of the last campaign, but the biggest blow was the loss of Jimmy Evans who, having won four Welsh caps while at The Kursaal, was sold to Burnley for £1,000. Also departing were Jimmy Bissett (Rochdale), Robert Booth (Swansea Town), George Halley (Bacup Borough), Walter Jennings (Boston Town) and Joe Humphreys (Burton Town). Initially, new recruits were thin on the ground with the only close season arrivals of note being Henry Dreyer from Crystal Palace, Tommy Evans moving south from Rotherham County, Ernie Edwards from Newport County and Billy Middleton from Aberdeen. Still scouring clubs outside the Football League for talent, Ted Birnie secured the services of goalkeeper Jimmy Maidment from Thomson's Welfare and from Midland Leaguers Scunthorpe United came inside forward Victor Whitham. The latter repaid the faith shown in him by scoring twice on his League debut at Merthyr Town in the opening game of the season. Indeed Whitham would net five in his opening three games, but then only scored a further five in the rest of the campaign.

The squad was bolstered at intervals throughout the season, with Jimmy Hodge arriving from Norwich City in September and in February, welcome experience was secured by the signing of Freddy Jewhurst from Charlton Athletic and Ernie Watkins from Birmingham City.

Some heavy defeats were sustained early on, 1-4 at Charlton and 0-5 at Newport County and a season of struggle was predicted by the press and supporters alike. Arguably the best result achieved in the first half of the campaign was a thrilling 4-4 draw at Luton Town over the Christmas period. The same month had seen an ignominious exit from the F.A.Cup at the sixth qualifying round stage, The Shrimpers going down 1-2 to Southern League Llanelly at Stebonheath Park.

There were some truly inexplicable results; in March, for example, Northampton Town were beaten 5-1 at The Kursaal, with Ernie Watkins notching a hat-trick, yet a week later the club played the reverse fixture at the County Ground and a team showing only one change were put to the sword by the humiliating score of 0-8.

A major blow was suffered in April when top scorer, Billy Goodwin, admittedly less prolific than in his first season, sustained a broken leg in the defeat at Brighton. To his credit though he was heard saying "tell the boys to play up" as he was stretchered out of the Goldstone Ground. Having suffered an appalling injury, often career ending in those days, Goodwin would have to wait two years before playing again, and then after eight appearances he would bow to the inevitable retirement.

The club were perilously close to the re-election zone throughout the campaign but had done enough to survive by a single point as the last weekend of the season came round. It was just as well as the trip to Plymouth resulted in a 1-7 battering.

1924/25 - Fitness The Key In Improved Fortunes

Ted Birnie had taken a serious look at the team's failings during the previous campaign and came

The crowd at the Goldstone Ground await the teams for the 1923/24 league match between Brighton and Hove Albion and Southend United.

to the conclusion that the players were less fit than their counterparts. Trainer Bill Cartwright was tasked with devising a tough regimen to improve matters; skipping and sprinting were introduced to training sessions and lengthy runs along the seafront to Thorpe Bay became the order of the day. The new, more professional outlook paid dividends, as the club enjoyed their most successful Football League campaign thus far.

Birnie had again been busy in the transfer market in a bid to find a successful formula. Leaving The Kursaal were Billy Evans (joining Queens Park Rangers), Billy Middleton off to Brighton, Jimmy Maidment to Newport and George Davies returning to Wellington Town. Tommy Evans and Joe Hall were also released without finding new clubs.

Joining Southend were Walter Bennett (from Chelsea), George Bissett (Pontypridd), goalkeeper Billy Hayes (Brighton), Elias MacDonald (Southampton), Tom Wolfe (Coventry) and Frank O'Rawe (Preston). Irishman Jim Donnelly would prove a more than useful addition, having signed from Accrington Stanley. However, the biggest success story of the season was a player the club already had on its books. Jim McClelland had joined Southend aged 21 in July 1923 from Raith Rovers. He had bided his time in the reserves, making an occasional first team appearance in the 1923/24 campaign. The new season had started somewhat inauspiciously when Birnie introduced McClelland at centre forward for the Bristol Rovers game at the start of October. The young Scot scored and it kick-started a run of seven successive League victories for the team, McClelland scoring seven goals in the impressive sequence. Counting two F.A.Cup ties with London Caledonians, McClelland's tally was eleven goals in nine starts.

By the end of January, a 3-0 defeat of Bournemouth saw the club move into the promotion places for the first time ever. However, a dismal run in February and March of eight games without a win would put paid to any lofty aspirations. By mid-March, Jim McClelland had scored 21 times in only 26 matches, so it was no surprise when bigger clubs beat a path to The Kursaal to watch the youngster. Second Division Middlesbrough won the race for his signature and paid

One of Southend United's new signings for the 1924/25 season, George Bissett, who joined from Pontypridd.

Southend an undisclosed fee, plus the services of Billy Hick. It was to prove an astounding bit of business as Hick would be Southend's top scorer for two of the next three seasons.

The final three games saw the club concede thirteen goals and slump to tenth in the final table. It was the side's highest finish to date, but such a dramatic loss of form must have been a bitter disappointment.

1925/26 - Cup Fever Hits the Seaside

Manager Tom Birnie was a busy man during the 1925 close season as he again reshuffled his squad. Leaving the club were Jim Donnelly, an ever-present from the previous campaign, who joined Brentford, Elias MacDonald returned north with Southport, Tom Wolfe moved to Fulham and Billy Thirlaway signed for Luton Town. Jackie Slater joined Grays Thurrock United and Charlie Dorey joined Guildford United; both members of the Southern League.

The Report of Directors for the year ending 2nd May 1925 showed Southend United having made a profit of £1,767 3s. 5d., a vast improvement on the previous year, when the club made a loss of £50 5s. 6d.

Boosting the squad was a triumvirate of signings from Leeds United; goalkeeper Billy Moore, Fred Graver and Tommy Bell all arrived at The Kursaal from Yorkshire. Dickie Donoven proved a prudent signing from Midland Leaguers Mansfield Town and from the north east came Jack French (Middlesbrough) and Jack Andrews (Shildon Colliery). Billy Shaw was another signing from the Midland League, transferring from Scunthorpe United. Hugh Morris joined from Nottingham Forest, having seen service with Notts County and Manchester City and Stephen Smith arrived from Charlton Athletic.

The board had spent the summer improving the ground and increasing the size of the terracing; The Kursaal could now accommodate some 18,000. The Football Association had amended the offside

Southend United Football Club, Limited.

Report of Directors.

1925.

The Directors herewith submit their Annual Report and Accounts for the year ending 2nd May,

The Directors are pleased to report a profit on the year's working of £1,767 3s. 5d., most of which has been brought about by reduction of working expenses and transfer fees received for players.

The Directors report that during the close season both teams have been considerably ....ed, and they anticipate a more consistent and successful playing record next season.

.... Board co-opt Mr. H. G. Flowers as a director, he being ful ....firm the appointment. ..... Messrs. P. G. Ga

rule, allowing one player between the last back and the goalkeeper. Birnie had hoped that the change to the offside law would benefit a passing team like Southend and this would prove to be correct. The new team took a while to gel and initially some hefty defeats were suffered, notably 2-6 at Plymouth on the opening day and a 1-8 thrashing at Millwall in September. Birnie introduced Billy Moore between the sticks in place of Billy Hayes and the change paid immediate dividends; a 4-1 victory at Watford and a 6-1 demolition of Northampton Town at The Kursaal.

The season progressed with some impressive wins, 5-1 at home to Merthyr and Crystal Palace plus a 4-1 triumph at Bristol City, but some equally poor results, 0-5 at Charlton Athletic and 0-3 at Crystal Palace, meant the club hovered around mid-table throughout the campaign. The season finished with a poor run-in of four games without a win, culminating in a 1-5 reversal at Penydarren Park against Merthyr on the last day of the season. The club finished eleventh in the table with 19 wins and 19 defeats from the 42 game programme. Three players managed double figures of goals during the campaign, Billy Shaw (21), Billy Hick (18), and Ernie Watkins (13). In a season of high scoring games, four players scored hat-tricks; Watkins (v Brentford), Shaw (v Bournemouth), Hick (v Newport) and George Johnson (v Crystal Palace). A new record gate of 13,438 attended the Boxing Day clash with Bristol City.

In January, Ernie Watkins was allowed to leave for Brentford, which meant Billy Hick became a regular at inside forward. In March, Birnie bolstered his squad by the signing from Liverpool of the diminutive forward Fred Baron.

The F.A.Cup proved tremendously exciting following the rule change allowing League clubs automatic progress to the competition proper. Enjoying home advantage throughout the cup

run, The Shrimpers dispatched Isthmian League Dulwich Hamlet by 5-1 in the first round. The second round saw a narrow 1-0 win over fellow Third Division side Gillingham. Southport, from the Third Division (North) made the long journey to Essex in the third round, suffering a hefty 5-2 beating. The fourth round paired Southend with Derby County. The Rams were leading the Second Division, having not been beaten all season. The attendance record was again beaten when 14,225 crammed into the seafront enclosure. A blow to the home side's aspirations was suffered on the morning of the match when George Bissett was forced to withdraw following the sudden death of his brother. Fred Graver was bought into the side and gave a man-of-the-match performance. By half-time, goals from Jack Andrews and Graver had seen Southend hold a shock 2-0 advantage. Billy Hick added two more in the second half, before Murphy reduced the arrears for the visitors. The stunning victory bought the club to national attention again and cheering at the ground was heard in Hadleigh, some five miles away. The reward was another home tie against Second Division opposition; Nottingham Forest however escaped with a narrow single goal victory in front of another record gate of 18,153, the winning goal coming from Duncan Walker.

The 1925/26 campaign proved to be a highly profitable one on and off the field.

The team that beat Derby County.

UPS AND DOWNS

1926/27- An Unexpected Slump

After a momentous campaign, the new season was highly anticipated around the town. Several players had departed; George Bissett had retired while Billy Hayes (Accrington Stanley), George Johnson (Newport County) and Frank O'Rawe (Brighton and Hove Albion) had decided to join other Third Division clubs. Three players, Ernie Edwards, Fred Graver and top scorer Billy Shaw had opted to join clubs outside the Football League. They joined Dudley Town (Birmingham League), Wallsend Town (North Eastern League) and Gainsborough Trinity (Midland League) respectively.

New signings were modest in number; Percy Beaumont came from Barnsley, and Harold Dennis from another Yorkshire side, Huddersfield Town. Walter Brayshaw signed from Blackburn Rovers and filling the understudy role to Billy Moore was Arthur Purdy of Luton Town.

The season started inauspiciously, The Shrimpers going down 1-5 to Swindon Town at the County Ground. However, a visit to Merthyr prompted a run of four League victories in a row in September. The moving of Billy Hick from inside forward to centre forward proved a master stroke on Ted Birnie's behalf, the robust north easterner becoming the undoubted star of the team, scoring 29 goals during the season. His two goals against Newport in October saw him commence a run of seven consecutive matches where he would find the net, a club record he would beat himself the following year. Eleven goals came to Hick in the seven match spell. It was not surprising, therefore, that the club would find itself in sixth place in the table as Christmas approached. In the F.A.Cup, Southend had again been paired with Dulwich Hamlet in the first round. Drawn away this time at the imposing Champion Hill ground, a 4-1 victory failed to herald the start of another cup run, The Shrimpers submitting to Second Division Reading at the next hurdle.

Then, a dramatic and inexplicable post-Christmas slump saw the club slide down the table. During February and March, a run of seven matches without a win was finally ended by a single Hick goal at home to Gillingham. The club seemed heavily reliant on Hick for goals and when he did not score, the side would invariably draw a blank. Solely due to having a fair number of points in hand from the first half of the season, and a truly abject Aberdare team, a re-election battle was never a real possibility, although a final placing of

Southend United's home programme for the 1926/27 league match against Northampton Town.

19th from 22 teams would have given cause for concern among the board and supporters alike.

1927/28- Birnie Masterminds a Revival

Relatively few players departed the club in the close season; Birnie's squad was small and needed increasing in numbers. He had lost Billy Goodwin to retirement following his abortive attempt to return from a badly broken leg; Percy Beaumont also finished with the professional game. Fred Jewhurst and Stephen Smith moved to Clapton Orient, although Tommy Dixon and Bert Rosier would make the reverse journey. Rosier, a 34-year old veteran with extensive experience with Brentford as well as Orient, was installed as new club captain. Seth Plum and Jimmy Frew joined from Chelsea while Alf Horne (Hull City) and John Fell (Leeds United) moved south to join The Shrimpers. George Falconbridge had shown sufficient promise at Ilkeston United and Tom Brophy came from Aberdare (now in the Southern League having lost Football League status). Goalkeeper Tommy Boyce was tempted from St.Mirren and Stan Sayer came from Lincoln City.

Tommy Dixon

The campaign got off to a flying start with four wins from the opening five fixtures. The highlight was a 6-1 drubbing of Crystal Palace at The Kursaal, with Dickie Donoven helping himself to four of the goals. There was still the odd heavy defeat on opposition ground, 1-5 at Millwall and 1-6 at Coventry City, but prospects of a best ever season were being spoken of as a real possibility. The thrashing at Highfield Road was the start of Billy Hick's all time record run of scoring in eight successive matches. This has only even been challenged by Brett Angell in 1991 and Freddy Eastwood in 2005, both of whom fell one match short of equalling Hick's achievement.

The F.A.Cup proved a fleeting affair, Wellington Town being narrowly defeated at The Kursaal; inevitably Billy Hick scoring the only goal, before a second round exit to Gillingham at the Priestfield Stadium.

During the campaign, skipper Bert Rosier was often found to be at loggerheads with Ted Birnie and eventually he was stripped of the captaincy (which was handed to Dickie Donoven), and placed on the transfer list.

In March, Birnie was desperate to recruit an experienced custodian to stand in for the injured

Billy Moore and swapped full back Tommy Bell for Portsmouth's John Jarvie.

The club's League form remained healthy and in March, the 7-0 victory over Queens Park Rangers at The Kursaal was their biggest winning margin since Southern League days, Billy Hick scoring a hat-trick in the demolition. The season was rounded off in style with Newport County being soundly beaten by five goals to one. The Shrimpers had achieved their highest League placing thus far of seventh, albeit nineteen points adrift of champions Millwall.

A season of great team spirit and huge achievement was somewhat tempered by the announcement that the board had accepted an offer from Bristol City for crowd favourite and prolific goalscorer Billy Hick.

1928/29- Shankly Shines in a Season of Stability

Manager Ted Birnie's major 1928 close season task was finding a replacement for the prolific Billy Hick; he opted to sign Jimmy Shankly, a big gangly front runner from Sheffield United. Another significant signing was Dave Robinson from Leeds United who would spend the next twelve seasons playing in the first team and another fifty odd years serving the club in various capacities. Other signings included Portsmouth's Sid Binks and John Townsend from Ebbw Vale. Shortly after the campaign started, Joe Johnson was signed from Leigh Amateurs and Cyril Oxley arrived from Morecambe. However, Oxley would struggle to command a place in the first team and moved on to Kettering Town in March.

Jimmy Shankly

Departing The Kursaal were Tommy Boyce, returning to Scotland with Clydebank, John Jarvie (Watford), Albert Purdy (Brentford) and Bert Rosier (Fulham). Seth Plum could not recover from an ankle injury and was forced into premature retirement from the game.

Any doubts about the new goalscoring hope, Jimmy Shankly, who had little pedigree in League football, soon dissipated. In the opening eleven fixtures of the campaign, the Scot scored an unbelievable fifteen times, including a hat-trick in a 5-2 thrashing of Norwich City at The Nest.

Results were indifferent however, often ranging from emphatic wins (5-1 against Merthyr and 5-3 against Norwich City at The Kursaal) to heavy defeats such as 1-4 at both Bristol Rovers and Watford. A festive cracker was served up at The Kursaal when a dramatic 4-4 draw was fought out with Bournemouth and Boscombe Athletic. A grave setback occurred at Newport in December when Fred Baron was stretchered off with a broken leg.

Jimmy Shankly, who strangely never truly won over the Southend fans due to his awkward style, scored 35 goals in the campaign, the highest ever seasonal total by a Southend player. This included the club's only goal in the F.A.Cup that year, a humiliating 1-5 reversal at Luton Town. Useful scoring support came from Jack Bailey, who scored 14 and the ever reliable Dickie Donoven, who chipped in with eleven. The club scored 80 goals in the League but conceded 75, leaving them marooned in a mid-table twelfth place from the 22 clubs with 15 victories and 16 defeats from the 42 match programme.

1929/30- Baron Takes Top Scorer Mantle

The usual transfer activity occupied manager Ted Birnie during the 1929 close season. Leaving the club were Jimmy Frew to Carlisle United and Hugh Morris to Newport County. Jack Andrews returned to his native north-east to join hometown club Darlington, Stan Sayer and John Townsend

chosing Southern League clubs, signing for Dartford and Grays Thurrock United respectively.

Filling the gaps in the squad were Fred Barnett, a useful signing from Tottenham Hotspur, Bob Ward from Manchester United, Tom McKenna and John Borland, two Scots plying their trade in Wales with Merthyr Town and the most significant capture, that of Mickey Jones from Everton, who would spend the next seven seasons at the club.

An opening day injury to leading scorer Jimmy Shankly gave cause for concern but Fred Baron, returning from a broken leg, stepped up to the challenge and would eventually score 22 goals in only 25 starts. For the first time ever, the club won its opening five League matches until Northampton won 1-2 at The Kursaal. This reversal proved to be a temporary blip as the team then went seven games unbeaten before the wheels came off in spectacular fashion, with a 1-5 drubbing at Swindon Town. Shankly returned to the team over the Christmas period and proved he had not lost his shooting boots, bagging four against Queens Park Rangers and five in a 6-0 demolition of Merthyr Town at The Kursaal.

The F.A.Cup saw Brentford beaten at The Kursaal in the first round. The good fortune of being drawn at home in the second round, however, counted for nothing as Southend surprisingly succumbed 1-4 to Third Division (North) York City.

Shankly sustained another injury at Brighton in March and his season was curtailed prematurely. Fred Baron returned to the front line with immediate impact, netting a hat-trick in a 6-0 win over Bristol Rovers at The Kursaal. Clapton Orient

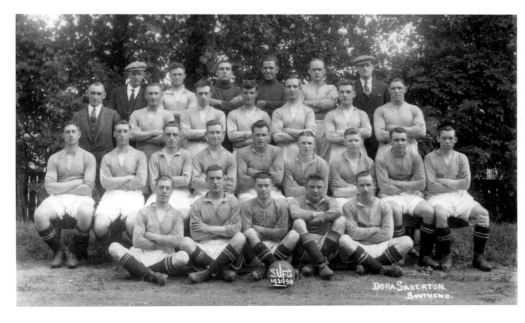

Southend United 1929/30

were also comfortably beaten by 4-1, however a late season collapse, with the team claiming only one point from the final six outings saw them finish in a disappointing eleventh place having headed the table for some of the campaign. The dramatic loss of form was compounded on the final day of the season when Fred Baron sustained another broken leg in the match at Northampton Town. He would only play another 13 games for Southend in the subsequent two years.

1930/31 - Influx of Experienced Players Precipitates Highest Ever Finish

Ted Birnie had the usual round of departing players to cater for during the 1930 close season, and with Fred Baron likely to miss the entire campaign, he had to strengthen his squad and rely on Jimmy Shankly remaining fit. John Armitage left for Northampton Town, John Borland signed for Barrow, Tom McKenna moved to Northern Ireland with Portadown and Joe Campbell joined Southern League Dartford for whom he would win two successive Southern League titles. In September, after four seasons at The Kursaal, Jack Bailey departed for the ill-fated Thames Association club.

Among the new arrivals to the Essex coast were Jim Nicol and Owen Williams from Middlesbrough. Owen Williams was quite a capture, having made his name with Clapton Orient gaining two full England caps before playing over 200 games for Middlesbrough. Joe Wilson also proved an excellent capture; despite having made just one solitary appearance for Newcastle United's first team, Wilson had decent experience in the northeast with the likes of Annfield Plain, Crook Town and Stanley United. Inside-left Tot Pike joined from Birmingham City; clearly he had developed as a player as Birnie had not offered him a contract following a trial in 1925. Full back Billy Gibson arrived from Blackpool and outside left Arthur Crompton signed from Tottenham Hotspur, backed with a decent pedigree in Forces football.

The opening game of the season saw a heavy home reversal, 2-4 at the hands of Crystal Palace but a win and a draw on the road at Brighton and Bournemouth put the team in good spirits for the next home game with Torquay United. A remarkable match ended 6-3 to Southend, with Shankly claiming a hat-trick and newcomer Owen Williams a brace. The club

Southend United's new signing from Middlesbrough, Owen Williams.

remained in the higher reaches of the table as Christmas approached, although away form was a worry with only wins at Brighton, Walsall and Norwich coming on the road in the opening ten away matches. An away draw in the F.A.Cup saw The Shrimpers bow out at the first round stage at Torquay United.

The December fixture against Clapton Orient took on new significance when the East London club had their Lea Bridge Road ground closed for safety concerns and announced that the fixture would be played at Wembley Stadium. A tiny crowd of 2,500 gathered at the legendary venue and The Shrimpers could not rise to the occasion going down 1-3, Southend's solitary Wembley goal coming from Mickey Jones.

The Boxing Day reserve team fixture against Southampton landed the club in hot water with the Football Association. The match had seen Southend forward Fred Baron dismissed from the field for violent conduct and the crowd reacted violently, the referee reporting the club, stating that he feared for his safety. The F.A. cautioned the club regarding the controlling of its' supporters and insisted the club print warning notices on the subject of crowd behaviour in the programme and on billboards around the ground for the rest of the season.

As the second half of the campaign progressed, The Shrimpers championship push was maintained and home form was excellent with notable triumphs coming against Newport County (6-2) and Exeter City (5-1), but a niggling run of injuries to Owen Williams, Arthur Crompton, Jack French and Dave Robinson put pressure on Birnie's small squad of professionals. Promotion prospects took a fatal blow over Easter when all three holiday fixtures resulted in defeats. It was perhaps a resignation to the inevitable that during April, the club arranged two additional fixtures. After the Easter defeats, prospects of winning the title seemed remote and as only the Champions would gain promotion, League leaders Notts County appeared to be home and dry. The extra games were a benefit match for Billy Moore against Everton, only the third Southend player to be honoured in this fashion after George Molyneux and Ernie Emery. The illustrious visitors won 2-6, although star attraction, Dixie Dean, couldn't play due to injury; he assisted as linesman for the match. A decent crowd of 8,164 ensured a decent payday for a

Sadly, Notts County did win the title and Southend had to settle for a final position of fifth. This was still the highest placing since the club were elevated to the Football League. Once again, Jimmy Shankly's goalscoring prowess was the eye-catching statistic from the campaign, the Scot bagging 28 in 41 League outings. Interestingly, the team remained fairly settled throughout the season and Mickey Jones, Fred Barnett and Billy Moore played every match of the campaign.

1931/32- So Close to Title Success but Promotion Eludes The Shrimpers Again

Manager Ted Birnie held the nucleus of his squad together for the 1931/32 season. Only bit-part players departed in the summer, Jim Nicol left for St. Johnstone while Billy Gibson and Bob Ward opted to pursue their playing careers

great club servant. Then Southend accepted an invitation to play a friendly match against the famous Jewish club Ajax, to be staged in Rotterdam. However, so concerned were the hosts by the growing reputation of Birnie's men that they called in a number of reinforcements, therefore making the opposition a Dutch "B" team. Even so, goals from Jimmy Shankly (2) and Fred Barnett saw a comfortable 3-1 victory.

The opening home game of the 1930/31 season saw Crystal Palace visit The Kursaal. If the football entertainment wasn't enough, you could always visit the Wall of Death, or even the Midget Mansion!

in Cheshire League football joining Macclesfield Town and Altrincham respectively. Ernie Hatfield joined Southend from Wolves and Arthur Thomson signed from Manchester United, having made a handful of appearances for the Red Devils. Cover for the ageing and increasingly injury prone Billy Moore was acquired in the shape of Bristol City's Dave Whitelaw and two players from local football were invited to join the squad, Buck Fryar arriving from Shoebury Town and Ken Mayes signing from Athenian League Barking Town.

In September, Owen Williams, frustrated at being unable to command a place in the team, opted to move back to his native north east with Shildon Colliery.

On the field, Southend could have scarcely made a more promising start to the season. The opening three fixtures resulted in victories and it was not until late November that the first defeat was incurred, a 2-3 reversal at Crystal Palace. Goalscoring was plentiful and indeed it was not until Christmas Day against Exeter City that the first blank was drawn in front of goal in a League encounter. The F.A.Cup proved once again to be a disappointment, a surprising 0-3 loss was incurred at Northampton in the second round, six weeks after winning a League fixture at the County Ground.

The New Year period tested the strength of the squad as Robinson, Dixon, Donoven and Barnett all spent periods on the sidelines with injury. However, once back to a full complement, coupled with the continuing development of Les Clenshaw in the reserve team, Birnie felt he was able to accept an offer from Brentford for Arthur Crompton.

A super run of eight victories in nine encounters put Southend within sight of the championship as the Easter

Top to bottom: Dave Whitelaw.
Action from a match at The Kursaal.
The players leave the field with The Kursaal waterchute clearly visible in the background.

fixtures were completed. The highlight in a rich vein of form was a 5-2 victory at The Kursaal over Mansfield Town, with young Clenshaw repaying Birnie's faith in him by claiming four goals.

However, a three match sequence of goalless draws in April left Southend in the wake of title rivals Reading and Fulham with two matches left. The Cottagers stood in pole position on 53 points, Reading a further point back. Southend were adrift by three points from the Royals and reliant on the other two slipping up. Southend beat Torquay and Reading walloped Clapton Orient 5-0 but Fulham's 3-2 win over Bristol Rovers ensured the title was going to West London with a game to play.

A tremendous season but ultimately a disappointing ending for Birnie's men, as title success had been a real possibility right up until mid-April. Once again Jimmy Shankly was the leading scorer with 20, the third time in four seasons he had scored twenty or more goals for the club.

1932/33 - A Disappointing Campaign as Mid-table Beckons

After such a good attempt at winning promotion in the 1931/32 season, Ted Birnie stuck with his squad for the new campaign, although the season would ultimately prove disappointing. The Shrimpers had suffered the enforced retirement of the prolific but injury prone Fred Baron and Jack French (Brentford) and Arthur Thomson (Coventry City) had moved on to pastures new. To try and build on his squad depth and strength, Birnie signed half a dozen players during the close season. Jack Morfitt arrived from Bradford Park Avenue with the reputation of being a useful utility player adept at playing across the front line or at left-half. Jack Robson signed from Derby County having had extensive experience at Reading, Harry Randle came from Birmingham City having come to prominence in the Midland League with Mansfield Town and Shirebrook, Billy Wootton (Port Vale) and Tom Wilson (Charlton Athletic) also signed up but would struggle to command a starting place. Wilson had a considerable League career behind him with Wigan Borough, Cardiff City and Charlton Athletic but could not displace Dave Robinson at left back. Harry Lewis, an inside forward, would prove a useful addition from Arsenal.

Birnie elected to start with Dave Whitelaw as his first choice goalkeeper but after a shocking 1-8

Jack Morfitt relaxes with a fan outside The Kursaal.

defeat at Torquay United, the veteran Billy Moore was hastily restored to custodial duties.

Form was indifferent throughout the campaign and a regular run of unbeaten matches proved frustratingly elusive. On New Year's Eve, Aldershot were thumped 5-1 at The Kursaal only for the side to lose 1-6 at Queens Park Rangers seven days later. The January home clash with Torquay United was marred by full back Dave Robinson sustaining a broken collar bone.

The F.A.Cup for once provided a useful distraction from League struggles. Exeter City were dispatched in the opening round in a replay at St.James' Park following a draw at home. In the second round, Southend were drawn at home to Scarborough from the Midland League; a Jack Morfitt hattrick paving the way for a comfortable 4-1 victory. The third round tie against Watford also required a replay, the sides having drawn 1-1 at Vicarage Road but Morfitt and Clenshaw earned The Shrimpers a Fourth Round tie against First Division Derby County. Mindful of their embarrassment at The Kursaal seven years previously, The Rams must have been concerned about history repeating itself. A 15,000 crowd enjoyed an electrifying game and Derby were grateful to scrape a narrow 2-3 victory. Tot Pike and another for Morfitt breached the visitors' defence but a brace from the prolific Jack Bowers and a third by Howard Fabian saw

Southend United stalwart Dave Robinson

the home side bow out of the competition. Jack Morfitt excelled himself by scoring seven goals in the six F.A.Cup ties.

Poor away form again resulted in the club being marooned in mid-table; a thirteenth place finish following a record of only 15 wins and 16 defeats from the 42 League matches was all that could have been expected. Goalscoring machine Jimmy Shankly had spent much of the campaign on the sidelines, haunted by injury, but his second goal against Luton in April meant he became the first Southend player to register 100 goals for the club. His deputy in the first team, Jack Morfitt, proved to be a worthy understudy, bagging 21 goals in only 33 appearances.

1933/34 - End of an Era as Birnie Bows Out

Following the disappointing 1932/33 campaign, Birnie decided to overhaul his squad. Out went Harry Lewis to Notts County, Tot Pike to Norwich, John Robson to Chester and Ernie Hatfield to Southern League Dartford. The biggest name leaving the club however was that of Jimmy Shankly; having scored 100 goals in 152 appearances, it was somewhat of a surprise that he was allowed to leave for Barrow.

New signings were George Robertson from Scottish Central League club Cambuslang Rangers and Albert Worthy from Lincoln City. Leo Stevens would prove a useful acquisition from Everton, Arthur Bateman signed from Grimsby Town but would stay only six months before leaving for Brentford, James Proudfoot arrived from Notts County with a decent pedigree after four years at Barnsley but only stayed for four months before leaving for Yeovil and Petters United. Harry Lane was arguably the best signing, joining from Birmingham City, and would go on to make over 200 appearances for Southend. The final signing was Hughie McMahon from Midland League outfit Mexborough Town.

The new team however started appallingly, the first 17 League fixtures yielded only fifteen goals and a meagre eleven points. Crystal Palace won 0-4 at The Kursaal on the opening day and heavy defeats were suffered on the road, 0-5 at Reading and 0-4 at Queens Park Rangers being but two. Ted Birnie's health was beginning to be a problem and, despite being only 55 years old, he contemplated early retirement. However, with the club in dire straits adrift at the foot of the table at Christmas, he decided to stay on and plot a course to safety.

The F.A.Cup saw a run to the Third Round, although a 0-3 defeat at Tranmere Rovers put paid to any prolonged interest in the competition. In the previous rounds, London Paper Mills had been narrowly defeated at their Dartford ground and Chester were beaten 2-1 in the second round at The Kursaal. The club also entered the new Division Three South Cup, but after receiving a bye in the opening round, The Shrimpers crashed out to Coventry City at Highfield Road.

The main problem was finding a regular goalscorer. The home fans had been spoilt with the abundant scoring enjoyed with the likes of Jimmy Shankly and Fred Baron; now profligate finishing saw the team squander many chances and points were being dropped on a regular basis. Over the Christmas period, results improved and coincided with Birnie's introduction of Leo Stevens into the forward line. He scored a hat-trick against

Bristol Rovers in a 3-0 victory and wins over Exeter City and Torquay United (both 3-1) followed, with Stevens bagging braces in both encounters. Results continued to improve, with the likes of Bournemouth (4-1 away) and Swindon Town (4-1 at The Kursaal) being defeated handsomely. By March, any thoughts of a re-election battle had been vanquished as Bournemouth and Cardiff City were beginning to be marooned at the foot of the table. So, with safety secured, Ted Birnie tendered his resignation in April. It would precipitate a contracted period of turmoil and speculation with the team collapsing to four defeats in the final five outings and finishing 16th in the table. The one highlight of a poor season was Leo Stevens, his strike in the final League encounter of the season, a 1-5 defeat at Bristol City, being his 20th of the campaign in only thirty appearances.

Boardroom in Turmoil as an Uncertain Future Haunts The Shrimpers

After twelve years and 558 games in charge, Ted Birnie's departure would inevitably be the end of an era for the club. However, his retirement due to ill health (he would pass away within eighteen months), coincided with six of the eight club directors resigning en masse, concerned about the direction of the club and their financial investments. Former chairman and owner of The Kursaal, David De Forest Morehouse, was among the departures from the boardroom. Indeed the Princeton educated businessman would also pass away within months of leaving the club.

The ownership of The Kursaal had passed to a board of trustees, under the leadership of Mr E.F. Williams, until Morehouse's two sons and daughter became of age. The club still had a lease at the ground, but with the large new Southend Stadium only just opened, rumours circulated that the club would decamp to the new venue off Grainger Road. The new stadium was owned by a company called The Greycing Company, a greyhound racing firm, whose leading light was Captain Tom McEwan. He swiftly joined the board of Southend United and within weeks a lease had been signed to confirm the change of home ground.

A new board and a bigger ground heralded a fresh start for the club, but they would need a new manager and mentor to achieve their grandiose plans of promotion from the Third Division. In fairness to the new board, the man chosen could not have come with a finer reputation and pedigree. As a player with Bolton Wanderers, Arsenal and England, David Bone Nightingale Jack had achieved everything possible and was regarded as one of the greatest players of the era. As son of the club's first manager, Bob Jack, and as successor to the popular Ted Birnie, the new man at the helm indeed had ample boots to fill.

1934/35- A Disastrous First Campaign At The Stadium for David Jack

Unsurprisingly in the tumultuous summer of 1934, many players departed and new manager David Jack had his own plans for the side. Tommy Dixon, the 35 year old veteran, decided to hang up his boots while Fred Barnett signed for Watford. Les Clenshaw joined Barrow and John Mustard left for Crewe Alexandra. Hugh McMahon joined Reading and Albert Worthy left for Rochdale after only a season at Southend. Harry Randle joined Gillingham.

Jack converted Jack Morfitt to a half back, having previously been mainly used across the forward line. George Robertson, Buck Fryar and the veteran Dickie Donoven, all survivors from Birnie's last squad would be reduced to bit part cameo roles in the side. Among a slew of signings from predominantly northern clubs were Billy Carr (Huddersfield Town), Billy Bushby (a forward from the Shildon Colliery club), Harry Johnson (Oldham Athletic) and a pair of signings from Sheffield United, Fred Cheesmur and Bert Oswald. Two interesting acquisitions came from Glasgow junior football,

David Jack

Jimmy Clark arriving from Benburb and Lawrie Kelly from St.Anthony's. From the Welsh amateur ranks came Bert Jones, signing from Ewyllrhsdyn. Namesake Benny Jones moved south from Nelson (now of the Lancashire Combination having been members of the Football League until 1931) and the only southern based player to join the squad was yet another Scotsman, Alex Stevenson, who had been plying his trade with Brentford.

The season opened brightly with decent wins at home against Aldershot and Bristol Rovers but a 0-2 reversal at Cardiff City precipitated a run of seven matches without a win. The run was only halted at the end of October when Millwall were narrowly defeated at The Stadium. Both Jack and the players blamed the horrendous state of the pitch following a prolonged spell of wet weather. Expensive remedial action was taken to allow improved drainage and home results duly picked up. Jack also boosted his squad by signing Norman Mackay from Plymouth Argyle and Jimmy Deacon from Wolverhampton Wanderers.

The F.A.Cup saw the club handed a home tie with Athenian League Golders Green in the first round. The result provided the club's biggest victory as a Football League club when the minnows were defeated by ten goals to one; Harry Johnson scoring five of the goals. The second round saw another match against a non-League side; this time Isthmian League side Wimbledon having the advantage of being drawn at home. A big crowd of nearly 11,000 gathered at Plough Lane hoping to see an upset, but a Fred Cheesmur

Southend United 1934/35

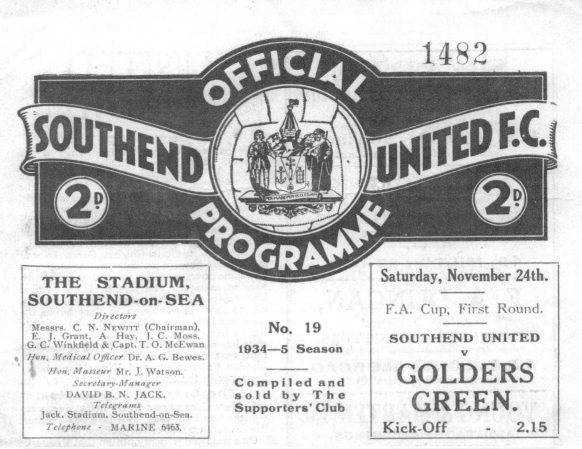

OFFICIAL SOUTHEND UNITED F.C. PROGRAMME

2ᴰ

2ᴰ

THE STADIUM, SOUTHEND-on-SEA

Directors

Messrs. C. N. Newitt (Chairman),
E. J. Grant, A. Hay, J. C. Moss,
G. C. Winkfield & Capt. T. O. McEwan

Hon. Medical Officer Dr. A. G. Bewes.

Hon. Masseur Mr. J. Watson.

Secretary-Manager
DAVID B. N. JACK.

Telegrams
Jack. Stadium, Southend-on-Sea.

Telephone - MARINE 6463.

No. 19

1934—5 Season

**Compiled and
sold by The
Supporters' Club**

Saturday, November 24th.

F.A. Cup, First Round.

SOUTHEND UNITED
v
GOLDERS GREEN.

Kick-Off - 2.15

---

hat-trick saw the visitors coast to an easy 5-1 triumph. However, ambitions came to end in the third round when Second Division Sheffield United outclassed Southend at The Stadium, scoring four times without reply. Interest in the Third Division South Cup ended at the first round stage after a replay with Brighton and Hove Albion.

As the League campaign progressed, wins became rarer, although some high scoring victories were attained, notably 6-0 at home to Bristol City and 6-1 against Reading. Newport County were defeated 5-0 at Somerton Park, but this was to prove to be the only triumph away from home during the season.

In the final reckoning, Southend finished 21st, four points behind Gillingham. The poor showing meant that in the season of change, having both a new manager and a new home ground, the club would have to launch a truly unexpected battle for re-election to the Football League, together with the equally abject Newport County club. In truth their re-election was a formality as there was weak opposition in the ballot. Southend's rivals were Bath City, making their third application for election, but they had little hope having finished only fifth in the Southern League (Western Section) eight points behind champions Yeovil and Petters United. The other applicant was Folkestone, champions of the Southern League (Central Section), who had not won a single vote with their initial application a year previously. The ballot was a resounding

The first round of the 1934/35 FA Cup saw Southend United thrash Golders Green 10-1. This is the programme for the match.

success and both League clubs comfortably retained membership. The voting went:

Southend United	48 votes
Newport County	43 votes
Bath City	1 vote
Folkestone	1 vote

1935/36- Better But Another Season of Struggle

David Jack was desperate to make a go of the job at The Stadium and sought new recruits throughout the summer. He went to his father, Bob Jack, still manager of Plymouth Argyle for help. The result was the signing of George MacKenzie, a future Irish international and Johnny Demelweek; MacKenzie would replace the veteran Billy Moore as goalkeeper after Moore had become only the second Southend player to pass the 300 appearances mark. Jack also divested Leeds United of three players during the close season when Joe Firth, Taffy Spelman and another Irish international Charlie Turner joined the club. Inside forward Len Bolan arrived from Tottenham Hotspur and the vastly experienced full back Jimmy Nelson came from Newcastle United. He had made his name with Cardiff City, making over 250 appearances and winning the F.A. Cup with them in 1927.

Departing The Stadium were Tommy Wilson, who had retired, and Joe Wilson, who joined Brentford. George Robertson signed for Chesterfield and goalkeeper Dave Whitelaw left for Gillingham. Two early Jack signings also left after only a season with Southend; Jimmy Clark returned to his native Scotland with Denny Hibernian and Alex Stevenson went to Ards in Ireland.

The season started in optimistic mood, an opening day 3-3 draw at home with Bournemouth and Boscombe Athletic was followed by a remarkable 7-1 drubbing of Crystal Palace at The Stadium. Leo Stevens scored a hat-trick in that game and would score seven in the opening three fixtures, the third being a 2-1 defeat of Luton Town at Kenilworth Road. Frustratingly, after such a prolific scoring salvo, Stevens suffered an injury hit season and would find the net only five more times.

When Millwall were defeated 6-0 at The Stadium, Southend held a handy position in the League table. However, the next eleven games before the year end would only result in one victory. The F.A.Cup beckoned once again and Newport County were defeated by a Harry Lane goal to nil at Somerton Park in the opening round. Round Two saw Midland Leaguers Burton Town visiting the Essex Coast but leaving with a 5-0 thrashing for their troubles, Bert Oswald claiming a hat-trick for The Shrimpers. In the Third Round, Southend were paired with Second Division Tottenham Hotspur. The first match, at White Hart Lane, was an epic encounter ending in a 4-4 draw, Len Bolan returning to haunt his former employees by scoring a hat-trick and Harry Lane grabbing a last minute equaliser. The tie was settled on a frosty Stadium pitch with the Londoners winning the replay 1-2, Bolan again netting for The Shrimpers. A record gate of 22,862 watched the replay generating receipts of £1,971. Newport County were again the opponents in the opening round of the Third Division South Cup and following a 3-0 victory at The Stadium, The Shrimpers received a bye in the next round. The Third Round saw a trip

to Crystal Palace, but a narrow 2-3 defeat saw the team exit the competition.

Bert Oswald sustained a serious injury in the home game with Aldershot in February and his place in the side was taken by George Willshaw, who had recently been acquired from Athenian League side Southall. The team enjoyed some-

Billy Moore

thing of a revival, winning five games and drawing one from a seven game sequence in February and March, however, a run of six defeats in the last nine games saw the season once again peter out disappointingly. The club finished 18th in the table, comfortably clear of the re-election places which were filled by Exeter City and once again Newport County.

On January 1st 1936, Southend United hosted West Ham United in the Annual Charity Football Challenge Cup. Medals (left) were awarded to all players who took part in the match.

Autographs

Unlike the players of today, players from the 1930s seemed to be able to sign their autograph and actually make it look like their name.

The set below are from 1931 and all the names can be read clearly. The set on the right are from the 1935/36 season and again, are fairly easy to read, including that of David Jack, who was the club's Manager at the time. Also noticeable is the fact that both the Assistant Manager Sidney Gibson and the Chairman Nevil Hewitt provided their autograph.

SHRIMPERS AT WAR

A poster advertising matches in the 1939/40 season. Unfortunately, due to the outbreak of war, some of these matches weren't played.

1936/37- A Top Ten Finish for Jack's New Team

After a disappointing 1935/36 campaign, David Jack dispensed with the services of several of his first team squad. Harry Johnson joined Exeter City and Lawrie Kelly also moved to the West Country with Bristol City. Fred Cheesmur left for Southern League Folkestone, a club he would enjoy a near fifty year association with as a player and trainer. Leo Stevens was allowed to move to Stockport County and Johnny Demellweek was released and was unable to find a new club. Veteran goalkeeper Billy Moore was contemplating retirement, having lost his place to George MacKenzie, but at the last minute was persuaded to sign up with Hartlepool United. Another long-serving player, Mickey Jones, opted to join Birmingham Combination outfit Shirley Town.

Newcomers to the team were initially thin on the ground, the only summer arrivals being Billy Dickinson from Rotherham, Jack Everest from Cardiff City and two non-League signings, Doug Wright (Chelmsford City) and Arthur Harris (Nuneaton Town). Billy Bryan was also engaged as reserve goalkeeper, joining from Walsall. Jack, however, augmented his squad throughout the campaign, Dickie Bird arriving from Sheffield United in October and two new signings from West Ham United came in the shape of Tudor Martin and Billy Adams.

The campaign got off to an amazing start. The third game in and hapless Newport County visited The Stadium, the perennial strugglers being battered 9-2 in a remarkable match, George Goddard with three and a brace for Harry Lane being among the goalscorers. Early results provided some modicum of optimism as in particular Billy Dickinson appeared to be a more than useful acquisition.

The Third Division South Cup provided a bye for The Shrimpers in the opening round but a 0-2 home defeat to Clapton Orient ended interest in the competition, Jack opting to field a weakened team. The F.A.Cup saw a Second Round exit, although both matches in the competition required replays. In the opening round, a 1-1 draw was secured at Selhurst Park before Crystal Palace succumbed to goals from Len Bolan and George Goddard in a 2-0 victory at The Stadium. The initial encounter with Palace was notable for the only playing appearance in a Shrimpers shirt for David Jack, the maximum wage rules precluding him from League activities. York City were the opponents in the second round and after an exciting 3-3 draw at home, The Shrimpers went down to a narrow 1-2 defeat at Bootham Crescent.

Back in the League, some hefty away defeats put paid to any genuine title aspirations. Queen's Park Rangers were 2-7 victors at Loftus Road and Newport County extracted some revenge in the return match at Somerton Park by winning 2-6. At the turn of the year, a run of four straight wins steadied the ship before an unexpected 2-3 home defeat to Bristol Rovers. The Shrimpers took that reversal in their stride and proceeded to dismantle Cardiff City in the next game at The Stadium; Harry Lane (3), two each for Doug Wright and debutant Tudor Martin, plus one for Bert Oswald saw an amazing 8-1 victory. Only one defeat in the next eight games saw The Shrimpers in a lofty position in the League table before an unfortunate injury to goalkeeper George MacKenzie was sustained against Brighton at the end of March. Billy Bryan was called up to the first team but hardly covered himself in glory, The Shrimpers failing to win any of their last six games. Another disappointing end to the season saw the team finish in tenth place, although it was a marked improvement on recent campaigns.

1937/38- A Dramatic Collapse Halts The Shrimpers Progress

David Jack retained the majority of his 1936/37 squad for the following season, with the only departees being Taffy Spelman moving on to Tottenham Hotspur and Dickie Bird, who was released. Billy Adams retired at the age of 35, but three new arrivals joined the club from Spurs, these being Sid Bell, Almer Hall and Charlie Jones. Keith Hague arrived from Derby County and once again Bob Jack helped his son out by allowing Johnny Milne to join from Plymouth Argyle. Ted "Gunner"

During David Jack's managerial reign, all players were issued with a "Training Rules and Players' Instructions" card. Smoking was not permitted in the dressing rooms and players were not allowed to go away for the weekend without the manager's permission.

Training Rules & Players' Instructions.

1. Players must attend the ground for training at 10 a.m. daily.

2. For all home matches, players, whether selected to play or not, must report at ground 45 minutes before kick-off.

3. For all away matches the actual time of departure will be stated : players must report at least 15 minutes before departure.

4. The attention of Trainers must be drawn *immediately* to cases of injury and illness.

5. No smoking is permitted in the dressing rooms, and players are requested to refrain from gambling.

6. Players must not bring friends without permission into the dressing rooms or into reserved accommodation on the train or conveyances when travelling to or from away matches.

7. Players are not allowed to incur any expense on behalf of the Club without first obtaining the consent of the Manager.

8. During the playing season players must not go away for the week-end without first obtaining the consent of the Manager.

9. Any player absenting himself from training or disregarding the above instructions without the necessary consent shall be held to have broken his agreement, and dealt with accordingly.

10. Trainer *must* report all breaches of rules to the Manager.

11. This card must be produced at all home matches. In no circumstances must players allow any other person to use it.

12. Players must report all breakages or damage to Club property.

13. The Directors request that every player will assist them to raise the tone of professional football generally. Everything possible is being done for your comfort and advancement, and any reasonable suggestion will be considered on its merits.

David B. Jack

Secretary-Manager

Hankey was signed on following a successful trial, having been demobilised from the Army.

The start of the new campaign saw home wins against Bournemouth, Brighton and Walsall counteracted by comprehensive defeats on opposition soil. Brighton defeated Southend on the south coast by 1-3 before going down 1-2 at The Stadium a week later. More worrying was the 0-5 reversal at Cardiff, in front of nearly 23,000 spectators at Ninian Park. The Third Division South Cup was once again a short lived affair with Exeter City defeating The Shrimpers 1-2 at The Stadium in the opening round. In the first half of the season, the only success away from home came at Northampton in September when goals from Sid Bell and Almer Hall secured a 2-0 victory. Home form remained impressive, notable wins coming against Torquay United (5-1), Reading (4-2) and Bristol City (5-0). Tudor Martin claimed a hat-trick against the men from Ashton Gate.

The turn of the year should have been celebrated in style but The Shrimpers went down to Bournemouth by seven goals to one at Dean Court. Revenge was then extracted from Cardiff City for the early season drubbing when the Bluebirds were vanquished 3-1 at The Stadium. Also in January, struggling Walsall were thrashed 5-1 at Fellows Park with George Goddard and Bob Oswald notching a brace apiece. Southend also exited the F.A.Cup in January at the Third Round stage in a replay at Barnsley. In the opening rounds the great amateur side Corinthians were defeated 2-0 in a match staged at the White City Stadium and a narrow single goal victory was enough to see off Athenian League challengers Walthamstow Avenue at their Green Pond Road enclosure.

In March, David Jack tried to strengthen his team with the arrival of Ernie Stokes from Torquay United. In the same month though, Harry Lane departed for Plymouth Argyle and Jack Everest went to Barnsley. The club suffered a dreadful run of form during March and April, with only a 4-1 home win over Aldershot chalking up a tick in the win column during the final thirteen matches of the campaign. Fifteen wins and seventeen defeats from the 42 matches resulted in another mid-table finish, 12th overall from the 22 clubs.

Tudor Martin was one of the season's success stories with 18 goals in all competitions; Billy Dickinson provided admirable support with a dozen goals.

1938/39- Twelfth Place Again for Jack's Underachievers

Following the disappointing end to the previous season, David Jack rang the changes in his squad during the close season. A major loss was Dougie Wright, who moved to Newcastle United for a fee of £3,250, although the Magpies softened the blow by making two of their squad players, Billy Forster and Billy Leighton available to Southend for no outlay in fees. The experienced centre half Charlie Turner moved to West Ham and George Willshaw signed for Bristol City. Tom McAdam transferred to Gillingham while the reliable goalscoring of Billy Dickinson was lost when he joined Hull City. Arriving at The Stadium was Eddie Davis, an Irishman from the Larne club and a third goalkeeper joined the books in the shape

of ex-Clapton Orient custodian Charlie Hillam. Jack Trainer arrived from Leeds United while an astute signing was Alf Smirk, who had been released by Sheffield Wednesday and had kept himself in shape by playing for the local bus company in Sunderland.

The opening fixture provided new opposition in the shape of Southern League champions Ipswich Town, who had been elected to the League in place of the previous season's basement boys Gillingham. Nearly 20,000 packed into Portman Road to watch the home side run out 2-4 winners; Billy Carr was injured during this fixture and would eventually have to retire from the game. Once again, the side's failure to build the odd decent victory into a sustained run of results proved a stumbling block. In September, away games saw a wretched defeat at Bristol Rovers (1-4) counteracted by a fantastic 4-0 victory over Bournemouth at Dean Court. The following month, a run of three defeats culminating in a 0-5 reversal at Clapton Orient, was ended by a comfortable 3-0 defeat of Watford at The Stadium, thanks to an Alf Smirk hat-trick. October saw the club stage one of its many "international friendlies" when Olympique Marseilles visited Essex. A tremendous encounter resulted in an honourable 2-2 draw.

The Third Division South Cup first round saw a defeat in a replay to Northampton, when the Cobblers triumphed 2-3 after extra time at The Stadium. In the F.A.Cup, Southend were again paired with the amateurs of Corinthians although this time

Southend United 1938/39

The Shrimpers had home advantage; another Alf Smirk treble resulting in a 3-0 success. A solitary Jack Trainer goal accounted for Port Vale in the second round, before the Third Round saw an apparently mundane fixture against Chesterfield cause all sorts of headlines. The initial encounter was abandoned when dense fog enveloped Saltergate with the sides level at one apiece. The re-staged game four days later resulted in another 1-1 draw, when Billy Bushby's spectacular volley levelled the game late on. The replay at The Stadium went to extra time and The Shrimpers led 4-3 when the referee awarded a second bitterly contested penalty within a matter of minutes. Len Bolan was dismissed for his protests; Sid Bell was booked for arguing and Alf Smirk also found his way into the referee's notebook for throwing mud at the Spireites George Milburn as he ran up to take the kick. Justice was done when Milburn's kick was saved brilliantly by George MacKenzie. The referee's report saw the three players fined and the club warned as to the conduct and control of their supporters. The cup run ended in the Fourth Round when Blackburn Rovers of the Second Division triumphed 2-4 at Ewood Park.

Back in the League programme, results remained inconsistent, with Jack frustrated by being unable to pick a regular starting eleven. All three goalkeepers suffered injuries at different times and only Johnny Milne, Alf Smirk, Sid Bell, Dave Robinson and Arthur Harris were consistent choices in the side. Potential regulars Bolan, Trainer, Bushby, Hague and Jackson all spent several matches on the sidelines with illness and injury.

As was common with many campaigns in the past, The Shrimpers suffered a post Easter slump. Over the holiday, two useful victories against Cardiff City and Northampton Town were accrued but this precipitated a run of five games without a victory or even a goal to celebrate. Only two wins in the final nine games of the campaign resulted in yet another mid-table finish.

1939/40 - The Shortest Season

New incumbents to the side for the new 1939/40 season were Tom Black from Plymouth and Jack Ormandy from Bury. Cliff Fairchild and Cyril Tucker were recruited from local football while Joe Sibley was signed professionally, having graduated from the junior ranks. Shortly after these signings, with War imminent, the Football Association declared that Rule 33 would be waived. This meant that no player serving in His Majesty's Forces could be signed on as a professional footballer. Walsall were defeated in the opening encounter but the following day it was announced that the German forces had invaded Poland. The F.A. were wary of the ill feeling their decision to press on with football during the First World War caused, but decided to carry on with the schedule as planned. After the third game, in with Southend lost 0-1 at Reading, the Government decreed that places

The programme from the only home league match that Southend United played in the aborted 1939/40 season.

of entertainment should now close for safety reasons and in support of those who had enlisted. The F.A. still had not cancelled the season but ordered clubs to "put players on standby", pending an emergency meeting to be held at Crewe. The meeting decreed:

- The order to keep players on standby to be withdrawn immediately.

- Signing on bonuses and expenses to be cleared immediately.

- Arrangements for refunding season tickets to be made.

- League matches played thus far to be counted as cup ties with reverse matches counting in the same manner if the programme could be resumed.

- Injured players to finalise claims.

- All inter-League matches to be cancelled and any alternative competition schemes to be deferred indefinitely.

This effectively abandoned the regular 1939/40 season after three rounds of matches.

Southend United During the 1939-1945 War

Although war with Germany had been officially declared, the Home Office were mindful that there had been little evidence so far that the Nazi's intentions included an attack on England. Therefore, being conscious of the need to keep the populations' morale as high as possible, the Home Office granted the Football Association permission to introduce regionalised league competition, albeit with several caveats.

- Crowds in restricted areas limited to 8,000 or half the official capacity whichever was least.

- Crowds in unrestricted areas limited to 15,000.

- Tickets to be purchased in advance (although this was subsequently relaxed).

- All matches would be staged at the discretion of the local Chief Constable.

- All activity relating to football would be subject to the Home Office Defence Regulations.

- All agreements related to the War effort must be unequivocally honoured.

Similarly to every club, Southend United were affected by a drastic reduction in available playing staff. Hankey and Singleton were serving in the Armed Forces, while many other players had returned to their hometowns, waiting for call up papers to arrive. Trainer was working on his family's farm in Ireland, Tucker had returned to Wolverhampton, Hague to Derby, Coyde to Newcastle (he had secured work as a plumber), Scaife returned to Boston and Downey to Liverpool. Others such as Len Bolan and Frank Walton took up war work, Bolan in a munitions factory and Walton at the Dagenham car plant.

Initially, Southend were placed in South Section "A", a ten team competition alongside the likes of Arsenal, Tottenham Hotspur, West Ham United and Norwich City. The need for crowd restrictions were never tested as the decimated teams attracted sparse crowds; an 1-8 defeat at Charlton Athletic in October drew marginally over 1,000 spectators and a 0-7 thrashing at the hands of Clapton Orient at The Stadium was witnessed by a paltry 912 spectators.

All clubs had to borrow players to field full elevens, using the authorised but almost feudal "guest player" system, allowing clubs to field players registered with others clubs without notice. Players often found it difficult to commit to playing matches, as their war duties often precluded their participation. Southend's young goalkeeper Ted Hankey fell foul of such preclusions when he sneaked away from his duties with the Royal Artillery to fulfil a promise to keep goal for Southend in a reserve team match with Reading. Despite playing under an assumed name, Hankey was caught by his sergeant major and was relieved of his sergeant's stripes for his troubles.

The club and players alike found the early months of the war a time of extreme austerity. The Player's Union issued grants in extreme cases and the clubs successfully lobbied the Union to authorise an increase in players' appearance fees to £2 a match and a win bonus of ten shillings was also authorised. As a club, Southend struggled in the Section "A" competition, competing against teams technically superior to them in status, albeit similarly hit by absentees. The competition

finished in January 1940 and with only four wins from 18 games, unsurprisingly the club finished bottom of the table. Arsenal won the competition with only one defeat but a testament to the affect on playing strength saw Tottenham Hotspur finish next to bottom, only four points ahead of The Shrimpers. The away match against Norwich was staged after the official end of the competition and resulted in a 2-3 win for The Canaries. However, the match was remembered for the terrible career-ending injury to Dave Robinson. "Cannonball", as he was known, was attempting to clear the ball, with no Norwich player close by, but he turned awkwardly and slumped to the ground. He was stretchered off and taken to the Norwich and Norfolk hospital, where a serious fracture of the right leg just below the knee was confirmed.

The dismal crowds that gathered for matches against famous but weakened opposition left the club in a terrible financial plight. Often matches were played on a Stadium pitch that had not had the grass cut as the club could not afford repairs to the lawnmower. Manager David Jack launched an appeal to raise £1,000 towards the clubs' salvation; within weeks, supporters and well wishers

Southend United's hastily arranged matches after the outbreak of war saw some very varied opposition visiting The Stadium; from works team Shorts of Rochester to the mighty Arsenal.

raised in excess of £500, which considering the dark times was a remarkable effort.

At the end of the competition, with the lucrative home match against star studded Arsenal being postponed, the club were in severe financial difficulties. The Southend Standard published remarks, attributed to Major Hay, that Southend United should and will close down rather than enter the supplementary competition. The club were losing in the region of £25 a week and attendances were abysmal.

The injection of finance from the appeal fund launched by David Jack allowed the club to participate in the second emergency competition from February 1940. This time, Southend was placed in Section "D", with more suitable opposition such as Aldershot, Brighton and Hove Albion and Bournemouth and Boscombe Athletic. The Football Association had also instigated the War Cup, a version of the F.A.Cup but without the participation of the non-League teams. The cup competition produced a great deal of interest and after defeating Watford 6-2 on aggregate in the opening round, Southend crashed out to a heavily augmented Nottingham Forest by a 1-4 two-legged scoreline.

Players still available to Jack at the start of the wartime campaign from his pre-war team had included the subsequently injured Dave Robinson, Len Bolan, Joe Sibley, Frank Walton, Alf Smirk, Sid Bell and goalkeeper Charlie Hillam. Guest players were used but less regularly than many other clubs. Jack utilised the services of the likes of Jack Holliday (Brentford), James Lovery (Bradford City), George Ludford and Jimmy McCormack (Tottenham Hotspur), Ted Reay (QPR) and Jack Sherborne (Chelsea) amongst many others. Two former Southend players returned to the town to don blue shirts once again, Dougie Wright of Newcastle United and Swansea Town's Harry Lewis.

Reporting of the matches proved to be an interesting exercise. Paper rationing naturally reduced the amount of column inches available but many reports were notable for the press not knowing some of the players due to the guest player system. Scribes would often resort to the ubiquitous "A.N. Other" or even "Newman" to attribute contributions from unknown players. Uniquely during wartime, the borrowing of players resulted in another general pseudonym being coined that of "A.G. Player" (A Guest Player).

As the second competition drew to a close, crowds again dwindled rapidly. Player's performances were understandably inconsistent and the familiarity of opposition drew lethargy from local supporters. In June 1940, a 2-2 draw with Watford was the club's seventh meeting in ten months.

As the war deepened and the threat of invasion became a very real possibility, the town of Southend and its strategic estuary location saw the staging of football matches becoming an increasingly peripheral activity. Warships were stationed in the Thames Estuary, often mooring in the deep water by the pier. The German airforce, the Luftwaffe, would use the Thames as a navigation point on the way to bombing raids in London. Southend itself was not immune from the bombing raids, suffering some 700 hits during the hostilities. The club suffered from one indirect fatality from the war; Club director George Winkfield, who owned a motor engineering firm, ran into severe financial hardship during the war and unable to see a future, took his own life by poisoning himself with carbon monoxide fumes.

Initially the club sought to stage matches at West Ham's Boleyn Ground but the formation of a London Junior League meant that this would not be possible. Hearing of Southend's plight, the directors of Chelmsford City offered to rent their New Writtle Street ground to Southend for a match-by-match rental fee. An agreement was settled, although the tiny crowds meant that Southend would often be unable to pay their hosts any rent at all.

The new 1940/41 season saw a third variant of emergency competition instigated by the Football Association. A total of 34 "southern" clubs (which included the likes of Mansfield Town and Stoke City) were lumped into one huge division. Clubs were free to arrange their own fixtures and the League table would be decided on goal average rather than points. This meant the amount of games played by each club varied wildly, Coventry City playing only ten matches while Stoke City completed 36 matches.

By August 1940, David Jack had been called up to utilise his financial qualifications to work for Barclays Bank. Weeks later the club lost the use of their ground as it was commandeered to aid the war effort as a training ground. Chelmsford City's manager Harry Warren was tasked with running two professional teams, his own side having turned professional in 1938. In these awkward circumstances, Warren was beginning to find fielding a decent team very difficult and often had little choice but to beg for players from other teams. Chelmsford City's ex-Hull City and Grimsby Town player George Baldry, Fred Chadwick and Dai Edwards (both Ipswich Town), Barrow's Bert Hollingsworth, Eric Jones (West Bromwich Albion), Norman Millar (an Irishman from Bournemouth and Boscombe) and Ernie Phypers (Doncaster Rovers) all made guest appearances for Southend. Warren was also able to draw on professional players assigned to the garrisons at Shoeburyness and Colchester and these players became regular choices in the team alongside existing personnel. Fred Jones of Ipswich Town was a notable success scoring frequently in his 25 guest appearances. Other regular guest players from the garrisons included Ralph Calland (Torquay United), Les Jones (Arsenal) and Jimmy McLuckie (Ipswich Town). Bill Parry and Allan Sliman of Chelmsford City also became regular starters for Southend during the 1940/41 season.

SOUTHEND UNITED 3

Colours—Blue and White.

RIGHT WING   LEFT WING

Rickett

2—Turton   3—C. Fuller

4—Leighton   5—Sliman   6—Parry

7 Jones,L.   8—Edwards   9—Jones, F.   10—Bell   11—Burley

The reader of this programme may have a relative or friend in H.M. Forces who would appreciate it being forwarded after having completed the:

RESULT {
     SOUTHEND UTD.........goals. Scorers.............................

     WEST HAM Utd. ....goals. Scorers.............................

Programme forwarded to.............................by.............................

11—Foxall   10—Goulden   9—Foreman   8—Macauley   7—Small

6—Barrett   5—Walker, R.   4—Fenton

3—Walker, C.   2 Savage

Conway

LEFT WING   RIGHT WING

WEST HAM UTD. 1

One of the home matches played by Southend United at New Writtle Street, Chelmsford during the 1940/41 season. The Southend United line-up contains some unfamiliar names, as many Chelmsford City players were included.

Harry Warren could still call on the services of a handful of Southend players, the likes of Sid Bell, Vic Wright, Billy Leighton, Frank Walton and Alf Smirk were often able to participate at short notice due to being locally stationed with the war police reserve. However, often the local players would be forced to play matches having had little sleep following a nightshift on duty at the garrisons and other military outposts. As the season progressed, more and more Chelmsford players turned out for The Shrimpers as the two clubs effectively fielded a joint team.

The matches caused some interesting stories; a guest player from Tottenham, Tom Paton, turned up to face his own club in a December 1940 clash. He thought the game was in Southend but arrived only to find the club had been relocated twenty miles north some four months previously. Another story involved Horace Rickett, the regular Southend goalkeeper. He was so incensed that Crystal Palace's fourth goal had been allowed to stand when Collins, the Palace forward, had clearly been offside that he refuse to carry on playing. This had followed a controversial third which had hit the bar and bounced down in front of the line but a goal was still signalled. Despite Southend already being reduced to ten men, Jim McLuckie being carried off with a badly twisted knee, Rickett staged a sit down behind the goal and despite the best efforts of Harry Warren and his team mates

he refused to return to the fray. Fieldus took over in goal and nine man Southend could not stop Palace winning 0-7.

Southend played 15 matches in the Southern Regional League before the London clubs agreed to only play each other in the remainder of the season. The remaining clubs formed another competition, the Football League South, where 14 more matches were contested. However, in a late reconciliatory move it was decided to add the games played and goals scored to the Southern Regional League table. In the "final" League table, Crystal Palace had the best goal average of 1.954 from 27 matches; Southend completed 29 matches but mustered only 64 goals for an average of 0.633 (goals scored divided by goals conceded). Only Southampton, Swansea Town and Clapton Orient fared worse.

The War Cup saw an excellent 4-3 aggregate win over Millwall in the First Round. An unkind draw saw Southend paired with War Cup holders West Ham United in the next round. Southend won the first leg 2-1 but went out on aggregate when the Hammers triumphed 1-3 in the second leg. The club gained a welcome cash injection when the games against West Ham attracted an excellent crowd for the time of 9,000 for the two games.

On June 4th the club held a meeting which agreed the motion to continue at New Writtle Street for the 1941/42 season. This was despite losses on the previous campaign exceeding £200 and regular difficulty in meeting the player's match by match fees of thirty shillings a man. Five days later the Football Association met at a Nottingham hotel and the competition saw clubs split geographically into two; League South and West. Southend were placed in the Southern section and the fixture list below was agreed, with a League Cup competition to start from December 27th.

However, the future looked bleak for Southend when all the London clubs voted en masse to form their own competition, the London League, in July 1941. The main issue was their unwillingness to travel to the more outlying clubs on the grounds of expense and inconvenience. The Football Association expelled the London clubs immediately which conversely gave the green light for the London League to start up. Much to the chagrin of clubs like Southend, their most attractive of opponents had been taken away and the rebel clubs' argument actually held little water when both Portsmouth and Aldershot were invited to join the new "London League". There was more than a little coincidence that both towns were navy and army bases awash with conscripted professional footballers looking for games to

1941/42 Proposed Fixtures		
August 30th	Luton Town	Away
September 6th	Luton Town	Home
September 13th	Southampton	Home
September 20th	Southampton	Away
September 27th	Arsenal	Home
October 4th	Arsenal	Away
October 11th	Charlton Athletic	Home
October 18th	Charlton Athletic	Away
October 25th	Crystal Palace	Home
November 1st	Crystal Palace	Away
November 8th	Norwich City	Home
November 15th	Norwich City	Away
November 22nd	Watford	Home
November 29th	Watford	Away
December 6th	West Ham United	Home
December 13th	West Ham United	Away
December 20th	Clapton Orient	Away
December 26th	Clapton Orient	Home

play. The London clubs immediately saw the attraction of playing these two sides, fortified by the likes of Tommy Lawton and Frank Swift, but the contradiction was clear for all to see.

The Southend club held an emergency meeting and unanimously decided to call a halt to the operation of the club for the foreseeable future, pending a cessation to the hostilities. The ad hoc arrangement of renting New Writtle Street was cancelled with immediate effect and the club become one of 21 Football League clubs who became dormant for the 1941/42 season. Major Hay stated that the club would remain loyal to the Football League, as the rebel clubs had no guarantee that they would regain their former status upon resumption of normal football competition.

The only football matches played at The Stadium between November 1941 and August 1945 were Charity Matches and Armed Forces representative games. One such match, the Army v Navy in 1942 saw the presence at The Stadium of one of the great names in football of the time, Arsenal's Alex James, a Scottish international forward who was stationed at the garrison in Shoeburyness. The Army XI triumphed by five goals to two.

By May 1945 the prospects for lasting peace looked probable and the Southend United board regrouped and elected to revive the club. It was unanimously agreed that the team would reform under the full time management of Harry Warren, who had served the ailing club well during their period of exile in Chelmsford. Warren busied himself with contacting players returning home from far flung places, assessing whether they were in a fit state of mind and body to rejoin the club. The club also applied to compete in the reconstituted F.A.Cup competition for the 1945/46 campaign.

The club had run up debts in excess of £2,000 during their dormancy and the overall debt had climbed to £7,657. The board dug deep to fund the restoration of the facilities and returfing of the pitch. However, the supporters were soon complaining that the club were charging excessive admission charges. Entrance had risen to 1s 6d but an extra charge of 9d was being asked for supporters to stand under the covered eastern stand. The team was placed in the eleven club Third Division South (Northern Section) which basically contained the teams from the north side of the River Thames. The first post-War match of the 1945/46 season for Southend resulted in a 1-2 defeat at home to Queens Park Rangers. The club struggled initially, as many players were either still overseas or needed at short notice for military duties at home. The Southend squad contained four players that were interned in the horrific Nazi prisoner-of-war camps, these being Bob Jackson, Sid Bell, Cyril Thompson and Alf Smirk. Thompson was extremely lucky to survive his ordeal. Having been captured at Dunkirk he was one of two thousand prisoners sent on the infamous 500 mile March of Death across Europe from Lamsdorf. He was one of a handful of survivors.

Being only a 20 game programme, the League competition was completed by the turn of 1946. Southend had performed admirably in the circumstances, a tiny squad augmented by guest players and players who only made a single appearance. The highlights were a 7-3 triumph over Notts County at The Stadium followed ten days later by a 6-2 home win over Watford. In the latter game, Alf Smirk scored four of Southend's goals. However, with ten draws in the 20 games, a final position of next to bottom, with only Mansfield Town below them, was a trifle hard on the players and management. The competition was won by Queens Park Rangers. The F.A.Cup was played over two legs and in the First Round Southend were drawn against Watford. Another Alf Smirk strike saw a creditable 1-1 draw in the first leg at Vicarage Road, however, a dismal performance in the home game saw The Hornets win comfortably by three goals to nil.

From a financial point of view, the Northern Section was a success for the club, with some unexpectedly large crowds gathering at The Stadium, helped by uniformed servicemen being charged at child rates for admission. Crowds in excess of 7,000 were attracted to the home games against Queens Park Rangers and Clapton Orient while the Christmas Day fixture against Ipswich Town saw 9,000 spectators drawn to the spectacle. Goals from Ernie Marshall and Joe Macklin secured a comfortable 2-0 win against the men from Portman Road. Another decent Stadium crowd in December saw a Services charity match staged between London District and Eastern Command. The London Services side, boosted by the presence of several Chelsea players who had taken part in the famous Moscow Dynamo match two days previously, won comfortably by four goals to one. A crowd of 3,000 was augmented by 1,300 locally based servicemen.

The second half of the season was given over to a complicated

Action from the 1946 F.A.Cup meeting between Southend United and Barnet. The Shrimpers made the most of a mudbound pitch and ran out 9-2 winners. The bottom picture shows Harry Lane scoring one of his hat-trick.

League Cup competition where again, Southend were placed in the North Section. Clubs would play home and away matches with the top two in the final table contesting the semi-finals against the top two from the South Section.

Yet again, Harry Warren was unable to pick a regular team, although the likes of Herman Conway in goal, Sid Bell, Bob Jackson, Frank Walton, Alf Smirk and Frank Dudley were available for the majority of matches. The team was again boosted by the presence of guest players, including Hull City's Stan Montgomery and Ken Bennett, an inside forward from Tottenham Hotspur. The club enjoyed a revival in playing fortunes during the League Cup competition and challenged for the top position until the final weeks of the season, when a run of four draws and a defeat in the last five matches saw them finish fourth in the table. Queens Park Rangers and Walsall qualified from

the North Section, although the competition would eventually be won by South Section winners, Bournemouth and Boscombe Athletic.

To the obvious encouragement of all involved at the club, the 1945/46 campaign posted an overall profit of £1,755.

Mercifully, unlike the First World War, no club personnel past or present were lost during the horrific six year conflict. Club chairman, Nevil Newitt, was awarded the George Cross for his services to the Bomb Disposal unit.

SHRIMPERS ON THE MOVE

Ted Hankey

1946/47 - Meagre Budget as The Shrimpers Regroup

Although the financial picture was improving, the board were determined to live within their means in the first proper post-War season. Manager Harry Warren was granted a squad of 24 players, although half of them would have to be on part-time contracts. Warren appointed former England full back Wilf Copping as trainer while veteran coach Bill Cartwright joined the ground staff at The Stadium. Messrs. J.H. Jacks Ltd of North Avenue made and donated a new set of blue shirts to the club. Season ticket prices for the new season were set at £5 for the stand and £2 for the ground. Southend were also treated to a fortnight of pre-season training under the auspices of the Football Association's top coach, the legendary Jimmy Hogan. Hogan was a coach ahead of his time, travelling Europe extensively, coaching in Austria, Hungary and Germany; he guided the Austrians to the 1936 Olympic Football Final. When the Hungarians scored their famous 6-3 victory over England at Wembley in 1953, they dedicated it to the influence of Jimmy Hogan.

Of the club's pre-War players only seven, Sid Bell, Ted Hankey, Arthur Harris, Joe Sibley, Bob Jackson, Alf Smirk and Frank Walton were offered new deals. Two prominent guest players during the second wartime campaign, Stan Montgomery and Ken Bennett, joined the club on a full time basis. Two local players that had made an impression in wartime matches, Cyril Thompson and Frank Dudley, were also signed up. Other wartime players who also made themselves available were Jack Gardiner, joining from the Holford's works team, Ron Humphreys, previously with the Snowdown Colliery Welfare club and also Bob Gibson and Tommy Linton, who joined direct from demobilisation. Both Tommy Tippett and Len Davies were offered contracts following the end of their conscriptions to the Army. Harry Warren also signed Dave Hamilton from Newcastle United, burly centre half Frank Sheard from Leicester City, while useful forward Harry Lane rejoined the club from Plymouth Argyle.

The season opened promisingly when Walsall were defeated 3-1 at The Stadium in front of 11,000 people, then a Frank Dudley strike earned a point at the newly renamed Leyton Orient. However, in the third game, a warning shot was fired when The Shrimpers went down to Reading by the embarrassing score of 2-7 at Elm Park. Warren rapidly steadied the ship and October's highlights included the infamous 3-1 triumph at Bristol

Southend United 1946/47

Rovers, when full back Bob Jackson assumed the identity of goalkeeper Ted Hankey, who had cut his hands on the train journey to Eastville. Jackson's heroics between the sticks earned a valuable away win and fooled the opposition and press alike.

In the opening round of the F.A.Cup, Southend were pitched against unknown opposition in the shape of Notts and Derby League outfit Brush Sports. Predictions of The Shrimpers coming a cropper at the tight Browns Lane enclosure were unfounded as a Cyril Thompson hat-trick helped pave the way for a comfortable 6-1 rout of the Loughborough based works team. Non-League opposition was the order of the day again in Round Two as a visit to Barnet was pulled out of the hat. Southend overwhelmed their Athenian League opponents, being 5-1 up at halftime and finishing the match victors by nine goals to two. Hat-trick hero in the visit to Underhill was Harry Lane, ably assisted by braces from Joe Sibley and Ken Bennett. Southend received a plum draw in the Third Round when a share of a 50,000 plus gate at Goodison Park was guaranteed when they were paired with Everton. Despite strikes from Thompson and Bennett giving the Toffees

The Southend United team leaving for their FA Cup match against Brush Sports.

The team that took on the Toffees. Southend United, sporting kit borrowed from Aston Villa, line-up before the FA Cup tie with Everton at Goodison Park.

food for thought, the First Division outfit eased to a 2-4 victory.

Back in League action, the forward line was missing the input of Frank Dudley, who had injured himself in the home defeat to Cardiff City. However, Cyril Thompson seized his opportunity and grabbed hat-tricks against Norwich City and Bristol City. The Norwich match came away from home and saw The Shrimpers record a highly creditable 5-1 victory. However, the team were still frustratingly inconsistent and this would ultimately hamper their promotion push. On Christmas Day, Watford defeated Southend by four goals to nil at Vicarage Road, only for Southend to turn the tables in the return match a day later running out 5-0 victors at The Stadium.

In the New Year period, a run of three defeats in four matches saw Harry Warren decide to strengthen his squad. Harvey Pritchard (known as John) joined from Manchester City while Ernie Brown arrived from Newcastle United. From Middlesbrough came defender Jack French, nephew of a pre-War Southend player of the same name. The team was also bolstered by the return to fitness of Frank Dudley, who would notch hat-tricks against Northampton Town and Exeter City. His

return to the side was much needed as Joe Sibley had departed to Newcastle United for the not inconsiderable fee of £7,000.

With promotion still looking out of the question; only the champions went up and Cardiff City were running away from the competition, The Shrimpers looked to finish as high up the table as possible. Goalscoring seemed to be easy for the side; Thompson would end the season on 27, while Dudley, Lane and Smirk would all reach double figures. Dudley's achievement of sixteen was particularly remarkable as he missed half the campaign through injury.

As the season wound down to a close, a frustrating slump in form saw the team fail to win any of the last seven games. A heavy 1-5 final day defeat to Port Vale saw Southend finish eighth in the table, a distant 22 points behind Cardiff City.

SOUTHEND UNITED OUT OF DEBT

£5,000 Liabilities Cleared in Year

SOUTHEND United start the New Year free of debt—the first time in the Club's forty years' history that there has been no deficit. During the past twelve months, liabilities of £5,000 have been cleared, and there is now no bank overdraft. Mr. C. Nevil Newitt, G.M., M.B.E., the Chairman of the Club, gave this information exclusively to "The Onlooker," of the "Southend Standard," at the week-end, and he will express his personal thanks to all concerned in a New Year message to be published in the programme on Saturday, when the United entertain Reading.

At the last annual meeting of the Club, in August, a profit of £1,755 was reported on the first post-war season, reducing the deficiency to £5,482, which included £2,929 share capital. At the previous annual meeting, which covered the war years, liabilities were £7,237.

All outstanding debts have now been cleared, and by the end of the season the Club should be in a sound financial position, for they can still count on substantial receipts from the F.A. Cup, and there will also be a useful sum from the Cup pool. In addition, if "gates" are maintained at the present level, further liabilities are not likely to accrue.

down at the end of the 1914-15 season, the debit was £3,028.

After the First World War, the annual meeting held in May, 1919, showed liabilities of £3,027, and the Roots Hall ground unavailable, being then in use as allotments, while the owners desired to excavate for sand. A move was made to the Kursaal, and a town's meeting launched. The first season there—the last campaign of the old Southern League—resulted in a profit of £3,357, due largely to success in the F.A. Cup (£877) and receipts from transfer fees (£1,380), so that the Club actually cleared off its liabilities and had £329 in hand. However, an order had been placed for a new grandstand, cost-

Despite a disappointing end to the playing season, financially the club were reaping the benefits of the start of the post-War crowd boom and closed the campaign completely debt free.

The local papers confirm that Southend United are debt free.

1947/48 - Another Top Ten Finish but Promotion Seems Unattainable

Harry Warren held onto the nucleus of his squad for the 1947/48 season, with only squad members and reserves such as Len Davies, Jack Gardiner and Dave Hamilton being released from the club. Veteran Arthur Harris decided to wind down his playing days back at Nuneaton Borough of the Birmingham Combination and another departure to the non-League game was Ron Humphreys, who joined Kent League outfit Folkestone.

Strengthening the squad was undertaken by signing Doug Beach and George Goodyear from Luton Town, the latter having come to Warren's attention during some wartime guest appearances for The Shrimpers. Jack Robinson arrived from Bury and Charlie Whitchurch trod the well worn path from Tottenham Hotspur. An intriguing acquisition was that of inside-forward Billy Pryde from Scottish junior club Bo'ness.

Off the field, the club announced that supporters would have to leave a 6d deposit, refundable upon return of their cups and saucers from their half time refreshments!

The season did not start too auspiciously when three of the opening five fixtures were lost by heavy scores. Visits to Bristol City (0-6), Ipswich

Town (0-4) and Walsall (0-6) gave grave cause for concern and Warren decided to leave Doug Beach and Frank Walton out of the defence. Stalwarts Sid Bell and Bob Jackson stood in and steadied the ship before Beach and Tommy Linton became the regular choices in the full back berths.

Away matches were still unrewarding, with the side having to wait until mid-November for a victory on the road; a visit to Eastville resulting in a narrow 2-1 triumph for The Shrimpers. The F.A.Cup draw produced an away tie against Newport County, and Southend's away day blues continued as, despite a Ken Bennett brace, the side went down 2-3 at Somerton Park.

In December, Warren decided that a new custodian was needed as Hankey's deputy Jack Robinson had done little to convince the manager that he was a reliable alternative. Warren plumped for Paddy Nash, who joined from Middlesbrough following a recommendation from Ayresome Park boss and ex-Shrimpers manager David Jack.

A harsh winter gripped Britain in December and only three games were played in that month. A home win over Bristol City and a rare away win at Bournemouth and Boscombe Athletic produced some festive cheer for The Shrimpers' faithful, however the match at Dean Court was marred when the home side lodged an official complaint against the referee when he appeared to blow up

Bob Jackson

some five minutes early. Upon appeal, the final result was upheld and Southend kept the points.

Fortunes improved at the turn of the year and the League encounter at Somerton Park provided revenge for the early F.A.Cup exit when Newport County were beaten 5-1 on their own ground, with Ken Bennett scoring a hat-trick.

In March, the squad was again bolstered by fresh blood when Tommy Edwards and Cyril Grant both moved to the Essex coast from Second Division Fulham. The signing of Edwards paid immediate dividends when he netted on his debut in a 4-0 victory over Aldershot. Meanwhile another capture saw Dennis Thornhill arrive from Wolverhampton Wanderers. The same month, however, saw the departure of long serving Alf Smirk, who returned to the North East by signing for Third Division (North) Gateshead.

Yet again a promising season was scuppered by a dismal run in the closing weeks, when a home win against Bristol Rovers became the only victory in the final nine fixtures. Southend's season petered out into a disappointing ninth place, some 18 points behind champions Queens Park Rangers.

1948/49 - A Season of Transition as Warren's New Squad Fails to Gel

Harry Warren realised that many of his squad from the 1947/48 season were not good enough or past their prime. The veteran Bob Jackson and inside forward Charlie Whitchurch decamped to Folkestone. The two leading scorers from the previous season, Cyril Thompson and Ken Bennett joined Derby County and Bournemouth respectively. However, making the reverse journey from those clubs were Robert Brown, a useful inside-forward, and Harry Gray an outside-right. Harry Warren also decided that Paddy Nash would be first choice goalkeeper with Ted Hankey providing back up. Jack Robinson, now third choice custodian, found himself surplus to requirements. Don Travis signed from West Ham United while

The "Player's Ticket", which was issued to all Southend United players, stated exactly what was expected of each player throughout the season. Rule 8 states that should a player be injured whilst riding in a motor car, it will be their own responsibility!

Jimmy McAlinden

Stan Bell was offered a contract after performing well for several local sides. David Lindsay, a Scottish full back, joined Southend from Sunderland while Avery Osmond arrived from Midland Leaguers Peterborough United. Finally Ernie Butler moved south from Stockton of the North-Eastern League.

Warren was faced with a squad of new names and unsurprisingly the team took time to gel. The opening weeks saw goalscoring becoming a major issue with Warren forced to experiment with Stan Montgomery and Jack French, nominally defensive regulars, as emergency forwards. The dilemma was all too starkly illustrated in October when five successive League encounters drew a blank for Southend's shot shy strike force. At the end of that month, Warren decided to take drastic action and approached the board with a request to sign a new player at what would be a club record fee of £6,500. Much to the manager's delight, the board acquiesced and Warren secured the signature of Northern Ireland international Jimmy McAlinden.

A 3-0 away win at Torquay United, with a brace for fit again Frank Dudley, was a rare ray of light in the gloom of the opening half of the season. Southend would hang alarmingly around the lower reaches of the table throughout the campaign and over the New Year period the goalscoring drought returned, forcing Warren again to delve into the transfer market, desperate for new forwards. He signed Freddie Morris from Barnsley and Jimmy Lawler from Portsmouth; Lawler eventually being successfully converted to a centre half role. The defence had been weakened by Stan Montgomery's departure to Cardiff City in December, but in his absence Jack French stepped up to become a first team regular.

For once, the closing months of the season saw Southend's results pick up considerably, thus surviving the dreaded end of season battle for re-election. In the final dozen fixtures, four wins and five draws saw sufficient points gained to avoid the bottom two places. These were filled by Al-

Goalmouth action from the 1948/49 Boxing Day match against Norwich City.

dershot and Crystal Palace, although Southend finished only one point clear of the Hampshire team.

It was in this season that the idea of a return to Roots Hall was mooted as the rental lease at The Stadium was due to expire in 1955.

1949/50 - McAlinden Inspires Rise from Mediocrity to Title Chasing Shrimpers

A significant body blow was dealt to Harry Warren's playing strength for the 1949/50 season as the useful goalscorer Frank Dudley was snapped up by Leeds United for a club record fee received of £10,000 during the opening weeks of the close season. The Yorkshiremen softened the blow by sending young centre forward Albert Wakefield in the opposite direction. Other departures from The Stadium included Harry Lane and Billy Pryde, who both retired, while George Goodyear joined Crystal Palace. Stan Bell returned to local football with the Monarchs club while Tommy Linton and Avery Osmond opted to pursue their playing careers with Kent clubs, Linton with Tonbridge of the Southern League and Osmond with the then professional Kent League club Betteshanger Colliery Welfare.

A whole host of newcomers arrived at the club in the summer, including two players signed from Southampton. Reg Davies would prove to be an astute signing but his colleague, the Australian born George Horsfall was an unmitigated disaster. Horsfall cost a transfer fee of £1,000 and was

repeatedly injured, only playing in the final game of the season before departing on a free transfer to Guildford United. Jimmy Clough, a pacy outside-left, arrived from Crystal Palace and Joe Loughran, a doughty full back, came from Burnley. Len Jones signed from Plymouth Argyle and Warren continued his penchant for giving local and non-League players a chance to shine, Les Stubbs signing from Great Wakering Rovers and Ron Gawler joining from Kent League Canterbury

Les Stubbs

City. Stubbs would eventually serve Chelsea with some distinction.

Despite an opening day defeat to Notts County at Meadow Lane, the injection of new talent paid dividends as the side were transformed from the underachieving outfit from the previous campaign. Newport County were put to the sword at The Stadium when newcomers Clough and Wakefield each scored twice in a 6-0 thrashing. After six games Southend topped the Division Three (South) table for the first time since 1931. However, away games would still prove somewhat of a stumbling block, but the visit to Swindon in November ended as a 2-2 draw after The Shrimpers had an incredible six goals disallowed for various infringements. In fact the first victory away from home did not arrive until mid-March when two Albert Wakefield goals ensured victory against Millwall at The Den.

By October, Warren had concluded that the left sided full back position was a weakness in the side, with the ageing Harry Gray being the unchallenged holder of the berth. Warren signed Harold Wallbanks from Fulham to replace Gray in the side. Wallbanks was one of three footballing brothers, Horace and Jim being the others, but he was universally known as "Choppy". Wallbanks would never be conclusively drawn on the subject of his nickname, popular theory citing his robust methods for retrieving possession, although the pragmatists stated it was merely a corruption of his place of birth, Chopwell in Tyne and Wear.

Wakefield's acquisition was proving to be a profitable one in front of goal; in the F.A.Cup two more for the Pudsey-born front man saw off Leyton Orient in the opening round. The Second Round saw Southend given a tough trip to Wrexham, but once again Wakefield scored both Southend goals in a 2-2 draw to bring the tie back to Essex. This time The Shrimpers made no mistake overcoming the Welsh side by 2-0 with goals from Wakefield again and Jimmy Clough. In December goalkeeper Tommy Scannell joined Southend from Tilbury, having starred in their run to the First Round of the F.A.Cup. The draw for the Third Round again saw Southend on their travels, paired with the 1948 finalists and First Division powerhouse,

Blackpool. A crowd of nearly 25,000 gathered at Bloomfield Road to see the home side, with Matthews and Mortensen in full flow, ease to a 0-4 triumph.

Back on the League trail, results were maintained with Freddie Morris proving an able foil to the prolific Wakefield in front of goal. The Stadium became something of a fortress with only Crystal Palace taking a point off their hosts between August and the end of January visit of Nottingham Forest. The first home defeat of the season came

Above: The Southend United players in training for the Leyton Orient FA Cup tie.
Below: The Southend United players' Christmas Party 1949.

in a thrilling match where, despite yet another brace from Wakefield, the points headed to the Midlands with the visitors edging victory by three goals to two.

March was a particularly exciting month as Southend maintained interest in the title race; Albert Wakefield again grabbed the headlines by scoring in six successive matches. As April progressed, led by captain and pivot McAlinden, promotion beckoned at long last. With only four games remaining a three way battle for the title was fought between Notts County, Southend and Northampton Town. The Cobblers visited The Stadium in late April for a crunch fixture, a crowd of 13,000 gathering for the event. However, the visitors dealt the home side's promotion prospects a fatal blow by taking the game by two goals to one. Southend's weary troops capitulated, drawing their final three games, finally finishing third, seven points adrift of worthy champions Notts County.

Southend United reserves were runners-up in the Football Combination Cup tournament of 1949/50.

1950-51 - McAlinden Ban Hits Promotion Aspirations

Southend were hit with savage news in May 1950 when influential skipper Jimmy McAlinden was banned by the Football Association for four months. His offence related to his time at Portsmouth when he was alleged to have received an "under the counter" signing-on fee from Pompey manager Jack Tinn. Southend were penalised for an offence beyond their control, while the hierarchy at Fratton Park went unpunished, as two directors originally banned for life were subsequently reinstated. McAlinden would miss the opening twelve matches of the season.

By Harry Warren's normal standards, the close season was relatively quiet. The most welcome signing was the return to The Stadium of Joe Sibley after two seasons at Newcastle United. Only two other players with previous League experience were added to the squad; goalkeeper Frank Coombs arrived from Bristol City while Bobby Harper, who had seen service with Newport County was also added to The Stadium ranks. Crichton Lockhart was signed from Surrey County League outfit Chertsey Town. Perhaps one of Warren's best ever signings was Sandy Ander-

Opposite Page: How the "All Football" newspaper covered the Jimmy McAlinden story.

son, a full back who had been playing for Scottish Junior club Newburgh when he was stationed at Shoebury Garrison as a physical training instructor during his National Service. Warren had been impressed by his playing ability and offered the flame haired Scot a trial. Anderson would be Southend's regular full back for the next twelve years.

Departing the club in the close season was Robert Brown (Shrewsbury Town), Jimmy Clough (Barrow) and Len Jones (Colchester United). Both Freddie Morris and Dennis Thornhill were forced into premature retirement through injury and veteran goalkeeper Ted Hankey signed for Tonbridge, while Harry Gray also moved to a Kent club in the shape of Kent League Ashford Town.

The season opened in spectacular fashion, a 5-1 victory being secured over Watford at The Stadium, Reg Davies and Albert Wakefield scoring two apiece. However, the next two home games against Millwall and Leyton Orient resulted in defeats and this set the tone for the rest of the campaign when results would be, as had been in many previous campaigns, frustratingly inconsistent.

Heavy away defeats were also suffered at Bristol Rovers and Swindon Town (both 1-4) and new keeper Coombs paid the price by losing the first team jersey to Paddy Nash and then Tommy Scannell. Nash kept goal when Swindon put paid to Southend's F.A.Cup ambitions for another season, when the Robins won 0-3 at the County Ground.

The inconsistency of the side was highlighted over the Christmas fixtures when the same side was often played home and away within 24 hours. On Christmas Eve, Bournemouth and Boscombe visited The Stadium and were handed a distinctly unfestive 6-1 battering. A day later the return match at Dean Court saw the home side exact revenge by three goals to one.

Warren had acted to shore up his leaky defence by signing Jimmy Stirling from Birmingham City in December, and by the turn of the year defeats became less frequent.

A remarkable game occurred at The Stadium in March when Swindon paid dearly for defeating Southend twice earlier in the campaign. Indeed the game looked already lost after 14 minutes with the visitor's two goals to the good. However, five goals before halftime from Tommy Tippett,

THIS WASN'T OUR 'CRIME'

McAlinden ban ruins promotion chance

By ALL FOOTBALL'S Own Correspondent

SOUTHEND UNITED are fed up. They believe their promotion chances have been ruined or seriously jeopardised by the Football Association's four-month suspension of Jimmy McAlinden, their captain and inside-right—a suspension which will have deprived the team of its schemer-in-chief for 11 matches during the most vital period of the season.

McAlinden was fined £50 and suspended until October 1 by a joint F.A. and Football League commission. It was alleged that in 1945 he had illegally accepted £750 as an inducement to return from Ireland to his then club, Portsmouth.

Two years ago Southend United paid a record fee for the club to obtain McAlinden's transfer from Stoke City to whom he had moved from Portsmouth.

Says indignant Southend manager Harry Warren: "It is grossly unfair that our club should have been so severely penalised for an incident which has nothing whatever to do with us, and which, in any case, occurred five years ago.

"We did not even secure McAlinden from Portsmouth, where the illegal payment is said to have been made.

"Last summer, we finished third in the Southern Section, level on points with the runners-up, Northampton. With runaway Notts County out of it, we believed that this season we had a first-class promotion chance.

"McAlinden is the 'brains' of our team. By the time he plays his first game on October 7 we will have been deprived of those 'brains' for the 11 opening matches, upon which depend largely a team's promotion chances.

"Is this justice?" Is it fair that Southend United should be punished for a 'crime' we didn't commit?"

Harvey Pritchard's contract for the 1950/51 season. He earned the princely sum of £8 per week, with an extra £4 if he was playing in the first XI.

Reg Davies, Cyril Grant (2) and Jimmy Lawler saw the home side turn the game on its' head. Tippett completed a hat-trick in the second half and Davies headed his second. Architect of the massacre was Jimmy McAlinden, who was irresistible as the fulcrum of the forward line.

Southend were enjoying an eleven game unbeaten run when they visited Newport County in late March, but the wheels fell off in spectacular fashion when The Shrimpers went down 1-6 at Somerton Park. In April, Southend lost the services of Reg Davies as the board found the £10,000 offered by Newcastle United too tempting to refuse. However, the season finished in optimistic fashion when Exeter City were beaten 5-1 at The Stadium, with Les Stubbs confirming his top scorer position with a brace. Stubbs netted 19 times in only 31 appearances and the side netted 92 League goals in total during the season with another four players netting a double figure tally of strikes. Wakefield scored 15 while Davies, Grant and Tippett scored a round dozen each. Overall the team finished in seventh place, 18 points adrift of runaway champions Nottingham Forest.

The season was rounded off with a match staged for the Festival of Britain, when Racing Club Malines from Belgium came to Southend. The tourists enjoyed their stay despite a 6-1 defeat.

1951/52 - Away Day Hoodoo Cost Shrimpers Dear

As in the previous close season, Harry Warren opted to keep the majority of his squad intact for the 1951/52 campaign; his sole summer signings were Dennis Thompson and Gordon Loukes from Sheffield United. Departing the club were Paddy Nash, who retired from the game and fellow custodian Frank Coombs, departing for Colchester United. Three other players on the periphery of the first team moved into the non-League circuit; Ron Gawler joined Ted Hankey at Tonbridge, Dave Lindsay signed for Southern League Yeovil Town and Frank Walton joined Dartford.

The campaign started none too auspiciously when The Shrimpers failed to register a victory in their opening five matches. The balanced was redressed somewhat by home wins over Brighton and Hove Albion and Northampton Town. However, a month into the season, Tommy Tippett departed for Bournemouth and Boscombe. In October, Aldershot visited The Stadium, and true to a history of being Southend's whipping boys, returned home with a 7-1 thrashing; a spectacular performance by the side saw braces from Jimmy McAlinden and Cyril Grant.

Despite indifferent League form, for once Southend enjoyed a decent F.A.Cup, reaching the Fifth Round for only the second time. Lady Fortune shined on The Shrimpers as home advantage was forthcoming in every round. Southend certainly found their shooting boots in the early rounds, defeating Bournemouth and Boscombe by six goals to one and then helping themselves to another five without reply against Oldham Athletic; Albert Wakefield netting a hat-trick against the men from Boundary Park to see his side comfortably into Round Three. Second Division Southampton were the visitors to Essex in the next round and returned to The Dell on the wrong end of a 3-0 scoreline. Bristol Rovers put up a better fight but goals from Les Stubbs and Jack French secured a narrow 2-1 triumph. So the Fifth Round was reached for the first time since 1926, and the club were hoping for a plum tie. However, the balls that came out the hat paired The Shrimpers with Sheffield United, then a mid table Second Division outfit. Despite going into the break one up

Jack French scores the winning goal in the 1951/52 FA Cup tie against Bristol Rovers.

thanks to the ever reliable Wakefield, goals from Alf Ringstead and Len Browning in the second half saw the Blades end Southend's interest in the competition.

The New Year saw a wretched turn of bad form, when five successive defeats, including 0-5 at Brighton and 0-6 at Bristol City, saw Harry Warren drop goalkeeper Tommy Scannell in favour of former junior Peter Heathcote. However, in February, Geoff Morton joined The Shrimpers from Watford and immediately displaced both men between the posts. The team promptly went on a five match unbeaten run, which included a 4-1 win at Leyton Orient, 5-1 at home to Watford (when The Shrimpers rattled in all their goals in the first half) and a revenge 5-1 thrashing of Bristol City.

The season finished well, with wins over Ipswich Town (5-0) and Newport County (2-1) and Southend ended up in ninth place overall, 18 points behind worthy champions Plymouth Argyle. Southend's failing was their desperate away form, 16 of the 23 matches ending in defeat. Conversely, home form was excellent, with only Millwall gaining a League victory at The Stadium during the campaign. Goalscoring showed a similar pattern,

56 coming at home compared to just 19 away. In all matches, Albert Wakefield led the way with 21, while Les Stubbs and Cyril Grant netted 18 apiece. Jack French contributed a more than useful eleven from his half-back berth.

1952/53 - Warren's Squad Depleted by Sales

There were only minor comings and goings during the summer of 1952, with Frank Burns from Swansea Town and Eric Duggins from Portsmouth being the only additions to Warren's squad. Departures were Choppy Wallbanks to Workington, Bobby Harper to Linfield in Northern Ireland, Gordon Loukes (Gravesend and North-fleet) and John Pritchard (Folkestone), none of whom had commanded a regular first team place in the previous campaign.

Once again Southend started well, winning four of the opening five matches, the only defeat coming in a thrilling match at Northampton when the home side triumphed by the odd goal in seven. Heavy away defeats punctuated the entire season, 1-5 at Bournemouth and Boscombe in September and during December, three successive away matches saw beatings suffered at Shrewsbury Town (1-7), Torquay United (2-4) and Bristol City (0-5). The Boxing Day clash at Ashton Gate was watched by a crowd in excess of 30,000 as attendances at football enjoyed an unprecedented boom period.

A major blow was sustained in November when free-scoring Les Stubbs joined First Division Chelsea for a fee of £10,000. Warren acted to fill the void in his team by signing Ron Mansfield from Millwall and Eric Marsden from Crystal Palace. Meanwhile, Joe O'Neil arrived on loan from Aberdeen, having been stationed at Shoeburyness on National Service. Marsden proved something of a stop-gap acquisition, as he had left for Shrewsbury Town by March. If the supporters were upset at the sale of Stubbs, as they vocally demonstrated on several occasions, Chairman Major Alfred Hay was certainly ill advised to appease them by saying the club would not sell any more players. Less than a fortnight later, Jackie French was sold to Nottingham Forest for an undisclosed fee. The clubs' coffers were further swelled in the same month when Newcastle were forced to pay an ex-

Southend United 1952/53

SOUTHEND UNITED F.C., LTD.
Tour France-Belgium
MAY 13th—25th, 1953

Directors :
Mr. Ald. H. H. Smith, (Chairman)
Dr. A. G. Bewes, (Vice-Chairman)
Mr. C. Nevil Newitt, M.B.E., G.M.
Major A. I. Hay, M.B.E.
C. O. Benson, Esq.

Guest: Mr. Coun. W. H. Cox
(Deputy Mayor of Southend-on-Sea)

Secretary-Manager: Mr. Harry Warren

Trainer : Mr. Wilf Copping.

Players :
Tommy Scannell   Jimmy Lawler
Jimmy Brown   Joe Sibley
Bill Pavitt   Jimmy McAlinden
Sandy Anderson   Cyril Grant
Eric Duggins   Jacky Bridge
Dicky Whitehead   Ken Bainbridge
Jim Stirling   Tommy Lowden

PLEASE . . .

1. Check your football outfit before leaving.

2. Remember your passport.

3. Do not take more than £5 British money out of the country.

4. Remember you are British.

5. Thoroughly enjoy every minute of this tour.

ITINERARY

WEDNESDAY, 13th MAY
Assemble Southend Stadium - 8.20
Bus leaves Southend Stadium - 8.30
Arrive Dover - approx. 12.00
Boat leaves Dover Main - 12.57
Luncheon in Steamer
Arrive Calais (Maritime) - 14.15
Train leaves Calais - 15-02
Arrive Hazelbrook - 16.08
Change
Leave Hazelbrook - 17.23
Arrive LENS - 18.24
Hotel de la Paix, Lens

THURSDAY, 14th MAY
MATCH v LENS F.C. - 16.00

FRIDAY, 15th MAY
Visiting Battlefields, etc.

SATURDAY, 16th MAY
Train leaves Lens - 9 23
Arrive Paris (Nord) - 12.55
Bus to Hotel Univers and Portugal.
10 Rue Croix Des Petite,
Champs, PARIS.

SUNDAY, 17th MAY
MATCH v C.A. MONTREUIL

18th & 19th MAY IN PARIS

WEDNESDAY, 20th MAY
MATCH v ANGERS F.C. floodlit

THURSDAY, 21st MAY, IN PARIS

FRIDAY, 22nd MAY
Train leaves Paris (Nord) - 11.20
Arrive Brussels (Midi) - 14.46

SATURDAY, 23rd MAY IN BRUSSELS

SUNDAY, 24th MAY
MATCH v
RACING CLUB MALINES k.o. 15.00

MONDAY, 25th MAY
Train leaves Brussels (Midi) - 7 33
Arrive Ostend (Quay) - 9.06
Boat leaves Ostend (Quay) - 9.45
Arrive DOVER (Marine) - 13-30
Bus leaves Dover on arrival
Arrive Southend - approx. 18.30

A player's Itinerary Card for the 1953 tour to France and Belgium. Players were reminded to remember they were British!

tra £2,000 for Reg Davies; a clause in the sale agreement was activated when Davies became a full international, as he was capped by Wales in a match against Scotland at Ninian Park. Added to Warren's transfer headaches was the female section of the supporters club passing a motion that the manager should sign better looking players in future!

With such erratic away form it came as no surprise that when an away tie to a non-League side was drawn out of the hat in the opening round of the F.A.Cup, Southend faced a potential giant killing. The opposition came in the shape of Southern Leaguers Bath City, who were forced to rapidly install crash barriers at the Bristol End of their Twerton Park ground as well as five sections of temporary terracing to cater for the 16,000 crowd. The extra expense was well worth it as the home-

sters won 3-1 with Ray Snook (2) and Bill Ellison ensuring Southend's first defeat to non-League opposition since becoming members of the Football League. A Cyril Thompson strike was scant consolation for a sorry Southend team.

The season wound on in a similar vein, decent home form but truly dismal away results preventing a serious title challenge. The only victories on the road came at Swindon Town (3-1) in September, Newport County (1-0) in December and in March at Exeter (2-0). Unusually for the era, Southend found goals at a premium after Stubbs' departure; Cyril Grant was top scorer for the season with a meagre 13.

Another top ten finish was secured for the fourth successive season as a final position of eighth was the outcome to a modest campaign. In truth, promotion seemed more distant than ever as Southend ended some 25 points behind champions Bristol Rovers.

The club ended the season with the first of several European tours; a short tour of France was completed before playing a return game in Belgium against Racing Club Malines.

1953/54 - New Look Squad Flirts with Relegation as Jimmy Mac Bows Out

To try and appease the discontent of supporters upset by the constant leakage of prized assets from the side, the board and manager Harry Warren had a busy summer of 1953 scouring the transfer lists for some players with League experience. Two new centre halves arrived in the shape of Jim Duthie of Hull City and Fulham's experienced stopper Bill Pavitt. Les Dicker arrived from Tottenham, while a brace of signings came from Southampton, Tom Lowder and Jack McDonald. A shrewd acquisition came in the form of goalkeeper Harry Threadgold, who would serve Southend with no little distinction for many years. The only non-League player signed in the close season was Doug Young from Isthmian League Walthamstow Avenue. Young came with some pedigree though, being an England amateur international.

Leaving the club during the summer was Ernie Butler, who joined Darlington, having not featured in a single first team outing for Southend during the previous campaign. The usual flow of older players to non-League teams continued with Albert Wakefield joining Clacton Town, Frank Sheard (Gravesend and Northfleet) and Ron Mansfield, who signed for Sittingbourne. A month into the new campaign Geoff Morton, now behind Threadgold and Tommy Scannell in the queue for the first team goalkeeper's jersey, opted to join Exeter City.

The opening seven fixtures provided a gloomy insight into the way the season would pan out. Only a Joe Sibley brace in a home win over Northampton Town provided two points in the win column, and more alarmingly, five of the opening seven games ended in defeat. A visit to Brighton resulted in a 2-3 reversal but was notable for the introduction of a startling new away kit, green and red quartered shirts. Results steadied somewhat and home wins over Bournemouth and Brighton saw The Shrimpers edge away from the foot of the table.

A super win over Norwich City at The Stadium in October, by five goals to two, saw the return to the first team after a lengthy absence through injury of Crichton Lockhart. Lockhart celebrated his return in style, bagging a well taken hat-trick against the Canaries. The F.A.Cup returned in November and once again Southend were handed a tricky looking tie away to non-League opposition. Mindful of their acute embarrassment against Bath City in the previous campaign, Southend were determined not to repeat that performance against Finchley of the Athenian League. An excellent crowd of 9,000 gathered at the Summers Lane ground and Southend made no mistake this time, with goals from Joe O'Neil, Joe Sibley and Jimmy McAlinden ensuring entry into the next round. The reward was a home draw against Chesterfield, but despite a Les Dicker goal Southend fell to a 1-2 defeat to the Spireites.

Back on the League trail, December proved a dismal month for The Shrimpers, a 3-0 home win on Boxing Day over Watford providing minimal consolation for humbling defeats at Bristol City (1-4) and Northampton Town (0-5). Results picked up in the New Year, with home form proving more reliable as the team moved away from the relegation zone. Warren was desperate for a reliable goalscorer; he had never truly replaced Les Stubbs, and in February finally got his man. 29 year old Roy Hollis joined the club from Tottenham, having come to the fore with Norwich City. Hollis scored on his debut, a 3-0 home win over Shrewsbury Town, and would proceed to score ten times in only 13 games, including a hat-trick against the luckless Walsall. Hollis would finish the season as second top scorer behind Ken Bainbridge, despite only playing a third of the games. In March, to the astonishment of many, Southend's reserve team goalkeeper Tommy Scannell was capped by the Republic of Ireland against Luxembourg.

The season finished on a sad note, with talisman Jimmy McAlinden announcing his retirement. His final appearance at home to Queens Park Rangers resulted in a standing ovation from the Southend supporters. With the fulcrum of the side

Albert Wakefield

A CENTURY UNITED

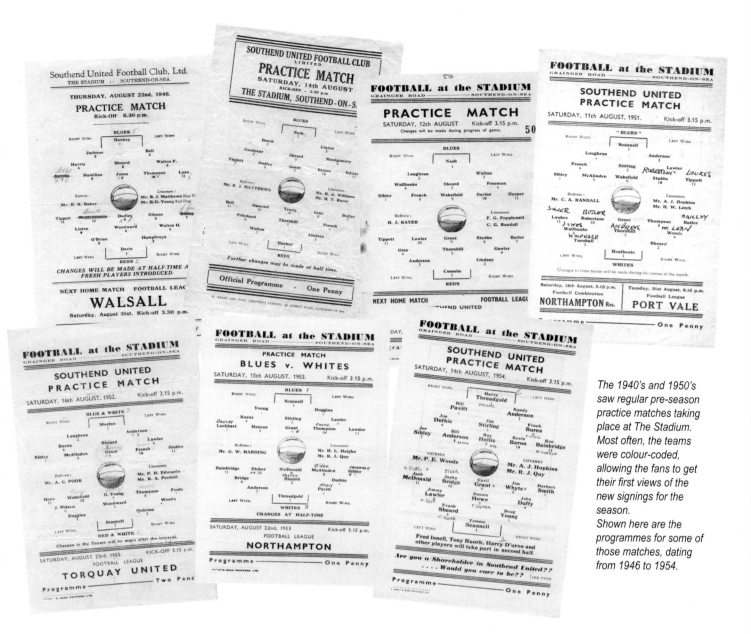

The 1940's and 1950's saw regular pre-season practice matches taking place at The Stadium. Most often, the teams were colour-coded, allowing the fans to get their first views of the new signings for the season.

Shown here are the programmes for some of those matches, dating from 1946 to 1954.

now gone, the season tailed off badly, with the club finishing 16th in the table. In truth, re-election never looked a real possibility as Colchester United and Walsall looked doomed from an early stage. However, a higher finish could have been possible without three of the final four games ending in defeat.

1954/55 - Baron and Hollis Hit Fifty Goals as Fortunes Improve

There was a relatively quiet close season for Southend United during the summer of 1954. Departing the club were Tommy Lowder, who joined Southampton, and Dennis Thompson, who joined Albert Wakefield at Clacton Town. Eric Duggins was also released. Harry Warren's signings had a distinctly celtic flavour. Billy Anderson joined from Hibernian, Jimmy Whyte from Third Lanark and John Duffy came from Celtic. A suitable foil for Roy Hollis was found in the shape of Kevin Baron, who arrived from Liverpool. Denis Howe

came south from Darlington and Bert Smith arrived from Aston Villa.

In a total antithesis to the previous campaign, the opening seven fixtures saw only one defeat, and that a narrow single goal reversal at Aldershot. Kevin Baron proved an instant hit, scoring eight times in those seven matches. Baron and Hollis would gel like no other combination; if one failed to hit the net, the other invariably would.

Roy Hollis

Despite the potency of the new strike force, away games were still an anathema to the team and before Christmas, some heavy reversals were suffered on the road to the likes of Torquay United (1-4), Southampton (0-3) and Leyton Orient (1-5).

The F.A.Cup proved an exception to the away day hoodoo when Bristol City were defeated 2-1 at Ashton Gate and Bradford Park Avenue were edged out 3-2 at their Park Avenue ground; Roy Hollis scoring all five goals in the opening two rounds. Southend were rewarded with a revisit to Goodison Park, eight years after their previous visit. The Shrimpers put up a good show against their illustrious hosts but went down 1-3 despite Kevin Baron scoring on his return to Merseyside. A share of the gate must have put a smile of the faces of the directors as at 53,043, this was the largest crowd ever to watch a game involving Southend United.

In December, Warren strengthened his options upfront by signing Gordon Barker from Bishop Auckland; the Northern League outfit had grabbed headlines by embarking on three consecutive F.A. Amateur Cup triumphs. The Christmas game saw Norwich City visit The Stadium and a spectacle was offered up, culminating in an honourable 3-3 draw, with Roy Hollis scoring a memorable hat-trick against his former employers.

Any hopes that this would be a promotion season at last were ended at the County Ground, Northampton on February 5th when Southend

crashed to a 2-6 defeat. This was a precursor to a run of nine games without a win, eight of which were defeats. The horrendous run was somewhat surprisingly ended at The Den against promotion chasing Millwall, when goals from Jimmy Whyte, Cyril Grant, Roy Hollis and Kevin Baron secured an unexpected 4-1 victory. Local rivals Colchester United were then dispatched 4-2 at The Stadium, as Southend were determined to finish the campaign strongly. The highlight of the run-in was a 4-1 win at Coventry City, courtesy of a Crichton Lockhart hat-trick.

The nightmare post-Christmas slump saw the club end with a record of 17 wins and 17 defeats for a final placing of tenth in the table. Southend scored 89 goals in the League and F.A.Cup with Hollis and Baron claiming fifty between them. Hollis top-scored with 32 and Baron provided admirable support with 18.

The season was rounded off with another European jaunt. Three Maltese clubs, Hamrun Spartans, Sliema Wanderers and Floriana were beaten before The Shrimpers were narrowly defeated 2-3 by Catania in Sicily.

Southend United 1954/55

1955/56 - In His Final Season Warren Leads the Club Back Home

Harry Warren had a great deal of work to do during the summer of 1955 to ensure the club's first season at the new Roots Hall ground would result in a serious tilt at the title. His defence was weakened by the retirement of Billy Pavitt and a further six players from the previous season's team joined the non-League circuit. Ken Bainbridge, a reliable goalscorer, and Les Dicker joined Chelmsford City, while Cyril Grant and Tommy Scannell joined Kent based clubs Gravesend and Northfleet and Folkestone respectively. Bert Smith joined Corby Town of the Midland League and Jack McDonald moved to the south-west with Southern League Weymouth.

Warren continued to scour clubs north of the border following the success of previous imports such as Sandy Anderson and John Duffy. New recruits offered contracts were John McGuigan, an outside left from St.Mirren, and full back Arthur Williamson from Clyde. Dickie Dowsett signed from Tottenham while Bill Brewster left Chelsea for the Essex coast. Northern Irish forward Sammy McCrory arrived from Plymouth and would have the distinction of scoring the first goal at the new ground.

An excellent crowd of 17,700 gathered at the newly built Roots Hall ground and the side gave them a display to remember, McCrory, Hollis and Dowsett ensuring a comfortable 3-1 win over Norwich City. Reading were beaten at Roots Hall a week later before Colchester United were humbled 6-3 at Layer Road, Roy Hollis scoring four of the goals. However, the optimism sweeping over the club suffered a dent in the fourth game when Reading extracted revenge at Elm Park by winning 1-4. That scoreline was also repeated at Dean Court in Bournemouth's favour; these defeats galvanised the team and a run of five consecutive victories saw the club at the upper reaches of the table. This run coincided with the recruitment of Barnsley's Harry May to the left back berth. After a third of the games, Southend lay handily positioned in second place.

The F.A.Cup proved a more enduring distraction from the League programme than had become customary. Queen's Park Rangers were comfortably beaten 2-0 at Roots Hall in the opening round, then Southern League Weymouth were narrowly defeated by a Crichton Lockhart goal to nil at their Recreation Ground home. The Third Round saw a tricky away tie at Second Division

Lincoln City successfully overcome, Southend winning 3-2 with Hollis grabbing a brace; the reward was a home tie against mighty Manchester City. A horrendously mud-caked Roots Hall pitch saw Bert Trautmann deny countless Southend efforts, as a Joe Hayes goal settled the match in the visitors favour. A new record attendance of 29,500 was set for an epic David v Goliath encounter. City would go on to win the competition, defeating Birmingham City 3-1 in the final at Wembley Stadium.

The League campaign saw away defeats at Brighton (0-4) and Norwich City (2-7) severely hamper championship aspirations. As usual, Harry Warren steadied the ship with useful wins at home against Colchester United (4-0), Exeter City (6-0) and Queen's Park Rangers (5-1).

Unfortunately, as in many previous campaigns, a late season slump ended promotion hopes once again. In the final nine games only two victories were forthcoming, and a 0-5 defeat at Millwall followed by a 2-3 reversal at home to Torquay United saw a disappointing climax to the season. Southend finished the campaign in fourth place on 53 points, but in truth were well behind Champions Leyton Orient (66 points), Brighton and Hove Albion (65pts) and Ipswich Town (64pts). Despite the dawn of a new era for the club at Roots Hall, another ended as in June, Harry Warren announced he was stepping down after 16 years in charge to take up a similar position at Coventry City.

Sandy Anderson

The Long-Awaited Return To Roots Hall

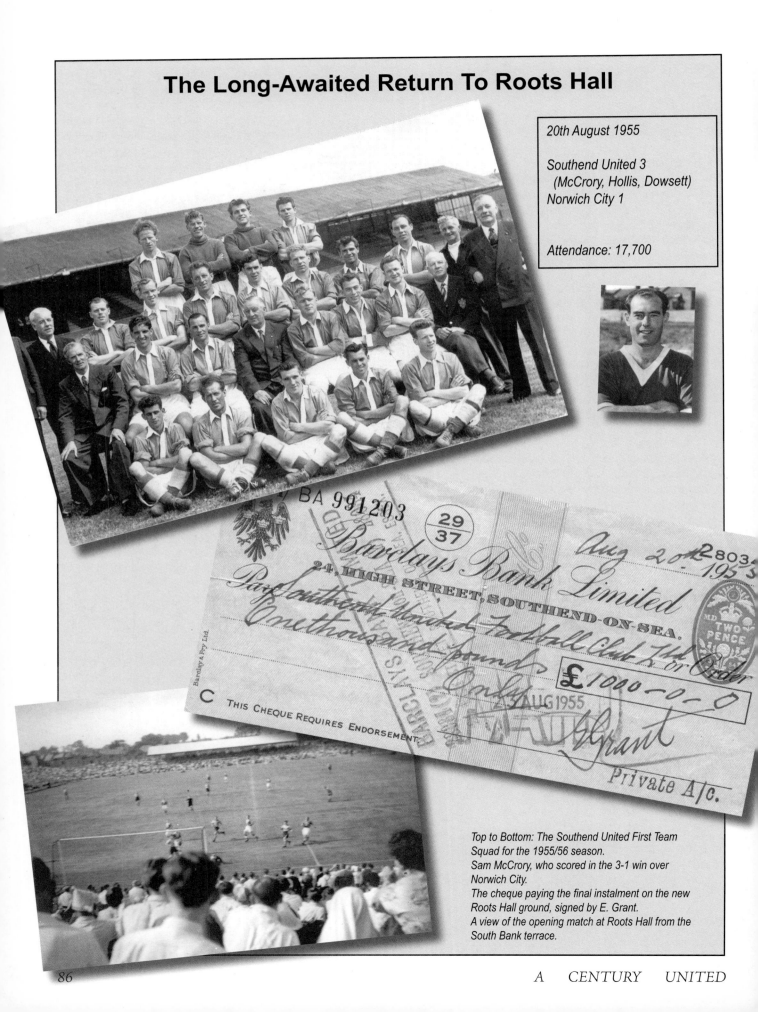

20th August 1955

Southend United 3
(McCrory, Hollis, Dowsett)
Norwich City 1

Attendance: 17,700

Top to Bottom: The Southend United First Team Squad for the 1955/56 season.
Sam McCrory, who scored in the 3-1 win over Norwich City.
The cheque paying the final instalment on the new Roots Hall ground, signed by E. Grant.
A view of the opening match at Roots Hall from the South Bank terrace.

"COME ON YOU WHITES"?

NEWS CHRONICLE POCKET PORTRAIT

H. THREADGOLD *(Southend)*

Harry Threadgold

1956/57- A Respectable Start for Eddie Perry

Harry Warren had left the Southend squad in pretty good shape for the new incumbent, so Eddie Perry had little rebuilding to undertake for the 1956/57 season. Indeed Warren's departure had been so hasty and unplanned that he himself had made four new signings prior to the offer coming in from Coventry. Warren's final signings for the club continued his liking for Scottish players, as all four had been plying their trade north of the border. Tom D'Arcy and Alex Duchart both signed from Hibernian while Jimmy Thomson and Ron Tulloch left Raith Rovers and Hearts respectively. Meanwhile Tony Ruark had been assimilated from local football and would get a brief run in the first team when Jimmy Stirling was injured in September.

Perry's only dealing in the transfer market was to return to his former club Fulham to persuade Brian Ronson to become back up goalkeeper to Harry Threadgold. The squad itself had been reduced in size, but the departing players had been on the periphery of the team anyway and the major names remained under contract. Departing Roots Hall were the veteran Joe Sibley, who had retired, and Dickie Dowsett, who joined Southampton. Frank Burns signed for Crewe while Billy Anderson (Weymouth), Doug Young (Folkestone) and Jackie Bridge (Gravesend and Northfleet) all moved to non-League teams. Bill Brewster and Harry May were also released with May eventually joining Southern League Gloucester City.

The season kicked off in predictably unpredictable style with some inexplicable results being produced. In September Exeter City beat The Shrimpers 1-6 at St.James' Park only for Southend to win the very next game 4-0 against Reading. An early season match saw The Shrimpers visit Highfield Road and their wily former manager plotted their downfall as his new charges cantered to a 0-2 win. Another strange result occurred in October when Aldershot beat Southend 3-5 in a thrilling game at the Recreation Ground. This pre-empted a run of eight matches unbeaten for Southend which saw them heading up the League table.

The F.A.Cup saw another lucrative run for The Shrimpers, with all four games being watched by five figure crowds. In the opening round, local rivals Colchester United were soundly beaten at Layer Road, with Sammy McCrory netting a hat-trick in a 4-1 win. In the next round, The Shrimpers were handed a tricky away tie at Southern League Hereford United. Despite trailing at half-time, The Shrimpers rallied in the second half and squeezed into the next round by three goals to two. The Third Round saw Liverpool come to Roots Hall, and although at the time a pre-Shankly Second Division club, they were still formidable opponents. In a breathless encounter, Southend recorded a famous victory when goals for Jim Duthie and Jimmy Thomson secured a 2-1 triumph. The reward given was an attractive home tie against First Division Birmingham City. The gulf in class soon showed as Southend were four down at the break and went on to lose 1-6, Hollis grabbing a consolation effort late on. However, the share of a near 29,000 gate came in handy.

The post New Year League programme was somewhat uneventful save for the odd punctuation of an unexpected result. Aldershot, who had struggled at the foot of the table all season, completed an unlikely "double" against Southend when they came to Roots Hall in March; a 2-4 victory for the visitors meant Aldershot had scored nine goals in two games against Southend.

A late March visit to Queen's Park Rangers resulted in a 0-3 defeat for The Shrimpers; Perry took the defeat in his stride and a simple tinkering with formation, Baron and Thomson switching roles, reaped immediate dividends. Conversely to many post-War seasons, Southend finished the campaign very strongly, remaining undefeated in the final nine outings. Notable results included a revenge 3-0 beating of Queen's Park Rangers and a "double" over Gillingham, 2-0 at Priestfield and 5-0 at home. A visit to eventual champions, Ipswich Town, resulted in a creditable 3-3 draw but sadly the match was marred by Jimmy Thomson sustaining a broken leg, which would keep him sidelined for eighteen months.

The side finished in a healthy seventh place and Roy Hollis was once again top scorer with twenty, although Sammy McCrory (18), Johnny McGuigan (11) and the luckless

Thomson (10) all managed double-figure tallies. Despite a sound opening campaign, Perry's sometimes over-intricate passing movements had not garnered universal acclaim, but he was determined to be his own man as Warren's imposing shadow still loomed large over the club.

Defensive stalwarts Sandy Anderson and Jimmy Stirling were rewarded for their loyalty with a benefit match against a Select XI. The club then signed Lou Costello, a young striker from Aldershot, before embarking on another European tour. The club's first port of call was Germany, where three games were played. An enthralling 6-5 victory was gained against Worms and Saarbrucken

Sam McCrory advertises the Empire News and Sunday Chronicle.

were also defeated (2-1). The only reversal came at Mannheim, where the home side won 2-4. The tour was extensively featured in the seminal "Kicker" magazine and Sandy Anderson gained widespread praise for his powerful shooting. The next stop was Vienna, where a narrow 1-2 defeat was sustained against an Austria "B" team. The tourists moved onto Czechoslovakia where four further games were undertaken. Victories came against Karlovy Vary (6-1) and Budêjovice (4-0), the latter seeing Costello score his first goals for the club as he deputised for Roy Hollis, who had to remain in England with business commitments. The other two matches against Carlsbad Dynamo and Pilsen ended in honourable draws. As the club returned home, they stopped off in Holland en route and a goalless draw was played out with Sparta Rotterdam.

A tragic footnote to the high profile tour was the death of new club chairman Arthur Bewes, who had been flown home having been taken ill in Czechoslovakia. He died a few weeks after returning to England and had held his post for only three months.

1957/58- Strong Finish Earns The Shrimpers a Place in the New National Third Division

Eddie Perry undertook a modest amount of transfer activity in the summer of 1957. Leaving the club for other Football League clubs were Ron Tulloch, who joined Carlisle United and Crichton Lockhart, who moved on to Rochdale. The usual flow of older players to non-League clubs continued when Jack French joined Folkestone, Jimmy Lawler (Chelmsford City), Jimmy Whyte (Sittingbourne) and Tony Ruark (Tonbridge). Perry's only summer signings were Canadian outside right Errol Crossan from Gillingham and Ray Smith, a half back from Luton Town.

The campaign could not have got off to a more spectacular start, with the opening four fixtures resulting in wins for Southend with no less than eighteen goals in the credit column. Exeter City were bested by 5-0 on their own ground in the season's opener, Roy Hollis claiming a hat-trick. Norwich City then visited Roots Hall but went down by five goals to two. Queen's Park Rangers were then thumped 6-0 at Roots Hall as Crossan and Sam McCrory recorded braces each. An early "double" was completed in the fourth game, when the return at Carrow Road took place and another McCrory brace ensured a 2-0 win against the Canaries. The bandwagon then ground to a

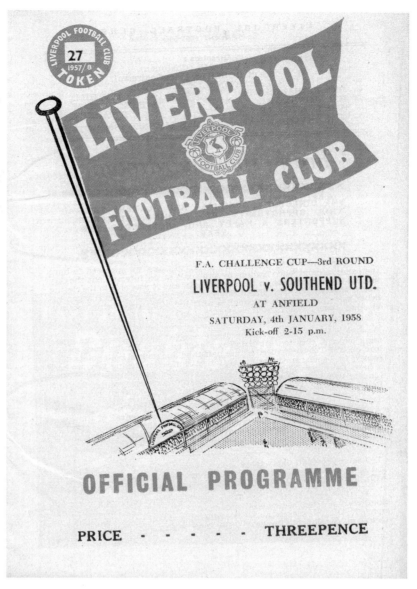

Southend visited Anfield in the FA Cup 3rd round, but after securing a draw, lost the replay at Roots Hall.

halt at Roots Hall when, despite two more for Errol Crossan, The Shrimpers sunk to a 2-3 reversal to Essex rivals Colchester United.

September and October saw a period when defeats outweighed victories but the highlight of the latter month was a McCrory inspired 4-1 defeat of Walsall at Roots Hall, the Irishman bagging a hat-trick.

The Shrimpers' manager seemed to have uncovered a gem in Ray Middleton, who joined the club in November from non-League Bulford United, when the youngster scored on his debut in a 5-1 win against Shrewsbury at Roots Hall, but after a handful of games it became clear he was not up to the professional game.

The F.A.Cup saw a tricky First Round tie, away to Western League Trowbridge Town, successfully overcome, thanks to two goals from Roy Hollis without reply from the home team. Torquay United were beaten in Round Two, albeit in a replay after a draw at Plainmoor. The Third Round paired Southend with Liverpool once again and the Second Division side must have still been smarting from their exit at Roots Hall the previous season. However, this time the tie was at Anfield in front of a 43,000 crowd, but a Johnny McGuigan goal in the second half earned The Shrimpers a replay. Despite a closely fought match at Roots Hall, the Reds went through by the odd goal in five.

The New Year saw some new arrivals to the club when Perry bolstered his options by capturing Duggie Price from Swansea Town and Willie Morrison from Sunderland.

In league action, Southend were enjoying a nine match unbeaten sequence when the club made the short trip to Layer Road in January; unfortunately, a Tommy Williams' goal for the U's put paid to the run. Despite the set back, The Shrimpers were soon on another unbeaten run, this time of eight matches, with the highlights being a 3-1 win at Port Vale, McCrory grabbing his second hat-trick of the campaign, and a 5-1 Roots Hall victory over Coventry City.

After successive away defeats to Brentford (2-4) and Gillingham (0-2), Southend finished the campaign in fine style with only one reversal occurring in the final nine outings. The season closed with the visit to Roots Hall of Northampton Town. Southend triumphed in an exciting encounter by 6-3 with McCrory netting a third hat-trick. His final goal against the Cobblers was his thirtieth strike in League matches and his seasonal tally of 33 was the highest achieved by a Southend player since Jimmy Shankly's record breaking 35 in season 1928/29.

Southend finished the campaign in seventh place, which was important in this campaign as

British Railways often ran train excursions to away matches; this one was for the December F.A. Cup fixture at Torquay. The fare of 28 shillings equates to £1.40.

the final table would see the top twelve staying in the Third Division with the top twelve from the Northern section. The regional divisions were scrapped in favour of a national Third Division and a new Fourth Division for those clubs from both Third Division North and South finishing in the bottom half of their respective tables.

Therefore Southend United became one of only six clubs to have maintained Third Division South membership throughout its existence between 1921 and 1958.

Interestingly, average crowds took a downturn during the season, partly due to fuel rationing bought on by the Suez crisis, but Supporters Club membership reached an all time high with 22,000 registered members.

The season was once again rounded off with a lucrative end-of-season tour; this time the club visited Holland, Germany and Austria. Southend's only defeat on the tour came against an Austria "B" national team when the hosts narrowly triumphed by 4-3 in Vienna. Notable wins were achieved against Groningen (2-1), Wacker

The squad pose outside Heidelberg Castle.

SOUTHEND UNITED IN GERMANY

CONTINUING THEIR TOUR OF GERMANY, Southend United visited the famous German seat of learning, Heidelberg University. Here they are outside Heidelberg Castle with Manager Harry Warren, Chairman Major A. I. Hay, M.B.E., and Coun. H. W. Cox.

Munich (3-0) and old acquaintances Sparta Rotterdam were also beaten by two goals to one.

1958/59- Big Spending Shrimpers Come Up Short Again

The main transfer of the summer of 1958 was the sale of John McGuigan to Newcastle United, Southend receiving a fee of £2,250 plus the services of Bill Punton in exchange for the outside-left. The only other newcomer was Colin Cairns, who completed his move from Camelon Juniors having had a trial at Roots Hall the previous spring. Also leaving Roots Hall were Dennis Howe (Aldershot), Ray Middleton (Luton Town) and Tommy D'Arcy, who failed to find another club initially, but later joined Queen of the South. Furthermore, the veteran Jim Duthie retired from the game during the summer. Eddie Perry was content to hold the nucleus of the squad together as they had served him well in the previous campaigns. His side would face new and untested opposition including Accrington Stanley, Stockport County, Bury and Rochdale, as the northern clubs had joined them in the unified Third Division.

The campaign kicked off in fine style with a 4-1 win at Bournemouth and Boscombe; inevitably Hollis claimed two to open his account for the season. However, defeats at Reading (0-3) and Chesterfield (0-4) exposed defensive frailties and a lack of fire power up front. The occasional big victory still came along as home wins over Queen's Park Rangers (4-0) and Doncaster Rovers (5-0) demonstrated, but more often than not

Alan Dicks

Southend United 1958/59

The Shrimpers would be limited to single goals in a lot of matches. Jimmy Thomson had returned to the side following a broken leg, but despite three goals in ten starts, he was not the answer to the shot shy attack. In November, Perry acted to bolster his attacking options; Indian born Bud Houghton was signed for £1,000 from Birmingham City while Les Stubbs returned from his successful spell at Chelsea. Southend laid out big money in securing Stubbs, a joint fee of £12,500 saw centre half Alan Dicks joining Stubbs at Roots Hall. At the same time, the half back line was strengthened by the arrival of Alec Stenhouse from Portsmouth. Leaving Roots Hall was popular forward Kevin Baron, who joined Northampton Town of the new Fourth Division.

Despite the new arrivals, another F.A.Cup embarrassment was suffered at the hands of non-League opposition. A goalless draw was played out at Roots Hall with Southern League Yeovil Town before the replay took place five days later. An expectant crowd gathered at The Huish to see the home side triumph with a single Johnny Dennis goal.

Perry's signings had the desired effect in the League matches; goals came more freely as wins over Mansfield Town (5-1) at Roots Hall and Notts County (4-1) at Meadow Lane would attest. However, the team were plagued with inconsistency, not helped by the necessity to rotate goalkeepers as Harry Threadgold proved next to hopeless under floodlights and would refuse to play evening games. A visit to Carrow Road resulted in a 0-4

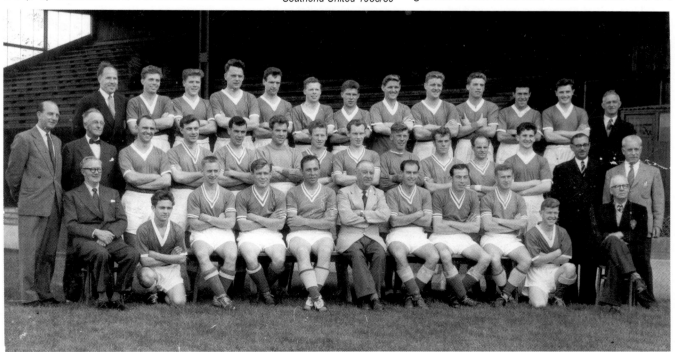

loss, and a week later Hull City took the points at Boothferry Park (2-3). A third straight loss was incurred at Roots Hall when Chesterfield stormed to victory by five goals to two, albeit with future World Cup winner Gordon Banks in goal.

The pattern of up and down results continued throughout the season; Bud Houghton was fast becoming a Roots Hall favourite when he bagged his first hat-trick against Accrington Stanley in early March. He would later exceed this achievement by scoring all four goals at Field Mill when Southend demolished Mansfield Town 4-1 on their own turf. To illustrate the perplexing nature of the teams' performances, in the latter part of the season, two 1-6 beatings were sustained at Bradford City and Brentford.

However, Southend rounded off the campaign in fine style when relegated Notts County were beaten 5-2 at Roots Hall with Hollis (2), Houghton (2) and McCrory scoring the goals.

Considering the hefty outlay on transfer fees, a final position of eighth must have been a disappointment, especially as there were now two promotion places available. These were filled by champions Plymouth Argyle and Hull City to add a geographical symmetry to the inaugural unified Third Division table.

How the local paper reported the Shrimpers change to white for the 1959/60 season.

At the end of the campaign Roy Hollis and John Duffy were rewarded with two joint benefit matches against Portsmouth and an All Star Select XI.

1959/60- It's "Come On You Whites" As Perry Calls it a Day

A deeply unpopular decision was taken during the 1959 close season, when the board announced that a motion had been passed to change the clubs' colours to all white. The board justified their decision by saying the blue kit was the most commonly used in League football, causing colour clashes and the white strip would show up better under floodlights. The blue colour was retained, albeit minimally, in the collar and a thin stripe on the shorts. Floodlights had finally been erected in the summer and were used for the first time, without any real ceremony, against Mansfield Town in September.

Eddie Perry again had the support of the board to invest heavily in new talent during the summer. The most notable capture was that of centre half Peter Watson, a £5,000 signing from Nottingham Forest. Ray Whale and Tony Forrester both arrived from West Bromwich Albion and new goalkeeper Norman Uprichard, an Irish international, joined from Portsmouth. Ron Fogg was recruited from Athenian League outfit Grays Athletic. There

WILL WHITENESS ADD BRIGHTNESS TO SOUTHEND UNITED?

This season the United, known so long as "The Blues," will appear in their new colours—white shirts with blue edgings. The group of directors, players and officials includes, left to right, back row: Stirling, Fogg, Uprichard, Threadgold, Watson, Anderson and Whale. Standing: Mr. Eddie Perry (Manager), Wilf Dixon, Stenhouse, Morrison, Smith, O'Neill, Walker, Kent, Melrose, Dunsmore, Forrester, Price, Dave Robinson and Mr. Nelson Mitchell. Seated: Hollis, Mr. C. O. Benson, Williamson, Mr. A. I. Hay, McCrory, Ald. H. H. Smith (Chairman), Houghton, Ald. H. W. Cox, Duffy, Mr. S. H. J. Bates and Costello. On ground: Duncan, Kellard, Ayres and Squibb.

were minimal departures from Roots Hall; Gordon Barker trod the well worn path to Chelmsford City while Brian Ronson joined Norwich City and Jimmy Thomson signed for Headington United of the Southern League.

The campaign got off to a disastrous start with only one victory, a narrow 3-2 win at home to Queen's Park Rangers, coming in the opening nine League encounters. Alarmingly, six of the nine matches resulted in defeats as The Shrimpers propped up the fledgling League table. A brace of September home wins against Bradford City and Shrewsbury Town allayed fears somewhat, but optimism was a scarce commodity around Roots Hall. The return match with Bradford resulted in a 1-3 defeat, but was notable for the debut of Bobby Kellard, a 16-year old who became the youngest ever Southend player at that time; he was still on junior forms as he was still too young to sign professional terms. He quickly became an England international at Youth level.

Perry, in attempting to answer his critics, pointed to some heavy wins, 7-1 against Tranmere (Hollis, McCrory and Price all netting twice) and 6-1 at home to Accrington Stanley. Cynics weighed in with the fact that defeats were still too frequent and those two victories came against sides that would struggle all season and, in the case of Accrington, against a club who would become defunct within three years.

The F.A.Cup saw the visit to Roots Hall of Oswestry Town, then of the Cheshire County League. Fortunately, Southend's forwards were on top form that day and the visitors were soundly beaten by six goals to nil. However, the clubs' foray into the competition ended at the Second Round stage when a 0-3 reversal was suffered at The Dell, home of Third Division rivals Southampton.

Norman Uprichard

After a winless January, the supporters dissent reached very audible levels and criticism of Perry's team selection and purchases abounded. His cause was not helped by the fact that his two expensive signings, Stubbs and Dicks, could not hold a regular place in the starting eleven. Perry pointed out that part of the problem with Stubbs was that the player was in dispute with the club as, apparently, the wage deal agreed for his return to the club was not entirely honoured. Indeed Stubbs had actually gone on strike until the matter was resolved.

Perry had been a more than adept player, winning three caps for Wales, but in truth was a poor man-manager and his tactics were often lost on his players. The crowd also questioned his passion for the role and it came as no surprise when he tendered his resignation in February 1960. The board accepted his resignation and Perry vowed to seek a job with more security outside of football. However, within months he returned to his former club Fulham, as chief scout.

Following Perry's departure, Major Alf Hay, the former club chairman, took over day to day team duties and signed a couple of new players in March, when Billy Wall and Peter Corthine arrived from Chelsea. Corthine arrived with a bang, netting on his debut to earn a valuable point at Newport County. However, The Shrimpers' all-time top scorer Roy Hollis moved on to Chelmsford City in March.

A decent run-in saw only two defeats in the last ten fixtures, resulting in the club finishing in a respectable twelfth place. Notable results included a 4-0 win at hapless Accrington's Peel Park home and a final day 3-0 defeat of Bournemouth and Boscombe at Roots Hall. Hay had done well in his temporary capacity, although he upset a lot of supporters by announcing that the popular Irishman, Sammy McCrory, would not be offered a new deal for the next campaign.

A notable achievement at the end of this season was that full back Arthur Williamson completed a fourth successive season as an ever present in the team. Duggie Price took the goalscoring plaudits with an excellent tally of 29; just as well

Roots Hall's terraces had additional uses - the players fitness was tested to the full.

Norman Uprichard signed for Hastings United. Ron Fogg opted for Weymouth while both Les Stubbs and Willie Morrison moved to Bedford Town.

The club kicked off the new season with the all white kit modified to white shirts and blue shorts. A ragged start saw a hefty 0-3 home defeat against Bury and a 1-5 loss at Walsall. Before the doom mongers got into full cry though, a timely 3-0 win at Saltergate against Chesterfield was accrued.

Unfortunately, defeats grew by the week and Broome called for reinforcements; a new keeper Peter Goy arrived from Arsenal in October as competition for the ageing Harry Threadgold. At the same time, winger Gordon Nutt also joined from Highbury and Ken Jones was offered a professional contract when he left the Army. The odd result offered some hope, notably a 6-1 thrashing of Watford at Roots Hall, with Bud Houghton bagging a hat-trick.

Alas, the writing was on the wall and Broome could not seem to turn the tide. A humiliating 2-5 defeat was suffered at Fourth Division Rochdale in the new League Cup competition; fortunately a similar embarrassment was avoided in the F.A.Cup against Southern League Clacton Town, The Shrimpers winning 3-1 at Old Road. Predictably, the next round saw an all too familiar demise, 2-3 at the hands of Gillingham. The team were in the bottom four when the Essex derby was lost at Layer Road, Colchester United running out 0-2 winners. After six months in charge, Broome was unceremoniously booted out by Chairman Alf Hay. It was a bleak time for The Shrimpers as spiralling debts of £25,766 were announced at the AGM. Alf Hay once again took over team selection duties, heading a selection committee, and some notable results were achieved. Newport County were beaten 4-2 at Roots Hall and Hull City were turned over on their own pitch to a single Jim Fryatt goal. To offset the mounting debts, Hay accepted a £2,000 bid from Southern League Oxford United for centre forward Bud Houghton.

as McCrory (11) and Hollis (9) had very lean campaigns by their own high standards.

Sporting the much talked about white kit, Duggie Price adds to his season's tally of 29 goals.

1960/61 – New Decade and a New Broome, but Frank Only Lasts Six Months in the Hot Seat

Like his predecessor Eddie Perry, the new Southend manager Frank Broome came to Roots Hall with a decent pedigree. A former Aston Villa and England winger, Broome had left the managerial post at Exeter City to take over on a week-to-week contract at Southend.

Broome signed five players during the 1960 close season, but had to largely rely on Perry's acquisitions. The newcomers were Charlton Athletic's Jim Fryatt, a prolific scorer and seen as the long term replacement for the departed Hollis. Full back Pat Holton arrived from Chelsea and Pat Laverty from Sheffield United. Two Scottish players also arrived at Roots Hall; George Duncan signed from Glasgow Rangers and, what became a very astute signing for the club, outside left John McKinven arrived from Raith Rovers.

Several of the older Southend players moved on to professional Southern League clubs and the unfortunate John Duffy had to retire through injury. Jim Stirling joined Poole Town and goalkeeper

Left to right: New signings John McKinven, Pat Laverty and Jim Fryatt.

A CENTURY UNITED

Considering his rhetoric regarding former internationals making poor managers, it was something of a surprise when Major Hay acquiesced to the appointment of former England player Ted Fenton as the new Southend manager in March. Southend were in a perilous position and faced a tough run in. In the third from last game, a 4-1 home win over Coventry, which

Southend United 1960/61, the team now sporting blue shorts with their white shirts.

included a Peter Corthine triple, saw Southend fifth from bottom, just outside the drop zone. On the last day of the season, Southend needed to beat Grimsby Town to ensure survival, although a defeat wouldn't necessarily mean relegation if Tranmere Rovers lost; Southend went down 0-1 at Blundell Park, but fortunately news filtered through the Tranmere had also been beaten, 1-4 at Notts County. Chesterfield, Colchester United and Bradford City were joined in the relegation places by the Prenton Park club, and Southend lived on in the Third Division.

The only crumb of comfort from a dismal season was the efforts of Fryatt and Corthine, as

The Southend-on-Sea & County Pictorial bring the news of Frank Broome's sacking.

both shared the top scorer's mantle with sixteen apiece.

1961/62- Fans' Anger at Fenton's Failures

The controversial white shirts were ditched in the summer of 1961 in favour of blue shirts with white vertical pin stripes and white shorts. The move was a popular one and so was Fenton's ditching of many of the previous campaigns poor performing squad. Distinctly less popular was the increase in admission charges to three shillings.

Leaving the club were George Duncan, who joined Chesterfield, while Gordon Nutt joined Eindhoven in Holland. Duggie Price moved to Hull City and both Pat Laverty (Wellington Town) and Alec Stenhouse (Bedford Town) joined clubs outside the Football League. Meanwhile Ray

SOUTHEND-ON-SEA & COUNTY PICTORIAL

"THE SOUTHEND AND WESTCLIFF GRAPHIC"
"THE LEIGH AND SHOEBURYNESS RECORDER"

With which are incorporated "THE SOUTHEND, LEIGH AND WESTCLIFF GRAPHIC"
"THE SOUTHEND PICTORIAL TELEGRAPH"

Price 2d.

Telephone 42261 (5 lines) Southend-on-Sea

Registered at the G.P.O. as a Newspaper

No. 3085

FRIDAY EVENING, DECEMBER 9, 1960

SOUTHEND UNITED MANAGER SACKED BY DIRECTORS

Southend's November road toll

ONE person was killed, 23 seriously injured and 59 slightly injured on Southend's roads during November.

The highest casualty figure was among motor cyclists. Seventeen were slightly injured and two seriously injured. Three pillion passengers were slightly hurt.

Pedestrians are also well up on the list, with one killed, eight seriously and seven slightly injured. seven pedal cyclists over . . .

AFTER only four months in the manager's "hot seat" at Southend United, Frank Broome got the sack this morning (Friday). This news will come as a big shock to United fans as nobody had even a remote clue that this was in the offing.

Before Thursday's annual meeting of the club, Mr. Broome was asked to resign because, they said, "we have not had the desired results."

Mr. Broome refused to resign, and today a hasty meeting of . . . directors resulted in Mr. . . .

house in Keith Way, Prittlewell, and has only partially decorated the rooms.

His wife and one of his sons . . .

Frank Broome at Roots Hall.

At work and at play.
Above: The Shrimpers sport their new kit for the 1961/62 season, with the controversial white shirts having been dropped in favour of blue with a white pinstripe.

Below: The training kit was not so smart, with the players expected to provide much of their own gear, a far cry from the pampered existence of today's players.

Peter Goy makes a great save in the match at Highfield Road, Coventry. Tony Bentley and Peter Watson look on.

Whale and Pat Holton were both released without finding new clubs.

Ted Fenton was swift to draw in new talent to his squad and arguably his best signing was the capture of full back Tony Bentley from Stoke City. Norman Bleanch arrived from Fenton's former club West Ham but was moved onto Bradford Park Avenue in a matter of months. Ray Brand was recruited from Millwall, Ray Goulden from Arsenal and Pat Kerrins from Crystal Palace, Fenton doubtless drawing on his immense knowledge of the London clubs. From Sunderland came Harry Grieveson while Bob Duncan was offered a contract after impressing with the junior team.

The multitude of new faces took time to gel and only two wins, both at home against Bradford Park Avenue and Coventry City, were forthcoming in the opening eight fixtures. More encouraging though was the decent performance against Second Division Stoke City in the League Cup and, although going down to a late goal, The Shrimpers performance against superior opposition was welcome news indeed.

The introduction of Ray Brand to the forward line paid dividends, as he score six goals in as many games during September and October. A notable

win was the 4-1 triumph over Port Vale at Roots Hall, although this came hot on the heels of a 3-5 reversal at Queen's Park Rangers. Sadly, the signs for another season of struggle were confirmed when, in the ten matches from the Port Vale win to the end of 1961, only two wins were achieved. This run included the customary early

Tony Bentley

F.A.Cup exit, when Watford brushed aside a sorry Shrimpers side at Roots Hall by two goals to nil.

In November, the board came in for severe and vocal criticism from the terraces, and the fans laid siege to the Directors' entrance following the home defeat to Northampton Town. They yelled abuse and called for the board to "buy or resign". Chairman Alf Hay failed to quell the stormy waters by saying the disturbance had been caused by "beatniks" and then pointed the finger at the clubs' "yobbo element". A public campaign to boycott the next home game was an unqualified success when only 4,754 turned up to watch the game against Halifax Town, the lowest crowd thus far at Roots Hall. The point had been made loud and clear; the current team was just not good enough.

New recruits did arrive, but hardly in the manner demanded by supporters. In December, Fenton strengthened his forward line by recruiting Ray Smith, a prolific local goalscorer, from the Basildon Town club. Fortunes took a turn for the better in January and the side went through the month undefeated, although the brief spell of good form ended in the first February fixture, a 1-3 defeat at Reading. Another new signing occurred in February when Norman Lee arrived from Bournemouth and Boscombe to give further options in midfield. However, big money signing Alan Dicks moved on to Coventry City.

Major Alf Hay MBE

Southend were facing another struggle against relegation, but the recall of the veteran Harry Threadgold in goal saw results improve dramatically. With Threadgold between the posts, The Shrimpers won five and drew five of their final fifteen encounters and finished the season in 16th place, six points clear of danger.

To bluntly illustrate the teams' shortcomings, Ken Jones top scored with a meagre 13 and the rising star of the team, Bobby Kellard, contributed eleven from his wing position. Worse still, Kellard had become frustrated with the team's poor performances and slapped in a transfer request.

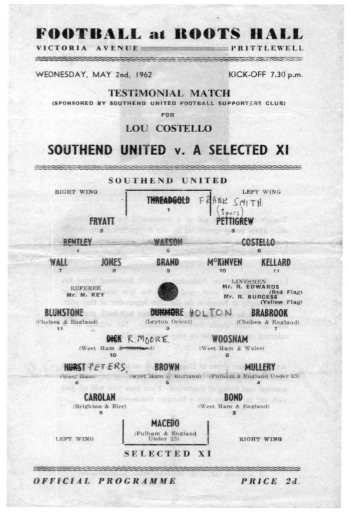

Long-serving Lou Costello was awarded a testimonial match at the end of the 1961/62 season, a Select XI providing the opposition.

Ted Fenton had stated that he was happy with the "satisfactory consolidation" of the team, days before announcing that half the squad would be released in an unprecedented clearout.

1962/63- Improving Fortunes Despite the Worst Winter On Record

Fenton's brutal cull was needed and paved the way for a bright new squad. Ray Goulden moved to Ipswich Town, and Jimmy Shiels moved to Northern Ireland with Ballymena United. Peter Corthine signed for Chelmsford City and Harry Grieveson opted for Sittingbourne while Pat Kerrins signed for Southern League Romford. Long serving full back Arthur Williamson was released and moved back to Scotland to run his family's butchery.

After the vocal protestations of the previous campaign, the board kept their word and dug deep into the transfer kitty. Ted Fenton returned to his former club West Ham United to sign Micky Beesley and Derek Woodley for fees of £4,000 each. Derek Tharme arrived from Tottenham Hotspur and Norman Liggitt came south from Middlesbrough. Scots born forward Ian McNeill was recruited from Brighton and Hove Albion and a month into the season, the board released more

New signings for the 1962/63 season, from left to right: Norman Liggitt, Micky Beesley and Derek Tharme. Below: Southend United 1962/63

funds to acquire Terry Bradbury from Chelsea for £6,000, but this was soon tempered by the departure of Bobby Kellard to Crystal Palace for a club record £30,000.

After a disappointing opening day defeat at Watford, Southend promptly won five straight matches, Beesley proving a particular hit, scoring eight times in the opening five fixtures. One of the early season victories was a 3-1 defeat of Shrewsbury Town, although a fortnight later, inexplicably, the return match resulted in a 0-6 hammering at Gay Meadow. Despite the odd heavy away defeat form was generally good although the club could have done without the 1-5 midweek defeat at Port Vale in September. Peter Goy was injured and Harry Threadgold still had his phobia of floodlights, so third choice keeper John Tennant was in the team and gave an erratic display between the sticks.

A run of four defeats in September was arrested by another sequence of five straights wins, such was the inconsistent form of the team. Pick of the wins was a 3-2 win over Bristol Rovers where John McKinven notched a superb hat-trick.

The club received a bye in the opening round of the League Cup, but were soon out of the competition following a 2-3 home defeat by Third Division rivals Notts County. The F.A.Cup was equally short lived, although Brighton were beaten in the

Bobby Kellard

opening round thanks to two Ken Jones goals at Roots Hall; Watford triumphed 0-2 at Roots Hall in Round Two.

In November, Fenton decided he needed a replacement for the veteran full back Sandy Anderson and he sourced John Neal from Aston Villa to fill the boots of the long time fan favourite. A month later, John Tennant was allowed to join Ashford Town of the Southern League.

After a single goal defeat to Hull City at Roots Hall on Boxing Day, the worst winter weather recorded gripped Britain. The club did not play another home fixture until March 9th, when the game with Halifax Town was given the go ahead. The Roots Hall pitch was heavily frozen and even the Thames was iced over during a bitter winter. Indeed, only three away games were completed in that time, leaving the club with horrific fixture congestion. Amazingly, from the turn of the year, the club went eight games unbeaten as a steady climb up the table began.

April was a hectic month with eight games played in a three week period. Perhaps this explained the two bizarre away defeats that month, 3-6 at Ashton Gate against Bristol City and 3-5 at Northampton Town.

Pitch Invasion Mars Local Derby

The 1962/63 home league derby against Colchester United was marred by crowd trouble at Roots Hall after fans invaded the pitch, angry that the referee, Mr. Bye of Bedford, had booked two of the Southend United players!

After an appeal by Ted Fenton and the appearance of three police cars, the crowd dispersed quietly, by which time Mr. Bye had been smuggled out of the ground.

Referee under fire at Roots Hall

Southend United 2, Colchester United 3

REFEREE Mr. P. Bye (Bedford) was smuggled out of Roots Hall on Saturday by another exit as a hostile crowd demonstrated outside the main entrance in protest against the booking of two Southend players—Smith and Kellard—in the second half of the match against Colchester, writes **ALLAN EDWARDS.**

The moment Mr. Bye blew his whistle for full-time the pitch was invaded from all four sides by hordes of fans, and the Police had to clear a path to the dressing rooms as the crowd shouted abuse.

After the fracas on the pitch, still-irate fans milled around the entrance and a long line of men, women and children stood on the edge of the car park, continually chanting for the referee.

Finally, three Police cars roared up, Manager Ted Fenton appealed to the crowd to think of the club, and suddenly it was over as fast as it had begun. Mr. Bye had by that time left the ground.

To win games Southend need the determination only an enthusiastic crowd can give them. On Saturday supporters showed they could produce a roar to match any at Hampden, and it almost brought the equaliser Blues deserved, but there was no excuse for the roar of anger which followed.

Mr. Bye roused the crowd by taking the names of Ray Smith and Bobby Kellard when they kicked the ball away after being penalised, but earlier took no action against a Colchester player for unfair tackling, apart from awarding Southend a number of free kicks.

However, it was no fault of Mr. Bye that United lost both points. A disastrous first five minutes, a third inexcusable slip just when they looked to be on top to stay, and the game seemed to be all over.

But what a treat it was to hear those frenzied roars after the break. They electrified the team, mistakes were forgotten, and this was suddenly the most exciting game seen at Roots Hall this season.

Ray Smith added to Mike Beesley's first-half goal, was injured a minute later, came back on after five minutes, and then almost snatched the equaliser, which was finally denied them only by Colchester luck.

Praise Colchester, though, for making the most of their few opportunities. The first one came when the game was three minutes' old. Centre-forward and captain Martyn King moved into the Southend penalty area without a defender within two yards of him. With all the time in the world he squared the ball to inside-left Bobby Hunt, who shot on the turn past a late-diving Harry Threadgold.

Second goal

Two minutes later there was a stunned silence when Colchester got a second.

This time King left Peter Watson leaden-footed, there was nobody else to cover, and once more Threadgold was nowhere to be seen as the leader drove low into a corner of the net.

Although completely rocked, Blues were not beaten yet, and they gradually forced their way on top, encouraged more and more by the crowd. The roar reached such a crescendo a goal had to come, and centre-forward Mike Beesley, who had been unlucky with a shot earlier, got it in the 20th minute.

A John McKinven centre laid it on. Woodley and Smith had their shots blocked, but Beesley's third-

time-lucky drive rocketed past Colchester 'keeper Percy Ames.

Blues threw everything at the Colchester goal in the next 10 minutes. Five corners came in as many minutes, a cannon shot from Bobby Kellard—he had a first-class game at inside-right—was headed round a post by centre-half Duncan Forbes more by luck than judgment, and a McKinven pile-driver was quickly kicked behind by right-back Richie Griffiths as Ames stood unsighted.

Third slip

Then came that fatal third slip which lost Southend both points. Left-half Ray McCrohan took a long throw-in, and Bobby Hunt, unmarked again, hooked the ball between a completely surprised Threadgold and the near post.

Colchester were never in the game during that temperature-raising second half, and it is a mystery how Blues failed to share the spoils.

Three minutes after the restart Ray Smith would have been clean through, moving on to a lob from Beesley, but right-half McCrohan leapt up to bring the ball down with his hands and stop a certain goal. Luckily for him he was just on the edge of the penalty area.

A few minutes later Derek Woodley slipped a beautiful ball through to Smith, who fumbled it, then recovered only to blast it over the bar.

Biggest blunder

Blues' long-overdue second goal came two minutes later, when Colchester made their biggest blunder. An Anderson free kick was headed about in the penalty area, inside-right Sammy McLeod tried to slip the ball back to Ames, but Smith was standing between them, and he made no mistake as the 'keeper raced out.

Smith left the field a minute later with a badly-gashed head after colliding with Duncan Forbes, and returned to become the unluckiest man on the field when, in the dying stages, he moved into position for a McKinven pass and beat Ames with his shot, only to watch the ball scrape off the wrong side of a post.

Southend United: Threadgold; Bentley, Anderson; Costello, Watson, Lee; Woodley, Kellard, Beesley, Smith, McKinven.

Colchester: Ames; Griffiths, Fowler; McCrohan, Forbes, Hunt, R. M.; Hill, McLeod, King, Hunt, R. R., Grice.

Southend United Manager Ted Fenton (above) appeals to demonstrators (below) to disperse after Saturday's match at Roots Hall.

A decent run-in saw a final placing of eighth achieved with a points tally of 50, eight behind promoted Swindon Town and a further four behind champions Northampton Town. Despite his opening salvo, Micky Beesley was overhauled by Ken Jones in the final weeks of the campaign to take the top scorers mantle. Jones scored nineteen and Beesley sixteen, although the latter stood on fifteen before sustaining an injury in the Boxing Day game. Winger John McKinven weighed in with a dozen goals.

At the end of the season, and despite the crazy fixture backlog, the club undertook a tour for the first time in a number of years. A short trip to Ireland saw matches played against Cork Hibernians and Dublin's Shamrock Rovers, but disappointingly the match that would have pitted Southend United against Southend United was postponed at the last minute. The hosts were based in the town of Waterford.

1963/64- Scots Imports Fail To Impress

Once again Ted Fenton was a busy man during the 1963 close season with further wholesale changes made to his squad. A new goalkeeper was needed as the long serving Harry Threadgold had hung up his gloves. Striker Jim Fryatt, who had never shown his prolific best at Roots Hall and was even played at full-back on occasions, transferred to Bradford Park Avenue. A further five players joined non-League clubs; veteran full back Sandy Anderson opted to wind down his playing days at Folkestone Town while Ray Brand and Derek Tharme moved close by at Hastings United. Norman Liggitt opted for Southern League King's Lynn and Billy Wall signed for Cambridge City, also members of the Southern League.

Fenton's reinforcements had a distinct Scottish flavour to them. Benny Friel (Dumbarton), Bobby King (Rangers) and Bobby Gilfillan (Raith Rovers) were joined in October by Bobby Cameron (Gravesend and Northfleet), Jimmy Conway (Norwich City) and Malcolm Slater (Montrose), all of whom were born north of the border. Other acquisitions included new goalkeeper Brian Rhodes from West Ham, who would start as second choice to Peter Goy, and Barry Ashworth, who arrived from Bangor City.

The season got underway to a decent start, the early highlight being a 4-1 victory over Barnsley, with Ashworth and Micky Beesley sharing the

Five of the six Scottish players who were with the Shrimpers during the 1963/64 season, top to bottom, left to right: Bobby Cameron, Benny Friel, Jim Conway, Bobby King and Bobby Gilfillan.

goals between them. However, heavy defeats away to Peterborough (0-3) and Port Vale (1-4) were a sign of things to come.

Between September 14th and the end of the year, only three wins from the 22 League encounters were forthcoming and another F.A.Cup first round humiliation was suffered against Southern Leaguers Yeovil Town. The League Cup saw the club reach the Third Round for the first time, but this was assisted by being granted a bye in the opening round. Port Vale were bested in the next round (2-1) but Second Division Swindon Town proved too strong, cantering to a 0-3 win at the County Ground.

The turn of the year started in spectacular fashion with a classic encounter at Loftus Road, home of Queen's Park Rangers. Jimmy Conway scored the winner four minutes from time to see Southend home by five goals to four in an amazing match.

Southend United on parade

Majority of the Southend United players in this picture are in the running for places in the team to meet Bournemouth in the opening match of the season at Roots Hall on August 24th. REAR (left to right): Terry Bradbury, Norman Liggitt, Ray Smith, Peter Goy, Lou Costello, John McKinven and Mike Beesley. FRONT (left to right): Ian McNeill, Ken Jones, John Neal, Derek Woodley, Tony Bentley and Peter Watson.

The Southend United team for the opening game of the 1963/64 season.

ver. Two players, Bobby Cameron and Brian Rhodes, emigrated to Australia, with Cameron joining the Adamstown club.

A desperately poor start for Southend saw only two wins coming from the opening dozen matches. Alarmingly, eight of these games resulted in defeats, with the defence leaking four goals on three occasions. Bristol City beat Southend both home and away by the same 0-4 scoreline and Peterborough also hit four in a 2-4 win at London Road. Fenton rang the changes to the defence, dropping Bobby King and shifting John Neal to left back. Lou Costello was restored to right back and, thankfully, Peter Watson returned from injury. Fenton also realised his squad was a little lightweight all round and called for reinforcements a month into the season; Andy Smillie was a welcome acquisition from Scunthorpe United while Colin Metcalf arrived from Norwich City.

The reshuffle worked and The Shrimpers won three of the next four games, Bobby Gilfillan netting six times, having rediscovered his goalscoring touch; the Scottish forward bagged a hat-trick against Workington at Roots Hall. The next two home games both produced remarkable 6-3 wins

A steady run of just two defeats in twelve matches during February and March meant that relegation was not a genuine threat, but at times the side looked bereft of ideas and former player Alf Smirk, now the reporter for the Southend Standard, labelled Fenton's charges as "ponderous and pathetic".

The highlight of the run-in to the end of the season was a 7-1 demolition of Shrewsbury Town at Roots Hall, Bobby Gilfillan hitting four of the goals.

Southend finished in 14th place, seven points clear of the relegation places which contained Millwall, Crewe Alexandra, Wrexham and Notts County. Micky Beesley top scored with a meagre 13 goals, with support coming from Ray Smith (12) and ten from Gilfillan. The main problem from a disappointing season was wretched home form, which saw only nine victories from the 23 matches. Ten of the home matches were drawn.

1964/65- Fenton Bows Out After an Uninspiring Campaign

A relatively quiet 1964 close season for Southend manager Ted Fenton saw only three new arrivals to the Roots Hall roster. Tony Howe signed from local rivals Colchester United, goalkeeper Ian McKechnie signed from Arsenal and Alec Hutton arrived from Scottish Junior football with Tulliallan Thistle. Departures included Ken Jones to Millwall, Peter Goy to Watford and Ian McNeill to Do-

The 1963/64 season saw low crowds on the South Bank and the club over £42,000 in debt. "Low crowds" was, of course, objective... things would get much worse in the 1980s.

"Gates" increase by £5,533 at Roots Hall, but—

UNITED NOW OVER £42,000 IN RED

ALTHOUGH "gate" receipts were up last season by £5,533 and the club received £19,000 from the Supporters' Club, Southend United lost £5,924 on the year and are now £42,642 in the red.

The loss was due to a big increase in wages, benefits and salaries and fees paid for new players.

Club, but it is interesting to note that since the broadside launched against the Press, the club have won only TWO OUT OF 18 GAMES.

for Southend. Bristol Rovers were the first victims, with John McKinven scored three and then Gilfillan went one better, netting four of the six against Essex rivals Colchester United.

Southend enjoyed a modest run in the League Cup, going out 1-3 to First Division Stoke City in the Third Round. Previously, they had disposed of Brentford at Griffin Park and Hull City in a home replay after a goalless draw at Boothferry Park.

The Christmas and New Year period saw a sustained spell of good results, notably a 4-1 win at Barnsley and a 3-1 victory at Shrewsbury Town.

The post-New Year period saw a couple of additions to the squad in the shape of Eddie May, an outstanding prospect with Athenian Leaguers Dagenham and centre forward Peter Bullock, signed from Birmingham City.

Towards the end of January, the wheels of the bandwagon fell off spectacularly, with home defeats to Scunthorpe United (0-1) and Mansfield Town (1-4). Fenton's men were, like countless Southend teams before them, dogged with inconsistency; a 6-1 home win over Oldham Athletic was followed up by a single goal reversal to Watford at Roots Hall. Big away defeats at eventual champions Carlisle United (3-4) and Mansfield Town (1-6) preceded a 5-0 home trouncing of Luton Town. The season was rounded off with an easy 4-0 defeat of Grimsby Town.

With such inconsistent results and a penchant for spectacular self-destruction, it was no surprise that the club finished in a mid-table twelfth place with a record of 19 wins and 19 defeats. Bobby Gilfillan was the man in form in front of goal, scoring 23 during the campaign, while the ever reliable John McKinven backed him up with eleven from his wide position.

Ted Fenton's contract was up at the end of the campaign and in a mutual decision with the board, it was not renewed. Fenton opted to take up that common post-footballing career of pub landlord.

In fairness to the former England international, Fenton's four years at the club were dogged with financial troubles and his hand was often forced into selling his better players to make ends meet. However, a lasting benefit of Fenton's era was his establishment of a robust youth system which would pay dividends for several years. Frankie Banks, Chris Barnard and Frank Mathews were

The ever-dependable Peter Watson.

all integrated into the first team after serving apprenticeships under Ted Fenton.

1965/66- Relegation Trapdoor Sucks in Williams' Sorry Shrimpers

The board sifted through numerous applications for the vacant manager's job and selected the name of Alvan Williams as their new man. He had risen to fame with Bangor City, where as assistant manager he coached the Welsh part-timers to a famous run in the European Cup Winners Cup.

Williams wasted no time in strengthening his squad. His major acquisition was Eddie Firmani from Charlton Athletic. He was a famous Italian international, who arrived at Roots Hall for a club record fee of £10,000, despite edging towards the end of his career. The other major summer signing was Mel Slack from Sunderland.

Departures were more plentiful; the supporters were particular upset at the sale of goalscoring midfielder Micky Beesley to Peterborough. Jimmy Conway and Benny Friel returned to Scotland, Conway to Partick Thistle and Friel rejoining Dumbarton. Lou Costello signed for Chelmsford City while Tony Howe moved to Eastern Counties Leaguers Clacton Town and Colin Metcalf opted for Wisbech Town of the Southern League.

The campaign commenced with a comfortable 2-0 win over Swansea Town, but doubts crept in when the next five games mustered only one point. Firmani would prove to be the main source of goals although once the enormity of his salary became public knowledge, a rift was caused in the squad.

In the League Cup, Newport County were dispatched after a Roots Hall replay in the opening round. In Round Two, Southend were leading at half time by a Firmani goal at Reading, then promptly conceded five in the second half. In the F.A.Cup, Southend won at home to Notts County and then accounted for Watford in the Second Round before being paired with Second Division Rotherham United. In a tight encounter at Millmoor, the home side won by the odd goal in five.

was this month that a major slump occurred; four defeats without scoring saw relegation confirmed with a game to go. A 0-1 defeat at Hull City meant the club would be playing Fourth Division football for the 1966/67 campaign. A 2-1 last day win over Reading was immaterial as Oldham, Mansfield and Bournemouth all had sufficient points to avoid the drop. Joining Southend in the drop zone were Exeter City, Brentford and York City, the first relegation The Shrimpers had suffered since joining the Football League in 1920.

Southend United 1965/66

The expensive signature of Firmani proved a poisoned chalice. Dressing room unrest was inevitable but his undoubted talent yielded 20 goals in a disastrous campaign. In such a wretched season, it was something of a surprise that a "Player of The Year" award was introduced, the inaugural winner being Tony Bentley.

Back on the League trail, single victories were punctuated by a procession of defeats. In November, the club suffered total humiliation when their record League defeat was handed out at Brighton, with Albion winning 1-9. More defeats were suffered at Watford and Gillingham, so Williams called for reinforcements.

A new goalkeeper, Trevor Roberts, was signed from Liverpool and Graham Birks signed from Peterborough. Alex Lumsden left Scottish Junior football and joined Southend from Camelon, followed by Tony Beanland from Southport.

Roberts tried manfully to shore up a leaky defence but had no answer to the five Swansea put past him or the four conceded at Swindon Town. The occasional victory appeased the crowd to some extent, notably a 5-3 win over Walsall and a 5-2 win at home to Gillingham. The latter match saw Firmani claim an inspired hat-trick.

Once again, the season was hampered by a harsh winter and was extended well into May. It

Eddie Firmani

See-Saw Shrimpers

Alan Moody

1966/67- Away Day Blues Cost the Shrimpers Dear

The board insisted that relegation would mean a tightening of belts; a tiny squad would undertake the first season outside of the Third Division. Williams' recruits numbered two; Johnny Baber was a useful signing from Charlton Athletic, while Colin Flatt was drafted in from Leyton Orient. Seven players left the club, although in the case of the impeccable Peter Watson, failure to recover from eye problems put paid to his professional career. Goalkeeper Ian McKechnie and young full back Frankie Banks signed for Hull City and another youth product, Chris Barnard, joined Ipswich Town. Terry Bradbury went to Leyton Orient and Bobby King went to Southern League Romford. John Neal joined Wrexham as trainer.

The campaign kicked off in optimistic mood, with the side unbeaten in the opening six encounters before a visit to Somerton Park resulted in a 0-3 reversal against Newport County. The side bounced back however, winning the next four matches, notably a 5-1 thrashing of Chester at Roots Hall, in which Ray Smith hit a hat-trick. The run also included a handsome 4-1 home win over Port Vale, made all the more notable by the appearance at centre half of Bobby Haddrick, who beat Bobby Kellard's record as the clubs' youngest first team debutant.

The early season saw the depressingly regular premature exit from the League Cup; a 0-2 defeat to Gillingham at Priestfield in a First Round replay. After a very decent start to the League campaign, October saw a run of four straight defeats and although November's results faired slightly better, the F.A.Cup campaign lasted just one game, which was a single goal defeat at Watford.

The strangely regular occurrence over the Christmas fixtures struck again, Boxing Day seeing a 2-5 defeat at Aldershot, only for the team to make amends a day later with a 4-0 triumph at Roots Hall. The New Year saw the useful acquisition of Steve Ingle from Bradford City, and an early contribution from the new man was a brace of goals in a 2-1 triumph at Barnsley. Departing Roots Hall in January was Malcolm Slater, who signed for Leyton Orient. In a season of fluctuating bouts of form, this came in the middle of five consecutive victories, the best win being a 4-0 drubbing of struggling Bradford Park Avenue.

In March, Williams decided to cut his losses with Firmani, selling him back to Charlton for £2,000.

Southend United 1966/67

1967/68- Best's Arrival Cannot Prevent Another End of Season Collapse

Ernie Shepherd began his first full season in charge by pruning his squad of players from the ultimately disappointing 1966/67 campaign. Leaving the club were Derek Woodley, joining Firmani at Charlton Athletic, whilst Colin Flatt (Wisbech Town) and Bobby Haddrick (Hastings United) opted to pursue their careers in non-League football. Alvan Williams returned to Roots Hall to sign three of his former charges; Ray Smith, Tony Beanland and Steve Ingle.

Just one month after offloading Firmani, Williams himself bowed out of Roots Hall, perhaps pre-empting the board, who were rumoured not to be considering a contract renewal. After decamping to Wrexham to become their first team manager, his assistant at Roots Hall, Ernie Shepherd, took over the day to day running of the team.

The run-in to the season highlighted the issue that blighted a potential promotion campaign, this being an inability to win on the road. The closing months saw defeats at Notts County, the eventual champions Stockport County, Luton Town, Barrow and Southport. In fact, the final five matches of the season saw goals dry up completely, with two against Luton Town at Roots Hall being the only time The Shrimpers troubled the scorer's column.

For the first time in sixty years, the club announced a share issue to raise a transfer kitty. It was a resounding success, with £30,000 being handed over for new signings. Shepherd's major summer signing was Phil Chisnall, a former Busby Babe, who cost a club record £17,000 from Liverpool. Also joining the club were Jackie Ferguson from Airdrieonians, Joe Ashworth from Bournemouth and Boscombe and Roy Walsh from Ipswich Town. Also moving down from Scotland was Jimmy Stevenson, previously with Hibernian. More reinforcements came in September, in the shape of Bobby Howlett from Chelsea

A night match under the floodlights at Roots Hall.

The disappointing run of form at a critical stage of the season saw Southend finish in sixth place, eleven points adrift of champions Stockport County. Completing something of a northern monopoly, also promoted to the Third Division were Southport, Barrow and Tranmere Rovers whilst bottom of the table were Lincoln City. Ray Smith top scored for Southend with 19, while goalkeeper Trevor Roberts took the "Player of the Year" trophy.

Left to right: Phil Chisnall and Sammy McMillan.

and Sammy McMillan, who made the reverse journey from Wrexham.

Once again the season started well, with only one defeat in the opening ten matches, and there was considerable optimism for a successful campaign. However, despite beating Brentford in the opening round of the League Cup, hopes for a cup run were short lived when Darlington triumphed 1-2 at Roots Hall in the Second Round.

In October, Alvan Williams had the last laugh on The Shrimpers, masterminding a 1-4 victory over Southend at the Racecourse Ground. The club's League form remained steady and they found themselves at the top end of the table. Phil Chisnall was finding the net regularly, ably supported by the ever reliable John McKinven from his left wing berth. As most supporters came to expect by now, the Christmas and New Year period saw the goals dry up somewhat and Shepherd scoured the market for potential new strikers. In the meantime, the inevitable early F.A.Cup exit duly arrived in a 0-1 defeat at the Goldstone Ground in the opening round.

In January, Shepherd found his man; Glaswegian forward Billy Best arrived from Northampton Town for £3,000. At first, the new man failed to set the world on fire, his first four games drawing a blank. However, after a goal against Halifax Town, the floodgates opened. Two more followed at Exeter, then a hat-trick against Chester at Roots Hall. His clever forward play saw Workington annihilated 7-0 at Roots Hall, Best having to be content with just one goal but contributing to nearly everything that was good about the display, the game being witnessed by a season best crowd of

13,871. In all, Billy Best scored 14 goals in just 20 games, but four defeats in the final six matches saw the club miss out on the promotion places, again finishing in sixth place. Another decent capture in the transfer market was Eddie Clayton, who arrived in March from Tottenham Hotspur.

Despite Best's sterling efforts, Phil Chisnall remained top scorer with 17 League goals, with McKinven just one behind, although he added a further strike in the League Cup. After such a promising start, the loss of form at the end of the season once again cost the club dear, finishing just four points adrift of the promotion places. Champions of the division were Luton Town with Barnsley, Hartlepool United and Crewe Alexandra taking the remaining promotion places. Bradford Park Avenue finished bottom of the table with a meagre haul of 23 points. Having played only twenty matches, Billy Best's strike rate of 14 goals in 20 games won him the "Player of the Year" title.

Billy Best

1968/69- Goal Crazy Shrimpers
Come Up Short Again

Ernie Shepherd had a relatively quiet summer of 1968, signing just three players for his squad. John Kurila, a Scottish centre half, arrived from Northampton Town and David Stone signed from Bristol Rovers. The third arrival was a new goalkeeper, Lawrie Leslie, a former Scotland international, to challenge Trevor Roberts for the first team jersey. Departing the club were Eddie May, joining Alvan Williams at Wrexham, Ray White (Bristol Rovers), Frank Mathews (Torquay United)

Top: Southend United 1968/69
Below: The players meet the press.

and Joe Ashworth (Rochdale). Jackie Ferguson returned to Scotland with Ayr United while Jimmy Stevenson signed for the then professional Southern League outfit Brentwood Town.

Shepherd's star signing of this season happened in September when Ian "Chico" Hamilton arrived at Roots Hall from Chelsea for the not insignificant fee of £5,000. The club ditched the royal blue shirts from the previous campaign and dark blue shirts were introduced instead. However, with remarkable alacrity, the Football League waited until April to tell the club they were unhappy with the colour as it was too close to the black referee's kit. Southend completed the final five fixtures of the campaign in borrowed kit.

The season started off with a win at home against Halifax Town, followed by a couple of draws. Predictably, The Shrimpers lacklustre form away from home, which was a feature throughout this decade, resurfaced with reversals

A CENTURY UNITED

at Lincoln City (1-2) and the ever fruitless visit to Newport County (1-4). Alvan Williams returned to Roots Hall again in September, but Shepherd had the last laugh on this occasion when an Eddie Clayton strike settled matters in Southend's favour.

September also saw a Second Round exit in the League Cup; a spectacular 6-1 victory at Dean Court saw Southend account for Bournemouth in the opening round before an away trip, this time to First Division Wolverhampton Wanderers saw The Shrimpers put up a sterling performance, but a single John Farrington goal saw the Midlanders home safely.

More new arrivals to the team came in October; Gary Moore, a tall centre forward signed from Grimsby Town, while Dave Chambers joined from non-League Cambridge United. Meanwhile, popular midfielder Andy Smillie left for Crystal Palace.

Back on the League front, October was a decent month, with Lincoln defeated at Roots Hall followed by a 6-1 thrashing of Exeter City at home, Billy Best scoring three times. Again, the month ended with a disappointing 1-3 reversal at home to Rochdale.

The F.A.Cup beckoned in November and Southend would achieve a new competition record which still stands to this day. In the opening round, home advantage was received and the opponents would be Southern Leaguers King's

Lynn. Any nerves about a potential banana skin were soon put to bed when Gary Moore opened the scoring after two minutes. Southend went on to win 9-0, with Moore and Best each scoring hat-tricks. Two further "goals" were harshly disallowed for offside and Norman Coe in the Linnets' goal made six wonderful saves to prevent a double figure rout. Southend were drawn at home again in the Second Round against another Southern League outfit, Brentwood Town. This time, Southend went one better, scoring ten against their hapless Essex neighbours. Moore again opened the scoring but then Reg Stratton had the audacity to equalise for the visitors. After that it was a procession for the Shrimpers; Gary Moore with four headers and Sammy McMillan had put Southend 5-1 up by the 70th minute, but then Billy Best took over. He scored the remaining five goals, with four coming in the final six minutes as the visitors completely crumbled. This meant for the first time in the competition's history, the same two players, Moore and Best, scored hat-tricks in successive ties. The cup run continued when Third Division Swindon Town were defeated 2-0 at the County Ground in Round Three but a trip to Third Division Mansfield Town in the Fourth Round saw The Shrimpers slump to a 1-2 reversal.

The matches leading up to Christmas and the New Year put Southend behind in the promotion chase. A humiliating Essex derby reversal to Colchester United (0-4) at Layer Road precipitated a run of poor form. York City and Chester left Roots Hall with all the points, while a fruitless visit to Belle Vue continued the malaise, with Doncaster Rovers winning 0-2. Shepherd dipped into the transfer kitty again to patch up his ailing side, former Manchester United player Frank Haydock arrived from Portsmouth, and another two Cambridge United players were persuaded away from the Abbey Stadium; full back Keith Lindsey and centre half Peter Robinson signed in January and March respectively.

Only five matches were played in January and February during another harsh winter, the highlights being a 4-0 win over Brentford at Roots Hall and, in the Essex derby, a brace for Billy Best helping Southend gain revenge over Colchester by three goals to one. The ship had been duly steadied and with only one defeat in March, Southend were right back in the promotion hunt. Due to the fixture pile up, Southend faced twelve matches in the

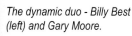

The dynamic duo - Billy Best (left) and Gary Moore.

final six weeks of the season; April saw some handy victories, 4-2 at home to Aldershot and 4-0 against Swansea Town, then Bradford Park Avenue were beaten home and away (5-0 and 3-0 respectively) on their way to a second successive bottom place finish. Newport County were defeated by a John Kurila goal to nil in the final match of April, leaving Southend really needing to win three of their remaining four matches in May. But as in so many other seasons, form deserted the team at the crucial stage; with all four away from home it was a tall order, but a narrow 3-2 win at Darlington gave a glimmer of hope. Then, defeats to Rochdale and Scunthorpe United put paid to any lingering hopes as seventh place was taken, five points adrift of the promotion places.

Once again it was a northern cartel in the promotion places, Doncaster Rovers taking the title ahead of Halifax Town, Rochdale and Bradford City.

Southend scored a remarkable 106 goals in all competitions, helped by the big F.A.Cup wins. Billy Best scored 31 times, ten coming in just four F.A.Cup appearances, with his strike partner, the much maligned Gary Moore, weighing in with 21. Chico Hamilton on 12 and Eddie Clayton with one less provided admirable support to the front pair. Despite the proficiency in front of goal, it was a defender that took the "Player of the Year" award, the always consistent John Kurila.

1969/70- Traumatic Season as Shepherd Quits and Hudson is Sacked

Ernie Shepherd was gutted by his side's inability to secure promotion, and the stress weighed heavily on the popular manager, now in his tenth year at the club. His summer 1969 captures were John Chambers from Aston Villa, and Owen Simpson from Colchester United. He also made further captures throughout the opening months of the season; goalkeeper Brian Lloyd arrived from Stockport County in September.

Departing Roots Hall were Southend's youngest ever first team player, Phil O'Connor, who joined Bexley United. David Stone joined Hastings United while Lawrie Leslie took up a coaching post with Millwall. Bobby Howlett joined Colchester United and Mel Slack departed for Cambridge United. However, the biggest loss was that of the mercurial Chico Hamilton, who signed for Second Division Aston Villa; a record fee of £40,000 softened the blow to a degree.

The Football League again upset The Shrimpers' board by decreeing that the popular Friday night fixtures would be restricted in number for the new season.

The League campaign kicked off in promising fashion, a win at Darlington (2-0) was followed by a 3-0 home win over Scunthorpe United and a draw at Lincoln City (3-3). Billy Best scored five times in these games, including yet another hat-trick in the Scunthorpe victory.

The League Cup provided an epic encounter with Brentford in the opening round. In the days before penalty shoot-outs gave a nail biting finale to cup-ties, endless replays could ensue to settle the outcome. A 2-2 draw at Roots Hall saw the sides go back to Griffin Park, but 120 minutes could not muster a single goal and a second replay was required. The rules in those days stated that if such a replay was needed then it would be contested at a neutral venue, so the sides met for the third time in nine days at Millwall's home at The Den. In another tight encounter extra time was again needed to separate the sides, but a Sam-

In 1969, Southend United were banned from wearing their dark blue shirts, as it was claimed they clashed with the kits of the officials. The Daily Express ran this cartoon in response to the ban.

Southend United 1969/70

my McMillan hat-trick saw Southend go through by three goals to two. Another replay was needed to see off Shrewsbury Town in the next round, but the run ended in the Third Round when Bradford City won 1-2 at Valley Parade.

Despite the excitement of their cup exploits, the club's League form collapsed. A 0-2 defeat at Swansea Town in September precipitated a run of eight games without a win. A tired and emotional Ernie Shepherd offered his resignation, which Chairman Bill Rubin reluctantly accepted, asking him to remain at the club as General Manager to support the new man at the helm, Geoff Hudson. Shepherd accepted the offer and his stint at the club continued. Hudson's first move was to ban players from drinking in the popular new bar at The Stadium, the Shrimpers Bar.

Hudson also wielded the axe, Graham Birks and Sammy McMillan (both Chester), John McKinven (Cambridge United) and Peter Robinson (Margate) all departed during his reign. He topped up his squad by signing Joe Jacques from Darlington and

Bill Garner

in November, a £15,000 fee saw centre forward Bill Garner prised away from Southern League Bedford Town. Hudson was unlucky with injuries; Haydock, Beesley and Lindsey all spent time on the sidelines while an outbreak of flu saw the club successfully appeal for two matches in December to be postponed. Goals were hard to come by and results failed to pick up to any real degree. An F.A.Cup defeat in a replay to Gillingham in the First Round put paid to hopes of cup glory. In the League, January and February saw the side hit rock bottom, defeats to Notts County (2-5), Crewe Alexandra (3-5) and Workington (0-5) saw the knives come out for the new man in charge. Three successive three nil away reversals, to Port Vale, Exeter City and Oldham Athletic, were the final straw and after just twelve matches in charge, Geoff Hudson was dismissed, with Shepherd returning to the hot seat while a new incumbent was sought.

The Southend board turned to legendary goalscorer Arthur Rowley as the new man at the helm. He brought in Pat Wright (on loan from

Derby County) and Maurice Kyle (on loan from Oxford United) to shore up the side and Billy Best returned to his sharpest form in the closing months, hitting four in a 4-3 defeat of Peterborough United at London Road and braces in home wins over Chester and Darlington. Southend, for once, enjoyed a successful end to a campaign, losing just three of the closing twelve matches, to avoid the re-election battle.

A final place of 17th was very poor but endemic of a traumatic season. The re-election battle was contested by Newport County, Darlington, Hartlepool United and Bradford Park Avenue, who finished bottom for the third straight season. Avenue's luck run out and Cambridge United were elected to the Football League in their place. At the other end of the table, Chesterfield were champions, with the promotion places filled by Wrexham, Swansea City and Port Vale.

Billy Best was top scorer again with 24 goals, but a lack of support from colleagues highlighted the problem suffered by the club all season, a chronic goalscoring deficiency. Gary Moore's proficiency in front of goal deserted him and he registered only ten goals during the campaign. Unsurprisingly, the ever popular Billy Best won the "Player of the Year" award for a second time

1970/71 – Rowley Fails To Inspire The Shrimpers

Having inherited a squad built by other managers,.Arthur Rowley quickly made changes to his Roots Hall squad; out went John Kurila, who joined Colchester United, and Pat Wright, returning to Derby County. John Chambers and Paul Vickery moved into the non-League game with Bromsgrove Rovers and Barking respectively, while centre half Frank Haydock emigrated to South Africa. Rowley's signings included Ian Cowan from Dunfermline Athletic, Kevin Fallon from Sligo Rovers and Alex Smith from Huddersfield Town. A month into the season, Bernie Lewis (Watford), Jimmy Lumsden (Leeds United) and John McMahon (on loan from Preston North End) augmented the first team squad. However, it was Ernie Shepherd's last signing for the club that would prove the most memorable, a mere £100 fee securing the services of local youngster Peter Taylor.

Despite the club being in the hands of the Football League's most prolific goalscorer ever, it was that very commodity that proved so scarce in the opening weeks of the campaign. In the open-

Peter Taylor

ing fourteen matches of the season, only seven goals were scored, four courtesy of the incomparable Billy Best. Only three matches were won, at home to Northampton Town and away to both Lincoln City and Hartlepool. A traditionally brief flirtation with the League Cup ended in a 0-3 First Round defeat to Second Division Charlton Athletic at The Valley.

In late October, goals became slightly more plentiful with some very welcome wins being achieved against Newport County (3-0), Brentford (4-3) and at newcomers Cambridge United (3-0). However, a consistent run of results proved elusive, with regular defeats being suffered on the road, notably 0-3 at York City and 0-4 at Peterborough United. Even home form was erratic, with several matches ending in tame draws when victory often seemed assured.

Arthur Rowley was given a three-year contract at £7,000 per year, a vast sum for a manager of a lower division club in those days.

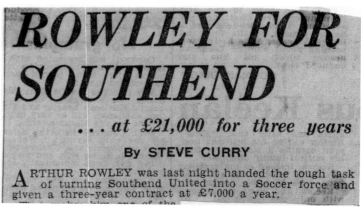

ROWLEY FOR SOUTHEND
...at £21,000 for three years
BY STEVE CURRY

ARTHUR ROWLEY was last night handed the tough task of turning Southend United into a Soccer force and given a three-year contract at £7,000 a year.

The ever-popular Terry Johnson.

The F.A.Cup proved more fruitful; in the opening round, Southern League Weymouth were put to the sword at Roots Hall, Bill Garner claiming four in a 7-0 demolition. Far more even was the Second Round tie with Athenian League neighbours Dagenham, a single Billy Best goal ensuring safe passage to Round Three where another home tie awaited. Unfortunately, Second Division Carlisle United were far too strong for Southend, returning to Cumbria with a handsome 0-3 victory.

Rowley called for reinforcements; Geoff Barker signed from Hull City, John Roberts from Bradford City, while Terry Johnson and Dave Elliott both joined from Newcastle United. John Piekalnietis arrived from Nottingham Forest and Mick Harmston came on a month's loan from Sheffield United. Leaving the club in March were David Chambers (York City) and Owen Simpson (Darlington).

Despite the changes, results did not improve; one week Darlington were defeated 4-0 at Feethams but a fortnight later the side lost by the same score at Bournemouth and Boscombe. Unusually, Southend had a strong finish to the season, winning three and drawing two of the last five fixtures, but an overall placing of 18th was a huge disappointment to Rowley, the board and supporters alike. The re-election places were avoided, Southend finishing four points clear of Lincoln City who finished fourth bottom; the bottom three places were taken by Newport County, Hartlepool United and Barrow. Billy Best was top scorer for a third straight season with 22 in all competitions, substantially ahead of Bill Garner

on twelve. Stylish defender Alex Smith was voted "Player of the Year".

1971/72 – Rowley's Men Storm Back to Division Three

After his initial season in charge ended in acute disappointment, Rowley spent the summer months devising his plan for the 1971/72 campaign. Newcomers to the club included George Duck, a young striker from Millwall, Ray Ternent came south from Burnley and centre half Brian Albeson arrived from Darlington. Two of Rowley's own acquisitions departed the club, Kevin Fallon joining Midland League club Ilkeston Town while Ian Cowan moved to Australia. Veteran Tony Bentley (Folkestone Town) and John Baber (Margate) departed, having given sterling service; Bentley would be awarded a second testimonial match against his former club Stoke City. Jimmy Lumsden took up a coaching role with Leeds United, Geoff Barker rejoined Hull City and Phil Chisnall signed for Stockport County.

The season started pretty poorly, with only a 3-0 defeat of Darlington earning a tick in the win column in the opening six fixtures. After an inglorious start to proceedings, a welcome Billy Best hat-trick saw off Grimsby Town at Roots Hall and further wins were then forthcoming against the likes of Doncaster Rovers (2-0 at Belle Vue) and Brentford (2-1 at Griffin Park) while Newport County (3-1) and Southport (2-1) made the long trek home from Essex empty handed. Sadly, a near 10,000 crowd watched Colchester United

Southend United's 11-day tour of Russia in July and August 1971 started at the Boston Hall Hotel, Westcliff on the day before departure where the Mayor of Southend Alderman Hector Hill wished them bon voyage. The next day saw the team catch BEA's morning flight from Heathrow to Moscow.

On arrival, the Shrimpers drove north to a hostel eight miles south of Kalinin, their first opponents on the tour, and after a good night's rest, the team staged a training session on their opponent's ground. Having been successful in a request to have the long grass on the pitch cut, the Shrimpers were less successful on the pitch where a single goal from Russian striker Mosalenko in the fifth minute consigned them to their first defeat of the tour.

The next stop of the tour was Tula, 100 miles south of Moscow, a full day's travel by road from Kalinin. With a team including three former internationals in their line-up, it was always going to be a difficult game for Southend United, and they eventually succumbed 1-2 in front of a crowd of 14,000, Peter Taylor bagging United's goal.

From Tula, the touring party flew 800 miles south to Sochi, a resort on the Black Sea, where the temperature reached 90 degrees, leaving the players with little choice than to take a dip in the welcoming Black Sea waters.

In Sochi, the Shrimpers met a Sochi Select XI, drawn from clubs in the Black Sea area, and they proved too strong in the wilting heat, running out 0-2 winners. Southend United even managed to have Bill Garner sent off, although it appeared to be a very minor incident that incurred the wrath of the Russian official.

Another flight returned the touring party to Moscow, where they spent two days in the luxurious Hotel Sputnik. Due to a fixture pile-up, the scheduled game against Lokomotiv Moscow had been cancelled, and an alternative match against the industrial city club of Shinnik Jaroslavl was arranged. A crowd of 12,000 witnessed a 0-1 defeat for United, their fourth defeat of the tour.

The next day, the touring party jetted back to London Heathrow from Moscow, having thoroughly enjoyed their tour.

The programme for the match in Shinnik Jaroslavl had both squads in Cyrillic. By looking at the Southend United squad list carefully (shown on the left of the programme page), some players names can be worked out, such as Alex Smith (5th in list), Ray Ternant (6th), Billy Best (9th) and Bill Garner (10th)

СОСТАВЫ КОМАНД,
выступающих в сегодняшнем матче

«САУСЕНД ЮНАЙТЕД»   «ШИННИК»

Директор клуба Джон ФОСТЕР   Старший тренер, мастер спорта, заслуженный тренер
Генеральный секретарь клуба   РСФСР Виктор Марьенко
            Давид ДУГАН   Тренеры мастер спорта
                                     Станислав Воротилин и мастер
                                     спорта Геннадий Епишин

Начальник команды АРТУР РОВЛИ   Иван Домантиевский
Тренер команды Лоури Лесли   Леонид Борисов
Джон Робиртс — вратарь   Владимир Чуркин
Кейт Линдсей — правый защитник   Николай Растегаев
Алекс Смит — левый защитник   Валентин Волков
Рон Тернент — полузащитник   Владимир Панков
Дэвид Эллиот — правый полузащитник   Валерий Клещев
Терри Джонсон — правый крайний   Александр Стенищев
Билли Бест — правый полусредний   Вячеслав Наумов
Билл Гарнер—центральный нападающий мс Владимир Коротков
Георг Мур — нападающий   мс Валерий Рейнгольд
Джо Пикалнитис — нападающий   мс Виктор Санин
Питер Хант — левый полусредний   Николай Вихарев
Бернард Левис — левый крайний   Игорь Вьюгин
Георг Дак — полузащитник   Анатолий Напреев
Джо Холден — полузащитник   Юрий Иванов
Дэвид Барнет — нападающий   Юрий Карнахин
Питер Тейлор — нападающий
Джо Жак — левый полузащитник

О составах команд, выходящих на поле, будет сообщено по радио стадиона.

ОЧЕРЕДНОЙ МАТЧ
на первенство СССР по футболу состоится на нашем стадионе в понедельник, 9 августа. Нашим гостем будет один из лидеров чемпионата «Днепр».

ЗАПИШИТЕ ДЛЯ СЕБЯ
Матч окончился со счетом _____
в пользу команды _____
Голы забили _____

Цена 5 коп.

Областная типография Ярославского управления по печати.
АК 03508. З. 5701—71. Т. 3500.

win the Essex derby by a single Steve Leslie goal.

In the League Cup, a Terry Johnson goal meant a replay against Aldershot after a 1-1 draw at the Recreation Ground. Sadly, a Bill Garner strike was not enough to prevent a surprise 1-2 reversal at Roots Hall. In the F.A.Cup, a Billy Best strike saw off eventual Third Division champions Aston Villa in the First Round in front of a near 17,000 crowd at Roots Hall. However, the joy was short-lived as Bournemouth and Boscombe put South-end out of the competition in Round Two.

A new goalkeeper, Derek Bellotti, arrived at the club in December, having signed from Charlton Athletic, although he would have to wait until February before he displaced John Roberts as number one choice between the posts.

March was the month where promotion became a very real possibility; of the seven matches played,

six were won and the match at Exeter City was a goalless draw. A Bill Garner hat-trick put paid to the challenge of Chester at Roots Hall in a 4-2 victory, followed by a 4-1 defeat of Crewe Alexandra. Back to back home wins were followed by two on the road, 3-2 at Darlington and 4-1 at Reading; this time, Billy Best was taking home the match ball.

April was equally profitable, with Reading again beaten 4-1, this time at Roots Hall and Northampton Town losing by the same score ten days later, being undoubted highlights. The championship was probably lost in the home game with Cambridge United, when 17,000 packed into Roots Hall to see if The Shrimpers could extend their 17-game unbeaten run. An early injury to goalkeeper Derek Bellotti put Southend in an awkward position and when substitute Peter Taylor, all of 5' 7", took over in goal, Southend were soon 1-2 down. Alex Smith took a turn between the sticks, but Southend could not summon an equaliser and

The management team - Lawrie Leslie, John Lattimer and Arthur Rowley.

three draws in the final three outings handed the title to Grimsby Town. The good news was that second place meant a return to Division Three after a gap of six seasons; joining The Shrimpers in the promotion places were Brentford and Scunthorpe, while hapless Barrow were voted out of the League in favour of Hereford United.

This time, the leading scorer crown was won by Bill Garner with 26 goals, Billy Best coming second with a mere 20 and Terry Johnson chipping in with a more than useful 13. The "Player of the Year" award was, for the only time in the club's history, shared between two players, Garner and the solid defender Brian Albeson.

1972/73 – Mid Table Stability for Rowley's Men

Arthur Rowley had a relatively quiet summer of 1972, securing the signature of just three players in the close season. Mike Harrison arrived from Birmingham City and Dundee United's Don Mackay was brought in as understudy to Derek Bellotti. Striker Bobby Bennett was signed from Athenian League Staines Town but would fail to make much of an impact on the first team. Rowley would bolster his squad extensively in the opening months of the campaign, with five more transfers being completed between September and

Bobby Bennett

November. Kevin Johnson arrived from Sheffield Wednesday and Paul Matthews from Leicester City. Alan Moody was an excellent acquisition from Middlesbrough for a fee of £15,000, whilst Chris Guthrie also arrived from the North East, the striker leaving Newcastle United for southeast Essex. Tommy Horsfall came up from the south coast, signing for Southend from Dover of the Southern League.

Leaving Roots Hall from the promotion winning squad were John Roberts, who joined Northampton Town, while John Piekalnietis (Yeovil Town), George Duck (Wealdstone) and Bernie Lewis (Chelmsford City) all opted to pursue their careers with non-League clubs. However, the major departure came in September when £80,000 took striker Bill Garner to First Division Chelsea, only 24 hours after he played for Southend against the men from Stamford Bridge in a League Cup tie at Roots Hall.

The season started off slowly, with only a 3-1 win over the newly renamed Swansea City earning any points from the opening five fixtures. This match saw Bill Garner score his last goals for the club before his big money move to Chelsea, his last appearance attracting some 24,000 to see a narrow 0-1 defeat for The Shrimpers. In the opening round, Southend had beaten Aldershot by two goals to one, although the 'Shots would gain a modicum of revenge in the F.A.Cup when they returned to Roots Hall and secured a 0-2 victory in a First Round tie.

In the matches after Garner's departure, the goalscoring onus fell on Billy Best, Gary Moore and Terry Johnson. Best and Johnson would contribute but Gary Moore went twelve League games without a goal, prompting Rowley to sign Chris Guthrie in November.

October and November were tricky months for the side, with only three home wins against Shrewsbury Town (2-0), Brentford (4-0) and Walsall (2-0) being secured, although useful points were gained in draws at Bolton Wanderers and Scunthorpe United.

Away form remained poor; December produced just one away point in a goalless draw at Charlton Athletic on Boxing Day, whilst long trips to York City (0-2) and Blackburn Rovers (1-2) proved fruitless, although the latter was memorable for Guthrie opening his goalscoring account for The Shrimpers. The side's indifferent form contin-

ued during January and February as Southend dropped perilously close to the relegation zone.

The return of Alex Smith, and Don Mackay coming in for Bellotti in goal, saw enough points secured during March to avert any real possibility of relegation. After a single goal reversal at Shrewsbury Town, The Shrimpers went on to secure five wins and two draws from the remaining seven games of the month. Any lingering doubts were erased during April, when York City were defeated 3-0 at Roots Hall followed by high scoring Easter victories against Port Vale and Chesterfield. The side from the Potteries were defeated 5-0, with Chris Guthrie claiming three and Best

Don Mackay

a brace. The following day, The Shrimpers hit five more against Chesterfield, Guthrie and Best scored twice and Gary Moore completed a good day for Southend's forwards. Despite losing the last two outings of the campaign at Halifax Town and Rochdale, Southend finished in a relatively comfortable 14th place. It should be noted that two of the sides that followed Southend up from Division Four, Brentford and Scunthorpe United, struggled all season and both dropped straight back down, accompanied by Rotherham United and Swansea City. Division Three champions were Bolton Wanderers and also promoted were Notts County.

Chris Guthrie scored an impressive fifteen goals in only 25 matches to finish as top scorer, while Billy Best scored twelve and Terry Johnson ten. Johnson would be awarded the "Player of the Year" trophy.

1973/74- Brace Ends Shrimpers Scoring Woes

Rowley once again had a quiet summer, electing to boost his squad in stages throughout the campaign. His summer captures all proved more than useful acquisitions; Dave Cunningham from Brechin City, Andy Ford from Bournemouth and Neil Townsend from Northampton Town would all serve the club well. Leaving the club were Alex Smith, who joined Colchester United, Peter Woods and Ray Ternent both of whom joined Doncaster Rovers and Mike Harrison, who opted for Yeovil Town. Dave Barnett, who had not figured in the first team for eighteen months, left to join Folkestone Town. Rowley's most controversial decision however, was to allow the hugely popular Billy Best to rejoin Northampton Town. Best would be left twelve goals adrift of Roy Hollis' all-time club record of 135.

The season opened with goals once again in short supply. In the opening ten League matches, only one game was won, 3-1 at home to Cambridge United, and only seven goals were produced in total. Alarmingly, six of those ten games ended in defeat for The Shrimpers. Additionally, Southend went out of the League Cup at the First Round stage, a Peter Taylor strike being insufficient to beat Portsmouth at Fratton Park, the Second Division side victorious by two goals to one.

Wary of his goal drought, Rowley signed two new strikers in October. Stuart Brace cost £7,000 from Grimsby Town while a £15,000 fee brought Willie Coulson from Newcastle United. Brace would

Chris Guthrie and Dave Cunningham

prove to be an instant hit, scoring on his debut against Walsall and hitting three against Huddersfield Town in a 5-2 home triumph. The new arrivals were somewhat tempered by the departure of home grown winger Peter Taylor to Crystal Palace for a record fee of £120,000.

In the F.A.Cup, Southend were drawn at home to Athenian League Boreham Wood and despite being held at half-time, second half goals from Terry Johnson, Stuart Brace and a penalty from Brian Albeson saw The Shrimpers safely through to the next round. Home advantage was again put to good use, Johnson and Brace combining to see off the challenge of Fourth Division Reading. Sadly, it was another Fourth Division side that ended Southend's interest in the competition, Peterborough United winning by three goals to one at London Road in the Third Round.

The opening months of 1974 saw a change in fortunes on the pitch; the defence had been fortified by the arrival of Dave Worthington from Grimsby Town and a new goalkeeper, Malcolm Webster, who had joined the club from Fulham. A handsome 3-1 win at Bournemouth at the end of

Malcolm Webster

January heralded a run of only one defeat in ten matches which saw the club move comfortably into a mid-table position. Another astute signing in this period was that of front man Peter Silvester, coming from the Canaries of Norwich City.

April was a strange month; two successive home defeats (1-3 to Chesterfield and 0-2 to Brighton and Hove Albion) were immediately followed by two successive away victories (2-1 at Walsall and 2-0 in the return at the Goldstone Ground). The final home game of the campaign saw an excellent 4-1 win over promotion challengers Grimsby Town, Brace haunting his former employers with two well taken goals.

Southend finished in twelfth place with a fairly even playing record, sixteen wins, sixteen defeats and fourteen draws. Stuart Brace was top scorer by some distance, with 22 goals, Chris Guthrie a distant second with only eight. However, it was Guthrie that would be awarded the "Player of the Year" trophy. In truth, Brace was an opportunistic beneficiary of Guthrie's excellent and often selfless hold up play.

1974/75- A Season of Struggle Back in Division Three

Arthur Rowley spent the summer of 1974 strengthening his squad for the new campaign. Tony Taylor was brought in from Crystal Palace for £15,000, whilst Alistair Love came in from West Bromwich Albion. Bob Worthington arrived from Notts County to join his brother Dave whilst Tony Hadley proved an excellent acquisition from Essex Senior League side Basildon United. The goalkeeping position was augmented by the arrival on loan of Norwich City custodian Mervyn Cawston.

Leaving Roots Hall were Derek Bellotti, who signed for Swansea City, Kevin Johnson, departing for Workington and Gary Moore, who joined Chester. Don Mackay took up a coaching position with Bristol City whilst Bobby Bennett linked up with Southern League Wimbledon.

The season opened perhaps unexpectedly well, with the first four matches resulting in victories. Three home wins were secured against Chesterfield (2-1), Plymouth Argyle (2-1) and Halifax Town (4-0), the latter thanks to a Chris Guthrie hat-trick. In between, Bury were defeated by a Dave Cunningham goal to nil at Gigg Lane.

Guthrie struck two more as Cambridge United were defeated 2-0 at Roots Hall and Southend also enjoyed a rare passage into the Second Round of the League Cup; this progress was short-lived, when Essex neighbours Colchester United eased to a 0-2 victory at Roots Hall.

While home form remained excellent, away day trips to Watford, Blackburn Rovers, Peterborough United and Swindon Town were fruitless as Southend's travel sickness returned with avengance. Home form suffered a temporary dip as three draws in October and November meant Southend slumped down the table, although a 4-1 victory at Deepdale against Preston North End gave some cause for optimism. Rowley made an excellent purchase in December when Alan Little was tempted away from Aston Villa to bolster the midfield department. Another signing from West Midlands football came in January when young midfielder Ronnie Pountney was signed from Bilston for a fee of £3,000.

In the F.A.Cup, Southend were paired with Automotive Products Leamington, a successful works team competing in the Southern League; a tight encounter at the Windmill Ground saw Southend scrape through by two goals to one. More non-League opposition was encountered in Round Two when Southend visited Lynn Road, home of Isthmian League Ilford. A slightly more comfortable ninety minutes were enjoyed, with Southend winning by a score of 2-0, giving The Shrimpers a Third Round tie with First Division Queen's Park Rangers, with home advantage in The Shrimp-

Mervyn Cawston

ers' favour. A compelling 2-2 draw was fought out at Roots Hall, before the superiority of the opposition showed in the replay at Loftus Road, with Rangers, boasting the magnificent Stan Bowles and future England captain Gerry Francis in their line-up, winning by two goals to nil.

After the turn of the year, League form went through the floor. Brighton and Hove Albion were defeated at Roots Hall in the first League game of 1975 but only a win against Huddersfield Town was forthcoming in the seventeen matches between then and April 5th. With such a desperate run of form, Southend were plummeting towards the drop zone. Finally, a couple of handy wins against Swindon Town (2-0) and Bury (1-0) plus a draw with Colchester United in the final four matches meant relegation was successfully avoided.

Bournemouth, Tranmere Rovers, Huddersfield Town and Watford made the drop into Division Four, while Blackburn Rovers (champions), Plymouth Argyle and Charlton Athletic rose to Division

Two. Southend finished in 18th place, four points clear of the drop zone. Two away wins and nine home draws were key indicators to a tough season. Chris Guthrie regained the top scorers crown with an excellent 17, while Stuart Brace's dozen were also welcome in a season that generated only 56 goals in all competitions. Alan Moody was voted "Player of the Year".

1975/76- Rowley's Flops Go Down Again

Arthur Rowley's 1975 summer signings for the club included Terry Nicholl from Sheffield United, Steve Goodwin from Norwich City and Stuart Parker from Blackpool. Meanwhile David Keefe, Paul Denny and goalkeeper Sean Rafter were offered professional deals, having graduated through the junior ranks. Making the reverse journey to Sheffield United was the popular forward Chris Guthrie, Dave Elliott and Alistair Love both joining Newport County. The final summer departure was that of Bob Worthington, who quit

Southend United 1975/76

the game to pursue a career in rugby union as a physiotherapist.

The new season started in optimistic fashion with an excellent win against Sheffield Wednesday at home, while a Peter Silvester hat-trick took the points in a dramatic 3-2 success at Fellows Park, Walsall. After a frenzied 3-3 draw at home to Port Vale, the next five League encounters were all lost and another season of struggle looked likely.

In the League Cup, the rules were changed to make the opening two rounds of the competition two-legged affairs. At home in the First Round First Leg, Southend defeated Peterborough United by two goals to nil to assert a decent advantage for the away match. However, the Posh roared to a 0-3 victory at London Road to make it through to the next round on an aggregate of 2-3.

In the F.A.Cup, Southend swept through the opening four rounds, enjoying home advantage in all ties. Swansea City were beaten by two Stuart Parker goals to nil in the opening round. Southern League Dover were the next team to bite the dust, beaten comfortably by four goals to one. Then, Brighton and Hove Albion and Cardiff City were beaten by the same 2-1 scoreline to see Southend qualify for the Fifth Round stage for the first time since 1952. Southend were drawn against mighty First Division Derby County and were decidedly unfortunately to lose out to a single Bruce Rioch goal at the Baseball Ground.

League form was beginning to become a major concern; despite respectable home wins against the likes of Halifax Town (4-1), Grimsby Town (5-2) and Colchester United (2-0), defeats were continuing to rack up at an alarming rate. A beleaguered Arthur Rowley could only bring in loan players at the turn of the year in a bid to improve his side's fortunes. His pair of loanees were Alan Glover from West Bromwich Albion and Bristol City's Steve Harding, neither of whom would make any sort of impact on the first team.

In February, an outstanding individual performance from Peter Silvester saw the former Norwich man hit all four goals in a 4-0 demolition of Brighton and Hove Albion. However, this excellent home win was followed by six games without one, which included a 1-5 battering at Preston North End. The club were plummeting towards relegation and, from the last thirteen matches of the campaign, only two wins were secured, 2-1 at Gillingham and 2-0 at home to Chester

Dave Cunningham and Stuart Parker celebrate a United goal.

Steve Goodwin

The team went into the final two matches needing to win both to stand any chance of surviving the drop. In the first of these matches, away at Wrexham, despite an Alan Moody penalty and an Alan Little strike, a 2-2 draw was worthless, as relegation seemed inevitable. The final game was at Hillsborough where Sheffield Wednesday needed to win to avoid the drop. In a "winner takes all" match, the Owls duly won and crept out of the drop zone thanks to two first half goals from Mick Prendergast and Eric Potts. A lone reply from Alan Moody was too little too late; Southend were doomed. Rowley's tenure, already under pressure from disgruntled supporters, was all but ended when Dave Smith was bought in as manager, with Rowley being offered a consultative role.

Joining Southend in the relegation places were Halifax Town, Colchester United and Aldershot. Hereford United were runaway champions, gaining promotion for the second time in their first four seasons of League membership. Also promoted were Cardiff City and Millwall. Southend had a sorry record, achieving only twelve victories from the 46 League encounters and suffering 21 defeats. Surprisingly in a desolate season, three Southend players managed to score a double figure tally of goals. Peter Silvester was top of the tree, scoring 23 in all competitions, Stuart Parker netted 15, while Alan Moody chipped in with ten goals from centre back, although he was the side's nominated penalty taker. Alan Little was voted "Player of the Year".

Alan Little

TURMOIL AT ROOTS HALL

Derek Spence

1976/77- Numerous Draws Cost Shrimpers Dear

Arthur Rowley's "consultancy" role was mainly assigned to scouting duties, as Dave Smith took charge of first team affairs for the 1976/77 season. Among Smith's first acquisitions for the club were Ken Price from Dudley Town, goalkeeper Neil Freeman from Grimsby Town, Dave Young from Charlton Athletic and winger Andy Polycarpou, who was recruited from local football. Youngsters Paul Clark and John Walker were offered professional contracts, having come through the apprentice ranks. In October, Mansfield Town's Micky Laverick was a further addition to the roster.

Leaving Roots Hall were half a dozen Rowley signings. Willie Coulson, often an erratic performer, returned to the North East with North Shields of the Northern League, Stuart Brace signed for Falmouth Town, then of the Western League, Steve Lamb joined Chelmsford City, Tony Taylor moved to Swindon Town and Malcolm Webster began a long stint at Cambridge United. Finally, Terry Nicholl signed for Gillingham.

The season started unusually with the opening round of the League Cup competition. Stuart Parker opened his account for the season in a 1-1 home draw with Brighton and Hove Albion, but the Seagulls triumphed by 1-2 at the Goldstone Ground to advance to the Second Round.

League form was fairly inconsistent, although only two defeats were suffered in the opening fourteen matches; another eight ending in draws. The F.A.Cup saw Southend progress to the Third Round for the fourth successive season. Exeter City were beaten 2-1 after extra time following a drawn game at St.James' Park. Goals from Parker, Tony Hadley and Ronnie Pountney saw Newport County easily beaten at Roots Hall, the South Wales side failing to muster any response. However, despite home advantage once again, Third Division Chester ran out easy 0-4 victors in the Third Round.

The season's best form came in November and over the Christmas period. A Stuart Parker hattrick assisted The Shrimpers to a 4-1 victory over Bradford City, while the festive matches saw Brentford (2-1) at Roots Hall, Doncaster Rovers (3-0) at Belle Vue, and Aldershot at home (5-0) all successfully vanquished.

In February, the decision was taken to sell Stuart Parker to Chesterfield; predictably the prolific front man scored in his final Shrimpers outing, a 2-2 draw with Bournemouth. His replacement shared the same surname; Derrick Parker arrived from Burnley, but despite scoring on his debut at Workington, took time to find his scoring touch. Also arriving at Roots Hall during this time was midfielder Colin Morris, who also moved south from Turf Moor.

The goalscoring drought really took hold in the closing months of the season. In the final nineteen matches, only 14 goals were scored as Southend faded away to a tenth place finish. A tally of nineteen draws meant an immediate return to Division Three was nothing more than a distant dream.

Cambridge United were worthy champions and Essex rivals Colchester United made it back to the higher level at the first attempt, Exeter City and Bradford City filling the remaining promotion places. At the other end, Workington were making their fourth successive application for re-election to the Football League. This time they ran out of luck and were replaced by Southern League champions Wimbledon.

Despite leaving the club in February, Stuart Parker was still the leading scorer with sixteen goals while ever present defender Andy Ford scooped the "Player of the Year" award.

1977/78- Shrimpers Promoted Under Smith's Guidance

Dave Smith wielded the axe on his underachieving 1976/77 squad, with nine players being released to other clubs. Steve Dyer joined Southern League Weymouth while Peter Silvester joined the growing exodus to the North American Soccer League with the Washington Diplomats. Andy Ford and Dave Cunningham signed for Swindon Town, Alan Little joined Barnsley, David Keefe moved on to Torquay United, Paul Denny joined League newcomers Wimbledon while Ken Foggo opted for a move to Chelmsford City.

Top to bottom: Paul Clark, Micky Laverick, John Walker and Alan Foggon.

Initially, only two players were signed during the close season, Alan Foggon, a striker, from Newcastle United and midfielder Peter Abbott from Crewe Alexandra. Smith added to his squad at intervals throughout the opening months, with the likes of Steve Yates (Leicester City), Gerry Fell

(Brighton and Hove Albion) and Graham Horn (Charlton Athletic) giving further options for Smith to find a successful formula. Midfielder Graham Franklin also joined the club in October 1977 from Eastern Counties League side Lowestoft Town.

The season kicked off with a decent run of eight matches unbeaten, the highlight being a comfortable 3-0 win against Bournemouth at Dean Court. The lowlight was seeing the run halted, with a 0-2 reversal at Doncaster Rovers. The month of September ended on a high note when Derrick Parker scored all four goals in a 4-0 home defeat of Torquay United.

The opening round of the League Cup competition ended in an all too familiar early exit when Northampton Town won both legs for a 5-3 aggregate triumph.

After an optimistic start to the season, October and November bought a downturn in fortunes, with a 3-0 win at Wimbledon and a single goal victory at home to Watford being the only successes recorded.

The opening round of the F.A.Cup paired Southend with Torquay United and the Gulls were beaten 2-1 at Plainmoor. In the Second Round, Southend were drawn against Automotive Products Leamington for the second time in three years. After a goalless draw at the Windmill Ground, a comfortable 4-0 victory was clocked up in a Roots Hall replay. In the Third Round, a trip to the Baseball Ground was the reward, and despite a tight battle and two Derrick Parker goals, The Rams went through by three goals to two.

After the F.A.Cup run, League form improved dramatically and included good home wins; 4-2 against Newport County, 5-1 against Bournemouth and 5-0 against Halifax Town. Promotion was a very real possibility as March progressed although heavy setbacks were suffered against fellow candidates Aldershot (0-3) and Grimsby Town (0-2). Smith steadied the ship admirably and in the closing seven fixtures an excellent record of five wins ensured a second place finish, albeit nine points adrift of champions Watford. Also promoted were Swansea City and Brentford. At the foot of the table, perennial strugglers Southport were voted out of the League in favour of Wigan Athletic.

Derrick Parker proved a prolific marksmen, top scoring with 23 goals with a good supporting cast in the shape of Colin Morris (13), midfielder Micky Laverick with nine and centre back Alan Moody also finding the net on nine occasions. It was the consistency of midfielder Colin Morris that gained him the nod in the "Player of the Year" award.

1978/79- Goal Shy Shrimpers Fail to Impress

Dave Smith made three significant signings for the 1978/79 campaign, Micky Stead, a right back from Tottenham Hotspur and commanding centre back, Dave Cusack from Sheffield Wednesday; the club parted with fees of £50,000 for each player and they would form the backbone of the club's defence for several seasons. The third new signing was that of Mervyn Cawston, the former Norwich City goalkeeper who, having been on loan at the club some three years previously, signed on a permanent contract after a lengthy spell in the United States with Chicago Sting of the North American Soccer League. Additionally, apprentice Jeff Hull, an attacking midfielder, was offered full professional terms.

Leaving the club were keeper Neil Freeman, who joined Birmingham City, Alan Foggon, who returned to his native North East with Consett of the Northern League and midfielder Peter Abbott, who on being released from his contract, gave up

Micky Stead

Southend United 1978/79

the game altogether despite only being 25 years of age.

There was a slow start to the campaign, the supporters having to wait until the fourth match of the season to cheer a victory, a narrow 2-1 Roots Hall triumph over Plymouth Argyle. The clubs' indifferent form saw only three wins forthcoming from the opening eleven League matches and the club were hanging around the lower reaches of the table. October saw a change of fortune, with three wins and two draws from the five matches, the best result being a 4-0 demolition of Blackpool at Roots Hall.

The League Cup proved to be its usual fleeting affair, despite the best efforts of Wimbledon's Dave Donaldson trying his best to help the club into the next round. The full back scored own goals in both legs, but the Fourth Division side still ousted their higher ranked opponents by four goals to two on aggregate.

The team's erratic form resurfaced in November and December with the only League success coming in the year's final game, away to Peterborough United, when a single Micky Laverick strike secured a welcome win on the road.

In the F.A.Cup, a home tie against Peterborough United saw a tight encounter at Roots Hall, with Southend progressing with a 3-2 victory. In Round Two, a Derrick Parker goal at Watford meant a replay was needed to settle the affair and, with the draw for the Third Round having already been made, the winner of the tie knew that a home match with European Champions Liverpool was lying in wait. Andy Polycarpou scored the only goal of the replay, securing the plum draw for The Shrimpers. The original match was post-

DAVE SMITH

OH YOU BEAUTIFUL BLUES!

EVEN Bob Paisley, who is usually as words as Liverpool are with their oppo relief after his European champions had b goalless draw by Southend United in la battle at Roots Hall.

FA CUP EXTRA

Southend scare Europe giants

Southend 0   Liverpool .... 0 : By BRIAN SCOVELL

THIRD DIVISION Southend provided further evidence at Roots Hall last night that this is the year of the underdog in the F.A. Cup.

They had the edge on the European champions and inspired their extrovert manager Dave Smith to say : 'We might go up there on Monday and win it. Dafter things have been done. I thought tonight we did the Third Division proud.'

Bob Paisley was happy to be able

had had some of that he might have scored from the game's best chance in the 25th minute when Gerry Fell's through pass left him clear with only Ray Clemence to beat.

Clemence, clad in track suit trousers raced out so far that Parker was flustered into shooting too early.

At times it was like watching tennis at Wimbledon, with the 31,033 record crowd enthralled as the ball pinged backwards and forwards with neither side retaining possession.

with his

THE STINGER

LIVERPOOL last night discovered that snow, like alcohol at a party, makes equals of the most unlikely people.

And none looked mor-

MERV BEATS THE SWERVE TO KEEP LIVERPOOL KINGS AT BAY

Miller: Southend 0 Liverpool 0

settle into   Yet, obviously, the odds are

Snow-stopper Merv holds champs

By ALEX MONTGOMERY
Southend 0, Liverpool 0

THE FA Cup threw up another unlikely hero in Southend goalkeeper Mervyn Cawston last night.

He was brought back from American football last summer for £20,000 and helped earn Southend a surprising third round

before the match, and although referee Keith Hackett never had any doubts about the game conditions

Smith added: "I thought we were the better side in the first-half, the second was 50-50.

"I was disappointed we

Just some of the newspaper reports that greeted the Southend United players when they woke the next morning, after their battling 0-0 FA Cup draw with European champions Liverpool.

Anton Otulakowski

poned as the icy conditions made the terracing too dangerous for supporters, so the re-staged game was played out in front of an all-time record home gate of 31,033. Southend played exceptionally well to hold their illustrious opponents to a goalless draw. In the replay, class shone through and Liverpool triumphed 0-3, although Southend gained a standing ovation from the Anfield faithful for their excellent performances.

Another astute Dave Smith signing came in March in the shape of West Ham United midfielder Anton Otulakowski, a fee of £50,000 once again changing hands. The run-in to the end of the season became a source of frustration, a 5-3 win over Swindon Town at Roots Hall in March being the undoubted exception. A run of six matches in April saw the side fail to muster a single goal and only a single point from a goalless draw with Peterborough United was accrued. The goal famine was ended by two Derrick Parker goals at the Vetch Field, although these were insufficient to prevent a 2-3 loss to Swansea City. A disappointing campaign was rounded off by a home defeat to relegated Tranmere Rovers.

Southend finished in thirteenth place with fifteen wins, fifteen draws and sixteen defeats. The lack of goals was a real problem, with Derrick Parker top scoring with a meagre tally of twelve goals. Despite only scoring a collective total of 51 goals in 46 League matches, Southend still managed a positive goal difference, the defence being forged into a formidable unit conceding

only 49 goals in total. Midfielder Ronnie Pountney was presented with the "Player of the Year" award. Alongside Tranmere in the drop zone were Peterborough United, Walsall and Lincoln City. In a tight championship battle, Shrewsbury Town edged the title by a single point from Watford and Swansea City.

1979/80- Shock Relegation Stuns Smith's Men

Dave Smith limited himself to only two summer captures, these being Micky Tuohy, a lanky striker from Southern League champions Redditch United costing £7,500, and midfielder Terry Gray, who moved from Huddersfield Town. In addition to these arrivals, two apprentices, Garry Nelson and John Keeley, were offered full professional contracts. Departing Roots Hall were Micky Laverick, making the reverse journey to that of Terry Gray, while defender Neil Townsend signed for Bournemouth. Finally, Steve Goodwin opted to pursue his career in Norway by signing for Jorvik.

Smith's plans for the 1979/80 season were sent into total turmoil before a ball had been kicked in anger when thirteen of the first team squad went down with a severe bout of food poisoning following a friendly encounter at Dover.

After both opening games were won, Micky Tuohy making a goalscoring debut against Carlisle United and a Colin Morris goal separating the sides

Southend United 1979/80

against Wimbledon at Plough Lane, the team hit an early season wall. From the next thirteen fixtures, only a 4-1 win against Plymouth Argyle at home resulted in success for The Shrimpers.

In the League Cup, a rare run was started off with a comfortable 6-2 aggregate win over Brentford. In Round Two, Southend were drawn against First Division Bolton Wanderers. In the first leg at Burnden Park, the prospects looked grim when Dave Cusack was harshly sent off for two bookable offences. However, the ten men galvanised themselves and produced Southend's first ever victory against top flight opponents. Two Colin Morris goals secured a famous 2-1 victory and when a goalless draw was played out at Roots Hall a week later, Southend were through to the next round. Opponents for the single legged Round Three tie were West Ham United. A Ronnie Pountney strike earned a 1-1 draw against the Second Division outfit and in the Roots Hall replay, over 22,000 watched a goalless draw. The Hammers won the toss for the right to stage the second replay, and this time they made no mistake by winning at a canter by five goals to one.

The players of 1980.

Southend United Football Club Limited

ROOTS HALL FOOTBALL GROUND, VICTORIA AVENUE, SOUTHEND-ON-SEA SS2 6NQ   Tel: 0702 40707

President: NELSON L. MITCHELL

Directors: FRANK H. WALTON (Chairman)   LESLIE H. LESSER F.C.A. (Vice-Chairman)
JOHN N. WOODCOCK   DONALD A. SMITH   CHARLES G. JANES   FRED BONFIELD   M. D. RUBIN   A. R. RUBIN

Manager: DAVE SMITH   Secretary: KEITH HOLMES, F.A.A.I., F.Inst.C.M.

Registered Office: Roots Hall Avenue, Victoria Avenue, Southend-on-Sea   Registration No. 89767 England

Back on the League campaign, home wins against Exeter City (4-0), Grimsby Town (1-0) and Chester (4-1) as well as a rare away success at Oakwell (2-1 against Barnsley) pulled Southend away from the lower reaches of the table as Christmas approached.

In the F.A.Cup, opening round opponents were Alliance Premier League side Wealdstone, who boasted a young left back called Stuart Pearce in their line-up. In a tight encounter at Lower Mead, a Johnny Walker goal saw a narrow 1-0 win for The Shrimpers. Non-League opponents were drawn again in Round Two, when Harlow Town of the Isthmian League were pulled out of the velvet bag. In a tough clash at Roots Hall, the lower ranked club more than matched their hosts and thoroughly deserved a replay. Embarrassingly, the second game, at the Sports Centre in Harlow, saw Southend go down to an ignominious one goal defeat.

In January, there was uproar when fans protested vehemently against the sale of Colin Morris to Blackpool for the unusual fee of £111,111. However, some recompense was forthcoming when Northern Ireland international striker Derek Spence moved in the opposite direction for an identical fee and another striker, Keith Mercer, was acquired from Watford for £80,000.

Results went from bad to worse as Smith's expensively assembled squad nose dived towards the relegation zone. In the final sixteen matches of the season, only thirteen goals were scored and only three of those matches resulted in victories. Southend finished in 22nd place, two points adrift of safety. Joining The Shrimpers in the relegation places were Mansfield Town, Bury and Wimbledon. Grimsby Town were Third Division champions, also promoted were Blackburn Rovers and Sheffield Wednesday.

Chairman Frank Walton led the criticism of the team's management and players. Assistant manager John Lattimer was dismissed while Dave Smith was given a severe warning that unless results improved dramatically by Christmas 1980, then he too would be shown the door. To make matters worse, the club reported a trading loss in excess of £50,000 for the campaign. Symptomatic of a dreadful campaign was the fact that Derrick Parker top scored, for the third successive season, with a meagre tally of ten goals. To make the point all the more obvious, Parker had actually left for Barnsley in February, yet no-one had managed to overhaul his modest total. On a posi-

A   CENTURY   UNITED

tive note, Ronnie Pountney was again a dynamo in midfield, becoming the first player to retain the club's "Player of the Year" trophy.

1980/81- Stylish Southend Cruise to Division Four Championship

An under pressure Dave Smith stuck by his existing squad for the 1980/81 season, only enhancing his selection possibilities by awarding Glenn Pennyfather a full time contract with the club after he completed a successful apprenticeship. Departing the club were Micky Tuohy, signing for a fee of £6,000 for Worcester City and Gerry Fell, who had struggled to make a first team appearance the previous season, who signed for Torquay United.

The season started with a two-legged defeat to Oxford United in the opening round of the League Cup. However, the League campaign got off to a blistering start with the opening four matches all resulting in victories for The Shrimpers, Derek Spence helping himself to five goals in the process. However, doom mongers grumbled when in late September and early October, three successive away matches resulted in defeats. Doncaster triumphed 0-1 at Belle Vue, Northampton Town tabled a 0-2 success and Peterborough United ran out 2-5 victors at London Road.

However, Roots Hall became a veritable fortress; no-one took League wins away from the sea-side, and only four sides managed so much

as a draw. From August to December, ten home wins in a row were secured without even conceding a single goal. In the eleventh match, Bradford City's Bobby Campbell managed to pierce the impregnable Shrimpers defence, but it mattered little as Southend coasted to another victory by three goals to one.

In the F.A.Cup therefore, it was something of a surprise when Hereford United came to Roots Hall and left with a 0-1 victory, the only side to do so in an otherwise memorable campaign.

League progress was ever onward; in March, Halifax Town were torn apart by five goals to one, replicating the exact score in the away game from the previous October. Although promotion seemed inevitable, Colin Murphy's Lincoln City were in hot pursuit and no slip ups could be sustained. When the title challengers met at Roots Hall, a huge crowd of 12,000 gathered as the two sides slugged out a goalless draw. The result confirmed Southend's promotion to Division Three and put them in the driving seat as far as the title was concerned. Three victories, two on the road at Aldershot and Torquay United, and a last day draw at home to Rochdale ensured Southend secured their first championship win since becoming a Football League club some sixty years previously.

Lincoln City were worthy runners-up while also gaining promotion were a somewhat distant Doncaster Rovers and Wimbledon. The champion-

Southend United 1980/81

Derek Spence and Dave Smith celebrate winning Southend United's first ever silverware, the Fourth Division Championship of 1980/81.

A CENTURY UNITED

The 1980/81 Fourth Division Championship medal

1981/82- Shrimpers' Promotion Challenge Falters in the Home Straight

Dave Smith kept faith with all his championship winning players for the 1981/82 season, opting not to strengthen his squad at all. The only departees were fringe players Andy Polycarpou, who joined Cambridge United and Jeff Hull, who joined Basildon United.

A major change in the Football League saw three points awarded for a win to encourage more attacking play. There was also a new competition instigated for the Associate Members of the Football League, full membership being restricted to the top two divisions. The new competition was called the Group Cup and took place in the pre-season period. Clubs were split into four team groups, Southend being allotted a place alongside Orient, Gillingham and Wimbledon. The visit to Brisbane Road resulted in a 0-2 defeat, while a goalless draw was achieved against Gillingham at the Priestfield. The only home game played saw Derek Spence score a fine goal but Wimbledon won by two goals to one, thus ending Southend's progress at the group stage.

In the League Cup, a two legged tie against Portsmouth saw the Fratton Park men triumph by four goals to one on aggregate.

On the League front, the season opened well with an Alan Moody goal earning Southend's first ever

ship winning side broke a veritable cornucopia of club records in a truly amazing season. Most wins (30), most home wins (19), fewest home defeats (0), fewest home goals conceded (6), most consecutive home wins (18) were but a few of the incredible feats achieved by a squad of just seventeen players.

"Player of the Year" Derek Spence top scored with 21 goals, ably supported by goalscoring attacking midfielder Terry Gray with 17 and fellow striker Keith Mercer with ten. Smith had proved the doubters wrong and won the championship with an exciting and pacy brand of football. His methodology was built on a solid defence, and Mervyn Cawston amongst others wrote himself in to Southend United folklore by keeping his goal intact at home for a record 987 minutes. He also saved six consecutive penalty kicks in a fabulous season which many supporters still fondly recall to this day.

Southend United 1981/82

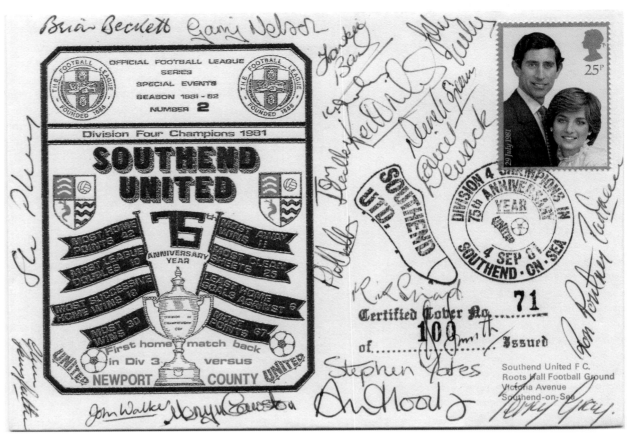

haul of three points from a single game, at Fellows Park, Walsall. Conversely, the campaign's opening home fixture against Newport County resulted in a Roots Hall horror show, the twin terror strike force of Tommy Tynan and John Aldridge wreaking havoc as the Welshmen won by four goals to nil.

After three successive away defeats to Carlisle United (2-3), Huddersfield Town (2-3) and Fulham (1-2), prospects looked grim, but Smith soon steadied the ship and four successive wins were enjoyed from the start of October.

In the F.A.Cup, the Bulls of Hereford United accounted for Southend's presence in the competition for the second consecutive season, this time winning 1-3 at Edgar Street in the opening round, with Southend goalkeeper John Keeley managing to lose a contact lens in the mud of the goalmouth early on in the game, which certainly didn't help the defensive performance on the day.

Progress in the League was swift and despite losing many of December's games, including the festive programme, due to some harsh weather, Southend went into 1982 standing in an encouraging third place in the table. Smith championed his troops by stating they were good enough to plough straight through the division for a second straight promotion.

Looking back with hindsight, it was a dismal run in February that probably cost Southend the

To celebrate the clubs' first game back in the Third Division, and also their 75th year of existence, a First Day Cover was issued for the match against Newport County.

dream of back-to-back promotions. In a month where five of the six matches were drawn, which including three goalless matches on the trot, and the sixth was a defeat at Bristol Rovers, the difference between three points for a win and one for a draw came sharply into view.

Smith addressed the relative barren spell in front of goal by purchasing a new striker, Steve Phillips arriving from Northampton Town for a bargain £15,000 fee.

His introduction to the team had the desired effect, with April proving a particularly profitable month; five wins and a draw from the six matches, the highlight being a spectacular 5-3 win at Turf Moor, home of eventual champions Burnley. Strikers Spence and Phillips helped themselves to a brace apiece.

Any lingering hopes of scraping into a promotion place disappeared altogether in May, when Southend failed to win any of the closing four matches and Burnley gained revenge for the previous month's defeat by winning 1-4 at Roots Hall and securing the title. Also promoted were Carlisle United and Fulham, while at the bottom Wimbledon, Swindon Town, Bristol City and Chester City found themselves relegated to Division Four.

Keith Mercer was top scorer with thirteen goals, Derek Spence's goalscoring touch deserting him; he managed only eight all season. New acquisition Steve Phillips notched an excellent ten

Steve Phillips

A CENTURY UNITED

goals from only eighteen games. Consistent defender Dave Cusack took the "Player of the Year" crown.

1982/83- End of Season Slump Signals End to a Golden Era

Despite the disappointments of the 1981/82 season, when a second straight promotion had looked a real possibility for much of the campaign, Dave Smith stuck with the players that had served him so well. In actual fact, the summer of 1982 must be one of the quietest in the clubs' history. The only departures were that of Terry

Southend United 1982/83

Gray, who joined Bradford City in August and Derek Spence, who moved to Hong Kong with the See Bee club. The only addition to the first team roster was that of young midfielder Adrian Owers, who graduated from the apprentice ranks at Roots Hall.

Once again the season started with the competition for the Football League's associate members, the Group Cup being remodelled as the Football League Trophy. The format was identical, with Southend pitted in a four team group alongside Colchester United, Orient and Watford. Southend once again performed poorly, losing to Colchester at Layer Road (1-3) and Watford at home (1-4) whilst the game with Orient at Roots Hall ended in a one all draw.

In the League Cup, now known as the Milk Cup, Southend were drawn against Second Division

Fulham and despite a Garry Nelson goal separating the sides at Roots Hall, the Londoners comfortably went through to Round Two, winning 2-4 at Craven Cottage.

The League campaign started with home form reminiscent of the great championship winning days, the first seven matches resulting in six wins and a draw. The run included a 4-0 dismantling of eventual champions Portsmouth and an exciting 3-2 win against Doncaster Rovers in which goalkeeper John Keeley became an early victim of the new professional foul rule. He received his marching orders with the score at 3-1, Keith Mercer donning the goalkeeper's jersey. Despite picking the ball out of the net from the resulting free kick, Mercer performed admirably to see Southend through to an unlikely victory.

The Shrimpers away form ranged from pitiful to downright abysmal, a 2-0 win at Dean Court against Bournemouth being a rare highlight in the opening months. The dichotomy between home form was amply illustrated a week after the 4-0 win at Roots Hall over Portsmouth, Southend travelling to Springfield Park, home of Wigan Athletic and going down to a four goal drubbing themselves. November ended with two notable away wins, 1-0 at Sheffield United and 3-1 at Walsall.

In the F.A.Cup, Southend were handed a tough opening round tie away to Bournemouth. Fortunately, the confidence gained by the win at Bramall Lane the previous week inspired a decent performance as two deflected goals saw Southend march on to the next round. The Second Round draw handed Southend a potentially huge banana skin when they were paired against ultimate non-League giant killers Yeovil Town. Home advantage fell in the favour of The Shrimpers, but the Southern League outfit were determined to put up a challenge. Inspired by the Bilston Rocket, Ronnie Pountney, who had one of his finest games in a Southend shirt, Southend ran out comfortable 3-0 winners, the tiny winger scoring twice. In the Third Round, home advantage again

Keith Mercer and Steve Phillips celebrate another goal.

favoured Southend as they were drawn against Second Division Sheffield Wednesday. A hard fought goalless draw was the outcome, with Southend having to play much of the second half with ten men following the dismissal of Micky Stead. In the replay at Hillsborough, the sides could not be separated from a 2-2 draw even after extra time, so the toss was made for the venue of the second replay. Southend lost the toss so it was another trip to South Yorkshire ten days later to try to settle the tie. Another close encounter ensued and only a goalkeeping disaster from stand-in keeper John Keeley saw the Owls go through by two goals to one.

That performance persuaded Smith to bring in a goalkeeper on loan as cover for the injured Mervyn Cawston and Martin Thomas stepped into the breach for six games during February. Results were generally sound, with as many wins and draws being accrued as defeats. The odd disastrous performance was still evident, none more so than the first game of March, when Newport County were the visitors to Roots Hall. The twin terrors of Tommy Tynan and John Aldridge again proved the undoing of The Shrimpers as the Welsh side won 1-4, Pountney notching a consolation strike. In March, supporters were

deeply aggrieved to see the sale of two popular players, Dave Cusack and Anton Otulakowski, to Millwall for a combined fee of only £60,000.

As goals were in such scarce supply, a young centre back Warren May, originally a schoolboy forward, was tried up front as an emergency measure. The move did not pay off and Smith bought in John Linford, who was struggling for first team games at Ipswich Town. The new man had a good impact, scoring in his first three appearances but Smith decided not to pursue any further interest after his loan spell ended. March ended with a decent 3-1 home win over Sheffield United, Steve Phillips hitting a hat-trick, this game also marking the only first-team appearance of Barrie Delf, a local league goalkeeper who was drafted into the team at the last minute after The Shrimpers found themselves keeperless through injury.

In the closing weeks of the campaign, Southend hit a wretched spell of form, failing to win any of their final nine matches. Trips to Cardiff City (1-4) and Exeter City (3-4) saw Southend ship four goals, as the side plummeted down the table. A final position of 15th was not reflective of the overall performance throughout the campaign, although many supporters felt it signalled the end to a golden era. However, none would have predicted the turmoil of the close season.

Portsmouth were worthy champions, confirming the title in a 2-0 Fratton Park win against Southend in the closing weeks of the season. Also promoted were Huddersfield Town and Cardiff City. Slipping down to Division Four were Reading, Wrexham, Doncaster Rovers and Chesterfield. Steve Phillips was top scorer with twenty goals, his nearest support coming from Garry Nelson and Keith Mercer who both scored nine apiece. The hard working Ronnie Pountney made history by becoming the first, and so far only, Southend United player to be voted "Player of the Year" for a third time.

Garry Nelson

A CENTURY UNITED

1983/84- An Impossible Task Ends in Relegation Once Again

The summer of 1983 was one of the most tempestuous in the clubs' history. Local butcher turned football magnate Anton Johnson had taken a controlling interest in the club from the Rubin family and, determined to make his mark, did so in dramatic fashion. In truth, there were rumblings among the supporters about Dave Smith's future when the side had finished the previous campaign so poorly, but surely none had expected him to be dismissed and in such an unsavoury manner. Smith was on holiday with his wife in Tenerife, when a message arrived addressed from the board, relieving him of his duties as manager of Southend United. Smith would return to the club and lock himself in the manager's office before successfully suing for damages.

As badly managed dismissals go, the board's handling of a popular manager was compounded by the fact that they had yet to decide on a replacement. So, with a matter of weeks to the start of the new campaign, Peter Morris, the former Crewe Alexandra manager, was drafted in, tasked with readying a squad of ten professionals, of which two were goalkeepers, into a side fit for Third Division football.

New Southend United manager Peter Morris introduces four of his signings for the 1983/84 season to the press and fans. Left to right: Greig Shepherd, Roy McDonough, John Fashanu and Mike Angus. Of the four, Fashanu never actually signed for the club and Angus made only one appearance.

Many of Smith's "old guard" had left the club. Long serving utility player Tony Hadley was allowed to leave for Colchester United, Phil Dudley joined Chelmsford City, Keith Mercer signed for Blackpool while the promising Garry Nelson went to Swindon Town. John Walker quit football altogether for a full time career with Essex Police.

Morris, a quiet likeable man with a decent knowledge of the game, began a seemingly impossible task of recruiting a veritable conveyor belt of new players. In came Greig Shepherd, a tall blond striker who had been playing in Hong Kong with Eastern Athletic. Alongside him would be Roy McDonough, a much travelled striker who joined from rivals Colchester United. The midfield was bolstered by the signing of Brian Ferguson from Hull City and Glen Skivington, a youngster from Derby who would fail to make an impact on the first team. Two defenders also arrived in the shape of Scunthorpe United's Mike Angus and left back Steve Collins, who joined from Peterborough United. Youth team forward John Gymer was also offered professional terms in a hectic month. Morris would continue to add to his tiny squad as the campaign got underway; in September, Billy Kellock, a fiery Scottish midfielder arrived from Wolves while former Welsh international Les Cartwright and goalkeeper Gerry Peyton were drafted in on loan from Cambridge United and Fulham respectively. In October, centre

back Chris Turner joined from Cambridge United and two months later Lil Fuccillo returned to England after a spell in the States with Tulsa Roughnecks. Morris would also sign former England forward Trevor Whymark from Grimsby Town and Kevin Steggles arrived on a brief loan spell from Ipswich Town.

With such a hotchpotch of signings and a squad of strangers, it was little wonder that the side struggled for results from the off. The side failed to win any of its' opening five League matches and in the Milk Cup, despite beating Wimbledon in the first leg at Roots Hall (1-0), the side contrived to lose the second leg by the spectacular scoreline of 4-6. The first League win of the season came in September at Roots Hall when, despite the dismissal of Steve Phillips, Southend held on to beat Millwall 3-2 in a stormy encounter. The month ended in optimistic vein when Southend went to Scunthorpe and triumphed 6-1 against an injury weakened side at the Old Show Ground. Steve Phillips signed off for his suspension with a hat-trick and full back Micky Stead claimed a rare goal with a long range effort. Sadly, it was to prove to be Southend's only success on the road until April. In a display of typically erratic form, Southend then lost three of the next four matches before walloping Brentford 6-0 at Roots Hall. November was a disastrous month and included a 0-5 drubbing at Sheffield United and an F.A.Cup exit at the hands of Plymouth Argyle in a replay at Home Park (0-2).

The storm clouds gathered over the club as the wretched form continued into December. Gillingham were Boxing Day victors with a 1-5 suc-

cess at the Priestfield, while Plymouth emerged 0-4 winners on New Year's Eve. Home wins over Wigan Athletic (1-0) and Lincoln City (2-0) did little to lift the despondency. However, the turn of the year proved to be an unmitigated disaster from which the side would not recover. In the eight games from January 2nd to February 14th, the side lost five and drew three, failing to score in the three matches in February.

With an Associate Members Cup tie approaching against Fourth Division promotion chasers Reading, Peter Morris and coach Colin Harper were relieved of their duties and the board justified their decision on the front cover of the Reading programme in no uncertain terms. They cited "despite our wholehearted support he has failed to bring the team to the required standard". In truth, many managers would have struggled given the circumstances and boardroom upheaval. The board announced that Chief Executive and former World Cup winning captain Bobby Moore would take the reigns in a caretaker capacity until the end of the season.

As so often happens, a change of manager had the desired effect and Reading were trounced 5-0 at Roots Hall in the opening round of the Associate Members Cup. Goals from Billy Kellock and Trevor Whymark accounted for Colchester United in Round Two as Southend won by 2-0 at Layer Road. In the Quarter Final, Bristol Rovers defeated their hosts by two goals to one at Roots Hall in a match that will be remembered for the quick thinking of Southend physio Buster Footman, who ran onto the pitch to free the tongue of Rovers' centre back Aiden McCaffery, who was convulsing horrifically after a clash of heads.

Moore's impact on the team failed to convert into League points, as the side stayed in the relegation zone for the remainder of the campaign. In March, Moore had bought in the veteran and flamboyant Malcolm Allison to help out with coaching but his stint was totally ineffective. The side's efforts were not helped by a fixture list that included nine matches in April alone; Southend failed to win any of their final three fixtures and were doomed long before a final day defeat at Wigan Athletic. Joining The Shrimpers in

1983/84 Southend United team group. Third from left in the back row is Tony Currie, whose injury during a pre-match warm-up meant that he never actually played a game for the Shrimpers.

The Anton Johnson Affair - In Our Darkest Hour

The chaotic sixteen month ownership by former butcher Anton Johnson saw Southend United at its' lowest ebb financially and on the pitch. Johnson had acquired 44.9% of the shareholding previously owned by the Rubin brothers Mark and Tony; the brothers themselves had inherited their large shareholding following the death of their father Bill Rubin. The financial picture at Johnson's ascent to ownership was far from rosy as relegation and dwindling crowds had seen the club accrue debts to the tune of £250,000. Shortly after Johnson had assumed his controlling interest, the players complained of late and missing salary payments, the first time this had happened at the club for 70 years. At that time, the club ran a highly successful loan club which was well subscribed to by supporters. However, it was soon reported that the loan club funds had been unashamedly plundered and the true financial picture was made public. The clubs' liabilities had risen dramatically to £700,000.

The matter of the disappearing loan club funds was passed to the police and within two months, the Standard Chartered Bank had banned any dealings in the shares owned by Anton Johnson, his associates and associated companies. Anton Johnson had employed a figurehead, local solicitor, Andrew MacHutcheon, almost as a "puppet" chairman. The pair's tenure at the club not only resulted in near financial ruin, but playing standards reached rock bottom. The demoralised squad, who were unsure whether they would be paid from one week to another, struggled at the foot of the Division Four table and played home games in front of the lowest crowds in the clubs' history. The home game against Halifax Town would attract a paying crowd of just over 1000.

The flamboyant businessman had previously been on the board at Rotherham United and Derby County, who had also suffered from severe financial troubles during his involvement in club affairs. With his shares effectively worthless following the ban from trading, Johnson had little choice but to leave the club and did so in October 1984 following his arrest by the police. The new regime, led by Vic Jobson, spent the next three years chasing Johnson, who had decamped to parts unknown, for debts amounting to £25,000. Other creditors also pursued him for debts in excess of £100,000. The High Court declared Anton Johnson officially bankrupt in his absence during a lengthy case in June 1988; all efforts to trace the runaway former owner, including the employment of private detectives, had produced nothing save for alleged sightings in the United States and Puerto Rico.

The court case unravelled some of the unsolved mysteries surrounding the clubs' disappearing funds. Anton Johnson had split his shares four ways between three associates, Geoffrey Myerson, William Harris and John Hillman, using a company called Splintcourt as a front for his business. Johnson's declaration of bankruptcy followed on from similar petitions against Myerson and Hillman. In October 1988, William Harris appeared in front of the High Court charged with fraud. He had been accused of orchestrating a deal in which the £70,000 lease payable to the club for the profitable Roots Hall Market, held every Thursday throughout the year, had been diverted elsewhere. It transpired that the £70,000 had been paid not to the club but instead had found its way to a company based in the Isle of Man. The owner of the company was Anton Johnson and the company's operations were run by Andrew MacHutcheon. The High Court judge Mr Justice Millet had branded Harris as "a liar" and ordered him to repay the £70,000 and all profits accrued since March 1984. Millet also described the still absent Johnson as a "confidence trickster", also awarding Southend United Football Club all costs totalling £250,000 following his edict that the club's board had undoubtedly fallen victim to a "concentrated fraud".

The whole affair had almost made the club extinct and only an emergency remortgaging deal with the Business and Mortgage Trust, generating £800,000 of working capital, provided salvation. Further welcome finance was forthcoming in personal loans from Ken Bates, chairman of Chelsea Football Club, and the owner of Oxford United Football Club, Robert Maxwell.

By Christmas 1985 it was widely reported that Anton Johnson and his associates had a *sine die* ban from involvement in any registered football club, for breaching Football League regulations. The most serious offence Johnson had been found guilty of was simultaneous involvement in more than one club, these being Southend United, AFC Bournemouth and Rotherham United. However, reports of the extent of the ban would appear to have been exaggerated as Johnson would soon be up to his old tricks.

In January 1997, Anton Johnson announced that he was the head of "an Irish consortium" that would buy controlling interest in Doncaster Rovers Football Club from Ken Richardson. Richardson had been jailed for his involvement in a fire at Rovers' Belle Vue ground which had resulted in extensive damage to the main stand. Richardson and his "general manager" Mark Weaver had been accused of systematic asset stripping of the club which led to its relegation from the Football League. Johnson had painted himself as something of a saviour, although fortunately for Rovers his consortium's bid would eventually fail.

In August 1998, he agreed to purchase a controlling interest in Scarborough Football Club. The deal was duly announced and Johnson declared the intention of "seeing Scarborough in the Premier League". By February 1999, former owner John Russell had returned to the helm at Seamer Road as Johnson had been successfully ousted having reneged on the terms of the acquisition.

In more recent years, Anton Johnson has been involved in the running of Basildon United Football Club.

the drop zone were Scunthorpe United, Port Vale and Exeter City. Leaving Division Three through the right end were champions Oxford United as well as Wimbledon and Sheffield United. Steve Phillips was top scorer again with 17 goals, while strike partner Greig Shepherd claimed a dozen in all competitions. In a season of little to cheer, veteran full back Micky Stead was voted "Player of the Year".

1984/85- The Lowest Ebb, Southend United on the Brink of Extinction

Chairman Andrew MacHutcheon announced that Bobby Moore had been given a four year contract as manager of Southend United and also stated that Roots Hall would become a mecca for local sports. Greyhound racing was being considered, but the first move was to introduce professional Rugby League to Essex by bringing the year old Kent Invicta side from Maidstone over to Southend. The move was an unmitigated disaster financially and an embarrassment to all involved. As boardroom wars deepened, MacHutcheon and directors Alan Gershlick and Vic Jobson were all forced from office in October, with former managing director of Rotherham United, John Adams, being appointed. Jobson would return as chairman once the Anton Johnson regime crumbled, but it was too late to stop another season of freefall.

Off the field activities would punctuate a horrific season; striker Steve Phillips was turfed out of his club home when mortgage arrears on a house in Leigh-on-Sea were passed onto a receiver. The club was also subject to a temporary ban from transfer activity when an instalment due for the transfer of Alan Rogers from Portsmouth was missed. Bobby Moore's hands were completely tied in terms of getting in new players and his only new signings were goalkeeper Jim Stannard, who arrived on loan from Fulham in September and

Tony Hadley, returning after a season's exile at Colchester United.

Departures meant the club would operate on a tiny squad for the new season. All-time appearance record holder, Alan Moody was released after a testimonial match, and joined Maldon Town. During the closing months of the previous season, Mervyn Cawston (Stoke City), Danny Greaves (Dagenham), Mike Angus (Darlington), Glen Skivington (Barrow) and Chris Turner had all left the club, Turner being forced into premature retirement with a back injury.

The season had started with an Essex derby at Layer Road, when a thrilling 3-3 draw saw the sides share the spoils. Southend's first victory of the campaign did not arrive until the end of September at the seventh attempt, when Exeter City were beaten by a Greig Shepherd goal at Roots Hall. Third Division Orient put Southend out of the Milk Cup in the opening round when they won 1-2 at Brisbane Road before holding Southend to a goalless draw in the second leg.

Glenn Pennyfather

A terrible 2-6 defeat at Aldershot in October followed by two successive 1-4 reversals, at home to Blackpool and away to Port Vale, confirmed the club would be facing another season of desperation.

In the F.A.Cup, Southend were paired with Essex rivals Colchester United in the opening round. A 2-2 draw was played out at Roots Hall, necessitating a replay at Layer Road. At the end of ninety minutes, the two sides were again locked at two apiece so extra time was needed. The outcome was settled when Glenn Pennyfather's full length diving header screamed past Mervyn Cawston into his own net.

The annual F.A.Cup demise signalled a moderately successful December, notable for midfielder Glenn Pennyfather and striker Steve Phillips both scoring in the same four successive League encounters. The New Year period heralded a run of five successive defeats, a 1-5 hiding at Chester City being followed by an even more ignominious defeat, 2-5 at home to bitter rivals Colchester United. Moore's decision to hand youngsters John Seaden and Micky Engwell first team debuts in this match raised a few eyebrows of concern.

The squad was depleted further in December when Greig Shepherd and Billy Kellock were allowed to leave for Peterborough United and Port Vale respectively. Moore was again hampered in his ability to bring in fresh faces, restricting his acquisitions to non-League players. Goalkeeper Jon O'Brien arrived from Maldon Town but conceded goals in every game he played in, while Barbadian Micky Welch, a prolific scorer in local football with Grays Athletic, was offered a trial but could not rise to the challenge. Moore could not really bring in any significant signings until March, when boardroom issues had been resolved to a degree. Then, Steve Collins went to Lincoln City before the experienced Steve Hatter joined from Wimbledon. Also arriving was young Charlton Athletic centre back Shane Westley, and on a two

The ever-friendly Billy Kellock signals his intentions for all to see, especially teammate Brian Ferguson.

month loan spell came Charlie Williamson, a left back from Sheffield Wednesday.

Progressively, results on the pitch went from bad to worse. In the last nine matches of the season, Southend managed to score in only two of them, a surprising 4-1 win away to Peterborough United, and the final game against Torquay United. The side lost their shape and discipline, Westley was dismissed for a reckless challenge at Darlington, Alan Rogers followed in the next game at Swindon, and Steve Hatter was sent off for fighting in a defeat at home to Wrexham, the visitors having two men dismissed yet still emerging victorious.

The prospect of Southend having to apply for re-election to the Football League for the first time in fifty years depended on the final game of the season. A re-election bid would have been a total lottery as Southend would have been at the mercy of many northern based members and in truth, the bad publicity surrounding the club would have been reason enough to cast them adrift. In the League table, Stockport County, Northampton Town and Torquay United were already consigned to the annual battle of currying favour, but

the final re-election place rested between Southend and Halifax Town.

Southend's final match was against bottom club Torquay United while Halifax Town hosted Swindon Town. A dour, tension filled encounter ensued at Roots Hall with the sides going in at half time locked at nil-nil, with scarcely a shot mustered at either end. The pressure was really on The Shrimpers as news filtered through that a Jeff Cook goal at The Shay had given Halifax a half-time lead. The second half continued in similar vein until Alan Rogers was up-ended in the area and Southend were awarded a penalty kick. In front of a handful of Torquay fans in the vast South Bank, Steve Phillips' kick hit the post and trickled tormentingly along the line before rolling into the net. Southend had survived; it mattered not that a Paul Sanderson strike had given Halifax a 2-1 win, Southend's marginally superior goal difference (-25 compared to -27) ensured a final position of 20th in the table. A handful of supporters danced in joy in the car park as the club had eked out a last ditch escape. The whole threat of re-election was later dispersed when all four League clubs were elected unopposed as Gola League champions, Wealdstone, withdrew their application for League membership.

In a desperate season, Steve Phillips was top scorer for a third consecutive campaign, with a remarkable 23 goals and was deservedly voted "Player of the Year".

1985/86- Moore's Men Mount a Challenge But Bobby Quits

It did not need a World Cup winning captain to determine that the Southend United squad needed major surgery following one of the most abject campaigns in the club's history. Bobby Moore set about the task in earnest during the 1985 close season. His goalkeeper was already in place, Jim Stannard having signed permanently the previous March, following an earlier loan spell, for a fee of £12,000. Following the mass departures from the previous season were Lil Fuccillo and Trevor Whymark, who both joined Peterborough United, whilst Micky Welch returned to Grays Athletic following his unsuccessful trial. Adrian Owers joined Southern League Chelmsford City as did ever popular midfielder Ronnie Pountney, cast aside at the ridiculously premature age of 30. Chairman Vic Jobson, never one to shy away from publicity, promptly announced that planning permission forthcoming, Southend would be playing at a new £14 million stadium for the following season. His plans were scuppered at an early stage starting years of acrimony between the club and the council.

Bolstering the ranks was Barry Silkman, a well travelled midfielder, who once commanded a sizeable fee when joining Manchester City. Bobby Moore went back to the West Ham United old boy's network, when 36-year old Frank Lampard joined Southend, as did ex-Hammer

Southend United 1985/86

Kevin Lock, who signed from Fulham. Despite the club's much publicised financial constraints, transfer fees were still being paid, albeit nominal amounts, Danny O'Shea arriving from Exeter City for £5,000. The most intriguing transfer of the summer was that of young Orient striker Richard Cadette, who had just completed his first season in the professional game having signed for Orient from Isthmian League Wembley. Orient had wanted £10,000 for the youngster, while Vic Jobson was adamant that Southend would pay no more than £2,000. The matter went to a tribunal to fix the fee, Jobson seething at the outcome of the fee being set at £4,000. It was to prove the steal of the century.

The opening day brought a draw at Gresty Road, Crewe being held 1-1 on their own ground. The next game was a Milk Cup tie at home to Gillingham where the same score was the outcome; Southend would lose the second leg 0-2 to exit at the opening round stage for the sixth consecutive season.

A late substitute in the Gillingham game was the new signing Richard Cadette, but there was little evidence of the dramatic impact he would have when he was handed his full debut in the home game against his old side Orient. His tremendous speed and skill on the ball saw the tiny front runner rattle in four goals and set up another for O'Shea as Orient were torn apart by five goals to one. The spectacular victory precipitated a run of five wins and a draw from the next six games as Southend rapidly climbed the early season table. In October, Roy McDonough returned to the club for a second spell following nine months at Exeter City.

As had been common in nearly all Southend teams since 1906, Moore's side was dogged by inconsistency, and defeats away to Mansfield Town (0-3), Port Vale (0-4) and at home to Colchester United (2-4) seemed to be expected by the fans.

In the F.A.Cup, Third Division strugglers Newport County came to Roots Hall in the opening round and returned to Wales with a single goal win, courtesy of Steve Mardenborough.

Any hopes of a promotion campaign ended with a dismal run in December and January. Out of nine fixtures, only two were won and six were lost including demoralising defeats at home to the all conquering Northampton Town side (0-4) and away to Orient (0-3). Moore tried to halt the slide

Top to bottom: Frank Lampard, Richard Cadette and Dean Neal.
Above right: Barry Silkman

in form by bringing in Dean Neal from Millwall and midfielder Gary Stebbing, who came on loan from Crystal Palace. Leaving Roots Hall was the prolific and popular front man Steve Phillips, who joined Torquay United.

In the Freight Rover Trophy, Southend were placed in a three team group with Colchester United and Northampton Town. At Layer Road, The Shrimpers were four down at half-time thanks to a Perry Groves hat-trick, and while Paul Clark pulled one back in the second half, the damage was done; Moore branded the performance "pathetic and spineless". In the home tie against Northampton Town, a meaningless fixture for The Shrimpers, Southend went down again, this time by three goals to one, a record low crowd for a first team fixture of 683 missing a spectacular long range goal from Frank Lampard. Despite the paltry crowd, amazingly this was not the lowest crowd in this unpopular competition during the season; a crowd of 461 watched Bury lose at home to Tranmere, while 279 hardy souls watched a meaningless encounter between Peterborough United and Aldershot. Amazingly, even this crowd was "beaten", the bottom of the barrel being a "crowd" of just 150 gathered for Halifax Town's 1-1 draw with Lincoln City.

Southend's campaign was dogged by bad luck as well; a harsh winter in the South East saw only one game played, another Essex derby defeat at the hands of Colchester United (0-2) at Layer Road. There was a full month between that match and the next at Stockport County, where a 1-2 defeat was tough on Southend as Paul Clark's shot had clearly hit the net but bounced out with such force that the referee refused to signal a goal, assuming erroneously that the ball had struck an upright.

With a mountain of games to play, morale was not helped by Barry Silkman walking out on his team mates stating he "did not care whether he kicked another ball for the club".

In March, apathy was reaching crisis point, only 1,006 paying spectators gathering for the 2-1 win over Halifax Town, a record low gate for a League match in the club's history. After a 2-3 defeat to bottom placed Preston North End, Frank Lampard quit the coaching side of his role at the club, and a month later Bobby Moore also resigned following the first team's abysmal 0-1 defeat to Isthmian League Walthamstow Avenue in the Essex Thames-Side Trophy. Despite unsuccessful efforts to change his mind, Moore offered to stay to the end of the season and strangely the final two matches resulted in two excellent home wins against Rochdale (5-0, with Cadette scoring three of the goals) and Port Vale (2-1). It would subsequently transpire that Moore's decision, with two years remaining on his contract, was mainly down to a pending court appearance for drink driving.

The club finished in ninth place, fifteen points adrift of the promotion places that were filled by Swindon Town, Chester City, Mansfield Town and Port Vale. The bottom four places, and hence the battle for re-election, were filled by Exeter City, Cambridge United, Preston North End and Torquay United; the Gulls finishing in last place for a second successive campaign. In what was to turn out to be the last ever re-election ballot, Enfield were the unsuccessful non-League applicants.

Richard Cadette scored an incredible 25 goals, although the lack of a reliable supporting cast proved to be the side's Achilles heel, midfielder Danny O'Shea being nearest to him with only nine goals. Unsurprisingly, Cadette was a hugely popular winner of the "Player of the Year" trophy.

1985/86 Player of the Year - Richard Cadette

Danny O'Shea　　　　*Steve Phillips*

WEBB, COLLYMORE AND FRY - THE THREE WISE MEN?

Stan Collymore

1986/87- Webb Quits Due To Board Interference with Shrimpers in the Home Straight

The Southend board were besieged with applicants for the vacant manager's post and a string of candidates were interviewed. Former England player Alan Mullery was one hopeful, as was former Tottenham Hotspur player John Pratt. The local papers declared that the favourite for the post was former Southend midfielder Eddie May. However, they were all wrong, as the board plumped for a late applicant, former Chelsea hero David Webb, who had previous managerial experience with Bournemouth and Torquay United.

Webb started by culling a number of Moore's squad, defenders Warren May and Steve Hatter joining Gola League side Maidstone United while goalkeepers Jon O'Brien and Barrie Delf joined Chelmsford City and Dartford respectively. Alan Rogers, a frustratingly inconsistent winger, left for Cardiff City, whilst young first year professional Terry Pryer was also cast aside. In September, the troublesome Barry Silkman and young forward Micky Engwell both joined Crewe Alexandra while Kevin Lock quit playing and took on the role of first team coach.

Joining the club were three players that were to become stalwarts of the Webb revolution. Dave Martin, a fiercely competitive midfielder, signed from Wimbledon, Peter Johnson, an elegant left back signed from Exeter City, while midfielder Derek Hall arrived from Swindon Town. Also joining from the County Ground was controversial full back Paul Roberts for his first spell at Roots Hall.

The League campaign kicked off with a disappointing 0-2 defeat at Peterborough United, old boy Greig Shepherd scoring the opening goal. Then came the League Cup (now known as the Littlewoods Cup) First Round tie against Third Division Brentford. A Dave Martin penalty separated the sides at Roots Hall, but a sign of better times ahead were clearly evident in the second leg at Griffin Park; a gritty determined display seeing Southend win again, this time by the odd goal in five. Their reward was a tie against First Division Manchester City over two legs, the first at Roots Hall. There were concerns that the now drastically reduced Roots Hall capacity of 12,000, due to the tightening of safety standards following the fire at Valley Parade and the riot at Heysel, would mean demand exceeding supply and the game was designated as an all ticket encounter.

Southend United 1986/87

performance before going down by two goals to one.

Back on the League front, optimism spread over the camp as a slew of results meant points were being chalked up regularly in the wins column. Highlights were 3-1 wins at both Lincoln City and Tranmere Rovers, a 5-3 home win over Rochdale and a 4-0 dismantling of Torquay United at Roots Hall. However, Webb's tough tackling side often fell foul of referees, both Paul Roberts (at Orient and Scunthorpe) and Roy McDonough (at home to Northampton Town and away to Swansea City), who to be fair was never a stranger to the referees' notebook, collected a brace of red cards each during the season. McDonough's dismissal for fighting in the Boxing Day game against Northampton Town proved a particular handicap as Southend went down to a heavy 0-4 defeat, although Dave Gilbert, McDonough's protagonist, would also see the changing rooms somewhat earlier than he would have anticipated.

However, the board were either over cautious or somewhat blind to the amount of support and goodwill the club had lost in recent times, a crowd of only 6,182 turning up for the match. In between the two legs, unexpected trouble brewed when Paul Roberts and Shane Westley were withdrawn from first team activity following a dressing room brawl. At the same time, Chairman Jobson, in a typical bout of petulance, threatened to resign when the council threw out his plans for a new stadium. After a 0-0 draw in Essex, the second leg against Manchester City was a tight affair, with City managerless following the departure of Jimmy Frizzell. Southend and particularly goalkeeper Jim Stannard, put up a tremendous

Glenn Pennyfather scores the Shrimpers' goal at Maine Road in the League Cup against Manchester City.

A CENTURY UNITED

Webb had pulled off another transfer masterstroke in October when, realising young John Gymer was ill-suited to a wide role, he secured the services of Martin Ling for £20,000 from Swindon Town. Ling's superb wing play and quality of crosses produced more openings for the likes of McDonough and Cadette and, as the latter was hitting the net regularly, a slurry of scouts beat a path to Roots Hall to watch the youngster. When asked of Cadette's future, Webb quipped that he "would rather sell his wife".

In the F.A.Cup, Southend were handed a tricky looking tie against relatively unknown opposition, Halesowen Town of the Southern League Midland Division. Home advantage proved critical as The Shrimpers ran out comfortable winners by four goals to one, McDonough claiming a brace. In the Second Round, Southend could have well done with avoiding recent nemesis club Northampton Town but once again were given a home draw. A spectacular encounter ensued with the two sides going hell for leather. The halftime score was one apiece but in the second half another six goals were shared, resulting in a four all draw, Cadette claiming a hat-trick for The Shrimpers. Five days later, the replay at the County Ground was shrouded in controversy when the Cobblers won another titanic encounter by 2-3 mainly thanks to two hotly contested penalties converted by Dave Gilbert.

Back on the League campaign, Southend were progressing well, hitting second place over the festive period and ending February with a decent run of four successive wins. Behind the scenes, Webb was involved in a string of rows with Chairman Vic Jobson, who constantly interfered with the playing side of the club. However, no-one predicted that the clash of strong personalities would result in Webb's shock resignation on March 2nd. He left Roots Hall claiming Jobson had treated him like "a dirty rag". In a move to ensure continuity, 28-year old captain Paul Clark was asked to take over as player/caretaker manager. Predictably, Webb's shock departure resulted in a slide in form, three of the next four games resulting

Jim Stannard

in defeats. Clark's confidence was not helped by Don Howe's last minute change of mind to come to the club to help out with the coaching side.

A win against Colchester United, 2-1, at Layer Road thanks to an amazing goal by Peter Johnson and a clincher from Cadette, were followed by successes against Orient and Cardiff City and the promotion bandwagon was back on the rails again. This opened a handy seven point gap between Southend and fourth placed Wolverhampton Wanderers, but the real test would come in April when the two sides vying for the third automatic promotion slot met at Roots Hall. A crowd in excess of 10,000, the club's largest gate in six years, gathered for the clash and after the smallest man on the pitch, Martin Ling, opened the scoring with a header, Southend defended resolutely to preserve a precious victory.

All the old doubts resurfaced that The Shrimpers would blow it, when two successive away defeats followed the euphoria of the Wolves game. A visit to Wrexham ended in a 0-4 defeat, but costlier still was an injury to Martin Ling, a fractured skull being the result of a reckless and almost criminal challenge by the Robins' Neil Salathiel; Ling would take no further part in the campaign. A 1-2 defeat to Burnley at Turf Moor followed, although nerves were steadied by a 3-1 win over Cambridge United in the final home game of the campaign. It meant that if a win was secured in a Friday night trip to Stockport County, then Wolves' home game against Hartlepool United the following day would be rendered meaningless, as Southend would have already clinched the final promotion place.

A large contingent of Southend supporters gathered expectantly at Edgeley Park, and Glenn Pennyfather paved the way for a memorable night with a goal in the first half. The prolific Cadette notched a nerve calming second and the Wolves supporters in the home end slunk disgruntledly out of the ground long before the final

Southend United in action during the 1986/87 season.

whistle confirmed Southend's promotion to Division Three.

The secret to the success was a settled side; despite the loss of David Webb, only eighteen players were used in League matches, and three of those made a very minimal contribution. Cadette was even more prolific than in his first season, scoring 31 times, and thus became the first Southend forward since Billy Best in 1969 to score thirty goals in a campaign. His main source of support came from the midfield with Glenn Pennyfather (14) and Derek Hall (11) having particularly successful campaigns in front of goal. However, it was the sheer consistency of ever present custodian Jim Stannard, an often unbeatable barrier, that gained him the nod in the "Player of the Year" poll.

1987/88- Bate Fiasco Pre-empts a Season of Struggle

Despite his young age, Paul Clark had done well to oversee the promotion run-in successfully and must have fancied his chances of gaining the manager's job on a permanent basis. However, authoritarian Chairman Vic Jobson, seemingly making a unilateral decision without consulting the rest of the board, chose the new manager himself. He plumped for Dick Bate, erstwhile former Boston United defender and coach with

Notts County, but with no experience at all as a manager at Football League level.

To the disappointment of many, although not a total shock, Richard Cadette was sold to Second Division Sheffield United. What was a total shock was the settling of a fee once again by tribunal, Southend cashing in their prized asset for a meagre £120,000; Chairman Vic Jobson vowed never to involve the club in such a method of settling fees again. Also departing the club were Jim Stannard, returning to Fulham for £50,000. Paul Roberts left for Aldershot, while John Gymer opted to join Crewe Alexandra as his first team chances had become very limited.

Dick Bate is offered a warm welcome by Paul Clark.

A CENTURY UNITED

Southend United 1987/88

The board offered financial support to the new manager and Bate set about purchasing new recruits. Priority was a new goalkeeper and a forward to replace the departed heroes. His choices were Eric Steele, a £10,000 capture from Derby County, who arrived with a decent pedigree, and the new goal getter was a man he knew from his days at Notts County. However, the relatively unknown Richard Young cost £25,000 and although he looked the part as a physically imposing front runner, his contribution to the club would border on the negligible. Roberts was replaced in the side by Chris Ramsey, who joined from Swindon Town for £14,000. He also captured Martin Robinson from Gillingham, who would make the headlines on his debut by netting twice in a 2-2 draw at Bury. Bate would also offer professional contracts to youth team graduates Justin Edinburgh, Paul Newell and Spencer Prior, following decent performances in pre-season matches.

The Littlewoods Cup saw a 1-2 defeat to Brentford in the away leg before a 4-2 triumph at Roots Hall overturned the deficit for an aggregate win. Little did Shrimpers fans know that they were watching the only victory the club would secure under the management of Dick Bate. The wheels would subsequently fall off in an unprecedentedly spectacular fashion. The third League outing of the season, away to Gillingham would result in an 1-8 humiliation, Southend's embarrassment being compounded by the fact that the Gills' would contribute their visitors consolation in the form

of a Gary West own goal. The next five matches were also lost, including heavy defeats at Notts County (2-6) and Port Vale (1-4). Bate was subjected to a vote of "no confidence" from the board and refused the offer to step down to a coaching role. Paul Clark was once again asked to step into the breach with literally hours to the kick off of the Littlewoods Cup Second Round tie with First Division Derby County. Despite the imposing presence of England keeper Peter Shilton in goal, Southend responded magnificently and a Roy McDonough penalty meant The Shrimpers held a precious lead for the second leg at the Baseball Ground. A doughty defensive performance saw a goalless second leg and a rare progression to the Third Round of the competition, where Southend were handed a trip to Second Division Ipswich Town. Southend were distinctly unlucky to lose by a single Graham Harbey goal that took a wicked deflection off Paul Clark. In the F.A.Cup, a typically early exit was experienced, Walsall winning 1-2 in a Fellows Park replay following a goalless draw at Roots Hall.

Clark acted quickly to bring in new faces; Adrian Burrows arrived on loan from Plymouth Argyle to lend some defensive solidity while Lee Nogan, a young Oxford United striker also arrived on loan to bolster the attack. A string of defeats in the League, notably after Burrows returned to Home Park, resulted in alarm bells ringing; Eric Steele was the major casualty, being replaced in goal by youngster Paul Newell after a 0-7 debacle at

Sunderland. However, it was the sale of Glenn Pennyfather in November to Crystal Palace for a record £150,000 that resulted in one of the clubs' most significant signings of the era. David Crown, a winger converted to a centre forward, was signed from Cambridge United for £45,000 and immediately results picked up, with wins over York City, 3-0 at Bootham Crescent, and an encouraging 4-1 win over Doncaster Rovers at home. Suddenly, the board decided to bring David Webb back as general manager whilst Clark would continue with team duties; Jobson how-

ever, having made his peace with Webb, said the returning hero would be "a giant fly on the wall" and within a short space of time he was handed full control of all affairs.

In the Sherpa Van Trophy, a win against Fulham and a narrow defeat to Brighton meant both Southend and Brighton went forward to the knockout phase. Strangely they were paired against each other in the First Round, with Brighton victorious by four goals to two at the Goldstone Ground.

Webb brought in some new faces in a bid to pull the side clear of the relegation zone. Paul Brush arrived from Crystal Palace for £12,000 and midfielder Peter Butler proved an excellent acquisition from Cambridge United for £60,000. Eric Steele had returned to goalkeeping duties, but his days were numbered when Paul Sansome arrived, initially on loan, from Millwall.

Southend were still precariously close to the relegation places but with Doncaster Rovers and York City doomed from an early stage, The Shrimpers still had everything to play for. Fortunately, two of the final three matches were against the already relegated sides both resulting in victories and Southend went into the final game, at home to Blackpool, knowing their fate was very much in their own hands. Grimsby Town had already joined the relegated clubs, leaving the final place to be filled by either Southend, Aldershot, Mansfield Town, Chesterfield or Rotherham United. It was the Millmoor club who was in the most threat-

Paul Sansome

A CENTURY UNITED

ening position with their final match being a home game against champions Sunderland. The Millers lost 1-4 to go down, but Southend cared little as their safety had been assured following an excellent display of free-flowing football, Blackpool being swept aside by four goals to nil. Following Sunderland into Division Two were Brighton and Hove Albion and Walsall.

David Crown was top scorer with 17 goals, strangely also topping the scoring charts at his previous club Cambridge United in the same season, no-one coming close to his tally of twelve. Roy McDonough chipped in with eleven goals, whilst wingers Martin Robinson (9) and Martin Ling (8) also contributed healthy tallies. It was hard working midfielder Dave Martin that took the "Player of the Year" mantle.

1988/89- Last Day Relegation Stuns Webb's Troops

David Webb opted to stick with his 1987/88 side for the new campaign, only offering professional terms to youngsters Danny Schneider, Matt Jones and Iain O'Connell during the summer. As expected, Paul Sansome made his loan move from Millwall permanent for a fee of £40,000 and leaving the club were Eric Steele, who joined Notts County, while Andy Rogers (Carshalton Athletic) and Dean Neal (Fisher Athletic) both chose to pursue their career on the non-League scene.

The season opened brightly with a 2-0 win over Bolton Wanderers, and Brighton were beaten home and away in the opening round of the Littlewoods Cup. However, in Round Two, Derby County extracted a modicum of revenge for the previous season defeat by winning 0-1 at home and then 1-2 at Roots Hall.

Away day disasters soon became an issue, with defeats mounting against the likes of Fulham (0-1),

Reading (0-4), Preston North End (2-3) and Brentford (0-4). By the middle of November, a run of five games without a win saw Southend entrenched at the wrong end of the table.

The club hoped a cup run would break the gloom, but the F.A.Cup interest lasted one game as Bristol City beat Southend 1-3 at Ashton Gate. The Sherpa Van Trophy qualifying group came soon after and two David Crown goals ensured victory against Lincoln City. Despite a 1-2 reversal in the other group game at Colchester United, in front of only 993 fans, Southend still qualified for the knockout stage. Southend were drawn away to Northampton Town and exited the competition following a 1-2 defeat after extra time at the County Ground.

Gary Bennett practices his shooting whilst David Crown looks on.

The players relax after a tough training session.

Webb strengthened the team by signing Gary Bennett from Chester City, who would soon become a terrace hero despite profligacy in front of goal that was unusual in his decent career. Webb also offered professional contracts to Andy Edwards, a young centre back released by West Ham United and Steve Tilson, a 22 year-old midfielder with Essex Senior League Witham Town, who had been recommended to Webb by ex-Southender Danny Greaves.

Southend gave themselves a good start to the end of the season in April when four successive wins were gained. However, relegation fears mounted when the next six games failed to produce any wins at all. So as with the previous season, Southend faced a nerve shredding last day climax to the season, only this time their destiny lay in the hands of other sides. Chesterfield, Gillingham and Aldershot had already been relegated, leaving the remaining place to be filled by Southend or Reading. Blackpool and Northampton Town's goal dif-

ference was better than Southend's, so even a handsome Southend win would not see those clubs in any danger. Southend's survival depended on Reading's result at Chesterfield. A goalless first half at Roots Hall against Chester City was tempered by the fact that Chesterfield were two goals to the good against Reading at Saltergate.

Top to bottom: Derek Hall wins a penalty against Wolves, whilst Steve Tilson looks on.
Roy McDonough scores an overhead kick against Blackpool.
David Crown scores against Bury.

A second half goal from Spencer Prior ensured Southend kept their end of the bargain, but Reading broke Southend hearts by rattling in four goals without reply, including two penalties, condemning The Shrimpers to relegation on goal difference with a record points tally for a relegated club of 54.

Wolverhampton Wanderers were Division Three champions, whilst also promoted alongside them were Sheffield United and Port Vale. "Player of the Year" David Crown scored a magnificent 29 goals but the deficiency in goals from other sources was all too clear, with Martin Ling being the closest to Crown with only nine goals; supporting strikers Roy McDonough (9) and Gary Bennett (2) offering little in the way of help.

1989/90- Webb's Wonders Bounce Back at the First Attempt

The shattering blow of relegation meant David Webb discarded several members of his squad from the 1988/89 campaign. One enforced departure was that of Shane Westley, who joined Wolves for a fee of £150,000. Also leaving were Martin Robinson and Danny O'Shea for Cambridge United whilst Derek Hall departed for Halifax Town. Peter Johnson was also on the move, signing for Gillingham. New faces included Andy Dixon from Grimsby Town and striker Mario

Walsh from Colchester United. Jason Cook and Peter Daley were two young midfielders picked up having been released by First Division clubs, Tottenham Hotspur and Liverpool respectively. Graduating from the ranks of apprentices were Paul Smith and Christian Hyslop.

The season got off to a flying start with five wins and a draw from the opening six encounters. The highlight was a 5-0 win at Aldershot, assisted by the home side's generosity with two own goals, David Crown scoring twice despite being booed with every touch for the "crime" of having played for Aldershot's arch rivals Reading. In the League Cup, now sponsored by Rumbelows, Southend were paired with Colchester United in the opening round. A sensational 4-3 win at Layer Road was followed by a 2-1 success at Roots Hall. Southend were then handed a plum Second Round tie against First Division Tottenham Hotspur. The first leg was at White Hart Lane, and The Shrimpers were more than happy to restrict their hosts to a single goal victory courtesy of a Terry Fenwick strike. In the return at Roots Hall, over 10,000 gathered to watch the likes of Paul Gascoigne and Gary Lineker parade their skills. A dramatic match saw Dave Martin give The Shrimpers the lead early on. Another from Gary Bennett put Southend ahead on aggregate before Paul Allen pulled the tie level on the stroke of halftime.

The match had already boiled up somewhat when Gary Bennett was forced to play on with a broken nose followed a heavy challenge by Gary Mabbutt, but after four minutes of the second half it exploded. Paul Stewart elbowed Sou-

thend full back Paul Roberts and was dismissed by referee Paul Danson. Stewart later claimed in the national press that Roberts had cheated and was successfully sued for defamation by the Southend player. The Moroccan born midfielder Nayim equalised on the night before Gary Bennett scored a third for Southend. However, rules stated that away goals counted double and despite constant pressure for a fourth goal, Spurs went down 3-2 on the night, their two away goals taking them through, the aggregate finishing 3-3.

The League campaign bubbled along nicely despite a run of four games without a win in December which followed on the back of an F.A.Cup humiliation at the hands of Southern League Aylesbury United. January saw a change in fortune, when three wins were secured including another five goal thrashing of Aldershot, when David Crown taunted the booing opposition fans with a superb hat-trick.

The newly responsored Leyland Daf Cup saw Southend progress from the group stages following a 1-0 win over Gillingham and a 3-3 draw at Cambridge United. Northampton Town were then defeated in the First Round by two goals to one as The Shrimpers qualified for the Second Round stage for the first time. However, hopes of an extended run were soon halted when Southend capitulated to Walsall by four goals to one.

In order to strengthen his squad in March for the end of season run-in, Webb secured the services of Andy Ansah of Brentford, while Dean Austin came from Isthmian League outfit St. Albans City for a transfer fee of £13,000. Another crucial signing was that of Ian Benjamin from Exeter City, who had terrorised Southend defences as part of the all-conquering Northampton Town side. Sadly, the popular Gary Bennett decided to return to the north-west with Chester City and left back

Gary Bennett scores against Spurs in the Rumbelows Cup at Roots Hall...

... and accepts the plaudits of the crowd.

Justin Edinburgh signed for Tottenham Hotspur for a record equalling transfer fee of £150,000.

Southend entered the run-in with a decent chance of promotion although defeats at Maidstone United (0-3) and at home to Chesterfield (0-2) made the likelihood of challenging Exeter City for the championship an outside bet. Indeed it was the third from last game of the season that saw the Grecians defeat Southend 2-1 at St.James' Park to confirm their title win. However, prior to then, Easter wins at Colchester United (2-0) and at home to Rochdale (3-2) gave Southend a real chance of a quick return to Division Three.

Southend went into the final match, away to Peterborough United, knowing that a victory would secure third place, Grimsby Town having already made sure of finishing in the runners-up spot. As it turned out, promotion rivals Stockport County, Maidstone United and Cambridge United all won their final matches but it mattered little as two more goals from David Crown ensured the required result was achieved at London Road. Cambridge United would gain promotion via the

Top left: The Shrimpers celebrate one of David Crown's goals at Peterborough.
Top right: David Crown is chaired from the pitch.
Below left: The team celebrate promotion in the dressing room.
Below right: The team return to the London Road pitch to celebrate their promotion.

play-offs while Southend supporters' delight of achieving promotion automatically was added to by the sight of arch rivals Colchester United being relegated to the Conference, as Darlington made a quick return to the Football League.

David Crown was once again leading scorer with a total of 23 goals, while Martin Ling provided useful support from the wing with eleven goals. The peerless goalkeeping of Paul Sansome saved Southend on many occasions and he was deservedly voted "Player of the Year".

1990/91- Super Shrimpers Achieve Double Promotion

Brett Angell

David Webb went on something of a shopping spree during the 1990 close season to fortify his squad for the new challenge of Division Three. The biggest signing was that of Brett Angell, who had won the Golden Boot in Division Four the previous season with 23 League goals for Stockport County; his services cost Southend the hefty fee of £100,000. Also joining the club were Chris Powell, a young left back released by Crystal Palace, as was midfielder Adam Locke. The experienced John Cornwell arrived from Swindon Town, while tall centre back Peter Cawley signed from Bristol Rovers. The final signing was Mark Hall, a young winger released by Tottenham Hotspur.

Leaving the club, however, was David Crown, who could not agree a new deal and was allowed to join Gillingham. The move would add more pressure to the shoulders of new signing Brett Angell, who was expected to fill the boots of a man who had been the clubs' top scorer for the previous three campaigns. Three fringe players opted to join non-League clubs during the summer. Paul Brush signed for Enfield, Matt Jones opted for Chelmsford City while Andy Dixon returned to the North East with Gateshead.

The season got off to a cracking start with five straight victories, the highlight being a 4-1 demolition of Cambridge United at the Abbey Stadium. However, the run came to a sudden halt when Stoke City won 0-4 against The Shrimpers at the Victoria Ground, although Southend's cause was not helped by the dismissal of Dean Austin and an own goal conceded by John Cornwell.

Chris Powell

Two of the ten goals scored against Aldershot in the Leyland DAF Cup.

In the Rumbelows Cup, Aldershot were narrowly beaten 4-3 over two legs, but in the Second Round, the team was well and truly slaughtered at Crystal Palace. The First Division side were on superb form as they run out 0-8 winners, with both Ian Wright and Mark Bright claiming hat-tricks. The second leg at Roots Hall was somewhat academic, but Southend put up a better performance, going down 1-2.

On the League front, the defeat by Stoke galvanised the team into winning five of the next six encounters, although the one loss was again a heavy one, this time Wigan Athletic running out 1-4 winners at Springfield Park.

SOUTHEND UTD.

Southend United 1990/91

In the F.A.Cup, it was another disappointingly early exit for Southend, when Leyton Orient triumphed 2-3 in a gripping encounter at Brisbane Road. In the Leyland Daf Cup, Southend were placed into a three team group with Aldershot and Reading. In the first game at home to Aldershot, the team went goal crazy, equalling the all-time club record victory by winning by ten goals to one against a hapless bunch of opponents. Southend were five up at half time and the match ended with Brett Angell hitting four and winger Steve Tilson claiming a sublime hat-trick. In the second group game, Reading were also put to the sword,

Southend running out 4-1 winners at Elm Park. The draw for the First Round of the knock out stages saw Southend handed home advantage against Maidstone United. A Brett Angell strike and an own goal saw Southend comfortably through to Round Two. Another home tie was secured and Torquay United were the visitors to Roots Hall. The game was goalless up until the 65th minute, when Southend promptly rattled in seven goals without reply, with Andy Ansah claiming the match ball for a hat-trick this time. In the Third Round, the run came to an abrupt end when Brentford outplayed The Shrimpers in a 0-3 reversal at Roots Hall.

David Webb secured the services of Pat Scully in January to bolster the defence, the Arsenal youngster having already won a full cap for the Republic of Ireland. A dip in form saw three of the four January League matches ending in defeat for The Shrimpers, although their position in the League table remained promising.

February and March brought enough wins to ensure a second promotion was a very real possibility, the best being a 4-1 triumph at Swansea City, a rare win on Welsh soil. Despite a slight goal famine in April, Southend drew at home to Cambridge United at the end of the month to ensure that promotion would be secured with a win at Bury in the last away game of the season. In a famous victory, a dramatic late Ian Benjamin winner secured the clubs' elevation to Division Two status for the first time in their history, despite having Pat Scully dismissed in the first half for an ugly challenge. The only matter left to settle was the outcome of the championship itself, but

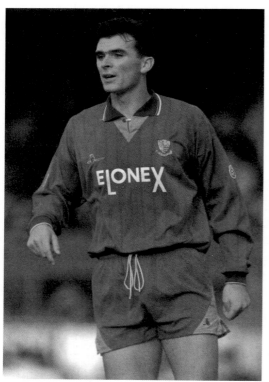

Pat Scully

a Marcus Gayle goal for Brentford at Roots Hall in the season's final match meant Cambridge United nipped in to steal the silverware with a last day win over Swansea City.

Brett Angell lived up to his billing by bagging 26 goals in all competitions and four other players also hit double figures in a triumphant campaign. Ian Benjamin scored 16, including his famous promotion securing strike, midfielder Dave Martin scored an incredible 14 times, with Andy Ansah contributing one less. Finally, elegant midfielder Steve Tilson found the net on eleven occasions. It was midfield powerhouse Peter Butler that won the "Player of the Year" award. Also gaining promotion to Division Two was Grimsby Town and, via the play-offs, Tranmere Rovers. Dropping down to Division Four were Crewe Alexandra, Rotherham United and Mansfield Town.

1991/92- Uncharted Territory for Shrimpers Ends in a Decent Showing

Manager David Webb kept faith with the majority of the 1990/91 squad that had taken the club into the previously uncharted territory of the second tier of the English Football League. In the summer of 1991 he snapped up the experienced former Ipswich Town winger Kevin O'Callaghan

Ian Benjamin celebrates after scoring Southend's first ever Division Two goal, against Bristol City.

on a free transfer from Millwall, while the versatile Andy Sussex joined the club from Crewe Alexandra. Promising young goalkeeper Simon Royce joined for £10,000 from Isthmian Leaguers Heybridge Swifts, although the fee would subsequently rise to £40,000. Leaving the club were Martin Ling, who rejoined Swindon Town for £15,000 and Jason Cook, who joined the growing band of ex-Southend players at Colchester United, as they were making a bid to regain their Football League status. Two fringe players who had struggled for first team opportunities were Iain O'Connell and Peter Daley, who joined Dover Athletic and Chelmsford City respectively.

The club's first ever League match at Second Division level resulted in a respectable 1-1 draw at home to Bristol City. Further optimism for a decent campaign was garnered when two successive away wins were achieved at Derby County (2-1) and Cambridge United (1-0). However, interest in the Rumbelows Cup ended predictably early when Watford won 1-3 over the two legs, as Southend were unable to overturn a two goal deficit from the away tie at Vicarage Road.

A temporary slide occurred in mid-September when The Shrimpers failed to win in four consecutive matches, although the run came to an end when a return to Vicarage Road was made for a

League encounter and Southend came home with the three points in a 2-1 victory, future Shrimpers' centre back Keith Dublin heading the Southend winner into his own net. This was the precursor to a remarkable match at Roots Hall; Southend were on a dismal run of missed penalties, stretching to four players and seven spot kicks. When a spot-kick was awarded in the home game with Charlton Athletic, young full back Dean Austin coolly put Southend into the lead. Both sides were then reduced to ten men when Steve Gatting was dismissed for a second booking for the visitors, followed by Spencer Prior when he conceded the games' second penalty. Fortunately, Paul Sansome made a magnificent save from Darren Pitcher. Charlton then equalised before Southend conceded a second penalty, this time Colin Walsh managing to hit the post and a valuable point was secured.

Southend entered the Full Members' Cup competition, now masquerading as the Zenith Data Systems Cup, for the first time following promotion. Southend were again paired away to Watford and this time progressed to the next round with a lone Andy Sussex strike. Hopes of a significant run were then ended in the next round when First Division Crystal Palace proved too strong, running out 2-4 winners at Selhurst Park, albeit after extra time.

Leading marksman Brett Angell then grabbed the headlines by setting a post-War club record of scoring in seven consecutive outings, although despite being constantly teed up for chances in the eighth match, a 2-1 win at home to Brighton and Hove Albion, he was unable to score again to equal Billy Hick's all time record of eight consecutive matches. The remarkable run coincided with a charge up the table, and on New Year's Day, due to an early kick-off time, a sensational 4-0 victory over once mighty Newcastle United saw The Shrimpers unexpectedly head the Division Two table for a few hours. The stunning win pre-empted the demise of the Magpies' manager, Osvaldo Ardiles.

One benefit of gaining promotion to the upper echelons meant that Southend were exempted to the Third Round of the F.A.Cup for the first time in their history. When the draw was made, the Shrimpers were handed a tough tie, away to First Division Everton. Despite the home side boasting the likes of Neville Southall, Peter Beardsley, Mo Johnston and Martin Keown in their side, the visitors put up a sterling performance at Goodison Park before succumbing to a single piece of

Top to bottom: Andy Ansah scores against Newcastle United.
Andy Ansah on the attack against Everton in the FA Cup.
Neville Southall makes an unbelievable save from Ian Benjamin.
Andy Ansah goes close at Goodison Park.

individual brilliance from England international Beardsley. Southall was also called upon to make one stunning save from Ian Benjamin, denying Southend the chance to take Everton back to Roots Hall.

Back on the League trail, any hopes of another promotion push were ended during a dismal run in February and March. A 0-2 reversal at The Valley against Charlton Athletic started a run of only one win in nine matches, as The Shrimpers headed towards mid-table. The one win that did come in that period was against a big name, goals from Angell and newly acquired midfielder Keith Jones secured a 2-0 win against north-east giants Sunderland. Jones had arrived at Roots Hall for a club record fee of £175,000 from Brentford the previous October and had proved an outstanding contributor to the Southend engine room.

In the home game with Middlesbrough, goalkeeper Paul Sansome's run of 150 consecutive first team appearances came to an end when he was red carded for being harshly adjudged to have pulled down the visitors John Hendrie and was suspended for one match. To add insult to injury, stand-in goalkeeper Steve Tilson could do little to stop Bernie Slaven converting the penalty kick to secure an undeserved three points.

Southend then suffered a poor run-in to the end of the season, with only a 2-0 victory at Plymouth Argyle registering three points in the final seven outings of the campaign. Considering it was the club's first ever campaign in such exalted company, a final standing of twelfth with seventeen

wins being accumulated was no little achievement. Brett Angell was once again top scorer with 23 strikes and although he kept up his excellent scoring ratio, it was noticeable that support from other areas of the field was markedly less evident than in the previous campaign, with Ian Benjamin and Andy Ansah trailing in his wake with a tally of nine apiece. It was no real surprise that Angell scooped the "Player of the Year" award for another productive season in front of goal.

1992/93- Arrival of a Footballing Genius Saves The Shrimpers

The general euphoria of surviving the first season in the higher division was tempered by the resignation in May of manager David Webb. It was the second time he had quit the club and it was once again due to one too many clashes with authoritarian chairman Vic Jobson. So in the summer the board set about the onerous task of replacing the club's most successful manager to date. The man they chose was Colin Murphy, who came with no little pedigree as a manager of lower division clubs since the mid 1970's. Meanwhile, reacting to the creation of the new Premier League, Division Two was renamed Division One.

The majority of the squad stayed at the club, with the exception of two notable transfers. Dean Austin followed Justin Edinburgh to Tottenham Hotspur for a new club record fee of £350,000, while influential midfielder Peter Butler moved to West Ham United for £125,000. His loss was felt the deepest, especially as Keith Jones would miss much of the campaign with a troublesome knee

Southend United 1992/93

injury. Murphy kept his transfer kitty intact, opting to sign only three graduates from the trainee scheme, those being Scott Ashenden, Jamie Southon and Jae Martin.

The new season started off with a desperate run of four straight defeats, before a brace from Ian Benjamin helped defeat Leicester City by three goals to one at Roots Hall. The League Cup, now sponsored by Coca-Cola, saw Southend enter at the Second Round stage with the draw pairing the club against Division One rivals Derby County. The Shrimpers edged out the Rams by a single Ian Benjamin goal in the first leg, however the return match at the Baseball Ground was an unmitigated disaster. Derby won comfortably, scoring seven without reply, Southend's cause not being assisted by Dave Martin putting through his own goal. Southend were undone by Derby's attacking frontline, with Paul Kitson, Marco Gabbiadini (2), Paul Simpson (2) and Tommy Johnson taking advantage of some shabby Shrimpers defending.

Stan Collymore

The Shrimpers fans were reacting badly to Colin Murphy's regime at the club. From September 18th to November 14th, the club played a total of ten League matches; no wins were forthcoming and only five out of the available thirty points were secured. The final three matches of that run resulted in defeats with the defence leaking three goals on each occasion. The fans were famously showing their discontent by staging a mass sit down protest at home games. Feelings were running high and "red cards" were handed out to all fans to visibly demonstrate their anger. Some of the cards had been given to players, and to the surprise of the supporters, several ran out for the home game with Oxford United with the red cards hidden under their track suit tops, before revealing them to the waiting crowd. Colin Murphy needed

a miracle to survive such vilification, and he went part way to salvaging his reputation by signing an unknown forward from the depths of Crystal Palace's reserve team. Stan Collymore made his debut in the home game with Notts County, which had been targeted by extremist supporters as a match to boycott to heighten the anti-Murphy rhetoric. A dismal crowd of 3,219 watched Collymore score twice in a stunning display of strength and power.

Southend had also made an early exit from the newly reconstituted Anglo-Italian Cup, a competition organised for Division One clubs to pit their skills against equivalent clubs from Serie B. The group stage of the tournament was held in the respective countries, Southend being pitted against Bristol Rovers and West Ham United. Qualifiers from the group stage would then be drawn in an "International" Group stage with Italian qualifiers. However, that proved academic as Southend lost both their domestic group games by three goals to nil.

Collymore's goals were bringing in some decent results, although defeats were still in plentiful supply. Barnsley were defeated 3-0 at Roots Hall with Collymore scoring twice alongside a rare goal from Chris Powell. The turn of the year brought another consummate home performance as Birmingham City were dismantled by four goals to nil. In the F.A.Cup, the Third Round draw gave The Shrimpers a home tie against Millwall, Collymore responding to some vile Millwall taunting by scoring the only goal of the game. Huddersfield Town were the opponents in the next round and in a tight encounter at Leeds Road, two more by Southend's new hero saw the club go into the Fifth Round draw. A trip to Hillsborough for the Fifth Round saw Southend pitted against Premier

Stan Collymore celebrates after scoring against Bristol Rovers.

League outfit Sheffield Wednesday. Despite a decent performance, two goals from Paul Warhurst saw the home side go through, and the Owls would eventually progress to the Final itself.

Despite some F.A.Cup excitement, the pressure was very much on the shoulders of Colin Murphy and another dismal run of form in March proved to be a final nail in his coffin; only a Collymore inspired win at Oxford United securing three points during March with two draws and three defeats forthcoming from the six matches played. Murphy was relieved of his duties, prior to Barry Fry masterminding an excellent 4-2 victory against Sunderland at Roker Park. The Shrimpers board had appointed Fry as Murphy's successor, and the ebullient former Barnet boss was tasked with ensuring Southend's survival with only nine games left to go.

Fry connected with Collymore immediately and the powerhouse forward responded with some of his greatest performances. West Ham, Bristol Rovers and Grimsby Town were all beaten at Roots Hall, although away wins were still a scarce commodity, trips to Barnsley, Leicester City and Cambridge United all proving fruitless. This meant survival went down to the final game of the season against Luton Town at Roots Hall, the Hatters also fighting for survival in a tight finish to the campaign. Only Bristol Rovers had been already relegated, so a titanic struggle with Luton ensued, Southend running out 2-1 victors. Southend fans invaded the pitch in joy and chaired their conquering hero Collymore off the pitch. A memorable day was completed when Luton fans joined the celebration as last day defeats for Cambridge United and Brentford meant Luton as well as a desperate Sunderland side both survived the dreaded drop. The champions were Newcastle United, with West Ham United also

being promoted. Swindon Town would join them in the Premier League via the play-off route.

Collymore's contribution to the season was immeasurable, his 18 goals in 33 games ensured First Division status was retained, and his huge popularity with the locals meant the "Player of the Year" ballot was a forgone conclusion. Incidentally, second top scorer was Ian Benjamin with eight goals, despite the much loved forward joining Luton Town back in November.

1993/94- Fry Slopes out in the Still of the Night and Spud Taylor Struggles to Survive

Despite hopes for the contrary, Stan Collymore's almost inevitable departure was confirmed in July when he joined Nottingham Forest, freshly relegated from the Premiership, for an initial fee of £2,250,000. Barry Fry, a consummate transfer market player, negotiated a plethora of sell-on clauses which would eventually see the club record fee enhanced to £3,570,000. Centre back Spencer Prior was also on the move for a sizeable fee, £200,000 taking him to Norwich City. Fry wielded the axe for several members of the 1992/93 squad; veteran Dave Martin was moved on to Bristol City after seven years at the club, Paul Smith was allowed to leave for Brentford where he carved out a highly successful career, while Christian Hyslop (Billericay Town) and Scott Ashenden (Hendon) opted for careers outside of the Football League. Mark Hall joined Fry's old club Barnet and young forward Steve Brown joined Third Division Scunthorpe United.

As was his trademark, Barry Fry went on a veritable summer shopping spree, signing nine new faces for the coming campaign. He returned to his old club, Barnet, to relieve them of four out

Southend United 1993/94

of contract players, midfielders Derek Payne and Jonathan Hunt as well as a pair of centre backs, Mick Bodley and Dave Howell. He also splashed some of the Collymore cash, investing a club record £400,000 in bringing full back Gary Poole to the club from Plymouth Argyle. The spectacularly coiffured Jason Lee joined from Lincoln City for £150,000 and the versatile Graham Bressington followed from Sincil Bank for a further £50,000. A more modest fee of £25,000 bought Gary Jones from Boston United, then of the Northern Premier League, while £100,000 bought striker Tommy Mooney from Scarborough. Always one to take a

gamble, Fry chanced £100,000 on the signature of former jailbird Ricky Otto from Leyton Orient.

Southend's opening fixture was a televised game against Nottingham Forest, and an expected quick return to Roots Hall for the departed hero Collymore, however a viral infection meant he was unable to play in the greatly anticipated match. The match ended in a 1-1 draw, Andy Sussex scoring for Southend with a Stuart Pearce penalty registering for the visitors. Southend's next game was the first competitive match for Millwall at their sparkling new stadium, the New Den. Again, the game was televised and

The Shrimpers somewhat spoilt the inauguration celebrations by triumphing by four goals to one.

Having been divested of so many key players in the summer, Second Division Barnet must have been relishing the chance for revenge when the Coca-Cola Cup draw pitted the two clubs together in the opening round. A dismal display by Southend in the home leg saw the North London side return home with a two goal advantage. A drawn game at Underhill meant the supposedly inferior opposition progressed to a Second Round tie with Queen's Park Rangers.

The early months of the season were a confusing mixture of brilliant performances and some truly abject displays from a team of apparent strangers. Among the good times were a 3-0 win at home to Peterborough United, a 1-0 win at Stoke City and a 6-1 thrashing of Oxford United at Roots Hall, where Tommy Mooney claimed a hat-trick. Poor performances were witnessed by away supporters who travelled to Grimsby Town (0-4) and Leicester City (0-3).

The Anglo-Italian Cup saw Southend successfully negotiate the domestic group stage, drawing with Luton Town and beating Wat-

Top to bottom: The players emerge for the opening day match against Nottingham Forest.
Andy Edwards shoots.
Andy Sussex scores.

ford at Vicarage Road. This put The Shrimpers into the International group stage. There were two groups of eight clubs, four English and four Italian, with the English clubs playing only Italian opposition for a total of four games each. The two highest placed clubs from both countries in each group would qualify for a national semi-final. The opening game did not go in Southend's favour, a 0-3 defeat against Fiorentina at the Artemio Franchi stadium was largely due to a brace from Argentine superstar Gabriel Batistuta. However, the second trip abroad had a better outcome when Cosenza from the deep South were defeated 2-1 on their own ground, even though the match was marred by an Italian player attempting to attack his tormentor in chief, Ricky Otto, with a hammer after the final whistle. Some quick restraining tactics from David Howell prevented some long lasting damage to the tricky winger. Another set back was suffered at home when Pescara outplayed their hosts by three goals to one leaving The Shrimpers needing to score heavily in the last game and rely on other results to progress. Padova were the final visitors to Essex and Southend duly rattled in five goals, with Gary Jones netting a brace. The result had the desired effect with Southend reaching the national semi-final against Group A qualifiers Notts County. In the first leg, a Phil Gridelet goal separated the sides at Roots Hall, but a repeat scoreline at Meadow Lane in County's favour meant the outcome would be decided on a penalty shoot out. County squeaked through 3-4 on penalties, with Graham Bressington missing the vital spot kick leaving

Southend to miss out on only their second Wembley appearance, and the first since December 1930. County qualified for the final against Brescia who had defeated Pescara in the Italian semi-final.

Southend's performances had meant the future of manager Barry Fry was subject to intense speculation. However, an approach from Birmingham City for his services was met with a firm rebuttal from the man himself, who stated he would not consider a move to St. Andrews under any circumstances. Four days later, Fry reneged on his word and took himself and assistants Eddie Stein and Dave Howell to the Midlands.

The new man at the helm was former Roots Hall favourite Peter Taylor, who was helpless to prevent a shell-shocked team going down 0-3 at home to West Bromwich Albion in his opening game in charge. However, this was somewhat forgotten when, in successive home games, Charlton Athletic were defeated 4-2 and Birmingham City were bested 3-1 in a white hot atmosphere at Roots Hall when the Southend faithful vented their anger at Fry's messy departure in no uncertain terms. However, the euphoria of defeating the returning traitor was soon dampened by a run of six successive defeats including a 0-1 reversal at Kenilworth Road in the F.A.Cup Third Round tie with Luton Town. In March, Nottingham Forest purchased another Southend United striker when Jason Lee moved to the City Ground for £250,000.

Taylor struggled to formulate a winning combination and in the final seventeen matches of the season the side only managed a paltry five victories. Fortunately, sufficient points had been gathered in the first half of the season to ensure relegation was never a real prospect and Southend duly finished in a reasonably comfortable 15th place. Much to the Southend fans' delight, despite a last day victory, Birmingham City were relegated when neighbours West Bromwich Albion also pulled out a last day victory. Also making the drop were Oxford United and Peterborough United. Runaway champions were Crystal Palace, while Nottingham Forest, fortified by 24 goals from Stan Collymore, made a quick return to the Premier League; joining them via the play-offs were Leicester City.

Tricky winger Ricky Otto was top scorer in a turbulent season with fifteen goals, with Brett Angell in second place with nine goals in only 23 games.

Ricky Otto

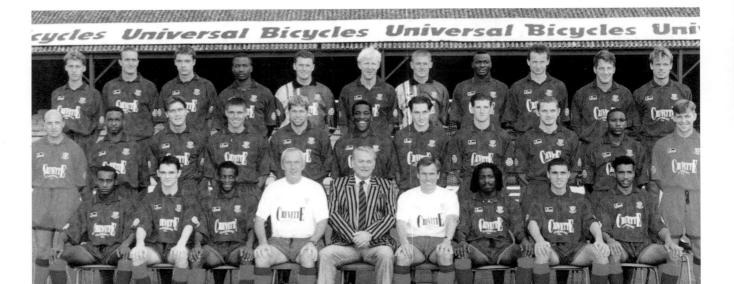

Southend United 1994/95

The popular and consistent left back Chris Powell was voted "Player of the Year".

1994/95- Thommo's Miracle Rescues Shrimpers from the Mire

Peter Taylor had a free rein to bring in his own players during the summer of 1994 and he did so with a plethora of new signings. Top of the list was the £250,000 capture of prolific Queen of The South marksman Andy Thomson. Peterborough United striker Dominic Iorfa arrived for a fee of £15,000, Mark Hone, a consistent full back with Southern League Welling United, also signed when £50,000 changed hands, three youngsters at the club were offered professional terms, these being Craig Davidson, Danny Foot and Declan Perkins and experienced centre back Keith Dublin arrived from Watford on a free transfer. Departing Roots Hall were Adam Locke, who joined near neighbours Colchester United, while midfielder John Cornwell was forced to quit the game through injury.

Despite the clutch of new players available to him, the season got off to a poor start. The first four League games failed to elicit a victory and the perennial early exit from the Coca-Cola Cup, this time at the hands of Watford, left an early season gloom enveloping Roots Hall. Taylor again entered the transfer market in a bid to kick start the campaign. Leaving the club were influential midfielder Keith Jones, a £150,000 acquisition for Charlton Athletic while Gary Poole became the first of many departures to Bir-

Andy Thomson

mingham City for a cut price fee of £50,000, the transfer registering a nett loss of £350,000 for the club. Moving in the opposite direction to Poole was Dave Regis, a burly striker arriving on a free transfer. Roger Willis signed for Southend on a free from Barnet while diminutive Leeds United striker Jamie Forrester arrived on a month's loan. However, the most significant capture was elegant midfielder Ronnie Whelan after a glorious and much decorated career at Liverpool.

The new signings at first struggled to gel; visits to Stoke City (1-4) and Wolverhampton Wanderers (0-5) resulted in ignominious defeats. However, immediately after the initial setbacks, an eight game unbeaten run, including five victories gave Taylor some welcome respite. Typically of his tenure though, the run was ended abruptly with a 0-5 thumping at Port Vale. Aside from a 4-1 home win over Reading in November, goals were a very scarce commodity and after the festive period the side began to ship goals at an alarming rate. Visits to Charlton Athletic (0-3), Burnley (1-5) and Grimsby Town (1-4) were nothing short of humiliations and when home form also buckled, with back to back defeats at the hands of Port Vale (1-2) and Watford (0-4), Taylor's position was rapidly becoming untenable. Two more departures to St.Andrews came prior to Christmas when Jonathan Hunt (£50,000) and Ricky Otto (£800,000) opted to link up with their former mentor Barry Fry.

In the F.A.Cup Third Round, Premiership side Southampton accounted for The Shrimpers interest in the competition with a comfortable 0-2 win at The Dell.

When the side suffered a run of four straight defeats, culminating in a 0-3 defeat against Bolton Wanderers at Burnden Park, Peter Taylor's resignation was accepted by the board. Former Sheffield United defender Steve Thompson was bought in as caretaker manager, charged with the not inconsiderable task of trying to ensure the clubs' First Division status.

Thompson made many changes to the formation; out went Paul Sansome in goal with Simon Royce being handed the jersey. Steve Tilson and Andy Sussex were restored to the midfield while Mick Bodley was bought back in place of Keith Dublin as Andy Edwards's partner in the rearguard. Finally, the off form Andy Thomson was replaced up front with Gary Jones, who had scarcely set the world on fire in his previous run in the first team.

The transformation in morale and results was nothing short of remarkable. Oldham Athletic were beaten 2-0 at Boundary Park followed by a 3-0 canter against Luton Town at Roots Hall. Chances of survival were boosted when Stoke City (4-2) and Burnley (3-1) were both beaten on the Essex coast. The season's final four games produced maximum points and included excellent wins at Tranmere Rovers (2-0) and Derby County (2-1). Thompson had masterminded a miracle escape from the drop zone and coaxed hitherto unseen form from want-away striker Gary Jones, who crashed in nine goals in twelve games.

In the final reckoning, Southend finished in a seemingly comfortable 13th place while Swindon Town, Burnley, Bristol City and Notts County filled the relegation places, which for much of the campaign appeared destined to include the Shrimpers. Leaving Division One through the right end were champions Middlesbrough. The Premiership was being reduced in size so second placed Reading had to be content with a play-off berth, which were won by Bolton Wanderers, who had finished in 3rd place. In a season which produced only 54 goals in all competitions, Gary Jones and Andy Thomson shared the top scorer's mantle with a meagre eleven apiece. The influential and truly gifted midfielder Ronnie Whelan was voted "Player of the Year".

Gary Jones

1995/96- Whelan's Band of Misfits Narrowly Avoid the Drop

The massively popular Steve Thompson was favourite to land a full time appointment at Roots Hall, but when the clubs' chief executive Peter Storrie decamped to relegated Notts County, he had no hesitation in offering Thompson the manager's post at Meadow Lane. The man given the job at Roots Hall was already there, Ronnie Whelan stepping up to a dual player/manager role. However, this role lasted just one game, as he was injured in the 1995/96 season opener at Portsmouth and never took the field again.

Leaving the club during the summer was midfielder Graham Bressington, injury forcing him out of the professional game at an unfortunately early age of only 29 years. The farcical £50,000 signing of David Roche from Doncaster Rovers the previous season ended with his dismissal from the club following his jailing for involvement in a shooting. Andy Edwards and Jae Martin left for Birmingham City with the former costing a fee of £400,000. Whelan's captures over the summer started with American international centre back Mike Lapper for an initial fee of £150,000, having been under contract to the United States Soccer Federation. Undoubtedly talented winger Paul Byrne was captured from Celtic for a fee of £50,000, promising young defender Leo Roget was also offered a full time contract. Whelan's own gap in the starting eleven was taken by a player well known to him from his days at Anfield, Mike Marsh joining the club for a record fee of £500,000 after a disastrous spell in Turkey with Galatasaray.

Whelan's initial impact in his new role was disappointing as one victory, at home to West Bromwich Albion (2-1), was forthcoming in the opening seven League outings. In the Coca-Cola Cup, Crystal Palace were again the opponents at the Second Round stage and despite a 2-2 draw at Roots Hall, Southend went out when the second leg at Selhurst Park resulted in a 0-2 win for the homesters.

September though, ended with an impressive run of three straight wins including a 3-1 triumph against Leicester City at Filbert Street, when the normally reticent in front of goal midfielder Julian Hails scored a remarkable hat-trick. Results in general were frustratingly inconsistent, a 2-4 reversal at home to Stoke City highlighted the defences' fragility but was notable for a debut goal for Norwegian trialist Petter Belsvik. He played three games but an option to sign him was not pursued and he returned to his native Norway

and became the all-time leading goalscorer in their top flight, beating the previous record of 135 goals held by Odd Iversen, father of one-time Tottenham Hotspur forward Steffan Iversen.

Southend's placing in the previous season's final table ensured their participation in the Anglo-Italian Cup once again. The competition had been re-organised to a straight international group. The two home games against Brescia and Foggia resulted in a 0-0 draw and a narrow 1-2 defeat. The away games saw trips to Reggio Emilia where local side Reggiana were held to a creditable 1-1 draw, but a trip to Salerno ended in a 1-2 defeat to Salernitana; Southend failed to qualify for the next stage in a competition eventually won by Notts County. In the F.A.Cup, a trip to Premiership side West Ham United resulted in a 0-2 exit at the Third Round stage.

In the second half of the season, the club's most impressive result was a 3-0 victory at Charlton Athletic, but defeats significantly out-numbered wins. In an attempt to halt the slide towards relegation, Whelan signed a bevy of new players. Another ex-Celtic player Mark McNally had joined in November for £100,000 and many more players arrived in the final stages of the season. Two costly new strikers in the shape of Barnsley's Andy Rammell (£250,000) and Dutchman Jeroen Boere, a £150,000 capture from Crystal Palace bolstered the forward line, whilst defender Mark Stimson arrived from Portsmouth for £25,000. Several loan signings were also made including

Southend United 1995/96

Thomson all mustered half a dozen goals apiece. The only player who featured in all 53 games of the campaign was goalkeeper Simon Royce and his brilliant displays undoubtedly kept the club in the division; he was recognised with a richly deserved "Player of the Year" award.

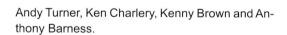

Andy Turner, Ken Charley, Kenny Brown and Anthony Barness.

The season slid to a terminal decline, only a 2-1 win at home to Ipswich Town salvaging a modicum of pride. However, sufficient points had been gathered earlier on in the season and coupled with a tight lower end of the table, Southend staved off relegation by the narrow margin of seven points. A final placing of 14th actually looked far more comfortable than in reality. Dropping down to Division Two were Millwall, Watford and Luton Town. Gaining promotion to the holy grail of the Premiership were champions Sunderland and second placed Derby County while Leicester City defeated Crystal Palace in the Play-Off Final.

In a troubled season, Whelan used a total of 31 players and the disjointed nature of the team was evident throughout the campaign. Top scorer with a miserly nine goals was Dave Regis, despite having left for Barnsley in February as a make weight in the transfer deal that bought Andy Rammell to the club. Paul Byrne, Mike Marsh and Andy

Mike Marsh

Roots Hall - From The Floodlight Pylons

Photographer Gary Bray was given access to Roots Hall from one of the most unusual positions back in 1984 - the floodlight pylons. Here are some of his views that most supporters would never normally get the chance to see.

Top: Two views of the South Bank car park, with the South Bank terrace clearly visible. The car park is now covered with flats.
Centre: A view of Roots Hall, taken during a Southend Sabres American Football match. Again, the vast South Bank terrace can be seen.
Bottom left: The managers' dugouts, overflowing with American footballers.
Bottom right: The South Bank car park, this time full of cars.

THE FALL AND RISE OF THE SHRIMPERS

Freddy Eastwood

1996/97- Whelan's Woeful Shrimpers Finish Bottom

Manager Ronnie Whelan had a few out of contract players at the end of the 1995/96 and the squad was freshened up in the summer break. The players leaving Roots Hall included a triumvirate of players who signed for Peterborough United, now managed by Barry Fry following his dismissal from Birmingham City. Declan Perkins, Roger Wills and Mick Bodley all signed on at London Road, the latter for a fee of £75,000. Reliable full back Mark Hone was allowed to leave for Lincoln City, while Danny Foot, never a first team regular, opted to join Southern League Crawley Town. Additions to the Southend squad in the close season were Paul Williams, a once prolific striker with Charlton Athletic but beset by a run of bad injuries, and Ritchie Hanlon, a youngster released by Chelsea. Whelan also cast his net further afield than normal by signing three Danish players; John Nielsen (Ikaast), Tony Henriksen (Randers Freja) and Peter Dursun (Aarhus) adding a continental flavour to the Essex coast.

The season could not have kicked off in better style, Andy Rammell scoring the quickest goal on the opening day after one minutes' play against Tranmere Rovers at Roots Hall, a John Morrissey equaliser for the visitors leaving the Shrimpers with only a share of the spoils. Perhaps a warning of the struggles to come was felt when the next three League games were all lost, including a 0-5 battering at Oxford United. In the Coca-Cola Cup, Southend gave themselves an uphill battle by losing the home leg against Third Division Fulham by two goals to nil, not helped by a harsh red card shown to Mike Lapper. A decent display in the second leg at Craven Cottage saw at least some pride restored with a gutsy 2-1 triumph.

That victory was the precursor to the season's most remarkable match. Eventual champions Bolton Wanderers were the visitors to Roots Hall and in a dramatic encounter, Southend ran out 5-2 victors, with Dutch striker Jeroen Boere netting twice and midfield maestro Mike Marsh in imperious form as the hub of the home side. However, the good feeling surrounding Roots Hall following

Jeroen Boere

these triumphs was short lived as the next four matches failed to muster a win and culminated in a 1-6 thrashing at Selhurst Park against Crystal Palace.

In actual fact, the three months between October and December saw Southend only accrue three wins, all at home, to Sheffield United (3-2), Grimsby Town (1-0) and Reading (2-1), in a total of seventeen matches played. The alarming run of form saw the side slump to the foot of the table and not even the introduction of some loan signings, Adem Poric (Sheffield Wednesday), Paul Read and Ian Selley (both Arsenal), could arrest the freefall. In November, Southend picked up what would be their only win on the road all season when a Larus Sigurdsson own goal gave them all three points from a trip to Stoke City.

Home form was scarcely any better as Barnsley, Huddersfield Town and Queens Park Rangers all gained maximum points from trips to Roots Hall, the latter courtesy of an own goal by Leo Roget as The Shrimpers pressed the self-destruct button once again. Roget was again in the headlines for the wrong reasons in the next game, a 2-2 draw with Oxford United. The coloured centre back was shown a second yellow card by referee Steve Bennett when the offence had actually been committed by Jeroen Boere; an appeal for mistaken identity was turned down. A miserable run of three successive defeats and Southend were consigned to bottom place in the table long before fellow relegation material Grimsby Town ran out 0-4 winners in an abject final day display at Blundell Park.

Southend United 1996/97

The New Year commenced with a 0-2 reversal at Filbert Street against Premiership side Leicester City in the Third Round of the F.A.Cup. Away defeats were coming thick and fast, including heavy ones to the likes of Sheffield United (0-3), West Bromwich Albion (0-4) and Wolverhampton Wanderers (1-4). In fact, the only point Southend picked up from away games between January and the end of the season came in April from a goalless draw at Swindon Town.

Southend only managed eight wins all season and finished nine points adrift of safety, being accompanied in the drop by Oldham Athletic and Grimsby Town. Champions Bolton Wanderers were joined in the Premiership by Barnsley and, via the play-offs, sixth placed Crystal Palace. Boere and Rammell both scored nine League goals each although the former Barnsley striker edged out the Dutchman overall by virtue of a lone Coca-Cola Cup goal against Fulham. In a season of few real candidates, ever present centre back Keith Dublin was voted "Player of the Year".

fer deal. Two of Alvin Martin's new signings would leave within a month, Carl Beeston joined from Stoke City and promptly left for Hednesford Town

Southend United 1997/98

1997/98- Martin Fails to Halt Slide as Southend are Bottom Again

Ronnie Whelan tendered his resignation as the season ended, not before controversially releasing popular midfielder Steve Tilson, due a testimonial match the following campaign, after nine seasons at the club. The board decided to give another untried former player the job of regaining First Division status, that man being Alvin Martin, the former West Ham United stalwart who had just retired from playing after a season at Leyton Orient.

Joining Tilson through the out door were veteran goalkeeper Paul Sansome, who joined Gravesend and Northfleet, Andy Sussex, who joined Tilson at Canvey Island, Ritchie Hanlon, who also went non-League with Welling United of the Southern League and American defender Mike Lapper, who returned home with Columbus Crew after Southend refused to pay an additional instalment due to the U.S.S.F. as part of his trans-

after nine games while George Parris' Southend career was even shorter; just one appearance after signing from Brighton and Hove Albion, the former West Ham defender joined St.Leonard's. Other newcomers were Nathan Jones, a left back making a second attempt at League football after a season in the Spanish Second Division with CD Numancia, young defender Ben Lewis was signed from Colchester United, while home grown youngsters Chris Perkins and Trevor Fitzpatrick were offered full time deals. Winger Adrian Clarke was offered a permanent deal following a promising loan spell from Arsenal at the end of the previous campaign.

If Southend harboured thoughts of an immediate return to Division One, the opening five fixtures proved conclusively that it would be far easier said than done, only one League win coming in that time, courtesy of a single Jeroen Boere strike against Burnley at Roots Hall. A rare Coca-Cola Cup success was enjoyed as the First Round paired The Shrimpers with Third Division Cardiff

City, a drawn away leg setting up a comfortable 3-1 home triumph as inconsistent winger Paul Byrne turned on an all too infrequent match winning display. Aside from a visit to Derby County's shiny new Pride Park home, the Second Round was one to forget as Paulo Wanchope ran the visitor's defence ragged with an inspired display in a 0-5 walkover. The home leg had also been lost for a 0-6 aggregate win for the Rams.

After the poor start to the season, Martin called on the West Ham United old boys network once again, bringing in midfielder Martin Allen on a month's loan from Portsmouth. He also gave a trial to Gabon-born forward Roger N'Zamba, who had been plying his trade in Italy with Triestina. In arguably the shortest Southend career ever, the new striker came on as a substitute for Jeroen Boere in the home game with Fulham only to be substituted himself twelve minutes later following a hamstring strain. He was never seen again.

Persisting with continental signings, Martin then offered contracts to Regis Coulbault and Sada "Pepe" N'Diaye, both from French football with the Toulon and Troyes clubs respectively. The gangly Senegalese born striker N'Diaye had an immediate impact, scoring a debut winner away to Plymouth Argyle, although that was to prove the highlight of his seven months at the club. A decent run of form was enjoyed during December, a 3-2 home win over Preston was followed by a trip to Gillingham; another away defeat looked on the cards with The Shrimpers trailing by a Nicky Southall goal as full time beckoned. However,

Martin Allen

two injury time goals from Coulbault and Boere secured a welcome three points. This game was followed up by a spectacular 4-4 home draw with York City, Adrian Clarke and Keith Dublin scoring a brace apiece.

In the Auto Windscreens Shield, a First Round exit was suffered as Wycombe Wanderers won 0-1 at Roots Hall in front of just 1,500 supporters. In the F.A.Cup, struggling Southend were handed a potential banana skin with an away tie to perennial Conference members Woking. In another game of late goals, two in the last two minutes from Nathan Jones and Phil Gridelet meant Southend were spared the embarrassment of an exit to a non-League outfit. Predictably, the inevitable exit came in Round Two when a trip to Fulham ended in a 0-1 defeat, although Southend's cause was not helped by some eccentric refereeing from Barry Knight who dismissed goalkeeper Simon Royce and defender Ben Lewis.

Former Welsh international goalkeeper Neville Southall was brought in on loan from Everton in December as cover for the suspended Royce, but his arrival coincided with a truly horrific spell of form. After Andy Thomson had scored in the 19th minute of a 1-2 home defeat to Luton Town on January 3rd, Southend failed to score in the next five League encounters, four of which were lost and included a 0-5 battering at Carlisle United.

In a bid to halt the slide towards Division Three, Martin bought in some more reinforcements. Simon Coleman joined from Bolton Wanderers and young midfielder Kevin Maher signed up, having been released by Tottenham Hotspur. Two new loanees also arrived in the shape of the vastly experienced centre back Richard Jobson from Leeds United and, later in

Regis Coulbault

March, Martin Aldridge, who arrived on loan from Oxford United.

The new look defence showed improved solidity as finally some much needed victories were racked up against the likes of Blackpool (2-1), Plymouth Argyle (3-0), Wigan Athletic (3-1 at Springfield Park) and Bournemouth (5-3). However, Southend seemed to exhaust their supply of goals in the home game with the Cherries as in the final seven games after that match, only two goals were scored and only two more points accrued.

A dismal end to a truly abysmal season saw Southend only muster eleven wins and 43 points all season and the club were stuck with the humiliation of successive relegations in last place. The Shrimpers finished ten points adrift of safety and joining them in Division Three were Brentford, Plymouth Argyle and Carlisle United. Watford were Division Two champions and also promoted were Bristol City. Grimsby Town, who had made the drop from Division One with The Shrimpers the previous season, made a quick return, winning the play-offs against Northampton Town.

Jeroen Boere was comfortably top scorer with 14 goals, his nearest form of support coming from Andy Thomson back on six goals. "Player of the Year" was the midfielder cum full back Julian Hails who had tried manfully in a woefully inadequate side. Manager Alvin Martin could never choose a settled side, enlisting a record number of 33 players during a wretched campaign, although his plight was not helped by a career ending injury to midfield talisman Mike Marsh against Bristol City in October.

1998/99- Little Change in Shrimpers' Fortunes as Martin Quits

Southend were back in the basement division for the first time in nine seasons and Alvin Martin faced a huge task to pull back team morale after the most dramatic slide in the clubs' history. There was a plethora of departures from Roots Hall following the disastrous 1997/98 season; star goalkeeper Simon Royce joined Premiership Charlton Athletic on a Bosman free transfer. Dutch striker Jeroen Boere joined Omiya Ardija in Japan's First Division, a move that went well for him, scoring nine goals in eleven games before

Southend United 1998/99

an incident in a nightclub saw him lose the sight of one eye, thus ending his playing career. Also leaving on a free transfer was expensive signing Andy Thomson, who never lived up to his potential, the Scot signing for Oxford United. Andy Rammell was another costly signing leaving for nothing when he joined Walsall. Phil Gridelet (Woking) and Ben Lewis (Heybridge Swifts) pursued their careers outside the Football League. Three of Southend's European players also returned to their homelands with John Nielsen joining Viborg, Regis Coulbault resurfacing with Hyeres and Pepe N'Diaye signing for Grenoble.

Alvin Martin signed three Manchester City players after they pruned their top heavy squad. Striker Barry Conlon cost £90,000 and lanky defender Dave Morley saw £10,000 change hands; Goalkeeper Martyn Margetson also arrived on a free transfer. Scottish striker Alex Burns arrived on a free transfer having spent a period in Holland with Heracles '74, the veteran defender Rob Newman signed from Norwich City and the equally experienced Mick Gooding arrived from Reading. Simon Livett return to the professional game after a spell with Grays Athletic, former youth team goalkeeper Melvyn Capleton rejoined the club from

Alex Burns

Leyton Orient and finally much travelled Miguel De Souza arrived from Peterborough United.

The season opened in fine style; on a blazing hot day at Scarborough, a delicious chip from Julian Hails secured a 2-1 win at Seamer Road. This was followed by a similar score at home to Shrewsbury Town, Alex Burns netting an injury time winner.

In the newly sponsored Worthington Cup, both legs against Gillingham were won by single goals scored late on, Rob Newman separating the sides at Roots Hall and Adrian Clarke netting an even later winner at Priestfield. Southend were drawn against Premiership opposition in the form of Coventry City and put up a very creditable performance at Highfield Road in the first leg, going down to a lone strike from Paul Hall. However, class showed through in the second leg where the Sky Blues ran out easy 0-4 victors.

On the League front, success during September and October was minimal, with only three wins recorded from the twelve games played. A 3-0 win at home to Rotherham United was the pick of the bunch, although a 2-0 "away" win against Brighton and Hove Albion during their enforced exile at Gillingham was also a welcome tonic. The match against Rotherham was also notable for the debut of the veteran Mick Gooding, bettering Neville Southall as the club's oldest debutant at the age of 39 years and 143 days. The match at Swansea City at the end of September was remarkable for the fact that Southend were reduced to eight men for the first time in their history when Julian Hails, Mick Gooding and Kevin Maher were all dismissed. Unsurprisingly, a 1-3 defeat ensued.

In November, a 1-4 reversal at Brentford immediately preceded the club's first ever home defeat to a non-League side in the F.A.Cup proper, Doncaster Rovers, then of the Football Conference, triumphing by a single Dave Penney strike at Roots Hall. The Auto Windscreens Shield was equally short lived despite the club receiving a bye in the First Round. The club duly visited Exeter City for a Second Round tie and were easily brushed aside by three goals to one in front of a spartan crowd of 1,143.

The highlight of the remaining matches of 1998 was an excellent 4-2 triumph at the Victoria Ground, home of Hartlepool United. The year ended on a down though when a trip to Torquay United resulted in a 0-2 reversal. The opening game of the New Year saw Rob Newman rescue a point in injury time at Chester City despite the home side playing with ten men for a considerable time following Sam Aiston's injudicious punch on substitute Mick Gooding.

After a home win against Scarborough, a five match run without victory meant the calls for Alvin Martin's dismissal were getting louder by the game. However, a decent loan signing of Brentford's Kevin Rapley saw the striker hit form with a burst of four goals in three games, deflecting the attention away from Martin's troubles for a brief while.

During January, Martin also signed experienced full back Martin Booty from Reading while his

team mate Barry Hunter, a Northern Ireland centre back, arrived on loan. Also arriving to address the lack of goalscoring output was Neil Campbell from Scarborough for a fee of £12,500, while another Reading player signed for Southend when Neville Roach joined, with £30,000 changing hands. The final new capture was German midfielder Lars Unger, linking up with Southend from Fortuna Dusseldorf.

Despite the influx of new blood, the results were still unacceptable; defeats at Cambridge United and Darlington weighed heavily on a beleaguered Martin and when a vocal tirade deafened him following a home defeat to Hull City, he threw in the towel. His assistant Mick Gooding presided over the 0-1 reversal at Rochdale before former Shrimpers' favourite Alan Little was ushered in as the new manager.

As often happens, the change of manager paid immediate dividends as Southend romped to a 3-0 win at Leyton Orient, Neil Campbell scoring two excellent goals having drawn a blank in his previous eight attempts. The honeymoon was sadly short-lived as the side failed to win any of the remaining four home games of the campaign, a dismal performance against Brentford summing up another wretched season, the 1-4 reversal seeing Lloyd Owusu score a hat-trick as he had also done at Griffin Park earlier in the campaign. Away from home, two wins were secured in the closing weeks of the season when Plymouth Argyle (3-0) and Barnet (2-0) were bested on their own grounds.

A final placing of 18th saw Southend only six points clear of the relegation spot occupied by Scarborough. Brentford won the League with Cambridge United and Cardiff City also gaining automatic promotion. In the play-offs, fourth placed Scunthorpe United defeated Leyton Orient in the final. Once again 33 players were used in a disjointed campaign, and somewhat symptomatic of a season of struggle, centre back Rob Newman top scored with a meagre eight goals. The shot shy forwards were headed by Barry Conlon with just seven from 36 appearances. Reliable full back Mark Beard was the fans' choice as "Player of the Year".

Mark Beard

Neville Roach

Southend United 1999/2000

1999/2000- Another Disappointing Campaign as Shrimpers Hit the New Millennium

Alan Little returned to his former club York City for several of his new signings during the 1999 close season. Scottish winger Gordon Connelly arrived for £50,000, while skilful midfielder Mark Tinkler joined for £40,000. Injury plagued striker Neil Tolson also arrived from Bootham Crescent on a free transfer. Before Christmas, Little would secure the services of two other players that had served him well at York, goalkeeper Mark Prudhoe signing from Northern Premier League Guiseley and Nigel Pepper arriving on an extended loan from Aberdeen. Another new striker to the club was much travelled Martin Carruthers who signed from Darlington for £50,000. A successful crop of trainee graduates were offered professional deals, namely Garry Cross, Leon Johnson, Danny Kerrigan and Tom McDonald.

Leaving Roots Hall were long serving Keith Dublin, who joined Farnborough Town, former captain Andy Harris who joined Leyton Orient, Lars Unger signed for Austrian club SW Bregenz, goalkeeper Martyn Margetson joined Huddersfield Town and Barry Conlon, who joined York City for £100,000.

Finally Alex Burns returned to his native Scotland by joining Raith Rovers.

The new campaign kicked of promisingly with five wins from the opening eight games, the highlight being a 4-1 home mauling of Halifax Town, although successive away wins at Hartlepool United and Macclesfield Town, both by two goals to one, also offered cause for optimism. Interest in the Worthington Cup, however, was short lived when Second Division Oxford United won both legs.

November and December bought a run of seven games without a win, only ended in the year's final outing when a single Martin Carruthers strike won the points at Plainmoor against Torquay United. This made up for an early F.A.Cup demise at the same ground when a Mick O'Brien free kick accounted for The Shrimpers. A home defeat to Cheltenham Town in the Auto Windscreens Shield completed an unwanted hat-trick of First Round exits in the season's domestic cup competitions.

The New Year started with a home defeat by Rotherham United followed by a humiliating 1-2 defeat at Barnet. Mark Prudhoe's display in goal at Underhill was deemed so poor he was substituted at half-time, Southend compounding their own misery by being reduced to nine men when Carruthers and Tinkler were red carded in a stormy encounter.

The side showed some steel in the next home game against Rochdale when they found themselves three goals down at half-time. A sterling comeback in the second half saw a point secured in a 3-3 draw when Leo Roget grabbed a late leveller. Other than Martin Carruthers, goals were in generally short supply so one time Southend target Steve Jones finally joined the club on loan from Bristol City. He made an instant impact, finding the net seventeen minutes into his debut in a 3-1 home triumph over Chester City. However, the next four games saw the side fail to score, although three points were obtained from goalless draws.

The supporters had suffered another season of frustration but the campaign ended on a high note when "Player of the Year" Nathan Jones marked his award with a truly spectacular winning goal against Cheltenham Town at Roots Hall. The prolific Martin Carruthers was easily top scorer with nineteen goals from 40 starts, while Neil Tolson contributed ten; the majority of these came early on in the campaign, which for Neil was blighted by injury.

Martin Carruthers

The Shrimpers finished in 16th place, comfortably clear of relegation but disappointing nonetheless. Chester City were relegated on the last day of the season following another miraculous escape by Carlisle United. Swansea City were worthy champions, just ahead of Rotherham United and Northampton Town, while gaining promotion via the play-offs were fifth place Peterborough United who successfully saw off Darlington in the final.

2000/01- Little Sacked as Webb, the Messiah, Returns to the Fold

Several players departed the club during the 2000 close season, notably Julian Hails hanging up his boots prematurely owing to a serious knee injury. Winger Adrian Clarke joined Conference outfit Stevenage Borough on a free transfer, while Steve Jones and Nigel Pepper rejoined Bristol City and Aberdeen respectively after extended loan periods. Alan Little was hampered in his expenditure during the close season as financial constraints weighed heavily on all areas of the club. Former Tottenham Hotspur trainee David Lee was offered a deal following good performances in pre-season matches while experienced left back Damon Searle was signed up on a free transfer from Carlisle United. Scott Forbes, a tricky winger, was offered a deal having most recently starred for Essex Senior League Saffron Walden Town. An experienced new goalkeeper was required but Little had to be content with securing the services of Brentford's Andy Woodman on a three month loan deal only. Youngsters Dave McSweeney, Leon Hunter and Craig Edwards were all offered first year professional contracts.

The season commenced with a reasonable run of results, Brighton and Hove Albion were defeated 2-0 at Roots Hall, newcomer Lee marking his debut with the winning goal. This was followed up

Southend United 2000/01

with hard earned draws on the road at Torquay United and Cardiff City. The Worthington Cup saw a tie against First Division Birmingham City pulled out of the bag, but the tie was all over after the first leg, when Southend capitulated 0-5 at Roots Hall, although a modicum of pride was restored when a goalless draw was played out at St. Andrews in the return. A couple of League defeats were suffered at home to Darlington and at Lincoln City but then a run of four matches unbeaten was achieved, culminating in a home win over Scunthorpe United. However, following that game the board decided that the team had not performed well enough and Little was relieved of his duties.

Much speculation abounded as to who would be the new man in charge and the Roots Hall faith-

Jay Smith scores against Cambridge United and celebrates with Mark Beard.

ful were delighted at the appointment of former manager David Webb for a third spell at the club. Nearly a thousand supporters made the long trip to Blackpool to welcome the returning Shrimpers' legend, with a late Trevor Fitzpatrick equaliser forcing a 2-2 draw to avoid a losing start for Webb. The new manager acted quickly to rebuild the squad on limited resources; striker Ben Abbey was acquired from Oxford United, while former Southampton trainee goalkeeper Daryl Flahavan was signed from Woking. Another arrival was diminutive midfielder Russell Williamson from Wimbledon.

In the F.A.Cup Torquay United, were defeated 2-1 at Roots Hall after a drawn game at Plainmoor. The Second Round tie paired Southend with local rivals Canvey Island with the non-Leagu-

A CENTURY UNITED

ers handed home advantage. Due to demand for tickets, a switch of venues was made and a crowd in excess of 11,000 saw a 2-1 victory for The Shrimpers. However, the ignominy of an exit to a non-League side was only postponed for a round when Isthmian League Kingstonian won at Roots Hall with a single goal after eight minutes from Eddie Akuamoah.

Southend were unbeaten in their first seven League matches under Webb before three successive defeats towards the end of November curbed the growing enthusiasm. Webb again dipped into the transfer market, acquiring Carl Hutchings from Bristol City, Shane Wardley and Tes Bramble from Southern League Cambridge City (the latter costing £7,500) while Michael Black was brought in from Tranmere Rovers. Webb also signed his son, Danny, a young forward from Southampton for £10,000. Around the same time Mark Tinkler, a decent performer in the Southend midfield, complained of homesickness and was allowed to return north by joining Hartlepool United. Defender Dave Morley joined Carlisle United while youngsters Garry Cross, Yemi Abiodun and Tom McDonald were all released to non-League clubs.

The Leyland Daf Vans Trophy brought the club's best run thus far in the competition for the League's Associate Members. In the opening round a very small crowd, given as 1,000, witnessed a 2-0 victory over Cheltenham Town, then two David Lee goals helped defeat Cambridge United 3-0 at Roots Hall in Round Two. Quarter Final opponents were Bristol Rovers and again home advantage was forthcoming for The Shrimpers, a Martin Carruthers goal setting up a semi-final clash with Swindon Town. The match against the Robins was locked at 1-1 when the match moved into extra time. Ties could be settled on the "golden goal" rule prior to the dreaded penalty shoot out, and Leo Roget duly obliged with a goal five minutes into the second period of extra time. This set up a two-legged Southern Section final against Brentford, who won both matches 1-2 to qualify for the Final against Northern section winners Port Vale.

Into the New Year, League form remained frustratingly inconsistent, 2-0 away wins being achieved at Leyton Orient and Brighton only to be undone by 0-3 home defeats by Halifax Town and Blackpool. More new signings arrived; Mark Rawle came from Boston United for £60,000 and combative midfielder Stuart Thurgood signed following a spell in Japan with Shimizu S-Pulse. Util-

ity defender Steve Broad arrived from Chelsea, initially on loan. Meanwhile, Martin Carruthers left for Scunthorpe United for a fee of £50,000, defender Leo Roget joined Stockport County and Trevor Fitzpatrick joined another ex-Shrimper, Pat Scully, at Shelbourne in Ireland.

In April, the home game with Mansfield Town had to be abandoned in tragic circumstances when referee Mike North collapsed and died on the pitch just before half-time. That month also contained arguably the season's most exciting encounter when a trip to Home Park saw a thrilling 3-3 draw with Plymouth Argyle, defender Rob Newman scoring a last gasp equaliser. The season petered out somewhat, although the restaging of the Mansfield Town game mattered little to either side given the sombre nature of the occasion and a 3-1 win for Southend saw the club finish in a comfortable eleventh place. A seasonal tally of 18 draws highlighted the side's failure to win a number of games when well placed to do so. The title was won by Brighton and Hove Albion while also promoted were Cardiff City and Chesterfield, despite the latter being severely handicapped by the deduction of nine points for eight instances of financial irregularities. Seventh place Blackpool won a place in the Second Division by winning the play-offs. Heading back to the Conference after nine seasons in the Football League were Barnet.

There was a three way tie for the top scorer title with Ben Abbey, David Lee and the departed Martin Carruthers all scoring on ten occasions. Consistent midfielder Kevin Maher, the hub of creativity in the side, was a deserving winner of the "Player of the Year" award.

2001/02- Rob is the New Man in Charge as Shrimpers are again Marooned in Mid Table

Despite making significant changes to his squad in the 2000/01 season, David Webb had a busy summer with plenty of new arrivals and departing players. Out of the club went David Lee, who left on a free transfer, signing for Hull City, injury plagued striker Neil Tolson, injury forcing him out of the professional game (he would soon resurface at non-League level with Hyde United) and dependable full back Martyn Booty joining Chesterfield. A clutch of out of contract players moved into the non-League circuit including Michael Black (Barking and East Ham United), Craig Edwards (Grays Athletic), Russell William-

Danny Gay

Back on the League front, several defeats raised eyebrows including reversals at Bristol Rovers (1-2) and Oxford United (0-2). On the flipside, a super Damon Searle strike gained a win at Rushden and Diamonds' Nene Park ground. After the home match against Cheltenham Town, when a Julian Alsop goal was enough to defeat The Shrimpers, David Webb resigned from the manager's job at Southend for the third time. On this occasion he cited health concerns as his reason for leaving; he had suffered with a minor heart scare in recent times.

Veteran centre back Rob Newman was asked to take care of the team, initially on a temporary basis. His early successes included a 4-2 win at home to Swansea City and a comfortable 4-1 success in the LDV Trophy First Round, defeating Conference side Stevenage Borough at their own Broadhall Way ground. However, interest in this competition ended in the next round when Second Division Bristol City won 0-2 at Roots Hall.

The team's inconsistency was frustrating for supporters and management alike and was amply illustrated in November when Macclesfield Town were defeated 3-0 at Roots Hall, only for the side to go down 0-1 at home to Plymouth Argyle in the very next outing. In the F.A.Cup First Round, a late Tes Bramble winner saw off the challenge of Luton Town at Roots Hall and the same player secured a replay in the Second Round 1-1 draw at Chesterfield. The Spireites were beaten in the Roots Hall replay to earn a home tie against Tranmere Rovers in the Third Round. A one man midfield master class from the visitor's Jason Koumas ensured a 1-3 defeat for Southend with Barrington Belgrave netting a consolation effort.

son (Chelmsford City) and Ben Abbey (Crawley Town).

Webb's new acquisitions included a trio of Yeovil Town players, Ben Smith, Gareth Risbridger and Barrington Belgrave, the latter costing a fee of £40,000. Another forward, Tony Richards arrived from Barnet for £36,000, tall centre back Leon Cort arrived from Millwall, while young goalkeeper Danny Gay was released by Norwich City and joined Southend as back up to Darryl Flahavan. Winger Jason Harris signed from Hull City but would leave for Nuneaton Borough after an unproductive three month spell. The most surprising capture was that of Dean Holness, a one time lower level non-League player who was better known for his role in Sky television football soap opera Dream Team.

The opening weeks of the campaign saw the first three games generate two wins and a draw. The best performance came at home to Halifax Town, a 4-1 success in which new boy Tony Richards scored a brace, although these would prove to be his only goals for the club.

The Worthington Cup saw the opening rounds being condensed down to one match affairs and Southend were drawn against Birmingham City for the second season running. The trip to St.Andrews resulted in a 0-3 defeat, Southend not helping their own cause after Phil Whelan conceded an own goal only sixteen minutes into the match. An ex-Shrimper took the opportunity to remind Shrimpers fans of his ability, Tommy Mooney returning to haunt the club with the other two goals.

Rob Newman

A CENTURY UNITED

In November, Steve Clark signed for the club from West Ham United for £50,000 while Marek Szmid (Manchester United) arrived on loan for a month and Roscoe D'sane arrived from Crystal Palace.

A trip to Spotland in December saw an interesting encounter, full back Steve Broad having given Southend a seventh minute lead against Rochdale, before goalkeeper Daryl Flahavan was sent off for handball outside the area. Danny Gay took over in goal and Southend's defence held out manfully for a much needed away win. The Boxing Day fixture against Rushden and Diamonds saw Southend two nil down at half time following a very poor display, but manager Rob Newman must have made the walls melt during the interval

Carl Hutchings

as The Shrimpers promptly rattled in four goals without reply in the second half.

In February, more transfer activity saw Carl Hutchings controversially decamp to Leyton Orient while Rio Alderton (Millwall) and loanee Brian Barry-Murphy (Preston North End) joined the club. Ian Selley rejoined for a second loan spell having previously done so in December 1996. Sadly, that month was a miserable one for results, a 2-1 home win over Bristol Rovers being the only success; a 1-5 reversal at Hartlepool United was especially humiliating, an injury crisis forcing manager Rob Newman to pick himself as an emergency centre forward.

The season wound down to a mid table finish, the highlight of the closing matches being a 3-1 win at home to Exeter City. The final three matches resulted in no wins and not even a single goal to cheer as the team signed off with a whimper. Another twelfth place finish was the result of a mediocre campaign, 21 defeats being a damning statistic, as was the meagre collection of only three away successes all season.

Tes Bramble was the only player to hit double figures with thirteen, with fellow front men Barrington Belgrave and Mark Rawle back on seven apiece. Goalkeeper, Darryl Flahavan, so often a barrier to more defeats, was voted "Player of the Year" although the award was greeted with boos at Roots Hall, the player having badly timed a transfer request after failing to agree a new contract. Halifax Town had the dubious distinction of being the only club to be automatically relegated from the Football League for a second time. Plymouth Argyle were worthy champions on 102 points, five ahead of Luton Town. Mansfield Town were also promoted despite being a distant third, while Cheltenham Town won the play-offs.

2002/03- Another Management Change Hampers Struggling Shrimpers

Manager Rob Newman had much work to do during the 2002 close season following the release of a number of players who were out of contract. Danny Kerrigan (Billericay Town), Marek Szmid (Sutton Coldfield Town), Ben Smith (Hereford United), Rio Alderton (Chelmsford City), Adam Wallace (Salisbury Town) and Scott Forbes (Canvey Island) all joined non-League clubs. Tony Richards, who had not figured under Newman or indeed since the early months of the previous campaign, has his contract cancelled by mutual consent and gave up the game altogether. Newman replaced these departees with more free transfer signings like Danny Maye, a left sided midfielder released by Port Vale and Jay Smith, a young central midfielder released by Aston Villa. Centre back Tom Jordan, son of former Scottish international Joe, was acquired from Bristol City, attacking left back Neil Jenkins arrived on a free transfer from Wimbledon, while the only fee

Neil Jenkins

paid out was £10,000 to secure the services of Graeme Jones from St. Johnstone. The striker had enjoyed a prolific spell at Wigan Athletic but had suffered more than his fair share of injuries.

The opening match of the season saw Southend show fighting spirit to twice come from behind to gain a draw at Hull City. Debutant Neil Jenkins levelled a Stuart Green opener but Stuart Elliott soon restored the lead for the Tigers. In injury time, Tes Bramble silenced a hostile Boothferry Park crowd with a last gasp equaliser. The enthusiasm gained from a hard earned point on the road was soon flattened by successive home defeats to Carlisle United (0-1) and Shrewsbury Town (2-3). A Worthington Cup First Round tie saw the seemingly annual early departure when Wimbledon won comfortably at Roots Hall by four goals to one.

The amount of regular defeats were becoming a concern; a visit to Rushden and Diamonds started badly when the team arrived late at Nene Park following a traffic accident and things went from bad to worse as Graeme Jones missed a penalty and the home side eased to a 0-3 victory.

After an injury time winner by Barrington Belgrave gave Southend the points at home to York City, the side then lost the next four League encounters; Swansea City (0-1) away, Hartlepool United (0-1) at home, Leyton Orient (1-2) away and Wrexham (0-1) at home. The defeat at Brisbane Road was particularly galling as Southend assisted their rivals greatly when defender Phil Whelan conceded a spectacular own goal.

Newman made some more signings to aid his ailing squad but none would make any real impact on the first team. Mark Salter arrived from Western League Frome Town, Tony Scully came from Cambridge United on a three month loan as did Danny Marney from Brighton and Hove Albion. The clubs' run in the LDV Trophy was restricted to just one match, Second Division Swindon Town running riot at the County Ground, winning 1-6, with Southend's misery compounded by the dismissal of Steve Clark.

More defeats arrived in November, the 1-2 reverse at Darlington at the end of the month being notable for Darryl Flahavan saving a penalty but then Tes Bramble sent a Southend spot kick way over the bar. In

the F.A.Cup, Southend needed an early own goal from Hartlepool United to get a draw at Roots Hall, but in an exciting replay, late goals from Leon Cort and Tes Bramble gained an unlikely away win. In the Second Round, Southend were drawn at home again, this time to Bournemouth of Division Two. It was a similar story to the previous round, Mark Rawle rescuing a draw to earn a re-match, but this time, the replay at Dean Court saw the home side running out 2-3 winners.

Back in the League, centre back Leon Cort achieved a remarkable hat-trick of headers against Boston United at Roots Hall in a 4-2 victory, thus becoming the first Southend hat-trick scorer since another unlikely player, Julian Hails, did so against Leicester City in September 1995.

As the League position of lower mid table was giving grave cause for concern, especially with two clubs now being relegated to the Conference, former Arsenal midfielder Stuart Robson was brought in to assist with first team training and another clutch of new recruits were signed. Daryl Sutch, an old acquaintance of Newman at Norwich City, joined in January while Ronnie Henry and Stephen Kelly, two young defenders, arrived on loan from Tottenham Hotspur. Irish international striker Dominic Foley joined on loan from Watford as did Gavin Strachan from Coventry City. Brett Darby, a striker released by Leicester, was offered a short term contract.

Darryl Flahavan

Worryingly, results failed to perk up to any real degree, indeed in the final thirteen matches of the season, only three were won and a sum total of nine goals were scored. Long before the season ended, and despite a 1-0 home win over Leyton Orient, Rob Newman was relieved of his duties. Robson, eyed with suspicion by many supporters, stepped in for three games before ex-Colchester United player and manager Steve Wignall was drafted in as Southend's ninth manager in ten years.

A desperate season wound down to a poor finish, the highlight of the closing months being a 3-0 win over Torquay United. Shrewsbury Town had already been doomed to the drop, but the second spot could be filled by either Exeter City or Swansea City as the seemingly perennial strugglers Carlisle United had manufactured another miracle escape and could not be caught by the Grecians. Swansea City had to ensure victory against Hull City to consign Exeter City to the Conference no matter what they achieved at home to Southend. The Grecians won 1-0 on a boiling hot afternoon at St.James' Park but Swansea's 4-2 success at the Vetch Field meant the win against the Shrimpers counted for nothing.

Champions were Rushden and Diamonds, who overhauled long time leaders Hartlepool United in the closing weeks, while Wrexham finished third. Gaining promotion through the play-offs were Bournemouth. Southend finished in a lowly 17th place in the table while Mark Rawle top scored with twelve goals in all competitions, one ahead of strike partner Tes Bramble; midfielder Kevin Maher set an unwanted club record with a seasonal collection of fourteen yellow cards. Stylish goalscoring centre back Leon Cort was the fan's choice as "Player of the Year".

2003/04- First Major Final for The Shrimpers as David Webb Makes Another Comeback

Steve Wignall had to perform the usual round of signing new players and releasing out of contract underachievers from the previous campaign. Phil Whelan was forced to retire, having failed to overcome a troublesome back injury while the veteran full backs Damon Searle and Daryl Sutch joined Chesterfield and Boston United respectively. Mark Rawle refused a new contract and opted to join Oxford United. The usual collection of departees to the non-League circuit included Stuart Thurgood (Grays Athletic), Mark Salter (Bath City), Steve Broad (Kingstonian), Barrington Belgrave (Farnborough Town), and Danny Gay (Hornchurch) while Tom Jordan and Brett Darby both signed for Southern League champions Tamworth. Goalkeeper Darryl Flahavan also left following the failure to negotiate a new deal, however, he would rejoin the club in September having failed to find another club.

Wignall's new captures included Mark Gower, a midfielder signed from Conference outfit Barnet for £25,000 and Drewe Broughton, a much travelled striker joining from Kidderminster Harriers. Jim Corbett, once signed by Blackburn Rovers for £500,000, left Ewood Park on a free transfer heading for Roots Hall. Defenders Mark Warren, Duncan Jupp, Jamie Stuart and Che Wilson arrived from Colchester United, Luton Town, Bury and Southern League Cambridge City respectively. Two new goalkeepers arrived, veteran Carl Emberson signing from Luton Town and youngster Ryan Robinson following Corbett from Blackburn Rovers, although both would eventually be eased out of the first team by the returning Darryl Flahavan. Midfielders Jamie Fullarton and Leke Odunsi signed from Brentford and Carshalton Athletic while former Aston Villa forward Michael Husbands was offered a deal following a successful try out in a friendly against Gillingham. In August, two new strikers were signed, Brentford's Leon Constantine was joined by Luke Nightingale of Portsmouth, although the latter would scarcely figure after being beset by injury.

A debut brace from midfielder Mark Gower saw Cheltenham Town beaten 2-0 on the opening day to temporarily quash the belief the many new faces would take time to gel. Sadly, the doubts proved well founded as six of the next seven League matches all ended in defeat and Southend exited the Carling Cup at the First Round stage when Swindon Town triumphed 2-3 at Roots Hall. The results failed to improve at all and following a 0-1 home defeat to Northampton Town in November, Wignall was shown the door.

Chairman Ron Martin asked David Webb to step into the breach on a temporary basis while a new man was sought and The Shrimpers favourite returned for a fourth, albeit brief, spell in charge. His first game was the Second Round LDV Trophy tie at Swansea City, the side having

Left to right: Mark Gower, Drewe Broughton, Mark Warren, Duncan Jupp.

progressed against Bristol Rovers in the previous round. Webb guided the side to a 2-1 win at the Vetch Field, not bad considering he had not realised the match was so imminent upon his arrival. The F.A.Cup tie against Canvey Island was next on the agenda and again the right result was achieved when Southend won a Park Lane replay 3-2, with Jay Smith grabbing a late winner in a game televised by the Sky. Webb then oversaw an abject 0-4 reversal at Yeovil Town before Steve Tilson, Youth Team Manager at Southend, was offered the job, initially on a caretaker basis.

As so often happens, the new man at the helm had an instant impact as Rochdale were systematically dismantled at Roots Hall to the tune of four goals to nil. Tilson soon made some changes to the squad, signing Mark Bentley for £10,000 from Dagenham and Redbridge, having been impressed with the player following matches against him during his Canvey playing days. Skilful front runner Lawrie Dudfield was signed from Northampton Town while Carl Pettefer and Nicky Nicolau were bought in from Portsmouth and Arsenal respectively. Wignall signings Emberson, Fullarton and Nightingale were all released.

In the F.A.Cup, success against Canvey Island bought a Second Round tie at home to Lincoln

Southend United line up before their first major cup final. Unfortunately, they froze on the day and lost 0-2 to Blackpool.

City and the Imps were duly dispatched by three goals to nil. The chance of a Third Round tie against a glamorous Premiership club did not exactly happen as The Shrimpers were paired with Conference side Scarborough. Jay Smith opened the scoring early for the home side but an unexpected replay was needed when the Seadogs levelled in the second half. Southend came undone on a dreadful pitch at Seamer Road when Mark Quayle scored late on to earn a Fourth Round tie against the might of Premiership Chelsea.

On the League trail, Southend enjoyed an eight match unbeaten run, Leon Constantine proving lethal in front of goal, hitting seven during that productive spell of points accumulation. In the LDV Trophy, Southend were steadily progressing through the rounds; Second Division Luton Town were the opponents in the Quarter Final and a super display at Roots Hall saw Southend win 3-0 with relative ease. However, in the semi-final, Southend were paired with Queen's Park Rangers, at the time runaway leaders of Division Two. The side put in the best display seen at Roots Hall for a number of years when Constantine, Steve Clark and two for Drewe Broughton saw an amazing 4-0 success. Rangers' manager Ian Holloway described the performance of his side as "humiliating". This set up a Southern Area fi-

nal with Essex rivals Colchester United. The first leg was at Layer Road and another inspired performance saw The Shrimpers bring a 3-2 lead back to Roots Hall. Nerves were put firmly on edge when, within ten minutes of the start of the second leg, Kemal Izzet levelled the aggregate scores for Colchester, but on the stroke of half-time, cult hero Drewe Broughton equalised and that proved to be the ticket to the final.

In their 98 years of history, the club had never qualified for a major final, the closest being a semi-final defeat to Notts County in the Anglo Italian Cup of 1994. Second Division Blackpool were the Northern Section winners and some 19,000 Southend supporters made the trip to the Millennium Stadium in Cardiff. A disastrous start saw John Murphy give Blackpool a second minute lead and the match seemed to get the better of The Shrimpers, most players appearing to freeze on the big day and it was no real injustice when Danny Coid netted a second in the 55th minute.

On the League front, form suffered from the distractions of the LDV run and after decent home wins against Scunthorpe United (4-2) and Darlington (3-2), the last five matches of the campaign failed to register a single victory. The side finished in a disappointing 17th place, although relegation was never a possibility as Carlisle United and York City had struggled all season. Doncaster Rovers were champions while Hull City and Torquay United were also promoted,

the latter with a last day win at Roots Hall. Fourth place Huddersfield Town made it up through the play-off lottery.

Leon Constantine was top scorer with 25 goals in all competitions, becoming the first player to exceed twenty goals in a season since Brett Angell in season 1991/92. Creative midfielder Mark Gower contributed nine goals during the season and won the "Player of the Year" award.

2004/05- Two More Finals as Tilly's Troops Gain Promotion

Although the success of reaching a major Final was no little achievement, the club must have been disappointed with the final League position of the 2003/04 campaign. Manager Steve Tilson however, must have been largely content with the majority of the squad as there was minimal movement in the transfer market during the 2004 close season. Tilson targeted some good quality players, bringing in local boy Adam Barrett from a stint at Bristol Rovers, while pacy forward Wayne Gray arrived on a free transfer from Wimbledon. Experienced Dutch goalkeeper Bart Griemink arrived as cover for Darryl Flahavan and two players returned to the fold after many years away, centre backs Spencer Prior and Andy Edwards. Departing the club were Leon Cort, who joined Hull City on a Bosman free transfer, top scorer from the previous campaign, Leon Constantine, who joined League One (the divisions having been renumbered again) Peterborough United after a protracted wrangle over a new contract, the unfortunate Leke Odunsi, who was forced to retire through an irreparable knee injury and the usual cluster of departees to non-League clubs; Steve Clark and Jamie Stuart (Hornchurch), Neil Jenkins (Crawley Town), Dave McSweeney (Billericay Town) and Mark Warren (Fisher Athletic).

The campaign did not start off too convincingly, with the team failing to win any of its opening five encounters, draws at Lincoln City and at home to Cambridge United being the only points accrued. More alarming was the meagre return of two goals in those games, one a penalty and the other coming from what was to prove the more than useful head of Adam Barrett.

ited to Barrett, his fourth in three games, but the defender later admitted to not touching the ball and the records debited David Bell with an own goal. A disappointing home defeat to Wycombe Wanderers (1-2) was followed by another success on the road, a 2-1 win at a desperately poor Notts County side, Adam Barrett maintaining his prolific run of headers with two more at Meadow Lane.

October began disappointingly with a very poor performance at Darlington which saw the homesters win by four goals without reply. Then, home wins against Boston United (2-1), Swansea City (4-2), Northampton Town (2-1) and Oxford United (4-0) saw the side storm up the table. The match against Swansea marked the debut of a new

Southend United 2004/05

A Barrett brace secured a win over Macclesfield Town at Roots Hall as August ended, the month also including a brave Carling Cup exit at West Ham United, Southend's profligacy in front of goal allowing the home side to win by two goals to nil.

September started with a 4-1 win at Rushden and Diamonds' Nene Park ground, the poor standard of the opponents allowing The Shrimpers to run riot as Lawrie Dudfield (2) and Tes Bramble scored the goals. The final goal was initially cred-

signing, Freddy Eastwood, who had arrived on loan from Grays Athletic with a view to a permanent deal. Rarely in the history of the club, arguably Collymore aside, has a single player made a more dramatic impact on the team. As the match kicked off the ball was played out wide on the left to Wayne Gray and his pacy cross was buried by Eastwood, 7.7 seconds into his Football League debut. The skilful front man would notch a memorable hat-trick before being substituted late on to a rapturous reception.

Freddy Eastwood celebrates two of his debut goals against Swansea City, (left) with Lewis Hunt and (right) with Wayne Gray.

In the cup competitions, the F.A.Cup was short lived as a tidy Luton Town side completely outplayed Southend at Roots Hall, winning at a canter by three goals to nil. Having had the taste of the LDV Final the previous season, the players set about this seasons' competition in fine, if nerve racking style, against Colchester United at Layer Road. Tes Bramble had given Southend the lead before Richard Garcia headed an equaliser in the second half. The match ended in a draw, The Shrimpers hampered by the harsh dismissal of Mark Bentley, and the dreaded penalty shoot out was called for. Miraculously, Southend rattled in all five penalties as Kevin Maher, Wayne Gray, Drewe Broughton, Lewis Hunt and Jimmy Corbett all found the net, the latter with his only touch of the game having been a late substitute. Colchester's Wayne Brown missed the target completely as Southend won 5-3 on penalties. In the next round, Southend's progress was somewhat easier, overcoming Shrewsbury Town at Roots Hall in an easy 4-1 victory. Good wins at Northampton Town (2-0) and at home to Swindon Town (2-0) saw Southend into the two legged regional final for the second year running and a superb Mark Gower winner saw Southend take a handy 2-1 lead into the home leg against Bristol Rovers. Goals from Wayne Gray and Freddy Eastwood meant a two all draw booked The Shrimpers a return trip to Cardiff for April.

On the League campaign, a 1-0 win over Chester City at Roots Hall in December saw Southend hit fourth place, a position they would hold until the start of February. The New Year games saw Southend defeat Rushden and Diamonds 3-0 at

Roots Hall and a trip to Aggborough bought a useful three points as Kidderminster Harriers were beaten 3-1.

Freddy Eastwood scored in six successive games during February and March as the side pushed for an automatic promotion slot. His attempt to equal Brett Angell's post-War record of seven straight matches was ended as he drew a blank at Cambridge United, although goals from Prior and Barrett secured the points at the Abbey Stadium. A win at home to Bristol Rovers (2-0) saw the club top the table and helped put the team in good spirits for the trip to Cardiff and their second successive LDV Trophy Final. The Northern Section winners were Second Division strugglers Wrexham and Southend put in a better performance this time, unfortunately being undone in extra time by goals from Juan Ugarte and Darren Ferguson. Meanwhile, Luke Guttridge joined the club from Cambridge United and would prove to be a useful acquisition.

The side had only five games to negotiate to ensure automatic promotion. The run did not start well with a 0-1 home defeat to Leyton Orient, but the long trip to Macclesfield Town saw two goals from Alan McCormack, on loan from Preston North End, secure a priceless away win. Another setback was suffered when Oxford United held out for a 1-2 home win after another lack lustre Shrimpers display, leading into a crunch game at home to leaders Yeovil Town; it was further despair as Phil Jevons scored the only goal of the game in front of a crowd of 11,735. Southend were still in third place and needed to match

Top left to bottom right: The captains line up before the kick-off, Freddy Eastwood shoots, Adam Barrett and Freddy Eastwood challenge for the ball, Freddy Eastwood shoots again, Mark Bentley tackles, Adam Barrett tries a flying header, Freddy Eastwood tries once more.

LDV Trophy Final - Millennium Stadium 10th April 2005

Swansea City's result on the final day of the season to ensure they took the 3rd and final automatic promotion place. Southend visited Grimsby Town while Swansea travelled to Bury and Swansea got off to the best possible start when Adrian Forbes opened the scoring in the first minute. The match at Blundell Park was tension filled and played out in desperately inclement weather for May. Michael Reddy opened the scoring for the Mariners but Freddy Eastwood notched an equaliser with twenty minutes left. Southend battered the Grimsby goal in search of winner, Mark Bentley coming closest with a shot that cannoned back off the bar. At Gigg Lane, despite a cruel rumour to the contrary, the Swans held on to win while Southend would have to settle for a play-off place. Swansea joined champions Yeovil Town and Scunthorpe United in the automatic promotion places whilst relegated to the Conference were Cambridge United and Kidderminster Harriers.

Having finished in fourth place, Southend were paired with seventh place side Northampton Town in the play-off semi-finals. After a goalless first leg at Sixfields, a lone Freddy Eastwood penalty separated the sides at Roots Hall, both matches being televised live on Sky Sports. This therefore ensured a third visit to the Millennium Stadium in the space of fourteen months, the opponents in the play-off final being Lincoln City, who had overcome the challenge of Macclesfield Town in the other semi-final. A modest crowd of under 20,000 gathered for the final and a tense match of few chances ensued. After ninety minutes, neither side had managed to score so extra time was needed. Interestingly, as Southend had wilted in the extended period against Wrexham earlier in the season, so Lincoln did so on this occasion. A tired looking Imps rearguard failed to clear a corner and Freddy Eastwood slammed the ball home from very close range. As Lincoln pressed for an equaliser, gaps opened up and after a thrilling run by Eastwood, the ball was laid off to Duncan Jupp who, having shown tremendous athleticism to run fully seventy yards to match Eastwood's run, coolly dispatched the ball into the corner of the net after a full 115 minutes of intense play. It was the full back's first goal for nearly ten years and a deserving winner. After a stuttering run in which many supporters thought the side had blown their chances, promotion to the Second Division was secured after seven seasons in the basement.

Freddy Eastwood enjoyed a magnificent first season, scoring 24 goals in only 38 starts. He

Adam Barrett

Freddy Eastwood shoots,
Freddy Eastwood scores,
Freddy Eastwood celebrates.

League Two Play-off Final, Millenneum Stadium, Cardiff

28th May 2005   Southend United 2 Lincoln City 0

Top left: Duncan Jupp celebrates his goal.
Middle left: Kevin Maher collects the Playoff Winners Trophy.
Bottom left: The team celebrate in the dressing room after the game.
Top right: Kevin Maher lifts the Playoff Winners Trophy.
Bottom right: Mark Bentley gets soaked while being interviewed on Sky.

was ably assisted by Wayne Gray on 13 while goalscoring centre back Adam Barrett chipped in with ten very valuable goals; on three occasions he registered braces. In a gruelling campaign, midfielder Carl Pettefer started all 58 matches, whilst out of several candidates, Adam Barrett's outstanding contribution to a successful campaign was rewarded with the "Player of the Year" trophy.

New recruits to the club were Mitchell Cole, like Eastwood joining The Shrimpers after a stellar season with Grays; he cost a fee of £45,000. The only other signing before the new season was that of striker Shaun Goater, the former Bermudan international, who had scored over 250 goals in an extensive career at the top end of the English game, being talked out of retirement by Tilson for one last fling.

Southend United 2005/06

2005/06 – Mighty Shrimpers Storm Straight Through to Win League One

Having achieved so much in the 2004/05 campaign, manager Steve Tilson was adamant that the players who had served him so well would be offered the chance to prove themselves at a higher level, so summer transfer activity was relatively quiet. Leaving the club was Michael Kightly, still a youngster but having failed to live up to not inconsiderable early promise; he joined Conference side Grays Athletic. The always inconsistent Tes Bramble was released to join Stockport County, while injury prone winger Jim Corbett signed for Margate. Nicky Nicolau refused to sign a new contract and opted to join Swindon Town while Lawrie Dudfield rejoined Northampton Town.

Many supporters predicted a season of stability in the new division as the club were operating with the smallest squad in the division. The step up in quality appeared immediately obvious as Port Vale came to Roots Hall in the opening game and outplayed their hosts to win 1-2 despite a spectacular overhead kick from Wayne Gray briefly offering a lifeline for The Shrimpers. However, optimism was restored when Southend went to Valley Parade and came away with a 2-0 victory against Bradford City, an ill tempered game seeing the hosts reduced to ten men early on before home striker Dean Windass was accused of biting Darryl Flahavan in a challenge that went unpunished by the referee. A debut goal from Shaun Goater ensured a share of the points at Walsall.

Top to bottom: Efe Sodje celebrates his goal against Brentford.
Freddy Eastwood scores one of his hat-trick at Chesterfield.
Freddy Eastwood gets another at Chesterfield.
Shaun Goater notches a header at Chesterfield.
Shaun Goater celebrates at Layer Road.

In the First Round of the Carling Cup, a young Southampton side completely outplayed Southend at Roots Hall, returning home with a 0-3 success. An early setback was suffered in the home game with Huddersfield Town when Eastwood was dismissed for violent conduct, when in truth the challenge was little more than a petulant shove. The club appealed the referee's decision but their chagrin was offended further when the player had an additional match placed on his three match ban, the Football League citing a "frivolous appeal" for the lengthened suspension.

Essex rivalry was re-established at League level for the first time in fifteen years, so the encoun-

ter at Roots Hall with Colchester United in September was eagerly anticipated. A brace from Shaun Goater and a brilliant individual goal from newcomer Mitchell Cole ensured a famous 3-1 victory, the derby success prompting a run of seven more wins, catapulting the side to the top of League One following a 1-0 home victory over former European champions Nottingham Forest. Boosting Tilson's attacking options was the arrival of Rotherham United's Jamal Campbell-Ryce, although his acquisition on a three month loan would result in a drawn out saga throughout the rest of the campaign. An ongoing battle with the Millmoor club would only be amicably resolved when a new board took over the Yorkshire club,

Campbell-Ryce finishing the season on loan to rivals Colchester United, although officially a Shrimper.

In the Football League Trophy, back to its generic name after sponsors Leyland Daf Vans went into administration, the spectacular success of the previous two campaigns was not repeated as a First Round exit was suffered in an embarrassing showing at Rushden and Diamonds. The F.A.Cup First Round draw saw a visit to Underhill to take on Barnet, fresh from their restoration to Football League status. A very early Freddy Eastwood strike separated the sides, but in Round Two, Eastwood netted again in a surprise 1-2 defeat at home to Milton Keynes Dons.

On the League trail, a memorable Freddy Eastwood hat-trick at

Top: Wayne Gray scores the Championship-clinching goal against Bristol City.
Centre: Wayne Gray celebrates.

Ashton Gate saw a hapless Bristol City side swept away on their own ground. Back at Roots Hall, a clash between first and second produced a crowd in excess of 11,000 as Southend took on Swansea City. In a battle billed as Eastwood versus Trundle, it was the audaciously talented Liverpudlian who held sway as the Swans triumphed 1-2. The defeat was the first in a run of seven games without a win as a minor slip down the table occurred and the harbingers of doom predicted further gloom to come.

The transfer window re-opened in January and a very shrewd signing of the experience centre back Efetebore Sodje was made for an undisclosed fee from Yeovil Town. Sodje would play 13 games for Southend, during which the side would concede only five goals, a true testimony

Bottom: Kevin Maher lifts the League One Championship Trophy.

to his impact on the side. Lee Bradbury, once a £3,000,000 signing for Manchester City, arrived on a short term deal from Oxford United. The New Year had started well, with a 2-1 win at Blackpool and Sodje's debut saw a hard earned point gained against Oldham Athletic at Boundary Park. Sodje's home debut saw him open the scoring in the game against promotion chasing Brentford, as Southend coasted to a 4-1 triumph, Bees manager Martin Allen nearly having a coronary caused by his touchline remonstrations at his badly-beaten troops. A goalless draw at Tranmere Rovers meant Colchester United briefly took top spot from The Shrimpers, although leadership was regained the following week when Swindon Town were beaten 2-0 at Roots Hall.

There was a poor showing on a pudding of a pitch at Griffin Park, Southend's 0-2 defeat to Brentford not being aided by Duncan Jupp's early own goal. However, faith was restored when another away trip produced one of the best Southend matches in recent memory. The Shrimpers were a goal down at halftime to Chesterfield at Saltergate when once again Freddy Eastwood took over the game in breathtaking fashion. A controversial penalty levelled the game and a truly brilliant second gave the visitors the lead. The homesters, galvanised by their perceived injustice of the red card shown for the penalty, quickly rattled in two more to retake the lead but Eastwood's third then levelled proceeding before the veteran Goater nodded a dramatic winner.

Another eagerly anticipated away trip was the visit to the hopelessly inadequate Layer Road for the return meeting with Colchester United. Ticketing arrangements had seen many Southend fans forced to purchase tickets for Colchester supporters' areas, although fortunately the match passed without incident. On the field, Southend totally outclassed their high-flying opponents, rattling in three first half goals without reply. So commanding was the lead, Tilson gave a debut to young midfielder Franck Moussa, a late substitute for Luke Guttridge, who became one of Southend's youngest ever debutants.

As with the previous campaign, Southend stuttered badly in the run-in although, rather helpfully, so did many of their challengers. Home defeats to Gillingham and Doncaster Rovers (both 0-1) really put pressure on The Shrimpers as the other clubs gained ground rapidly. A brave draw in a titanic encounter at Swansea City's new Liberty Stadium put Southend's destiny back in their own hands, the final day meant a Southend win would

ensure the title, although anything less could let arch rivals Colchester United in should they triumph at Yeovil Town. A tension filled Roots Hall watched as Bristol City were a much different proposition from the ragged outfit that had surrendered so meekly to The Shrimpers at home earlier in the season. A tight match meant Southend fans were glued to radios and mobiles for news from Huish Park, but fortunately Colchester could only manage a goalless draw and a late winner from substitute Wayne Gray ensured only the second championship win in 86 years as a member of the Football League.

Joining Southend and Colchester in the Championship were Barnsley, who defeated Swansea City in the play-off final. Going down to League Two were Hartlepool United, Milton Keynes Dons, Swindon Town and Walsall. Freddy Eastwood topped his opening season's tally with a magnificent 25 goals, which also earned him a share of the Divisional Golden Boot, Billy Sharp of Scunthorpe United equalling his total. The veteran Shaun Goater, who bowed out of the game in fine style, contributed eleven goals while Wayne Gray added nine including the championship clincher. The contest for "Player of the Year" had a variety of candidates, from a magnificently consistent Darryl Flahavan in goal to the inspirational captain Kevin Maher and the midfield dynamo Luke Guttridge. However, due to being the difference maker in so many games, the outstanding Freddy Eastwood was a truly deserving winner.

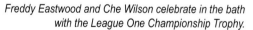

Freddy Eastwood and Che Wilson celebrate in the bath with the League One Championship Trophy.

Southend United 2006/07

Season 2006/07- Season of Struggle Ends in Relegation despite Glory of Man U Triumph

Manager Steve Tilson rang the changes to his squad despite the success of the last campaign. Shaun Goater and Bart Griemink had retired, the latter after a long battle against a catalogue of knee injuries. Right back Duncan Jupp and midfielder Mark Bentley opted to join Gillingham, feeling their chances in the Championship would be restricted. Wayne Gray also opted to stay in League One by joining Yeovil Town. Carl Pettefer, reduced to a bit part role in an injured plagued 2005/06 season attempted to revive his career at Conference side Oxford United. Veteran centre back Andy Edwards also moved into the Conference with Aldershot Town.

Tilson bolstered his squad with the some expensive acquisitions. Highly regarded centre back Peter Clarke was prised from Blackpool for £250,000, while striker Billy Paynter cost £200,000 when joining from Hull City. Simon Francis had impressed Tilson with displays for the Football League under-21 side and £70,000 was sufficient to secure his signature from Sheffield United. Both Matt Harrold (£90,000) and goalkeeper Steve Collis arrived from Yeovil Town, although Collis would miss three months of the campaign with appendicitis. Left back Steve Hammell, a full cap for Scotland, arrived from Motherwell while young striker Gary Hooper followed the well trodden path from Grays Athletic, joining former colleagues Freddy Eastwood and Mitchell Cole at Roots Hall. Tilson's final summer capture was the former England striker Michael

Ricketts, arriving on a free transfer after a lean time at Leeds United.

The campaign started reasonably brightly, an opening day victory against Stoke City coming courtesy of a Freddy Eastwood penalty. A second home win followed against a poor looking Sunderland team but away defeats at Crystal Palace, Queen's Park Rangers and Leicester City made for a stark introduction to life in the Championship, a division replete with more than a dozen ex-Premiership clubs. The Carling Cup made for some light distraction as wins at Bournemouth and at home to Brighton and Hove Albion set up a first ever visit to Elland Road against Leeds United. Meanwhile, Southend cut their losses with Michael Ricketts, injury prone and seemingly unwilling to get anywhere near fit; the former Premiership star was released from his contract.

Back in the League, progress was depressingly slow, successive defeats to Cardiff City (0-3), Derby County (0-3) and Coventry City (2-3) plunged Southend into the bottom three by early October, a position they would not escape for another five months. The Carling Cup tie at Leeds resulted in an excellent 3-1 win for The Shrimpers, 18 year old Gary Hooper impressing with a well taken brace. Scenes of unprecedented fervour occurred when Southend were drawn at home to Manchester United in the fourth round, the first ever competitive match between the two clubs.

The Sky Sports cameras arrived at Roots Hall for the anticipated mauling by the Carling Cup holders of the Championship basement dwellers; a

Southend held out for the most famous victory in the club's one hundred year history. Their exploits garnered headlines around the world.

Back on the League trail, the run without a win extended to an unwanted club record of seventeen matches until a late Alan McCormack goal secured the points in a 2-1 win against Southampton. McCormack had joined the club on loan from Preston for the second time, a move that would be made permanent when the transfer window reopened in January. Prior to that game, the

home defeat against a ten man Hull City in the League had dumped The Shrimpers to the foot of the table. Household names abounded, as the Red Devils fielded ten internationals including golden boys Wayne Rooney and Cristiano Ronaldo. However, in one of those inexplicable changes in football fortune, the side without a win in twelve League matches battled hard and the Southend boys to a man held firm, with Darryl Flahavan in incomparable form. Chances for an real upset were few and far between so when youngster David Jones upended Jamal Campbell-Ryce about 22 yards from goal, the set piece took on real importance. The angle favoured the left foot of Hammell but with his trademark self confidence and audacity Freddy Eastwood stepped up and planted an unstoppable right footed shot into the top corner, past a helpless Tomasz Kuszczak in the North Bank goal. Despite intense pressure,

Top to bottom:
Freddy Eastwood scores against Manchester United.
The scoreboard says it all.
The players celebrate after their famous victory.

195

Essex derby at Colchester United ended in controversy and a 0-3 defeat following the comical dismissal of Kevin Maher, who was swiftly joined in the dressing room by Mark Gower, injudiciously tackling the culprit immediately after getting booked for arguing over Maher's red card. 2006 closed with a dismal run of three League games without a goal and the Carling Cup run came to an end when the quarter-final was settled with a hotly disputed Jermaine Defoe goal from an off-side position, minutes from the end of extra time.

In November, Tilson secured the services of Spanish midfielder Arnau Riera on loan from Sunderland, although injury reduced his contribution to next to nothing. Money from the Carling Cup run was made available to fund the purchase of Irish striker Richie Foran from Motherwell for £200,000 during the January transfer window, and rumours of Freddy Eastwood's impending departure to any number of Premiership clubs thankfully proved unfounded.

January proved to be an historic month for the club. After more than twenty different planning applications to the Borough Council since 1985, when a relocation to a new stadium was first mooted, the club successfully applied for a new facility. On January 24th, Southend Borough Council unanimously voted for permission to build a 22,000 capacity stadium and associated retail outlets on the Fossetts Farm site on Eastern Avenue. The new site application also depended on Rochford Borough Council passing plans for an overflow car park and a flood attenuation facility which abutted onto land under their control. The gathering of Rochford Council the following night saw the motion successfully passed by a majority of thirteen councillors. However, the plans were subsequently pulled in for a public enquiry by Secretary of State Ruth Kelly.

The same month brought the F.A. Cup Third Round with a home tie against Barnsley. A late and hotly disputed equaliser meant the tie was taken to a replay at Oakwell after a 1-1 draw at Roots Hall. The Shrimpers made no mistake in the second match when goals from skipper Kevin Maher and Lee Bradbury earned a comfortable 2-0 victory. The draw gave Southend another trip to White Hart Lane, although this time they were no match for their Premiership rivals, a Freddy Eastwood penalty was scant consolation as Spurs ran out easy winners by three goals to one.

January's League fixtures provided a glimmer of hope when wins were secured at Cardiff City

(1-0) thanks to a truly spectacular strike from Lee Bradbury, followed by a very much unexpected 3-1 triumph at League leaders Birmingham City. A home win against West Bromwich Albion ensured nine points were obtained from just four League fixtures. The next month also provided some cheer for battle hardened Shrimpers fans, fellow strugglers Queen's Park Rangers being put to the sword by five goals to nil, skipper Kevin Maher rounding off a virtuoso performance with a brace of goals in injury time. However, a run of four games without a win immediately after the Rangers game sent the chances of survival back into the distance.

The Shrimpers entered March with renewed vigour when a home draw with Leicester City and a win at Portman Road saw Southend gain ground on faltering rivals. A win against freefalling Burnley at Roots Hall would take the Shrimpers out of the bottom three for the first time since October and a dull encounter was settled when two minutes into injury time, Richie Foran latched onto a weak defensive header to secure a vital three points. Sadly, hopes faded somewhat when a late David Healy equaliser prevented another Roots Hall win against rock bottom Leeds United and a dismal display at Hull City ended in a 0-4 thrashing. The arrival from Charlton Athletic of lithe forward Lloyd Sam did little to lift the circling gloom, the youngster returning to The Valley after two substitute appearances when he contracted a hernia injury.

As the end of season approached, Tilson's men floundered and five of the final six games of the season ended in defeat. The only bright note was an excellent 3-2 win at play-off chasing Preston North End, with three high quality goals from Kevin Maher (2) and Alan McCormack, the latter a spectacular volley which clinched the Echo's Goal of the Season award. The defeats consigned The Shrimpers to a quick return to League One. Once mighty Leeds United were also relegated, even before a ten point deduction was imposed for entering administration due to financial difficulties. The League table did not lie, six home wins all season and a miserly tally of 47 goals were indicative of a long hard season at the elevated level. The supporters chose captain Kevin Maher, consistently influential throughout the campaign, as the Player of the Year with Darryl Flahavan a close runner up having turned in some outstanding performances in goal. Veteran centre back, Spencer Prior, received a warm ovation from Southend supporters upon the announcement of his retirement to the warmer climes of Australia.

THE GROUNDS OF SOUTHEND UNITED

Roots Hall Main Stand 2006.

The Grounds

Roots Hall (1906 to 1914)

The Roots Hall from which Southend United's ground is named was an 18th century house on West Street, set in four acres of pastoral land. A previous house called Rowards Hall had stood on the same location from the 16th century. The last owner of Roots Hall was Daniel Gossett, who acquired the estate in 1876; he lived there for twelve years until 1898 and within a year of selling up, the house had been demolished and the whole area was turned over to recreational use. Initial occupants were Prittlewell Cricket Club, although the site was available to all-comers who could afford the rental. Southend Athletic briefly played there until moving back to the Marine Park ground on the seafront. Athletic were contemplating a move back to Roots Hall in 1906 when the newly formed Southend United secured a three year lease on the ground.

A pitch length embankment was created on the west side of the ground and local company Ducat's, owned by the father of prominent local player Andy Ducat of Woolwich Arsenal and England, were engaged to construct a grandstand on the eastern side of the ground. The timber stand was 122 feet long, straddled the halfway line, and had room for 200 on wooden benching. The new ground was not without its limitations however; the embankment often became very muddy during inclement weather and the players had no changing facilities other than a small hut. After the first month, the hut became a tea bar when a more suitable changing arrangement was provided by the directors. The pitch, although possessing a greatly admired surface, had a substantial longitudinal slope from south to north. It was enclosed by a white picket fence which in hindsight had been constructed too close to the touchlines, with a clearance of a mere seven feet. This was deemed dangerous to spectators and players alike with the occasional over-enthusiastic crowds causing crushing at the front. The initial 1906/07 campaign saw the directors sublet the ground to Southend Corinthians, who staged home games when United were away. This was primarily to offset the capital required for launching the club.

The first major improvements came in 1909 when the grandstand was re-roofed, although its construction meant a more obscured view due to the large number of weight-bearing struts used. The supporters funded the erection of a new stand on the west side of the ground in the same year. This was the first in a long line of donations and assistance provided by the supporters. This committee was chaired by Mr Tom Byford and Mr. A. Cooke was engaged as architect. The initial plan was for 125 yards of cover, around the same length as the grandstand opposite. The new cover would have a central section subject to an additional admission charge of 3d, with the remainder of the stand to either side being free to patrons. The first estimate of £350, which had concrete terrace covered with a roof supported by steel stays, was deemed too expensive and Mr Cooke submitted an alternative plan using timber in place of steel at a projected cost of £137. The committee then heard a counter proposal from Mr.Bremner's firm whose estimate came in under £100. This was accepted by the committee and then plans for raising the finance were discussed. The supporter's committee secretary, Mr. A. Howard, declared £10 had been raised by a whist drive; the remainder would be paid to a group of guarantors from the admission charges raised from League matches. The clubs' directors agreed the scheme on the proviso that admission from English Cup ties would go to club funds.

Despite the improvements, any crowd over 5,000 caused severe congestion problems and the record gate of 7,200 in November 1909 for the visit of Northampton Town generated reports of several crushing injuries to spectators. The complaints of visiting journalists were heeded when a press box was added in 1912. Previously, reporters had to make do with an open gantry mounted on the grandstand roof.

The club's headquarters remained at The Blue Boar Public House whilst the administrative office was in West Street, so the need to fully enclose the ground was considered an unnecessary expense. In July 1910, the open nature of the ground allowed the first manned flight in the borough; George Barnes took off in his Hunter monoplane in front of a crowd of 2,000 but strong winds saw him promptly crash in the adjacent field.

In September 1912, the pitch was hired out by the Southend Rugby Club when they entertained London Welsh. In 1913, the board tried to purchase the ground from its owner, George Radford, but a settlement could not be reached, the club under-

Top to bottom: The original Roots Hall entrance can be seen here on the left, in West Road.
The layout of the Roots Hall pitch, with fencing to hold back the crowd.

A   CENTURY   UNITED

taking some improvements to the ground during the summer of 1913. New entrances were created in Gosset Avenue to ease congestion and the supporters stand was re-roofed. The war intervened and relations between owner and tenant worsened following a dispute over rent arrears; football had been suspended and the club sublet the ground to the army for recreational activities. The grandstand suffered substantial damage to the roof during a gale in 1916 and Radford decided to cut his losses and auctioned off the assets. Messrs A. Provost and Sons held the auction and the stand was dismantled and sold for £92 10s to a local timber merchant, Flaxmans, to repair buildings damaged in a Zeppelin raid. A total of 1,100 feet of fencing from the pitch raised £15 10s and the tea hut just £2 10s. Even the shirts, footballs and corner flags went under the hammer. The pitch was soon dug up and turned over to allotments to aid the war effort.

The Kursaal (1919 to 1934)

Marine Park was opened on Southend seafront in the 1890's for leisure pursuits and boasted a beautiful flower garden and a trotting track. The tracks were popular in Victorian times for mod-

The Kursaal ground, with the watershute clearly visible.

est athletic games, cycling and carriage driving or "trotting" as it was known. The trotting track at Marine Park was sufficiently large to have a football pitch in the middle; dressing rooms were located at the Beach End of the ground. The first team to play there were Southend-on-Sea Football Club in 1897/98; they wore white shirts and blue knickers, the team changing its name to Southend Athletic in 1900 and becoming the pre-eminent team in the borough, albeit in the sedate surroundings of the South Eastern League. The ubiquitous domed entrance building was opened in July 1901 and the area became known as The Kursaal.

The ground was unused following Athletic's demise and in 1910 the trotting track was dug up and part of it was rented out as an amusement park, the venue being renamed Luna Park. In 1912 an American, Clifton Jay Morehouse, purchased Luna Park, restoring the venue to its former name of The Kursaal, having been impressed by a similarly named leisure facility in Ostende. A wealthy man, Morehouse had made his fortune by inventing the gas radiator in the United States. The Morehouse family would fund additional attractions at The Kursaal such as a scenic railway, and convert the domed building into a magnificent ballroom. Clifton installed his

Above: View of the first Greyhound meeting at The Kursaal, from the Watershute.

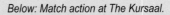

Below: Match action at The Kursaal.

The Kursaal - Home of Southend United 1919 to 1934

A   CENTURY   UNITED

Above: Work being carried out on the club accomodation in the Western Stand.

Below: A composite view of The Stadium under construction.

The Stadium - Home of Southend United 1934 to 1955

son, Captain David De Forest Morehouse, as managing director of the business; his vision was to own the most popular attraction in the country. However, funds were not limitless and when he heard that the local football club were bereft of a home ground, he enclosed the north-east corner of his Kursaal grounds as a football pitch. He became actively involved in the revival of the club following the Great War and a lease was signed, initially for a year, in April 1919 with an option to purchase the site for £9,500 in the future.

A large amount of work was needed to ready the ground for the first season, in fact the work was so hectically scheduled, a pre-season friendly against West Ham United had to be postponed. Entrances were built at the north and south ends, with access being gained from Woodgrange Drive and Beresford Road, Cumberland turf being laid on the pitch area, providing a most suitable surface. Embankments were constructed around the ground using 5,709 individual turfs although this nearly ended in disaster during the particularly arid summer of 1919. The new pitch was enclosed by a fence with a nine foot clearance, wary of the problems at the Roots Hall ground.

There were no stands or covered accommodation but the pavilion in the south-east corner was luxurious. It housed a boardroom, clubhouse and

Crowds pack The Kursaal for the 1922 League game against Newport County. Again, the watershute can be seen in the background of the top picture.

gymnasium and the changing rooms had large communal baths and a hot geyser; the match officials were afforded their own facilities as well. The rear of the pavilion had living quarters which were rented to United's trainer, Jack Campbell. During the first season, two small temporary stands were erected on either side of the ground, and at the end of that initial season it became obvious that Southend would be part of the Football League's expansion plans, so more security was needed and a four year lease was agreed. Once the club's new status was confirmed, the board engaged established stadium builders Humphreys of Knightsbridge, to construct a grandstand at The Kursaal. The London firm were contractors for the great Scottish stadium constructor, Archibald Leitch, who was consulted on the project. The eastern, Arnold Avenue, side was chosen and a 1,500 seater stand, costing £5,000, was erected with terracing and other improvements for an additional £3,000 also being provided. A further £500 was spent on increasing the size of the bankings on the remainder of the ground.

The board boasted The Kursaal could hold 23,000 spectators although only 11,661 turned up for the big Cup tie that season against Tottenham Hotspur, the club blaming the low turn out on disparaging remarks in the London papers about the facilities on offer at The Kursaal. The most

A CENTURY UNITED

remarkable feature of The Kursaal was opened in 1921, when the world famous Waterchute was erected behind the Woodgrange Drive end of the ground. Surely there cannot have been a more unique backdrop to a Football League venue.

By 1924, the ground was sufficiently admired to host Essex County representative matches and the Essex Senior Cup final of that year was contested between Ilford and Grays Athletic at The Kursaal. The ground's all-time record gate of 18,153 was established in February 1926 for the F.A.Cup visit of Nottingham Forest. The next innovation was the introduction of greyhound racing to The Kursaal, the track being illuminated by 50 floodlights of 1,000 candlepower each. However, the experiment played havoc with Bill Fitch's immaculate pitch and the wear and tear caused four games of the 1927/28 campaign to be postponed. There were also further problems with local religious groups vehemently opposed to Sunday race meetings. However, the main issue was with the Football Association, who frowned upon dual use grounds and in particular dog racing, standards of playing surfaces and fears regarding player hygiene being their main concerns. In March 1928, the Football Association decreed that the Electric Hare Greyhound Racing Company must leave The Kursaal ground by June 1928 or the football club would be expelled from the Football League. The experiment lasted a year and despite decent crowds, was a financial loss making venture.

A new stand was constructed on the west side of the ground by local firm, Flaxmans, and was completed by December 1928. It was 180 feet long and could house 3,000 spectators under its 25 foot high roof. It was a further six years before the supporters committee funded the installation of glass screen ends to lessen the voracity of sea winds howling through the stand. Some of the grass banking was also terraced with concrete.

The club was in a state of upheaval at the end of the 1933/34 season, with a major shake up in the boardroom leading to the appointment of former England captain, David Jack as manager. The new board were determined to usher in a new era in the clubs' history and decided to break the lease with The Kursaal's owners and move across town to the newly opened Southend Stadium. The cessation of the lease cost the club £250 and The Kursaal kept all the stands and other facilities. David De Forest Moorhouse had died in November 1934 and The Kursaal's trustees decided to abandon the football ground. The

West stand, scarcely six years old, was ripped up and replaced by the Cyclone Roller Coaster, purchased from the Brussels Exhibition. The pitch was dug up and the East stand stood in solitude for a further two years before being ignominiously dismantled in the summer of 1936.

The Kursaal as an entertainment site boomed until the late 1970's, when it went into an alarming decline. The amusement park was demolished and the area sold for housing, Prospect Close covering the old pitch. The ostentatiously domed ballroom was only saved by a preservation order, as The Kursaal lay forlorn and unloved for two decades, before investors bought the site and opened a bowling alley and leisure facility, restoring the old building to its former glory.

Southend Stadium (1934-1955)

There could scarcely be more of a stark contrast between the Southend Stadium and Southend United's previous ground at The Kursaal. The old ground was cramped and atmospheric, while the new home was capacious, airy and, because of the greyhound track, somewhat desolate. The new ground also suffered from a problematic pitch, the clay based surface was inherently rutted and the thinly sown grass left the pitch bone hard in summer and a quagmire in the wet months of winter and spring. The Stadium was originally planned in 1932, primarily for the use of greyhound racing. Interestingly, a previous initiative to introduce the sport to The Kursaal ground four years earlier had ended in dismal failure. Planning permission was obtained for the site of a former brickworks off Grainger Road and the owners set about raising the capital needed by launching a share issue. This was massively oversubscribed and everything was in place for building to begin.

The new venue was officially opened on May 19th 1933 and at this stage consisted of the large main stand on the west side of the ground, replete with 2,000 tip up seats, and extensive uncovered terracing all around the remainder of the ground. Over at The Kursaal, there were changes afoot in the boardroom when long time chairman and leading light, David de Forest Morehouse stepped down in March 1934 and Captain Tom McEwan was appointed to the board. McEwan was heavily involved in the Greycing Club, owners of the new Stadium and with the lease on The Kursaal barely two years from expiry, it was no

little surprise when Southend United applied to the Football League for permission to change their home ground for the 1934/5 season. Despite previously showing reticence towards dual purpose venues, the Football League authorised the move on 4th June 1934 and an initial seven year lease was signed, although this was soon extended to twenty-one years.

In the summer of 1934, the main priority was the pitch, which was marked out, north to south, with the dimensions of 112 yards by 72 yards. The pitch was sown with 25 bushels of grass seed and it took sufficiently well for the initial game to take place on 25th August, this being a reserve fixture against Tottenham Hotspur. A huge crowd in excess of 8,000 turned up to witness a 2-6 victory for the Londoners. The inaugural first team game saw a 2-1 triumph over Aldershot on 29th August in front of 7,456 spectators and three days later, 11,389 (£680 receipts) gathered for the visit of Exeter City.

Initial impressions of their new home were favourable and the 1934 Football Encyclopaedia described it as "one of the best grounds in the south". The huge 6,500 capacity Sutton Road terrace was soon covered with a large, cavernous roof, enlarging the covered capacity to some 9,000. The Stadium also now boasted three entrances on the Grainger Road, Maldon Road and Sutton Road sides of the ground. Entrance fees were fixed at a shilling for standing and two shillings for seating, however the pitch was a huge problem following heavy rain throughout October. Groundsman Bill Fitch laid extensive herring bone drainage at a cost of £1,000 to try and remedy the situation, but this turned out to be little more than a temporary fix. In the summer of 1935, the seeded pitch was dug up and replaced with 28,000 meadow turfs bought from a farm in

This aerial view of The Stadium has been doctored slightly, with the addition of the words "Southend United F.C." to the roof of each of the stands.

Fambridge. Even though this vastly improved matters, the clay base meant the pitch would always be bumpy in dry weather and periodically stones from the old brickworks would force their way to the surface.

Attendances were excellent and when the club drew Tottenham Hotspur in the F.A.Cup Third Round on 11th January 1936, an all time record gate was set. Gate receipts of £2,913 were raised from a huge crowd of 22,862, although contemporary reports in the Southend Standard state the figure to have been 23,634, a further 2,000 eager spectators being locked out when the game kicked off. The Stadium soon became a mecca for local sports, with greyhound meets being staged twice during the week and on Saturday evenings, boxing matches also becoming an occasional crowd puller. During the 1937/38 season, crowds were beginning to dwindle and the sole reason was discontentment with the view provided of the action. Furthermore, there was a growing nostalgia among supporters for the old ground; The Kursaal's remaining edifice, the East Stand, had been demolished in the spring of 1938. The players were also unhappy with the impersonal surroundings and could rarely feel any 'heat' generated by a partisan home crowd, a valuable asset resulting in many famous victories at the cramped Kursaal.

Both the Southend board and The Stadium owners were considering ground improvements when the site was requisitioned by the Army Officer Training Corps in August 1940. The football club was relocated to Chelmsford City's New Writtle Street ground and within a month, all greyhound racing was suspended due to the hostilities. The club returned in June 1945 to find all pre-war records had been destroyed and considerable damage had been sustained by the pitch.

Substantial returfing was needed and a claim of £271 was successfully claimed against the War Department. Repairs to the perimeter fence were also needed to prevent unobstructed free views.

Post war crowds boomed for both sports, but the beginning of the end for football came in 1953 when The Stadium owners refused to enter negotiations with the football club regarding the provision of floodlighting. With the twenty one year lease due to expire in 1955 and the deep unpopularity of the venue with supporters, the board began to search for a new site which eventually resulted in the club's return to Roots Hall in August 1955. The 1954/55 season was to prove the last for Southend United at The Stadium, av-

competition. However, Pegasus fell into a dispute with The Stadium owners and were unceremoniously booted out of the ground at the season's end. They started the 1972/73 season with an 1-11 defeat at Tiptree United and promptly folded when an abortive attempt to use the Melbourne Stadium at Chelmsford foundered.

The 1970's saw a downturn in attendances for greyhound racing, not helped by several dog doping scandals which saw numerous bookies turn their back on the races at Southend. The Stadium owners also failed to convince the council to grant permission for an additional track to host speedway and stock car racing. By the 1980's, the venue became a huge monument to yesteryear,

erage crowds went down to under 9,000 and the final match was staged on 30th April 1955, when Brentford were beaten 3-2. Football continued for many years, with The Stadium staging local finals, as well as United's reserve and youth team matches throughout the late 1960's and early 1970's.

Senior football returned for the 1971/72 season, when local amateur side Pegasus Athletic (formed in 1968) successfully applied to join the new Essex Senior League. They rented The Stadium to stage home games, groundsharing with Southend United's 'A' team, who competed in the same

Clearing the snow for the Christmas Day match against Ipswich Town in 1948.

with crowds rarely topping 400 for greyhound racing and the only well attended event being the annual fireworks display. Pleas to the council to rescue the venue were ignored and the last race meeting was held on Boxing Day 1985. The site was sold to developers and within two months The Stadium was razed to the ground. On the site now stands Currys and Matalan superstores, with the only indicator to its sporting past being the road that bisects the old pitch, which is called Greyhound Way.

New Writtle Street, Chelmsford City FC (1940-45)

When The Stadium and the town itself became a restricted area due to the War, the club had to look elsewhere to stage their wartime matches. The immediately obvious choice was Chelmsford City's New Writtle Street ground. Then a Southern League club, Chelmsford's stadium in those days was vast with a capacity of some 18,000. A match-by-match rental of £10 was agreed, although Southend United were soon in debt to the tune of £310. Crowds were often less than 1,000 and the club called a halt to their tenancy in October 1941, a few months into their second season.

It has to be said that Southend took somewhat of a liberty with their hosts, what with unpaid rent, missing equipment and, to cap it all, divesting them of their manager, Harry Warren, when football resumed after the War. In truth, he had already been looking after The Shrimpers during those wartime matches.

New Writtle Street was opened in February 1925 and four years later the main stand, costing £1,500, was opened. In 1938, a large barrel-roof covered terrace, opposite the grandstand, was opened and the grandstand was doubled in length in the same year. In the immediate post War years, the ground was augmented with substantial terracing.

The all-time record gate at New Writtle Street was set just after the War when 16,807 saw the Southern League local derby with Colchester United. Floodlights were first erected at the ground in 1960 and later still, in 1962, there was a cover put over the terrace at the Wolseley Road end. The much loved barrel-roof "barn" stand was

dismantled in 1989 as part of an ill conceived plan to rotate the pitch through ninety degrees. This was to facilitate a rebuilding programme but the club had planning permission declined. This, in truth, was the beginning of the end for New Writtle Street and with City's debts mounting, they were forced out of the ground when it was sold to property developers. The last first team match at the ground was against Clevedon Town on August 16th 1997, the club being forced into groundshares with Maldon Town and Billericay Town. New Writtle Street met with an almost indecently hasty burial, being razed to the ground in July 1999. Housing and an Esporta sports centre now stand on the site.

Roots Hall (1955 to date)

A lot had happened to the site of the clubs' first ground since its days as a World War One allotment. It was sold to the Southend Gas Company after hostilities ceased and the company plundered the vast amount of sand on the site and sold it during the post-war building boom. After the resources were exhausted, the area was bought by the Gas Light and Coke Company; the former sand quarry being used as a dumping ground for all sorts of rubbish.

Immediately after World War Two, the area had a rough circular track laid around the perimeter and was used for a short while for the local cycle speedway team, the Prittlewell Pirates. In 1948, the site was bought by Southend Borough Council.

When the problems at Southend Stadium became insurmountable, around February 1951, the club began the search for a new ground. The local council suggested a return to Roots Hall as the lengthy spell of quarrying had left a natural bowl shape which would save on costs. The Supporters Club established a trust fund to raise the lion's share of the capital.

The fund raising scheme was not without controversy. The Supporters Club chairman Nevil Newitt was soon at loggerheads with the rest of the Trust's board. His major concern was the ambitious scale of the proposed stadium; he would resign his position before the project began in earnest, stating that it would be a "retrograde step". Eventually, the project was indeed downsized to a 35,000 capacity stadium costing a projected £100,000. In March 1953, Chairman Major

New Writtle Street, Chelmsford.

Roots Hall: Work to start within a few days

WITHIN a few days bulldozers will arrive at Roots Hall, and work on the first stages of Southend's new permanent home will commence.

The bulldozers will start to clear the site and make the preparations for the installation of drainage.

Meanwhile, offers of assistance continue to flow into the Supporters' Club and to the United, and one additional offer of material help comes from Messrs. Stanfords to supply the sanitary equipment at the Roots Hall ground.

Blues ultimately plan to have their grandstand the entire length of the pitch, and this will be fitted with approximately four to five thousand seats.

The total capacity of the ground will be just over 40,000.

Under the conditions of the donation of £1,000 from Mr. Teddy Grant, the terraces behind one of the goals will be covered, but eventually United hope to have covered accommodation in all sections of the ground.

Admission to the ground will be gained from entrances at Shakespeare Drive, Victoria Avenue (entrance also for cars), Roots Hall Avenue, Fairfax Drive, etc. There will be accommodation for 300 cars.

Surveying the land which is to be Southend United's new home, on Tuesday, were Mr. A. I. Hay, M.B.E. (Chairman of Southend United), Mr. Arthur Drewry (President of the Football League) and Mr. Harry Warren (Southend United's manager).

The local paper announcing the start of work at the Roots Hall site.

Hay and Alderman Bert Smith approached new groundsman Sid Broomfield, saying they had a "little job" for him.

Broomfield and a small band of men began clearing the Roots Hall site in preparation for building to commence. During the clearing of the site, ro-

Roots Hall from the air - Spring 1955.

man coins and burial pots were discovered, attesting the site's ancient history. The Trust had acquired the site a year previously for £11,258. Within months, the site was ready and players and supporters alike pitched in to make the thousands of concrete blocks for the proposed main stand on the east side of the ground.

final terrace was a huge success, with a capacity of 13,500.

The project was successfully completed on time and under budget at £73,997, every penny bar a £5,000 grant from the Football Association having been raised by the Trust Fund. The club kicked off the 1955/56 season at the new ground and a crowd of 17,700 saw the ribbon cutting ceremony conducted by F.A. Secretary, Stanley Rous, F.A. Chairman Arthur Drewry and the president of the Football League, Arthur Oakley. Norwich City provided the opposition and the Southend players put on an excellent display, comfortably winning 3-1.

In April 1955, Boulton and Paul of Norwich were engaged to erect the steelwork for the North and West stands. Sid Broomfield and his crew of two men had the arduous task of terracing the open South Bank. The 72 step "Kop" terrace was a real labour of love, often the men would return to work in the morning to find their work undone by heavy overnight rain, which would sweep mud down the banking. In the end, the

In 1957, the Roots Hall pitch was dug up to lay new drains. The pitch was then re-seeded, leaving it with a look of Wimbledon (tennis, not Plough Lane!)

MONDAY, May 20th.—Work goes ahead at Roots Hall on the playing pitch. A rubber-tyred grader is spreading 2,400 cubic yards of mixed clinker and ash over the old pitch.

Initially, the grandstand was half its eventual size, financial constraints not allowing the extensions to the full pitch length until 1967; the extension joints to the roof can clearly be seen to this day. Similarly, the North Bank cover extended to the width of the penalty area and the West Stand only had one of the eventual two barrel roofs, covering the rear section of terrace. Again, the 1967 improvements saw the final construction completed. The intervening years saw unexpected expenditure on a new pitch, the original often being reduced to a quagmire, with much merriment being made in the press of "Southend-on-Mud". Furthermore, in 1959, £15,000 was spent on floodlights so the club could join the fad for evening kick-offs.

Total expenditure on the ground by 1967 had reached £100,268 but the construction won widespread praise. So much for Nevil Newitt's parting shot that "no-one on the project knows anything about building".

In August 1973, the club seriously considered a £1.1 million project for a new cantilever grandstand but the plans were eventually shelved. The ground remained untouched until 1989 when The Taylor Report and the subsequent revision of the 1975 Safety of Sports Ground Act meant the end for the South Bank. The Taylor Report into the Hillsborough Disaster had recommended that terrac-

son wasted no time in selling off the majority of the unusable terrace. Flats, called Priory Court, were erected in no time at all and Sid Broomfield must have been heartbroken to see his hard work destroyed. The South Bank was reduced to the front fifteen or so steps of terracing; it was indeed a sorry sight.

In the early 1990's, the wooden bench seating in the main stand extensions were replaced with black plastic seats that had previously been in service at the Stretford End of Manchester United's Old Trafford ground. The provision of plastic seating saw the end of cushion rental at the ground which had seen a steady trade for more than three decades.

Building the Priory Court flats on the South Bank.

As Southend progressed to the First Division, the

ing at senior football grounds should become obsolete by 1994. The Safety of Sports Ground Act, itself a legislation on the cause and effect of a crowd disaster at Ibrox Park in 1971, and its accompanying Guide to Safety at Sports Grounds, "The Green Guide" meant that the traditional British football ground would become a legacy of the past. The Green Guide correctly recorded that all crowd fatalities in British grounds, with the notably exception of Valley Parade which had been caused by a discarded cigarette in an ineptly stewarded wooden stand, had been due to overcrowding on terraces. The guide stated that the safety of spectators could be monitored most effectively in all seater stadiums. As a consequence, the capacity of the South Bank terrace was savagely cut to 1,500 and Chairman Vic Job-

Taylor Report required the club to convert Roots Hall into an all-seater stadium. The West Stand and North Bank had blue and yellow tip up seats bolted onto the existing terracing. The North Bank became the away end and suffered from a lack of consideration for sightlines when the seating was installed.

The reduced South Bank terrace was replaced in 1994 when Dutch firm Ballast-Nedam built a double tier 2,000 capacity stand that was christened the Frank Walton Stand. In the same year, unsightly flat roof extensions to the West Stand saw this stand connected to the North Bank and the new South Stand.

Roots Hall now and then.
Top: The South Stand with Priory Court looking over it; the pitch has just been re-seeded for the 2006/07 season.
Middle left: Mowing the hallowed turf.
Right: A familiar sight; market day at Roots Hall.
Below: Roots Hall from up the floodlight pylons.

A CENTURY UNITED

THE MANAGERS OF SOUTHEND UNITED

Bob Jack

Bob Jack

Aside from being a high quality outside left, Bob Jack was a great manager and administrator. Although Jack would play a vital role in Southend's formative years, his name is undoubtedly synonymous with Plymouth Argyle. His playing career started with Alloa Athletic in 1893 and within two years he moved to England with Bolton Wanderers, a club two of his sons, David and Rollo, would also serve with distinction. After 125 games for Bolton, Jack moved to Preston North End in August 1901, and around the same time showed his early interest in administration by becoming an executive member of the Player's Union. After a short stay at Deepdale, followed by similarly brief stints at Glossop North End and Burslem Port Vale, Jack began his long association with Plymouth in August 1903, becoming their first registered professional player. After 106 games for Plymouth, his third season at Home Park was marred by a dispute with the board of directors. He took little persuading therefore, to move to the new Southend club on July 30th 1906.

He used himself sparingly as a player in his first two seasons at Roots Hall, although his vast experience was brought to the fore when the club gained promotion to the top flight of the Southern League in 1908. Whilst in the area, he became a prominent bowls player with the Westcliff club and was Essex singles champion for a time. Later, in 1922, and ignoring his birthplace, he would represent England against Scotland at the sport.

After two Southern League Division Two titles and decent showings in the First Division, it was no surprise that Plymouth came back with a lucrative offer to return to Home Park as manager. Although having officially retired from playing that summer, Jack was forced to don his boots again in December 1910 when Argyle were short of players at Coventry. Under his guidance, Argyle were Southern League runners up in 1911/12 and a year later swept to the title. Jack would remain at Plymouth for the next 28 years, masterminding Argyle's ascent to the Football League after the Great War. They became a formidable side under Jack and incredibly were runners up in the Third Division (South) for six straight seasons between 1921 and 1927, when only the champions were promoted! By the 1929/30 season, Jack and the Argyle board were coming under pressure from supporters and local press who, fed up with being the also-rans, were vocally suggesting that the club were lacking ambition and worse, were deliberately faltering in the home straight. Jack hit back in the only way he knew how, by producing a devastating Argyle team which swept to the championship, winning 30 of their 42 games, coasting in by seven points from runners-up Brentford. Although struggling in their first Division 2 campaign, Jack would guide Argyle to fourth place in 1931/32 and fifth in 1936/37.

Bob Jack retired at the end of the 1937/38 campaign and moved back to the Southend area. Unable to resist the lure of the game, he took an offer from his son David, then Southend manager, to become chief scout at the club. Bob Jack died in the town in May 1943 at the age of 67, and after his long association with Plymouth, it came as no surprise that his ashes were scattered at his beloved Home Park.

George Molyneux

George Molyneux

Charged with filling the sizeable boots of Bob Jack, George Molyneux came with impeccable credentials, four full England caps and a wealth of experience with Southampton and Portsmouth. He had arrived at Roots Hall in the club's inaugural season at the age of 31, as captain on a salary of £2 10s a week. He represented the club with distinction, rarely turning in a poor performance and his enormous frame often intimidated opponents before a match started. However, his stint as player-manager was a disaster, with the club eventually losing their First Division place, although Molyneux retired in February 1911 as his performances had begun to falter as his advancing years, he was by now 36, caught up with him. He turned out for Colchester Town for a couple more seasons and also represented the Army during World War I, when he enlisted as a private.

He worked in Southend for many years at the Corporation Sewage Works in Eastern Avenue, before his death from cancer of the tongue in 1942. George Molyneux was the first of a number of great players who failed to make an impact as a manager of Southend United.

Joe Bradshaw

Joe Bradshaw started his playing career with Woolwich Polytechnic and later played for West Norwood before stepping up to the Southern League with Southampton. A short spell followed with Woolwich Arsenal before his father, Harry Bradshaw, then manager of Fulham, signed him for The Cottagers in March 1904. Although a reasonably talented winger, Joe hardly figured in the first team during his five seasons at Craven Cottage and a subsequent campaign at Chelsea in 1909/10. A brief stint at QPR followed before he joined Southend in February 1911 as player-manager.

His versatility was quite remarkable, playing in all outfield positions, as well as in goal, during his first campaign. In his first full season at Roots Hall in 1912/13, Bradshaw, now retired from playing, guided The Shrimpers back out of the murky waters of the Southern League Division Two as runners-up to Cardiff City. During his reign at Roots Hall, Bradshaw was hampered by the club's severe financial position and also had to deal with a fractious and divided board of directors. The 1914/15 season was overshadowed by the darkening cloud of war against Germany, but Bradshaw soldiered on manfully, even donning his boots again when numbers were short. The club shut down at the end of that campaign and the manager joined up in May 1915. Nobly, he left the club without pursuing the not inconsiderable amount of £50 owed to him in wages.

He survived four years of grim battle in various postings in France and in Theux, Belgium; it was from the latter that he sent a communication to the club's directors urging an early revival of the club once the hostilities had ceased, also offering any help needed once he was demobbed.

Bradshaw returned to England on leave in April 1919, only to find the same board had given the manager's job to Ned Liddell, despite protests from supporters who vocally stated their displeasure at Bradshaw's treatment. Southend's loss was all too apparent when his successor lasted barely a season in the post. Bradshaw himself was free to accept the manager's job at Swansea Town, which he did in June 1919. He oversaw their elevation to the Football League and in 1924/25 guided them to the Championship of the Third Division (South) by a point, following a tense battle with Plymouth. The following campaign saw The Swans reach the semi final of the F.A.Cup, although they lost 0-3 to Bolton Wanderers at White Hart Lane; their League campaign also bore fruit, with a highly creditable fifth place finish in Division Two.

Bradshaw's success in Wales saw him lured to Fulham for the 1926/27 campaign, but he spent three largely disappointing years at Craven Cottage and during that time The Cottagers were relegated to Division Three (South). He was dismissed at the end of the 1928/29 season, despite his side netting over 100 goals, and ironically was replaced in the hot seat by Ned Liddell. His last post in football management was a four season stint at Bristol City, but a desperate campaign during 1931/32, which saw The Robins win only three games, resulted in his services being terminated.

Disillusioned with the game, Bradshaw spent the rest of his career in the insurance industry. Contemporary writing cites Bradshaw as one of the most courteous, knowledgeable and enthusiastic managers, which makes the board's decision to overlook him in favour of Liddell back in 1919, all the more perplexing.

Edward 'Ned' Liddell

A consistent centre-half or left-half during a lengthy playing career, Ned Liddell started out in his native North East. He turned out for East Bank Black Watch, Whitburn and Seaham Harbour before making the long journey south to join Southampton in December 1905. He spent the 1906/07 season with Gainsborough Trinity (then in the Football League), before a six season spell at Clapton Orient saw him play over 200 games for the O's. During this spell, Liddell was selected for a representative match for London against Birmingham.

He joined Southend in October 1913, but after less than a year at Roots Hall he moved to Arsenal in September 1914. This was his last campaign as a player, although he remained on the backroom staff at Highbury throughout the war, his age meaning he avoided the call up. During the war he represented Essex in matches against the Army, captaining the side on one occasion.

MR. E. LIDDELL,

late of Woolwich Arsenal and Clapton Orient F.C.'s, writes:—

"The store of energy and stamina required under the trying conditions of first-class football matches needs constant replenishing and for this purpose I have proved that there is nothing to equal Phosferine.

When playing for Woolwich Arsenal and other clubs it was essential that I should be fit and in the pink of condition, and I found that a course of Phosferine during training was all that was needed. It quieted jangling nerves and braced up the whole nervous system in a way that was really wonderful.

At the first approach of that run-down feeling that comes to us all at times I have found by resorting to Phosferine the threatened breakdown is banished, and restored health and strength soon follow."

Secretary, Southend F.C.

65, Beedell Avenue, Westcliff-on-Sea.

This well-known Professional Football Player states that he always experienced the most complete sense of "fitness" and the greatest increase of endurance whilst taking a course of Phosferine—Phosferine banished the "used up" limp feeling which naturally succeeded the struggle of his many hot contests, and also enabled him to be certain of the nerve force to uphold himself with distinction.

When you require the Best Tonic Medicine, see that you get

PHOSFERINE

A PROVEN REMEDY FOR

Influenza	Neuralgia	Lassitude	Nerve Shock
Nervous Debility	Maternity Weakness	Neuritis	Malaria
Indigestion	Premature Decay	Faintness	Rheumatism
Sleeplessness	Mental Exhaustion	Brain Fag	Headache
Exhaustion	Loss of Appetite	Anæmia	Sciatica

Phosferine has a world-wide repute for curing disorders of the nervous system more completely and speedily and at less cost than any other preparation.

Ned Liddell used his fame to endorse Phosferine whilst manager at Southend United.

The board of Southend United somewhat surprisingly offered Liddell his first managerial post in April 1919 and he readily accepted and oversaw the first campaign at the club's new home, The Kursaal. Amongst his first signings was Lot Jones from Manchester City, who would become the club's first international. A modest season saw the club gain election to the Football League when the Southern League First Division was voted in "en bloc". During the close season, Liddell talked to QPR about their vacant position as manager and hastily signed a deal before Southend United came back with a better offer. He spent four seasons at Rangers, before returning to Southend as assistant to Ted Birnie in the 1924/25 season. He then accepted the chief scout post at Fulham, before replacing Joe Bradshaw as manager in May 1929. However, he had an uneasy relationship with the chairman John Dean and was dismissed in April 1931.

He scouted for West Ham between 1931-36, before being offered the manager's job at Luton Town. It was at this club he achieved his only managerial success when The Hatters captured the Third Division (South) title in 1936/37, two points clear of runners-up Notts County. He left Luton in February 1938 and subsequently scouted for Chelsea, Portsmouth, Brentford and Spurs during a lifetime in the game.

Tom Mather

Tom Mather did not play football but had a sound background in administration. He was initially assistant secretary at Manchester City, before serving Bolton Wanderers in a similar capacity. He was promoted to manager in 1915, but after the war found he had no job to go to when Bolton installed Charles Foweraker in his place. In truth, he had been manager in name only, as he had been called up to serve in the Royal Navy and Foweraker had deputised in his absence. His wartime adventures included a lucky escape from enemy U-boats in the Atlantic Ocean.

It was something of a surprise when Mather beat off stiff competition to secure the Southend job in May 1920. Sadly, his first season at The Kursaal was a disaster, with the team finishing 17th in Division Three (South), despite reaching the third round of the F.A.Cup. The following season was worse, with Southend propping up the table throughout the campaign and, despite being presented with a gold watch by the board before

Ned Liddell

the F.A.Cup tie with Worksop Town, it was no surprise when, in January 1922, Mather became the first Southend manager to be dismissed. Unbeknown to Mather his successor, Ted Birnie, was watching from the stand at Worksop. His dispirited team failed to turn things around and, at the end of the season, the club had to apply for re-election to the Football League.

Mather joined Stoke City as manager in October 1923 and oversaw some very dark days at the Victoria Ground. The Potters finished sixth in Division 2 at the end of that campaign, but severe financial problems meant many of his team had to be released and others were forced to take pay cuts. Some of his players, angry at the turn of events, turned up at the ground and launched a violent attack on the club's offices and dressing rooms. However, better days dawned and despite relegation in 1926, the club won the Division Three (North) title at the first attempt in 1926/27. The club narrowly missed out on promotion to Division One in 1931/32, when they finished two points adrift of runners up Leeds United, the failure being tempered by the events of February 10th 1932 when, after a lengthy personal crusade, he was able to persuade an ardent Port Vale supporter to allow his son to sign for the rival club; the youngster's name was Stanley Matthews.

Mather guided Stoke to the Second Division championship in 1932/33 with a single point margin over runners-up Tottenham Hotspur. In 1934, Stoke reached the F.A.Cup quarter final but lost to Manchester City at Maine Road, which attracted a record gate of 84,569. Mather joined Newcastle in June 1935, but found his hands tied by a troublesome board of directors. When the 1939/40 season was abandoned after only three games due to the outbreak of war, Mather left St. James Park.

After the war he became manager of Leicester City, but resigned before the season's end. He finished his career with a nine month stint with Kilmarnock in Scotland, although this too proved unsuccessful.

Ted Birnie

Ted Birnie

Described as a commanding left half with excellent heading ability, speed and also a good reader of the game, Ted Birnie began his playing career in the North East with Sunderland Seaburn. Having represented Northumberland County, he also trained as an engineer before his football career progressed sufficiently for him to join Newcastle United in June 1898; subsequently he spent seven seasons with The Magpies. After a season with Crystal Palace, a fee of £100 took him to Chelsea and after four seasons at Stamford Bridge, he spent his final campaign as a full time player at Tottenham, although he never truly recovered from a broken leg sustained at Chelsea.

In August 1911 he accepted the post of player-coach at the German club Mulheim however, with war looming, Birnie returned to England in early 1913 to become player-manager at non-League Newcastle City. He resurfaced in August 1919 as assistant trainer and scout of Sunderland, followed by a brief spell as trainer at Rochdale.

He joined Southend in January 1922, but could not help the club from finishing bottom of the table, seven points adrift of Exeter City. Southend improved immeasurably under Birnie's stewardship, especially after he brought former Chelsea colleague Bill Cartwright in as trainer. The team had a brilliant F.A.Cup run in 1925/26, reaching the fifth round, the furthest the club had ever been in the competition and he turned the team into promotion candidates, finishing third behind Fulham and Reading in 1931/32.

Birnie gained a reputation as a shrewd judge of a player's ability and his thrifty nature and financial acumen meant he was able to retire at the age of 55 in May 1934. However he was beset by ill health and died at Christmas the following year.

Three views of David Jack.

David Jack

One of the greatest English players of the era, David Jack initially showed little interest in following his father's footsteps into the professional game and indeed, had a promising job in the Civil Service. However, with his father being manager of Plymouth Argyle at the time, he played as a youngster for Plymouth Presbyterians, then represented the Royal Navy during World War I before making a few guest appearances for Chelsea.

When football resumed after the hostilities it was no surprise that the 20 year old signed for Plymouth. His undoubted talent caught the attention of Bolton Wanderers, who paid £3,000 for his services in February 1921. During his time at Burnden Park he gained fame as the scorer of the first Wembley F.A.Cup final goal, against West Ham United in 1923, and also scored the only goal when Bolton again won the F.A.Cup against Manchester City three years later.

In October 1928 Arsenal caused uproar when, just two years after the austerity of the General Strike, they parted with £10,890 for Jack's signature, comfortably a new British record transfer fee. Under the great Herbert Chapman, David Jack and Arsenal became the best player and team in the land. He was part of the feared Arsenal front line, which also included Cliff Bastin, Alex James, John Hulme and Jack Lambert. The Gunners won the F.A.Cup in 1930, Jack's third winner's medal, and won the League championship in 1931, 1933 and 1934.

David Jack captained England, winning nine caps, and represented the Football League on five occasions. His playing career finished with 301 goals from 595 games and at the age of 35, and having learned much from the great Herbert Chapman, Jack was looking to move into management. A flurry of interest ensued, but Southend beat off all competition and Jack signed on for an annual salary of £750, by far the highest in the Third Division, his fond memories of his childhood in the area helping the Shrimper's cause. The enormous salary precluded him from playing for his new club as the maximum wage for a player at the time was £8 a week. He did play in several friendlies and also gained dispensation to play at Crystal Palace in an F.A.Cup tie in November 1936.

His five seasons at Southend were average at best, with tenth place in 1936/37 the team's best showing. Although he shared his father's enthusiasm for talent scouting, he lacked his father's shrewd eye and indeed, when Bob Jack retired from the Plymouth job, his son was quick to enlist his services as chief scout.

When the Second World War broke out, Jack took a job with Barclays Bank and handed over control of the team to Chelmsford City's manager Harry Warren, as the clubs were sharing the New Writtle Street ground. Jack then managed a greyhound track in Sunderland before becoming Middlesbrough's manager in September 1944. His best campaign at Ayresome Park was 1950/51 when Boro finished sixth in the First Division, thirteen points adrift of champions Tottenham Hotspur. He resigned in April 1952 and became a publican in Islington before returning to football in August 1953, beginning a two season stint at Dublin outfit Shelbourne. He then returned to the civil service, working for the Air Ministry, however, he was not done with football or Southend and was working for the club as a part time scout when he died in London in September 1958, aged only 59.

Harry Warren

Harry Warren was born into a footballing family. His father Ben won 22 caps for England and

Harry Warren

made 250 appearances for Derby and nearly 100 for Chelsea. Tragically, Ben Warren died from a brain tumour at the age of 37 in 1917. Harry Warren was only 11 at the time and soon took a job in the office of the local mine, where his interest in administration was garnered at an early age.

His own playing career started with Gresley Rovers and he later signed for Blackpool in 1924. Never more than an average player, Harry Warren then played for Exeter City, Merthyr Town and Sheffield United, mustering only 33 league appearances between them. In 1930 he joined Notts County, but was never selected for first team duties.

His league career came to an end at the age of 29 in 1931 when he accepted the player/manager post at Southern League Folkestone, however his playing career was soon curtailed by a knee injury. He adjusted to the job superbly and gained a reputation for harnessing local youngsters and turning them into Football League standard players; in his time as manager, 25 footballers moved into the Football League from the Kent club.

These players included the likes of Viv Woodward (Fulham), Alex McIntosh (Wolves), Jack Acquroff (Hull), Jack Vinall (Sunderland) and Bob Iverson (Tottenham). In April 1939, Harry Warren joined Chelmsford City as manager, impressed with their ambition of attaining Football League status. During the war, Southend's coastal location meant it was a restricted area and the club entered into a groundsharing arrangement with Chelmsford at New Writtle Street.

Warren took over managerial duties of The Shrimpers in August 1940 with the club in disarray. Warren refused to take a salary and occupied his time working for the Ministry of Food, the Home Guard and was also a volunteer fire officer. With his zeal for organisation, Southend could not have a better man in charge when normal footballing activities resumed in the 1946/47 season. Southend developed into a magical team with great goalscoring prowess and he guided the club to third place in 1949/50 and fourth place in Division Three South in 1955/56, his last in charge, as well as reaching the fifth round of the F.A.Cup in 1951/52.

His huge respect among the Southend faithful meant he could have had a job for life, but somewhat surprisingly he opted to join Coventry City in June 1956. It was to prove a disastrous move and his roster was soon split in a wage dispute. His calm, collected manner failed to gain the respect of the dressing room and his transfer budget was severely restricted. He was sacked in September 1957 and was replaced by Jimmy Hill.

His partnership at The Stadium with Wilf Copping was seamless; Warren, the aloof genial general, and Copping the motivating man manager. It was no surprise that considerable success and respect was achieved.

Warren returned to the town following his dismissal at Highfield Road and used his vast administration experience in working for the firm of solicitors Bates, Son & Braby. He regularly watched The Shrimpers until his death in 1968 and his well attended funeral was testament to the esteem the town held him in.

Eddie Perry

Eddie Perry

Eddie Perry started his playing career with the works team Tredomen Engineering, a mining company, having gained local celebrity status as a violinist and vocalist. It was whilst with Rhymney that the young centre forward was offered a trial with Swansea Town. Although unsuccessful, he later joined Merthyr Town and Bournemouth and Boscombe Athletic, without ever breaking into the first team. Perry finally made his League debut with the short lived East London outfit Thames Association and his decent scoring record of 16 goals in 25 appearances secured a move to Fulham in May 1931. Although never a regular at Craven Cottage, he scored 36 goals in just 64 appearances.

In November 1936, a transfer fee of £1,500 took him to Doncaster Rovers, Perry making over 100 appearances before the outbreak of World War II. It was during his stint at Belle Vue that he belatedly won three full caps for Wales. During the war he played for Fulham once again and guested for Brentford in the 1942 London War Cup Final; he remained at Fulham in various capacities after the war, including those of coach and chief scout and was responsible for the discovery of the great Johnny Haynes. He also spent two summers in Norway as an emissary from the FA, trying to revive the game in the formerly Nazi occupied territory.

Perry joined Southend in July 1956 with the onerous task of filling the not insubstantial shoes of the ever popular Harry Warren. His record was reasonably successful, although missing first team games in favour of scouting missions did not sit too well with the board and supporters alike. His enthusiasm for developing young talent could not be faulted and under his watchful eye the club established a youth team for the first time in 1957. However the club made a poor start to the 1959/60 campaign and it was no real surprise when Perry resigned in February 1960, citing lack of team building funds as his reason. This was denied by the board, who referred to the £12,000 spent on Chelsea duo Les Stubbs and Alan Dicks, who were far from being regulars in The Shrimpers line-up. Perry then resumed his favoured career of scouting, once again with Fulham.

Frank Broome

A useful centre forward, Frank Broome began his playing career with local outfits Boxmoor United and Berkhamsted Town. He moved into the professional game with Aston Villa in 1934, becoming a good goalscorer at Villa Park, netting 78 goals in 136 league outings before war halted his career. He played one wartime international and won seven full England caps, including the infamous 1938 match against Germany in Berlin, when the FA forced the English players to give the Nazi salute to a watching Adolf Hitler during the German national anthem.

After the war he was free to join Derby County and in October 1949 moved on to Notts County. In his first season at Meadow Lane he won the Division Three South championship, and although used as a winger at County, he still contributed a decent goalscoring total, and was invited to join the FA tour to Australia in 1951. He then had a short spell at Brentford before joining Crewe Alexandra in October 1953. His playing career finished with a short spell at Shelbourne towards the end of the 1954/55 campaign, and he returned to Notts County as assistant/trainer in June 1955, taking over as caretaker manager in January 1957. At the end of that season, Tommy Lawton was brought in as manager with Broome stepping down to assistant; he found this position awkward and resigned in December 1957. He then spent two years in charge at Exeter City before joining The Shrimpers, on a week to week contract, in May 1960.

Despite signing five new players in the summer, the club started poorly and Broome was the target of abuse from supporters who feared his side lacked the passion for a fight. Southend's chairman, Major Hay, agreed and Broome was dismissed within four months of the new season; Hay stated Broome's time at the top had left him out of touch with the lower division clubs.

Disillusioned, Broome moved to Australia and was very successful as manager of Bankstown in New South Wales, and Sydney club Corinthians. He returned to England in May 1967 to become Exeter's manager for a second time. He departed St. James Park in February 1969 and spent much of the 1970's coaching in the Middle East.

Frank Broome

Ted Fenton

Ted Fenton was a youth player with West Ham United but was released and played for amateur outfits Ilford and Colchester Town, before West Ham came back to him and offered him a contract in November 1933. A useful wing-half, Ted Fenton played 176 games for the Hammers before, like many of his contemporaries, the outbreak of war interrupted his career for six years. His younger brother, Benny, played alongside him at Upton Park. He played in the 1940 War Cup Final and played in a wartime international versus Wales whilst he was a physical training instructor during campaigns in North Africa and Burma.

After the hostilities, Fenton joined Southern League Colchester United as player/manager and under him the Essex club had a great run in the F.A.Cup of 1947/48 reaching the fifth round before losing to Blackpool. In June 1948, Fenton returned to West Ham as assistant manager to Charlie Paynter; he succeeded Paynter in August 1950 and in 1958 won the Second Division Championship, returning the Hammers to the top flight for the first time in 26 years. He also established a renowned youth team at Upton Park, which bore fruit for many years after his mystery departure from the club in March 1961, the reason for which neither Fenton nor the board were prepared to offer an explanation.

Ted Fenton

From more than 40 applicants, Fenton successfully applied for the vacant Southend job and in his first season steered the team clear of the relegation places in Division Four. The next four seasons were less than inspired, with mid-table placings, and Fenton was dismissed in May 1965. He was restricted during his time as Southend United manager, budgeting constraints meaning he was often forced to sell his better players. As he had done at West Ham, Fenton focused on youth development and a string of youngsters progressed to the first team.

He never returned to the game following his dismissal, working as a publican and also running a sports shop in Brentwood for several years. Upon retirement he moved to Gloucestershire. Ted Fenton was killed in a car accident in 1992, aged 77.

Alvan Williams

Renowned as a strict disciplinarian, Alvan Williams was a huge man and compared favourably in stature to much missed former manager Harry Warren. Although born in Anglesey, Williams started his playing career with Stalybridge Celtic before joining Bury in December 1954, and subsequently played for Wrexham, Bradford Park Avenue and Exeter. However, it was only with Bradford Park Avenue that he established himself as a regular in the team; always unconventional, he lived in a caravan throughout his stay at the club. A well built half back, Williams had a reputation for very powerful penalty kicks, which were rarely missed.

He had to retire from playing at 28 through injury and he became assistant manager at Bangor City, presiding over their famous run in the European Cup Winners Cup of 1963, when they were only finally beaten in a replay at Highbury by Italian giants Napoli. He became manager of Hartlepools United in February 1964 and caused something of a stir by helping the club avoid a sixth straight season of applying for re-election to the Football League.

He joined Southend in June 1965, promising to transform the club and weed out any deadwood among the playing staff. His explosive temper and foul mouth (few could believe he was a vicar's son) failed to get the best out of his squad and a terrible season ensued, a club record 1-9 defeat at Brighton being the nadir in the campaign, resulting in the club's first ever relegation to Division 4. However the 1966/67 season began brightly and Williams' defensively-minded team were pushing for promotion throughout the season. Sadly, there were still rumblings among the board and supporters about Williams' penchant for brandy, and with the threat of dismissal looming, he resigned to take up the vacant manager's job at Wrexham, taking several Southend players to the Racecourse Ground with him, including top scorer Ray Smith and John Neal. He was only in charge at Wrexham for a year when a drink-driving ban saw the board force him to resign and hand over the reins to Neal, who had become his assistant.

Williams was now 46 years old and became a publican in North London. In 1978, he was landlord at the Robert Lee pub when he ended up in a fight with a 19 year old student who he was trying to eject from the pub. The student died from a brain haemorrhage and Williams was charged with murder. The case was heard at the Old Bailey, but was thrown out when witness testimonies fell apart. Williams admitted the lesser offence of affray and received a year's imprisonment, suspended for two years. Following this ordeal, Williams relocated to Croydon briefly before returning to North Wales. He was a publican in Bala for many years and received an award from the North Wales FA for a lifetime's contribution to football shortly before his death in 2003.

Ernie Shepherd

Ernie Shepherd was a good amateur player, having represented Derne Valley Schools as a youngster. He played for Bradford Rovers and was an amateur for both Bradford City and Fulham before turning professional at Craven Cottage in 1936 at the age of 25. His league debut, against Luton Town, came in the last game before war was declared and the 1939/40 season was abandoned. During the war he guested for Huddersfield Town, Brentford and Bradford City and in the unofficial 1944/45 season, he netted 26 goals in 45 games for The Bantams.

Shepherd achieved a remarkable feat in the 1948/49 season when he played for three clubs who were all promoted, although he failed to make enough appearances to win a medal at any of them. He had started the campaign at Fulham, who would be Second Division champions, before moving to West Bromwich Albion in December

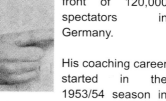

Ernie Shepherd

1948. The Baggies finished runners up to Fulham at the end of the season, although by March 1949 a £4,500 fee took Shepherd to Hull City, who became clear winners of Division Three (North). He finished his league career at QPR where from his outside-left role he scored 51 goals in 219 appearances. Probably the pinnacle of his playing career was being selected to represent London against Berlin in front of 120,000 spectators in Germany.

His coaching career started in the 1953/54 season in Iceland and he then held similar positions at Hastings United and Bradford Park Avenue, before becoming trainer at Southend United under the Eddie Perry regime in 1959. In 1966 he became assistant manager to Alvan Williams, taking over from the outspoken Welshman in April 1967, initially in a caretaker capacity. His initial sorties into the transfer market were not terribly successful, with Phil Chisnall (Manchester United) and Eddie Clayton (Spurs) failing to set Roots Hall alight. However, he soon became a shrewd player in a cut-throat market and Billy Best, Chico Hamilton and Peter Taylor were all hugely popular Shepherd captures. Interestingly, all those and several others were sold on for large profits. He also used the Park Side team as a nursery club for the senior team, his single minded goal being promotion back to Division Three`, which sadly ended in failure and left Shepherd on the verge of a nervous breakdown. He resigned in October 1969, but was persuaded to stay on as General Manager with Geoff Hudson as team manager. When Hudson was dumped after twelve games, Shepherd again took over the hot seat for two months before Arthur Rowley arrived at Roots Hall. Shepherd then managed Pegasus Athletic, a top amateur side playing at the Southend Stadium in the Essex Senior League competition.

In August 1973, he joined Orient as trainer/assistant manager and his aptitude for spotting young talent was highly successful at Brisbane Road; he was responsible for that rich vein of top players produced at the club in the mid 70's including John Chiedozie, Glenn Roeder and the late Laurie Cunningham. During his time at Orient he also held a part time post as England youth coach to Don Revie.

In 1976 he took a six month contract to coach Al Wasl in the United Arab Emirates and he stayed in Dubai for a remarkable ten years, leading Al Wasl to four league championships.

He retired in 1986 and returned to live in the Southend area, passing away at his home in Eastwood in March 2001 at the age of 81.

Geoff Hudson

Geoff Hudson

Geoff Hudson was a decent, if nomadic, full back who clocked up 337 League appearances for Bradford Park Avenue, Bradford City, Halifax Town, Exeter City, Crewe Alexandra, Gillingham, Lincoln City and Rotherham United in a twenty year career, the highlight of which was a Division Four champions medal in the 1963/64 season when at Gillingham. He was an already well qualified coach when he joined Southend as team manager, having had a spell as trainer coach with Cambridge United, then a Southern League club. Within weeks he was promising "promotion to Division Three by 1971 or his resignation". He never had the chance to fulfil his promise as he was dismissed within three months, with the club in the re-election zone in Division Four.

Arthur Rowley

Arthur Rowley was quite simply the most prolific goalscorer in the history of the English game. He scored an incredible 434 goals in 619 appearances, a total that is unlikely to ever be beaten. His formative playing career started with Wolverhampton School's representative games and occasional games for Wolverhampton Gas Works and Blakenhall St Luke's. He was on amateur forms with Wolves and West Bromwich Albion during the war but it was as a guest player, at the age of 15, for Manchester United in a wartime game that he made his debut. He played alongside his elder brother Jack, also a great goalscorer, who scored over 200 goals for the Old Trafford club; Arthur also guested for Middlesbrough, Brighton and Lincoln City during the hostilities.

When football resumed for the 1946/47 season, he started scoring prolifically for West Bromwich Albion, and in December 1948 he joined Fulham in a move which ironically saw Ernie Shepherd move in the opposite direction. In July 1950, Leicester City paid £12,000 for his services and he repaid them with a remarkable 200 goals in six seasons; in 1956/57 he scored 44 goals for The Foxes.

He became player/manager of Shrewsbury in June 1958 when a £7,000 fee took him to Gay Meadow and he took his new club to promotion to Division Three in his first season. In his second, the club finished third, just outside the promotion places and in 1960/61, The Shrews reached the semi-final of the inaugural League Cup competition, losing narrowly 3-4 on aggregate to Rotherham United. He retired from playing in April 1965 at the age of 39. Strangely he was always overlooked for a full England cap, although he won a 'B' cap and represented the Football League against the Irish League in October 1956. He joined Sheffield United in July 1968 but never saw eye to eye with general manager John Harris. He was dismissed under something of a cloud just a year into the job, although his squad was essentially the one that won promotion to Division One at the end of the 1970/71 season.

Arthur Rowley

Rowley joined Southend in March 1970 on an annual salary of £7,000 and in his second full season, 1971/72, he guided The Shrimpers back to Division Three when they finished runners up to Grimsby Town. However, after three modest Third Division campaigns, relegation at the end of the 1975/76 season saw Rowley dismissed by the board. An introverted man, Rowley was beleaguered by a 'Rowley out' campaign and spent his last months in charge relying heavily on his assistant Jack Burkett. Rowley was briefly kept on in an advisory role and was rewarded with a testimonial match against Leicester City. However, he soon left Roots Hall to become assistant manager at Telford United, then managing Oswestry Town, a Northern Premier League outfit, for several years before retiring to spend more time with his other passion; horse racing.

He retired to his adopted hometown of Shrewsbury and still lived there when he died in December 2002.

Dave Smith

During his playing days, Dave Smith was never more than a modest full back, not helped by some chronic bad luck with injuries. He started his career with East Craigie in Scotland, but joined Burnley in September 1950. He spent ten seasons at Turf Moor, making just 108 appearances, although incredibly he would break his leg five times, which severely limited his opportunities. The last two seasons of his career were spent with Brighton and Bristol City. He then rejoined Burnley as assistant manager before earning valuable coaching experience in Libya.

He joined Sheffield Wednesday as coach in June 1965 and was on the Wembley bench when the club reached the 1966 F.A.Cup Final. He joined Newcastle United as senior coach in July 1967, staying until the end of the 1970/71 season; during his time there, Newcastle won the 1969 Fairs Cup Final against Ujpest Dosza. Smith then spent three seasons as assistant trainer and reserve team manager at Arsenal, and in April 1974 he successfully applied for the vacant managerial job at Mansfield Town. In his first season he guided The Stags to the Fourth Division title, losing only six games and in 1975/76 the club reached the semi final of the Anglo Scottish Cup and the fifth round of the League Cup. In the league, Mansfield

struggled, although Smith successfully steered them clear of relegation.

It was still something of a surprise when he was dismissed at the end of the campaign, joining Southend and guided them to promotion in 1977/78, although the club slipped back down just two seasons later. The 1980/81 campaign saw Smith mastermind the club's greatest ever season, resulting in the Division Four title coming to Roots Hall and all sorts of club records being shattered. His style of sympathetic man management with a tough edge reaped dividends and the club enjoyed a golden spell under his guidance. Something of a maverick, Smith persisted with wingers when the genre had long disappeared from the majority of English teams. The 1982/83 season was something of a disappointment and there were a few rumblings amongst The Shrimpers supporters. However, it was a tremendous shock when new chairman, the controversial Anton Johnson, sacked him by telegram whilst Smith was on holiday in Tenerife. On his return, Smith, still possessing keys to his office, locked himself in and staged a lengthy

Dave Smith

Dave Smith, hard at work in the Manager's Office.

sit-in protest. He successfully sued the club for damages and the rest of his contract was paid in full; his shell-shocked team were relegated the following season.

Smith moved on to Plymouth Argyle and took them to promotion from Division Three in 1985/86. He almost took them to back-to-back promotions but the club faded in the home straight, finishing seventh in 1986/87. In June 1988 he began a seven month spell in charge of his hometown club Dundee, before returning to the south coast with Torquay United. He had a successful time at Plainmoor, overseeing a shock F.A.Cup defeat of West Ham United in January 1990. He surprisingly left the club in April 1991, with the club in the play-off picture in Division Three.

He left football altogether and took up a career in writing children's books. In July 2004, Plymouth and Torquay staged a benefit match for the popular Scotsman.

Peter Morris

A decent quality midfielder in his playing days, Peter Morris' fledgling career took off playing youth football for Langwith Boys Club, New Houghton Baptists and Ladybrook Colts. He signed professional forms for Mansfield Town in November 1960 and made his debut under the legendary Raich Carter at the age of 17. He later became The Stags youngest ever captain and stayed at Field Mill for nine seasons. Mansfield fans were horrified when the board accepted just £15,000 for his transfer to Ipswich Town in March 1968; his addition to the team ensured Town won the Division Two championship and promotion to Division One. Having played over 200 games for Ipswich, he moved to Norwich for £60,000 in June 1974 and played in the League Cup Final of 1975 when The Canaries lost 0-1 to Aston Villa at Wembley.

Morris returned to Mansfield in July 1976 for £10,000 to take up the player/manager role, ironically replacing Dave Smith at the helm. He guided The Stags to the Third Division title and their first ever promotion in his debut campaign, although the club went straight back down the following season. Morris joined Newcastle United in February 1978 as assistant manager to Bill McGarry and after a year at St James Park he moved to Peterborough United as manager, narrowly missing out on another promotion when The Posh finished fifth in Division four during 1980/81; ironically, Southend swept to the championship. He was replaced in May 1982 by Martin Wilkinson and was briefly out of the game before being offered the manager's job at Crewe Alexandra in November 1982. From there he joined The Shrimpers in August 1983, although the board's dallying in making a decision left Morris with little time or money to assemble a squad for the 1983/84 season. In fact, on his arrival, the club had only ten registered professionals of which two were goalkeepers. He arrived at Roots Hall amid the anarchy of the Anton Johnson era and really stood little chance of halting the club's slide back down to Division Four.

Morris lasted just six months and his unceremonious departure, along with coach Colin Harper, was announced in the club programme prior to an Associate Member's Cup tie at home to Reading in February 1983. He then spent a year out of the game before resurfacing as manager of Nuneaton Borough. During 1986, he spent several months coaching Aajar Sporting in Saudi Arabia, returning to England in January 1987 as Leicester City coach under Bryan Hamilton. He returned to non-League management in June 1988, beginning his first spell as Kettering Town manager. In his first season, The Poppies had a great run in the F.A.Cup, defeating league clubs Bristol Rovers and Halifax Town before succumbing to Charlton Athletic in the fourth round. In an amazing first season, he guided the club to the runners-up spot, behind Maidstone United in the Conference, missing out on promotion to the Football League by eight points. He stayed at Rockingham Road until June 1992 when he moved to Boston United.

In September 1993, he returned to the Football League as assistant manager of Northampton Town under John

Peter Morris

Barnwell; he was caretaker manager at the County Ground in January 1995 until the arrival of Ian Atkins. He then spent several seasons at Kings Lynn before returning to Kettering in June 1998. Again, in his first season, the club finished an unlucky second in the Conference, this time four points adrift of champions Cheltenham Town. However by February 2001, with The Poppies well on their way to losing their Conference status for the first time, Morris was dismissed. He returned to management again in June 2002 with a second spell in charge at Kings Lynn.

Bobby Moore

Bobby Moore's achievements as a player are known the world over and he was widely regarded as the game's most elegant defender. His early career took in games for Woodford Youth Club, as well as representative games for both Barking and Leyton schools. He joined the apprentice ranks of West Ham United, turning professional in June 1958. His first medal came in the 1959 FA Youth Cup, when The Hammers were beaten finalists.

At Upton Park, Moore won an F.A.Cup winner's medal in 1964 and a League Cup winner's medal two years later. Victory against Munich 1860 saw a European Cup Winner's Cup medal added to the burgeoning Moore trophy cabinet, this sitting

Bobby Moore

alongside his 1964 Footballer of the Year trophy. He was selected on twelve occasions for Football League representative honours and gained eight under-23 caps to add to numerous caps at youth level. Bobby Moore made his full England debut in May 1962 in a 4-0 defeat of Peru in Lima. He captained his country for the first time just a year later, aged only 23, against Czechoslovakia in

Bratislava. In July 1966, of course, he raised the Jules Rimet trophy as England became World Champions on that famous day at Wembley Stadium. Bobby Moore went on to make a then record 108 international appearances, with his final appearance coming against Italy in 1974.

After 642 games for West Ham, Moore was somewhat surprisingly sold to Fulham for £20,000 in March 1974. He reached another F.A.Cup final in 1975 with Fulham, but was on the loser's side this time as his new club lost 0-2 to his beloved West Ham. He spent the summer of 1976 playing for San Antonio Thunder in the NASL before returning to Fulham. He left Craven Cottage in May 1977 and spent another season in America playing for Seattle Sanders, where he reformed his great friendship with the legendary Pele, who was playing for New York Cosmos at the same time.

In February 1978 he took a player/coach position with Danish club Herning and his first managerial role came in December 1979 with non-Leaguers Oxford City, with whom he stayed until May 1981. He spent the 1982/83 campaign in Hong Kong as manager of Eastern AA and in August 1983 he was offered the post of chief executive at Southend United. However, by February 1984 he found himself thrust into the manager's hot seat when Peter Morris was dismissed. Initially he was in a caretaker role but took on the job full time that summer, despite being unable to prevent relegation to Division Four.

He presided over Southend's poorest ever campaign in 1984/85 when a re-election application was avoided only on the last day of the season and crowds regularly dipped below 2,000. The following season was scarcely better and Moore resigned on April 25 1986.

He spent the summer of 1986 working for TV and radio at the Mexico World Cup before moving into public relations; he had a brief spell as 'sports editor' for the ubiquitous Daily Sport. Despite resigning his managerial job, Bobby remained on the Roots Hall board until 1992.

Tragically at the relatively young age of 51, Bobby Moore died of bowel cancer in February 1993. Unequivocally one of the greatest and most respected sportsmen this country has ever produced.

David Webb

David Webb's playing career started as an amateur with West Ham United. However, it was with Leyton Orient that he turned professional in May 1963, establishing himself as a regular at right back before moving to Southampton in March 1966. With Webb adding extra steel, The Saints gained promotion to Division One at the end of that season, as runners-up to Manchester City. A transfer fee of £40,000 plus an additional player took David Webb back to London in February 1968, this time to Chelsea and under the management of Dave Sexton he was successfully converted to centre back.

In April 1970, Webb famously scored in the F.A.Cup final replay victory against Leeds at Old Trafford; a year later he won a Cup Winner's Cup medal when Chelsea defeated Real Madrid 2-1 in Athens. In December 1971, when both Peter Bonetti and John Phillips were injured, Webb kept goal for Chelsea against Ipswich, keeping a clean sheet in a 2-0 victory at Stamford Bridge. Webb was back at Wembley in March 1972, this time in the League Cup Final, unfortunately appearing on the losing side as Stoke City triumphed 1-2.

Webb left Chelsea in June 1974, having made 299 appearances and scoring 33 goals, a transfer fee of £100,000 taking him the short distance to Queens Park Rangers. His best season at Loftus Road was the 1975/76 campaign, when Rangers were Division One runners-up, just a point behind champions Liverpool. He subsequently played for Leicester City, Derby County and AFC Bournemouth, eventually clocking up over 700 appearances in a lengthy career.

David Webb

He became coach at Dean Court in May 1980 and succeeded Alec Stock as manager seven months later, guiding The Cherries to promotion from Division Four in 1981/82, but was dismissed in December 1982 following a 0-9 defeat at Lincoln City; his reply to Bournemouth was to sue the club for unfair dismissal. In February 1984 he took over at cash-strapped Torquay United, but due to the troubled financial position, Webb, who also had a major financial stake in the club, was forced to make several tough decisions which soon had him at loggerheads with the Plainmoor faithful. But Webb was

Above: David Webb collecting a Manager of the Month award

never short of confidence and he picked himself to play after a three year hiatus, aged nearly 39, against Chester City in November 1984, responding to his critics by scoring the only goal of the game. He played a further game for The Gulls in January 1985 against Crewe Alexandra. Sadly, the season finished poorly with Torquay having to apply for re-election to the Football League for the first time since 1927/28. After two games of the 1985/86 campaign, Webb gave up the manager's job, handing over to reserve team boss John Sims, so he could concentrate on his job as Managing Director. Although he returned the club to a modest profit of £77,000, Webb departed Plainmoor amid bitter acrimony in May 1986.

Webb quickly gained employment as manager of Southend in succession to Bobby Moore and within a few months, The Shrimpers were promotion contenders, although he would walk out on the team in March 1988 following one row too many with meddlesome chairman Vic Jobson. Erstwhile deputy Paul Clark carried on Webb's groundwork and The Shrimpers were promoted at the end of the campaign.

Webb worked as a car dealer before returning to Roots Hall in December 1988 as general manager, his stormy relationship with Jobson temporarily patched up. This spell at the club started with relegation to Division Four in 1988/89, before starting a period of unprecedented success at the club which saw successive promotions in 1989/90 and 1990/91. During the club's first ever Division Two season, Webb had the club famously top of the table on New Year's Day 1992 when Newcastle were hammered 4-0 at Roots Hall. However by March 1992, his relationship with Jobson had broken down irreparably and he announced his intention to quit at the end of that campaign.

In February 1993, he took over as manager of Chelsea in a temporary capacity, following the dismissal of Ian Porterfield, however his three months in charge failed to convince Ken Bates to offer him a contract. In May 1993, Webb took over team and financial affairs at Brentford, but with acute debts, Webb was forced to sell a number of players, much to the displeasure of Bees fans, who pilloried him as an asset-stripping charlatan. His unpopular spell at Brentford ended in 1997, although he took them to the brink of promotion to Division One in 1996/97.

After several years out of the game, David Webb returned to Roots Hall for a third time in October 2000 following the dismissal of Alan Little. Webb had only just got back into football that summer having been charged with overseeing Yeovil Town's progression to full-time football; in excess of 1,000 Shrimpers supporters travelled to Blackpool to hail the return of the messiah. Following a modestly successful year in charge he resigned, citing a health scare as his reason for leaving.

Remarkably Webb stepped into the breach once again in November 2003 for a four game spell in charge of The Shrimpers, after the departure of Steve Wignall. By the close of 2005, David Webb purchased a controlling interest in Yeovil Town Football Club and had appointed himself as managing director, but his stint at the club was a brief one as he sold his share in the club within six months.

Although vilified by some of his former clubs, David Webb will always be highly regarded by Southend fans and is rightly lauded as one of the club's greatest ever managers.

Paul Clark

Paul Clark started his career as a youngster with Southend United and soon won seven England Schoolboy caps, as well as caps at Youth level. e made his first team debut in August 1976 as a substitute for Steve Goodwin in a 1-2 League Cup defeat at Brighton and Hove Albion. After 35 first

Paul Clark

team games he was transferred to Brighton and Hove Albion, where he was to become a regular in midfield. Whilst at the Goldstone Ground, he was briefly loaned to Reading in October 1981 before returning to Roots Hall in August 1982.

He became hugely popular for his buccaneering style and crunching tackles, eventually clocking up in excess of 300 appearances for The Shrimpers. His career took an unexpected turn in March 1987 when David Webb's shock departure saw Clark take over as caretaker manager. He managed to steer the club to promotion in a famous last game victory at Stockport County and was optimistic that despite his youthful age, 29, he would be given the job full-time. His hopes were dashed when Dick Bate was appointed instead, but after Bate's disastrous spell in charge, the club once again turned to Clark in September 1987. The

impact was immediate, with the team defeating Derby County in the Littlewoods Cup.

Despite the team's shocking start to the campaign, Clark managed to guide the team to 17th place at the season's end, but with the 1988/89 campaign starting very poorly, after only four league wins in the first nineteen games, Clark was replaced by David Webb, who had returned to Roots Hall as General Manager. He remained as a player, but signed for Gillingham in June 1991, therefore missing out on the club's first ever Division Two campaign.

He retired from playing just 13 games into the 1993/94 season, briefly turning out for Chelmsford City before becoming assistant manager to Tommy Taylor at Cambridge United. The pair moved to Leyton Orient in November 1996 and stayed for several seasons until the axe fell in November 2001. Since then Clark has remained in the game as a local media pundit.

Dick Bate

Dick Bate failed to make the grade as a professional footballer, only ever holding amateur

Dick Bate is welcomed to Roots Hall by Paul Clark

forms with Sheffield Wednesday and York City. He failed to break into either club's first team and soon became a PE teacher; he played for several non-League teams including Alfreton Town (68-71), Boston United (71-76) and Frickley Athletic (76-79). In 1977/78, Bate was player/manager at Mossley whilst becoming a highly qualified FA coach.

He accepted the post of youth team coach at Sheffield United in 1978 and after two seasons at Bramall Lane, spent five years as the FA's North West regional coach. In 1985, Bate spent a brief spell as assistant manager of the England youth team; his next move came in June 1985 when he became coach to Jimmy Sirrel at Notts County. However, it came as a real surprise when Bate landed his first managerial post in June 1987, Southend chairman, Vic Jobson, lauding him as "the right man for the job" and if qualifications counted for everything, he would have been proved right.

Jobson's unilateral decision to appoint him against the wishes of the rest of the board backfired massively. He lasted just ten games in charge, with the only win coming in a Littlewoods Cup triumph over Brentford. The Shrimpers failed to win any of their opening eight league games under the new man and heavy defeats were sustained at Gillingham (1-8) and Notts County (2-6). Several of Bate's new signings, Eric Steele, Richard Young and Chris Ramsey, performed poorly and it was no real surprise when the autocratic Jobson wielded the axe just two months into the campaign.

Bate became assistant manager at Lincoln City under a future Southend boss, Colin Murphy, having briefly coached at Hereford United before this. In June 1988, Bate accepted an offer from the Malaysian FA to become national team coach, returning to England in January 1990 as reserve and youth team coach at Leeds United. More recently Dick Bate was named national team coach of Burkina Faso, as well as holding several FA coaching positions, including being the England under-19 manager.

Colin Murphy

Never more than an average player during a career with Cork Hibernians, Wimbledon, Hastings United and Crystal Palace reserves, it was with the latter that he sustained a career ending knee injury. He already had some managerial experience after his player-manager role at Hastings and for the 1971/72 season he became coach under Theo Foley at Charlton Athletic. In November 1972, he became youth team coach at Nottingham Forest, and then coach at Derby County under Dave Mackay. Murphy took over as manager at the Baseball Ground in November 1976, but he had a torrid time at the helm and was dismissed in September 1977, after big money signings Derek Hales (£300,000) and Gerry Daly (£175,000) failed to settle; he was replaced by Tommy Docherty.

He was not out of work for long, becoming Jimmy Sirrel's assistant at Notts County a month later, then his next port of call was Lincoln City, taking over as manager from Peter Daniel in November 1978. He spent seven seasons at Sincil Bank, guiding them to promotion from Division Four in 1980/81 as runners-up to Southend United and he nearly made it back-to-back promotions the next season when The Imps finished fourth, just a point behind promoted Fulham. At the end of the 1984/85 season he moved on to Stockport County, but stayed there only three months into the new campaign before receiving a financially lucrative offer to coach in Saudi Arabia.

Murphy returned to England in November 1986 and took his old job back at Edgeley Park. Again his stay was brief, resigning at the end of the 1986/87 campaign, returning to Lincoln as manager after the club had dropped out of the League. Under Murphy, The Imps stormed straight back, winning the Conference title by two points from Barnet, but in May 1990 he left Lincoln again to become youth team coach at Leicester City; the following campaign saw him at Luton Town as assistant to David Pleat.

Murphy joined Southend in May 1992, but always struggled to fill David Webb's boots. In November 1992, he signed a young reserve team player from Crystal Palace who would become the club's greatest ever player, Stan Collymore eventually being sold for a fee of £3.57 million, which stabilised the club's precarious finances for many years. Despite this masterstroke, the results never came and with his eccentric programme notes

Colin Murphy

The Words and Wisdom of Colin Murphy

When Colin Murphy took over the reigns at Southend United, he brought with him a whole new world of programme notes. Whether his ultimate failure at Southend United was down to his tactics, or the fact that the players couldn't understand the language he used is not known, but reading through his page from the opening home programme of the 1992/93 season, it is evident that he did not attend the "Barry Fry School of Football Management"!!

"These notes I am writing as we travel to play Newcastle and if the players play as spiritfully as they sound then for sure we will be in for a performance which will reflect some form of credibility on what will be one of the most difficult stages of the season.

Enough has been written about the past. Wonderment and disenchantment pondered about its motives. Philosophies expressed about repairing and planning for the future.

For sure continuation of negative campaigns may well see the club relegated and one would have thought that nobody or no groups of people would be as futile, self-centred, or indignant enough to place themselves in a position where they consider they are more important than the importance and well-being of the establishment.

Alternatively innovation of positive enthusiastic and behavioural and attitudal policies will see the Club mount a serious challenge for the Premier League, a dream for us all. Thereby placing credence on a contribution of modest genuine supporters' natures, that everybody can be proud of. Because they will seem to have had the most incisive productive effects. Effects that nobody would have dared envisualised two months ago.

Having made these two poignant observations it will be interesting to observe those who will unreservedly act in the interests of the players of the players' interests as it were.

Now, all we, that is Bob, I and the players ask, is a fair even chance, no more, no less. The same which would have been given to any other group of people at the Club charged with attaining Premier Division status. Then we will deserve what we get. Either the Lavish of the Press or the Scathing of the Criticism.

With Football Management becoming more and more diverse as the seasons escape us I am sure none of us, least of all yourselves will lose the sight of the main and maybe the only task in hand, winning football matches."

Over the years I have been constantly asked what is the main job of the Football Manager and in its crude final analysis it is to win football matches."

"ALTERNATIVELY INNOVATION OF POSITIVE ENTHUSIASTIC AND BEHAVIOURAL AND ATTITUDAL POLICIES WILL SEE THE CLUB MOUNT A SERIOUS CHALLENGE FOR THE PREMIER LEAGUE..."

and bizarre training methods (often preferring tennis balls to footballs), the Roots Hall faithful never took to him. The beleaguered Murphy was finally dismissed in April 1992 with the club in the relegation zone.

In November 1994, Murphy became manager of Shelbourne in the League of Ireland; a modestly successful campaign saw the Dublin club reach the Cup Final, although they went down 1-2 to Derry City. In May 1995, Murphy resigned to take up the manager's position at Notts County and his first campaign saw him guide County to fourth in the Second Division, although The Magpies would lose the play-off final to Bradford City. County fans heavily criticised Murphy's team selection and tactics and when the team started the following season poorly, Murphy was moved to General Manager to allow Steve Thompson to take over team affairs. The rot continued and the pair were dismissed in December 1996.

Murphy was out of the game for a while but resurfaced as national team coach of Burma in December 1999. In July 2000 Murphy agreed to take over at Cork City, but without a ball being kicked he walked out to take up Peter Taylor's offer of a coaching position at Leicester City. In November 2001, Murphy returned to Stockport for a third time, this time as Director of Football to support novice manager Carlton Palmer. In October 2002, Murphy once again linked up with Peter Taylor, becoming assistant manager at Hull City.

Barry Fry

Barry Fry began his long footballing career at Manchester United as an apprentice, winning seven England Schoolboy caps. He signed professional forms in April 1962 but never made the first team, joining Bolton Wanderers in May 1964, but made only three appearances that season. In July 1965, he moved to Luton Town, but only started six league games. He joined Southern League Gravesend and Northfleet, but after twenty games Fry moved back to the Football League in December 1966, signing for Leyton Orient where again he struggled to gain a regular midfield position.

He was released at the end of the 1967/68 season, returning to the Southern League with first Romford and then with Bedford Town, where he became something of a legend for his

Barry Fry

audacious free kicks. He then spent a six month spell at Stevenage Town, becoming a manager for the first time in July 1972, when he took over at Dunstable Town. It was a torrid time for Fry personally as a failed horse racing business saw him declared bankrupt. Fry's spell at Dunstable attracted all sorts of headlines; his first game in charge saw a paying crowd of 34 at Creasy Road, so he decided to think big, pulling off the signing of the legendary George Best. Best's first game at Dunstable, against Manchester United, attracted a record gate of 10,000. He then signed ex-England international Jeff Astle, who rewarded Fry, particularly in the 1974/75 season when his 34 league goals secured promotion from the Southern League North. His time at Dunstable was overshadowed by the controversial chairman Keith Cheeseman, whose cheques bounced all over the place and was eventually jailed for six years for bogus loan applications. On his release he was again jailed for blackmailing a bank manager into laundering fraudulent US bonds. Fry lasted two and a half exciting years at Dunstable before being sacked.

He joined another Southern League club, Hillingdon Borough in September 1976, the following campaign seeing him return to Bedford Town, this time as manager. In August 1978, he began his first spell in charge at Barnet. The club was struggling to survive financially, but Fry produced an attractive team and attendances grew rapidly, a steady stream of players being sold on to Football League clubs. Fry was manager of Maidstone United from January 1985 to July 1986, before returning for a second spell in charge at Barnet. He had tremendous success but found his club being Conference runners-up on no less than three occasions, 1986/87, 1987/88 and 1989/90. However, in 1990/91 he finally achieved his ambition by taking Barnet into the league, winning the Conference title by two points from Colchester. In his first League campaign, Barnet reached the play-offs, but lost to Blackpool. His time at Underhill was in many ways similar to his Dunstable days, as he had a tempestuous relationship with another controversial chairman, the notorious ticket tout Stan Flashman. Fry was sacked or resigned on numerous occasions, but always reinstated. He averted the financial collapse at Barnet by remortgaging his house and when, in November 1992, Barnet were charged by the FA over inconsistencies in their bookkeeping, Fry fell out with Flashman for the last time. It was no surprise that when he was offered the vacant job at Southend, he resigned again, this time for good.

He did well at Roots Hall, pulling the club out of the relegation zone of Division One before the end of the 1992/93 campaign and then masterminded the sale of Stan Collymore to Nottingham Forest. The Shrimpers started the 1993/94 season well, but when Karren Brady approached him to join Birmingham City, Southend fans were relieved when Fry declared " There is no way I am leaving Southend." Fry, and his backroom staff, Eddie Stein and David Howell, resigned four days later and went to St Andrews. Fry soon raided his old club by signing Ricky Otto (£800,000) and Andy Edwards (£400,000) and endured several heated receptions on his return to Roots Hall. Fry spent a fortune on players with little success and it was no real surprise when he was sacked at the end of the 1995/96 season. He was offered several jobs but took up the offer from an old friend, Chris Turner, to take over at Peterborough United. Not only was he manager, Fry was to own the club as well. However he had been royally misled to the size of the club's debts, some £3 million, and he was soon in dire straits. Financial salvation eventually came when Peter Boizot bought

a controlling interest from Fry. Despite never gaining universal favour at London Road, Fry has served the club in various capacities over eleven seasons.

Peter Taylor

Peter Taylor's fledgling career started as a schoolboy player for Canvey Island. He joined Southend United in 1970 as an apprentice and quickly made his first team debut, aged only 18, against Barrow. During the 1971/72 season he volunteered to keep goal for The Shrimpers against Cambridge United when regular custodian, Derek Bellotti, was injured, but became a first team regular during the 1972/73 campaign in his normal left-wing position with a series of dazzling performances.

In October 1973, Southend received a record transfer fee of £120,000 from Crystal Palace for his services and despite being a Third Division player, Taylor was selected to play for England on four occasions during his spell at Selhurst Park. In September 1976, Taylor joined Tottenham for an initial fee of £200,000 (this later doubled). His first season ended in relegation to Division Two, although the club regained their top flight status at the first attempt. He then signed for Leyton Orient for £150,000 in November 1980 and later played for Oldham Athletic (loan), Maidstone United and Exeter City. He wound down his playing career at Heybridge Swifts and Chelmsford City, followed by his first spell of management at Dartford, where he enjoyed modest success.

It was somewhat of a surprise when he was announced as successor to Barry Fry at Southend; his term in the Roots Hall hot seat

Peter Taylor

was not a success and the fans who adored him as a player, hounded him as a manager. A run of three straight defeats in February 1995 prompted Taylor to throw the towel in. He resurfaced as manager of Dover Athletic, then a Conference side, and was surprisingly appointed as England U21 manager under Glenn Hoddle; Taylor was a resounding success, with the team unbeaten during his year in charge. The FA were strongly criticised for not renewing his contract in favour of Howard

Peter Taylor

£20,000 taking him to Bramall Lane. He played 20 games for The Blades but was released at the end of the 1988/89 campaign.

Now 34, he rejoined Lincoln City, initially as a player, however with The Imps in dire straits, next to bottom in the Fourth Division under Allan Clarke, the ex-Leeds forward's dismissal gave Thompson the chance to cut his managerial teeth. He transformed the side, which lost only three of their last eighteen games of the season, finishing comfortably in a mid-table position. He spent three seasons at Sincil Bank, with his best performance coming in his last campaign, 1992/93; it was something of a surprise when he resigned in May 1993. In early 1995, he joined Southend United as Director of Football, but within a month beleaguered manager Peter Taylor had resigned and Vic Jobson, the Shrimper's chairman, offered Thompson the job in a caretaker capacity. The side stormed up the table after flirting with relegation all season, losing only four of his fourteen games in charge. The previously ineffective Gary Jones was transformed under Thompson, bagging nine goals in the last dozen games. Thompson was offered the job full-time, but was coaxed to Notts County by ex-Southend Chief Executive Peter Storrie. He was initially assistant to Colin Murphy, but took over team affairs when Murphy was moved to a General Managers role.

The pair were dismissed after a shocking run in December 1996, Thompson returning to the

Wilkinson. However, his profile was sufficiently increased to obtain a run of managerial jobs at Gillingham, Leicester City, Brighton and Hove Albion, Hull City and most recently Crystal Palace.

Steve Thompson

An uncompromising centre back, Steve Thompson's career was slow to take off, with lengthy spells at non-League Worksop Town and Boston United. He was 24 before he joined the professional ranks, when a £15,000 fee took him to Lincoln City in April 1980. After 150 games for The Imps, including a promotion success in 1980/81, Thompson moved on to Charlton Athletic, where he became a regular and won promotion to Division One in 1985/86, when his side finished runners-up to Norwich City. He moved on to Leicester City for £40,000 in July 1988, but frustrated by lack of first team opportunities, soon moved on to Sheffield United; a transfer fee of

Steve Thompson

game in July 1997 when he joined the coaching staff at Sheffield United. He was appointed caretaker manager in March 1998 after Nigel Spackman's resignation and despite four wins and four draws in his twelve games in charge, and an F.A.Cup semi-final appearance, the board decided against offering him the job permanently. He initially stayed on as assistant to new incumbent Steve Bruce, but resigned in November 1998. More recently, he was re-appointed Notts County manager in June 2006.

Ronnie Whelan

Ronnie Whelan started his legendary career at Home Farm, making his League of Ireland debut at the age of only 16. He soon won schoolboy, youth and amateur caps for the Republic of Ireland before joining Liverpool in 1979, soon becoming one of Anfield's favourite sons. He was voted PFA Young Player of the Year in 1980 and eventually played 506 games for The Reds. He won every medal available (1 European Cup, 6 League titles, 1 F.A.Cup and 3 League Cups) and won 53 caps for Ireland, the last two as a Southend player. He graced two World Cups (1990 and 1994) and the 1988 European Championships.

Whelan joined Southend as a player in September 1994 and had a successful first season, however an injury in the opening game of the 1995/96 season enforced his retirement from playing. He had already been given the manager's job in the close season and guided the club to 14th in Division 1. However, the following campaign was an unmitigated disaster, with The Shrimpers meekly surrendering their First Division place after six seasons. Whelan tendered his resignation in May 1997, returning to football in the 1998/99 season as coach of Greek club Panionios, whom he guided to the quarter finals of the last European Cup Winner's Cup competition. However, when league form suffered, he was dismissed at the season's end. He then coached Cypriot club Olympiakos Nicosia and has subsequently developed a career as a media pundit.

Ronnie Whelan

Alvin Martin

After the disastrous Whelan experiment, it was something of a surprise when Vic Jobson chose another managerial novice as his replacement. His plan backfired massively as Martin took a dispirited club to a second straight relegation. Martin had a memorable career with West Ham, whom he joined as an apprentice in 1974, signing professional forms in July 1976. He won England Youth and 'B' caps, as well as 17 full international caps during a career of almost 550 games for the Hammers; he won an F.A.Cup winner's medal in 1980 and a Second Division winner's medal in 1980/81.

Alvin Martin

After 19 seasons at Upton Park, he finished his playing career with a single campaign at Leyton Orient, from where he took up the vacant managerial job at Roots Hall. The first season was a real eye opener as a financially struggling club finished bottom of Division Two, winning only eleven games all season. He appointed the experienced Mick Gooding as his assistant for the 1998/99 campaign, but to no avail as the club struggled at the foot of the Third Division and after a succession of crowd demonstrations, a tearful Martin resigned after a home defeat to Hull City.

Martin found his stint as a football manager so harrowing that he turned to a career as a radio pundit instead.

Alan Little

Alan Little was a combative midfielder who always suffered from comparisons to his more talented elder brother Brian. Brian was already a first-teamer at Villa Park when Alan signed professional forms for the Midland club in January 1973. Alan made only three first team appearances for Aston Villa before joining Southend United in December 1974. In his first season, 1975/76, despite relegation to Division Four, Little was voted the club's player of the year. Little moved on to Barnsley in August 1977 and in the 1978/79 campaign, Little contributed seven goals in a successful promotion campaign

Alan Little in his Southend United playing days

which saw The Tykes gain fourth place in Division Three.

In September 1979, Little sustained a serious injury at Sheffield United which saw him sidelined for two months; he played only once more for Barnsley, moving on to Doncaster Rovers in December 1979. He stayed at Belle Vue until October 1982 when he joined Torquay United then after a season at Plainmoor he spent two campaigns at Halifax Town before finishing his League career with a dozen games for Hartlepool United. In July 1988, he became assistant manager to John Bird at York City; Bird left in 1991 but Little stayed on in a similar capacity under John Ward. When Ward quit for Bristol Rovers in May 1993, Little stepped up as full time manager. In his first season, York finished fifth in Division Two, but after flirting with relegation in 1995/96 and 1996/97, The Minstermen finally succumbed in 1998/99, although Little had been replaced by Neil Thompson in December 1998.

Little joined Southend as manager in March 1999 and the effect was dramatic, the team recording a comfortable 3-0 success at bitter rivals Leyton Orient. However it was to prove to be a false dawn, as the club faired only averagely under his tenure. Fans often criticised his, and assistant Mick Gooding's, visible lack of passion during games. When The Shrimpers had a disappointing start to the 2000/01 campaign, Little was relieved of his duties, a 1-0 home win against Scunthorpe failing to save his neck.

Rob Newman

A wholehearted competitor who amassed over 700 appearances in a lengthy playing career for Bristol City and Norwich City, Newman began as an apprentice at Ashton Gate, signing professional forms in October 1981. He spent ten seasons with The Robins before moving to Carrow Road for £600,000 in July 1991, where he was instrumental in The Canaries best ever season, finishing third in the inaugural Premiership campaign of 1992/93. The Canaries then enjoyed a memorable run in the UEFA Cup, with Newman again the strongman in midfield, defeating Bayern Munich before losing to Internazionale in the Third Round. In 1997/98, his last at Carrow Road, Newman was loaned out to Motherwell in December 1997 and Wigan Athletic the following March.

Rob Newman

seven seasons, making 336 appearances and scoring 27 goals.

In August 1984, he joined Brentford for whom he was again a regular at centre back and after two campaigns at Griffin Park, Wignall signed for Aldershot in September 1986. He had five seasons with The Shots, playing his final League game against Halifax Town in November 1990 when he initially became the coach at the Recreation Ground, and was manager when Aldershot dramatically collapsed in March 1992 and were expelled from the Football League. He stayed to become the manager of the newly formed Aldershot Town, albeit in the reduced surroundings of the Diadora League Division Three. Wignall took the club to two promotions before becoming manager of Colchester United in January 1995. At Layer Road, he guided the U's to the Auto Windscreens Trophy final in 1997 and the following season took the club up to Division Two via a play-off victory over Torquay United. He was then the manager of Stevenage Borough before rejoining another club

After seven years at Norwich, Newman was released at the season's end; he joined Southend as a player in July 1998 and soon became reserve team manager. When David Webb dramatically resigned in October 2001, Newman was handed the managerial reigns, but although clearly passionate and popular among the fans, the results did not materialise. When Stuart Robson was appointed first team coach in January 2003, the writing was on the wall. With both men vying for control, the team suffered and Newman was sent packing the following March.

After his stint at Roots Hall, Newman briefly turned out for Chelmsford City while scouting for West Ham United. He soon returned to management with Cambridge United, then moved to Bournemouth as assistant to Kevin Bond.

Steve Wignall

Steve Wignall was a junior at Liverpool but ultimately failed to make the grade at Anfield. A tall centre back, he finally signed a professional deal with Doncaster Rovers in March 1972, however, he had to wait for his first team debut which arrived eight months later in a 0-2 home defeat to Crewe Alexandra. He soon became a first team regular at Belle Vue, clocking up 141 appearances, before joining Colchester United in September 1977. He served the U's for

Steve Wignall

he had served as a player, Doncaster Rovers in May 2000, succeeding Ian Snodin. Failure to regain their Football League status cost him dear, being dismissed in March 2002 in favour of his coach David Penney.

Wignall was out of the game for some time before becoming a surprise choice as Southend manager in April 2003. His time out of the League game was all too evident and his apparent lack of emotion did not sit comfortably with the Roots Hall faithful, it coming as no real surprise when his brief tenure in charge was ended in November 2003, following a home defeat by Northampton Town. He is currently assistant manager at Wivenhoe Town.

subsequent reigns of Colin Murphy and Barry Fry, Tilson would lose his place in the team.

In September 1993, he was briefly loaned to Brentford, but Tilson's guile and ability was re-harnessed by Peter Taylor and he was restored to the team. After nine seasons at the club, Tilson was unceremoniously discarded by then manager Ronnie Whelan after nearly 300 appearances; he was callously denied a testimonial match. He was offered deals by Leyton Orient and Lincoln City but opted to join rising non-Leaguers Canvey Island. He served the Islanders for five seasons, contributing over 100 goals during their rapid rise to prominence, the zenith of his Canvey career coming in May 2001 when he skippered The

Steve Tilson

Steve Tilson

Steve Tilson is the epitome of a local boy made good. Working on a building site, the youngster would watch Southend United from the terraces when his commitments with Essex Senior League outfits Basildon United and Witham Town permitted. It was with the latter club that Tilson would receive the break he craved, as the mid-Essex club was managed by Danny Greaves, a former Shrimpers player who still had strong connections with the club. Greaves recommended the deftly talented youngster to Southend manager David Webb and Tilson was offered a contract after just one reserve team outing.

He played in the Shrimpers' midfield during the successful 1989/90 and 1990/91 promotion campaigns; in the latter he was an automatic choice on the left side. Tilson contributed a respectable eleven goals from midfield, including a hat-trick in a 10-1 Leyland Daf Cup victory over a hapless Aldershot. The 1991/92 season, the clubs' first in the Second Division, he would play every game for Southend, however under the

Gulls to an F.A. Trophy final victory over Forest Green Rovers at Villa Park.

Tilson returned to Roots Hall in 1999 as Director of Youth football and the outstanding injustice of his denied testimonial match was rectified in March 2003 when a fixture was arranged against an Ex-England eleven. A bumper crowd was testimony to his popularity and reflected the affection held for him by the Roots Hall faithful. When his former mentor David Webb made it clear that his fourth stint as Shrimpers manager would be as brief as possible, Tilson was requested to run the first team following Steve Wignall's dismissal. Initially in a caretaker role, and ably assisted by another former Shrimpers player Paul Brush, he successfully guided the team away from the dreaded Conference relegation zone. Tilson also guided Southend to their first ever national final in March 2004, but it ended in a 0-2 defeat to Blackpool in the LDV Trophy final at Cardiff. His first full season in charge, 2004/05, was dramatic with a skilfully constructed squad again reaching the LDV Trophy final at Cardiff, although another 0-2 defeat, this time in extra time, to Wrexham saw The Shrimpers again return home empty handed. The club challenged for promotion throughout the campaign but had to go through a tortuous play-off route to gain a well deserved promotion; this time The Shrimpers were on the right side of a 2-0 scoreline over Lincoln City.

Tilson had masterminded the club's first promotion in fourteen years, and promptly took them up again by storming straight through League One with an amazing championship win. Steve Tilson thus joined a select band of managers who had guided a team to back-to-back promotions, but he was the first to do so as the manager of the same club that he had also achieved the identical feat with as a player.

Steve Tilson

SOUTHEND UNITED IN PRINT

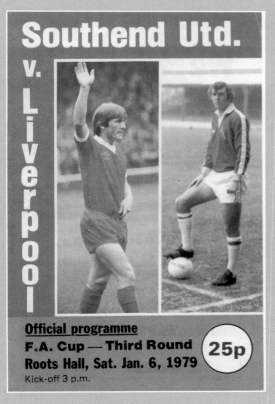

Southend United's first foray into full colour - the F.A.Cup Third Round match against Liverpool, January 1979.

Programmes

The Programmes of Southend United

Southend United have been known to issue programmes for their matches from very early on in their history. The first home match at which a programme was made available to the spectators was the first home game of the 1908/09 season on the 12th September 1908 against Millwall Athletic. This tall, thin single sheet of card, folded in a similar fashion to today's Chinese takeaway menus, contained many adverts along with the team line-ups, and cost the princely sum of 1d.

Way back in the pre-league days, many clubs issued programmes sporadically, and some did not issue at all. It is very hard to definitively determine into which category Southend United fall, as very few issues from the first twenty years of the life of the football club have survived, but it is commonly agreed that they did issue on a very regular basis, and that their programme was one of the better ones of its generation.

The programme from the 1910/11 season was along similar lines to that of the 1908/09 season. A single sheet of stiff card, tri-folded into the aforementioned "takeaway" shape contained very brief information to keep the spectators entertained during the half-time interval. The front contained details of the club itself, along with its officers of the day, and also contained the first advertisements which would be a recurrent factor in this, and every programme ever produced by the club. Opening the programme, the line-ups for both teams (Southend United numbered 1 to 11, the opponents numbered 12 to 22, although actual shirt numbering was yet to be introduced) was flanked by a range of advertisements and also the fixtures for both the first team and the reserve team. The reverse of the programme gave the fixtures for the half-time fixture board, along with an offer for the spectators to visit the Hippodrome after the match. The programme in itself measured eleven inches high and over five inches wide, even when folded, so its little wonder that so few of them have survived the intervening ninety or so years, as well as two world wars.

The first change in style came in the 1914/15 season, when Southend United issued what was their first programme in a format that is recognisable to football fans of today. Measuring a fairly standard eight-and-a-half by five inches, the eight-page issue was printed on fairly flimsy green paper, and cost the spectator 1d. As well as the half-time scoreboard and the team line-ups as before, this

The first ever Southend United programme was for the visit of Millwall on Saturday 12th September 1908. The programme is printed on card and measures 15.25 inches by 10.25 inches; hardly the size to be kept in fine condition in the overcoat pocket of a spectator. Once folded, the programme is still fairly unwieldy at 5 inches by 10.25 inches, but is more manageable. The programme is printed in blue ink, although there is some bordering on the front cover in red.

The first team fixtures for the season were included on the inside pages, and included matches against such teams as New Brompton, London Caledonians, Hastings & St. Leonards United and Croydon Common. There were also games against clubs that were to become old adversaries, including Brighton, Brentford, Crystal Palace, Northampton, Swindon and Exeter City.

This Programme is Printed by..

LONDON ORDERS RECEIVE SPECIAL ATTENTION.

ELLIS LTD.

They undertake all kinds of PRINTING in the very best styles by up-to-date methods.

FINEST COLOUR WORK IN THE COUNTY.

Enquiries and Inspection invited.

TELEPHONE— 25 SOUTHEND.

TELEGRAMS— ELLIS, SOUTHEND-ON-SEA.

22 LONDON ROAD and 14 CLARENCE STREET, SOUTHEND-ON-SEA; and 137 CHEAPSIDE, LONDON, E.C.

Southend United F.C. Ltd.

ROOTS HALL, WEST STREET, PRITTLEWELL.

Members of the Essex County F.A., Southern League Div. I., South Eastern League Div. I., and United League.

Champions 1906-7 and 1907-8 of the Southern League Div. II.

OFFICIAL PROGRAM.

1d.   1d.

For half-time results by the Code see opposite pages

Directors: Alderman Prevost, J.P. (Chairman), Geo. H. Hogsflesh, Esq. (Vice-Chairman), C. A. Stein, Esq., T. A. Buxton, Esq., W. J. Ellis, Esq., Oswald Trigg, Esq., R. A. Jones, Esq., Oliver Trigg, Esq., J. W. Davies, Esq., Councillor Richardson, E. A. Broadhurst, Esq., Donald Taylor, Esq.

Secretary and Manager: ROBERT JACK, Registered Office, Roots Hall, West Street, Prittlewell.

BLUE BOAR HOTEL, PRITTLEWELL.

(OPPOSITE THE FOOTBALL GROUND).

Headquarters of the Southend United Football Club Ltd., and the Southend Harriers.

Proprietor - - THOS. A. BUXTON.

First Team.

1908				Result For Agt
				0 1
Sep 5	New Brompton	s L	A	
12	Millwall	s L	H	
*19	London Caledonians	K C	H	
26	Coventry City	s L	A	
Oct *3	Bristol Rovers	s L	H	
10	Watford	s L	A	
*17	Norwich City	s L	H	
24	Reading	s L	A	
31	Southampton	s L	H	
Nov 2	Queen's Park Rangers	s L	A	
*7	Leyton	s L	A	
14	West Ham United	s L	H	
*21	Brighton and Hove Albion	s L	A	
23	Brentford	U L	A	
28	Crystal Palace	s L	H	
Dec 2	Hastings & S. Leonards Untd.	U L	H	
*5	Brentford	s L	A	
9	Queen's Park Rangers	s L	H	
12	Luton	s L	H	
16	New Brompton	U L	A	
19	Swindon	s L	A	
25	Portsmouth	s L	H	
26	Northampton	s L	A	
30	Gravesend	U L	A	
1909				
Jan 2	New Brompton	s L	H	
9	Millwall	s L	A	
13	Hastings & S. Leonards Untd.	U L	A	
*16				
20	Gravesend	U L	H	
23	Plymouth Argyle	s L	A	
27	New Brompton	U L	H	
30	Coventry City	s L	H	
Feb 3	Exeter	s L	A	
*6	Bristol Rovers	s L	A	
10	Brentford	U L	H	
Feb 13	Watford	s L	H	
17	Croydon Common	U L	H	
*20	Norwich City	s L	A	
27	Reading	s L	H	
Mar *6	Southampton	s L	A	
13	Leyton	s L	H	
17	Crystal Palace	s L	A	
20	West Ham United	s L	A	
24	Exeter	s L	H	
*27	Brighton and Hove Albion	s L	H	
Apr 3				
9	Portsmouth	s L	A	
10	Brentford	s L	H	
12	Northampton	s L	H	
13	Plymouth Argyle	s L	H	
17	Luton	s L	A	
21	Croydon Common	U L	A	
*24	Swindon	s L	H	

s L—Southern League Div. I.
U L—United League.
K C & *—Football Association Cup Dates.

There were many interesting advertisements included in Southend United's first programme. R.A. Jones, who would become a regular advertiser and supporter of the club over the forthcoming years, had a prominent advert above the team line-ups in the centre spread. Harrington's High Class Mineral Waters was another local company who would support the club over the years, and they were joined on the inside pages by carpenter and joiner Geo. E. Wells, and J.W. Cheesman, who was a Motor, Cycle and General Engineer.

On the back cover, T.J. Johnson of Hamlet Court Road stated that the "Rectus Flannel Shirt" was "a boon to chilly mortals", retailing from four shillings and sixpence. Brockman & Shepherd were purveyors of home-killed meat and Holloway of The Broadway, Southend had a "great reputation throughout Essex" for his false teeth. His prices started at only twenty shillings (the equivalent of £1 today) for a set, and he was one of the few advertisers who had a telephone; his number was Southend 55.

Thomas Buxton was also an advertiser as well as a director of the club, with the Blue Boar being described as the headquarters of Southend United Football Club and the Southend Harriers.

TRY E. BRIDGER & SON'S FAMOUS BREAD

NOTE ADDRESS 120 LEIGH ROAD.

Teams for To-day

SATURDAY, SEPT. 12th, 1908.

SOUTHERN LEAGUE, Div. I.

Referee : Mr. G. MILLAR, Norfolk.
Linesmen : Messrs. A. E. Wood and H. Vine.

SOUTHEND UNITED.

Colours : Royal Blue Jerseys, Black Collars and Cuffs, White Knickers.

RIGHT.   Cotton 1   LEFT.

Thomson 2   Molyneux (Capt.) 3

Emery 4   Leslie 5   Blott 6

Birnie 7   Frost 8   T. S. C. Little 9   Wright 10   Caldwell 11

KICK-OFF **3.30** p.m.

Hunter 12   Twigg 13   Tellum 14   Cunliffe 15   Dean 16

Blythe 17   Comrie 18   Frost 9

Jeffrey 20   Stevenson 21

LEFT.   Joyce 22   RIGHT.

MILLWALL.

Colours : Navy Blue Jerseys, White Knickers.

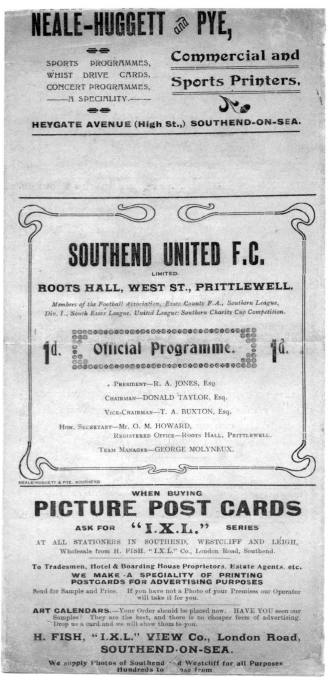

1910/11

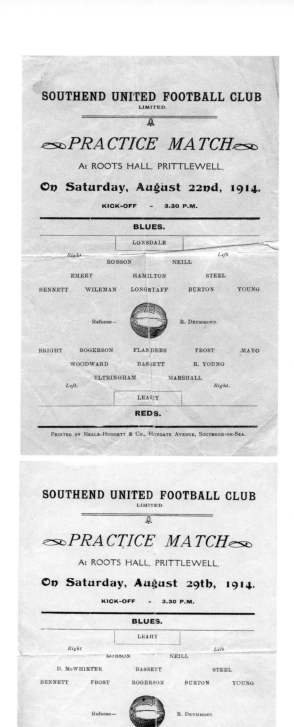

1914/15 single sheet practice match programmes.

programme also contained the first editorial content, reporting on previous matches, player injury news and war news.

The early 1910's also saw the introduction of the pre-season practice match, along with the standard single-sheet programme, a publication that would continue well into the 1960s. The single sheet offered the line-ups of the two teams, usually designated Blue and Red or White, and very little else.

It is also worth noticing that, far from some of the illustrations in this book being printed at the wrong angles, many of the programmes were produced and printed on a very low budget, meaning that the paper was of low quality, the printing was poor and very often off-centre and

the content crammed with filler and advertisements. Again, this was something that can be seen in programmes right up to the 1970's and sometimes beyond. It is only with the advent of high-quality, affordable printing that the standard of programmes has reached a level to which all clubs can aspire.

Due to the close-down of the club during the Second World War, no programmes were issued until

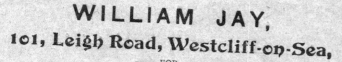

WILLIAM JAY,
101, Leigh Road, Westcliff-on-Sea,

------FOR------

Shop, Office and Bar Fittings and High - Class Decorations.

Shop Fittings and Sundries of every description in Stock.

Next King's Hall, Hamlet Court Road.

Telephone No. 581.

Southend United Football Club, Ltd.

Roots Hall, West Street, Prittlewell.

Members of the Football Association, Southern League Div. 1, South-Eastern League and English Cup Competitions

HEADQUARTERS :

THE "BLUE BOAR" HOTEL, PRITTLEWELL.

Proprietor—ARTHUR G. H. HUNT.

1D · OFFICIAL · PROGRAMME · 1D

Saturday, October 3rd, 1914:
SOUTHEND UNITED
v.
WEST HAM.

NEALE-HUGGETT & CO., SOUTHEND.

DENTISTRY
By FRANK McFARLANE,

154, Hamlet Court Road, Westcliff-on-Sea.

(Over Achilles Serres),

Hours—9 till 8.
Wednesdays—9 till 1.   Late Address : 72 LEIGH ROAD, WESTCLIFF-ON-SEA

1914/15

with advertisements, along with the first team fixtures and results for the season so far. The centre pages had the team line-ups and league tables for both the first and reserve teams, with page six having half a page of editorial and team news. The final two pages were advertisements, leaving the purchaser with approximately one and a half pages of content and six and a half pages of advertisements!

The programme for the 1930/31 season was the first that could truly be called a programme in the form that we know them today. As well as being of a standard nine by six inch size, it had twelve stapled pages and a cover printed on paper of a different colour to the rest of the programme - very advanced for the year of issue! Without raising the cost price (2d), the programme now contained two pages of United Gossip, Supporters' Club Chatter, team line-ups, first and reserve team fixtures, league tables and the half-time scoreboard, along with the standard Kursaal advertisement on the cover. By now, The Kursaal had become a big attraction and was advertising a motor car driven on the Wall of Death. The back cover was advertising "Talkies at Garon's Cinema", which featured "Music! Sound! Dialogue! Colour!", the price of admis-

the resumption of football in the 1920's.

The majority of clubs who issued programmes in the 1920's produced a large-format issue, often produced on very thin paper of varying pastel colours. Southend United were no different in this respect, although they bucked the trend in the 1930's by moving to a "proper" match programme, unlike teams such as Tottenham Hotspur, who continued issuing tissue paper-like four-pagers into the 1960's.

The Southend United programme for the 1926/27 season comprised of eight large format pages. By now, the price of the programme had risen to 2d, although it was doubtful whether the spectator was actually getting any more content for their money. The front page, containing the obligatory Kursaal advertisement that would be prominent for many seasons to come, led the reader to pages two and three, which were again packed

1926/27

sion being just 1/-.

The 1931/32 programme was identical to the previous seasons, except the alternative colour cover was dropped and the badge included. The Kursaal and Garon's Cinema advertisements were still in their regular places, and it was interesting to see an advertisement for Andrew Ducat Ltd., who had a sports shop in Hamlet Court Road.

Having found what the club deemed to be a winning formula, it was no surprise to find the only change for the 1932/33 season was another redesign of the cover. The United Gossip section had also been reduced to just one page, but the Supporters' Club Notes had been enlarged accordingly; already it was becoming apparent just how much the Supporters' Club would contribute to the advancement of Southend United in the years to come.

The 1933/34 programme was completely unchanged from the previous season, however the contents of the 1934/35 had a bit of a redesign. The United Gossip was spread across pages two

*Left to right:
1931/32, 1932/33*

for local companies that would, just like Southend United Football Club, stand the test of time and continue trading for many years into the future, including Howard's Dairies, the Southend Standard, the Alexandra Hotel and Liddiard's, whose shop outside the entrance to Roots Hall on Victoria Avenue still trades today (although under a different name).

Top to bottom: 1933/34, 1934/35, 1935/36

The 1936/37 programme again stuck with the tried and tested formula, although the advertisers were now beginning to realise that there was good money to be made from football spectators. Westcliff-on-Sea Motor Services had begun to run regular trips to Southend United's away matches, and advertised them in the programmes. It would cost the true fan only 3/6 (17p) to travel to Clapton Orient, whilst a trip to the wilds of Aldershot, Reading or Brighton would each cost 8/- (40p).

and three, with the Supporters' Club Notes across pages four and five. With the team line-ups still resident in the centre pages, the fixtures for the first team and reserves were joined on pages eight and nine by a new section, Who's Who in Southend Football Circles, a small biography of a local footballing hero. With the league tables and club goalscorers on pages ten and eleven, the newly laid-out programme was an excellent read, and the price was still the same at 2d.

The 1935/36 programme again retained the previous season's design and layout, along with the 2d price. The advertisements were now a mix of local businesses and attractions, with The Kursaal still occupying the front cover, both the "magnificent ballroom" and the "kinema" being main attractions, along with "12 full-size billiard tables". The lure of the cinema and theatre in general was also clear to be seen, as Garon's were still providing details of their cinema presentations on the back cover, with King's Cinema in Hamlet Court Road, the Gaumont Palace, the Plaza Super Cinema and the Talza Little Theatre Company all paying for space within the pages of the programme. There were also advertisements

The first major change in programme design for five seasons took place for the 1937/38 season. Out went the advertisements on the front cover, to be replaced by an aerial photograph of The Stadium, along with details of the match and the names of those currently serving the club on the Board of Directors. The long-standing patronage of The Kursaal was not lost, but they moved their advertisement to the centre pages; the rest of the contents were unchanged from the previous season.

The 1938/39 season saw a programme of exactly the same size and dimensions of previous seasons; twelve pages packed with cinema advertisements, local companies and the basic football information required by all spectators and supporters, including fixtures, league tables and goalscoring charts.

The 1939/40 season became the first of only three seasons where the programme design was changed during the course of the season, although the reason for this change was not at all

Left to right: 1937/38 and the only home League issue from 1939/40, before war was declared.

to do with marketing or supporter comments like the future changes would be.

The first home match of the 1939/40 season against Walsall saw a standard programme issued, the same in every way to that issued for the last game of the previous season. However, this was to be the only official home match of the season, as war was declared and emergency football begun to be organised.

The outbreak of war not only changed the face of football on the playing side, but it had a profound effect on things such as the printing and issuing of football programmes. Due to rationing and the lack of people available to work at places like printers, the programmes issued by all clubs were pared down and more austere issues were produced. The programmes issued by Southend United for the remainder of their home matches in the Sectional League and the League Cup comprised of four pages printed on reasonably thick paper of varying colours; white, light blue, pink, yellow and orange are all known to exist.

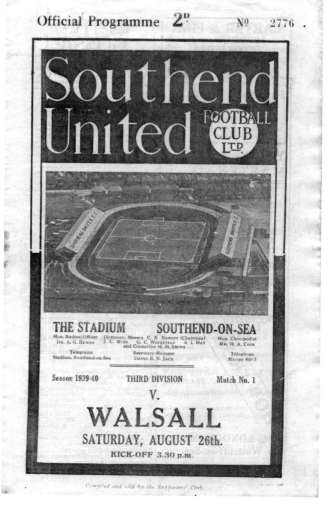

Once again, The Kursaal returned to the front cover, with the inside reserved for the team line-ups, United Gossip and Supporters' Club Notes. The back had details of fixtures and results, along with an advertisement for Garon's Cinema.

The 1940/41 season produced even more difficulties for the Southend United Football Club. Having been evacuated from The Stadium, the club made a temporary home at a different Stadium, that being the one in New Writtle Street, the home of Chelmsford City.

Along with a change of printers, Southend United took on the look and design of the existing Chelmsford City programme, thus leaving the club with its first complete change since the beginning. The front of the eight page programme contained the usual details of the Directors, Manager and Honorary Medical Officer, along with the address of the club, including a note stating that this was "due to Southend evacuation". For the first time in living memory, there were no advertisements in the programme for either The Kursaal or Garon's,

A 1940/41 programme, issued during Southend's stay at Chelmsford.

mainly due to the fact that it was highly unlikely that anyone from Chelmsford would be travelling to enjoy the attractions in Southend during these war-torn times. Page Three was entitled Club Notes and gave details of recently played and forthcoming matches. The centre pages showed the team line-ups (with both teams now numbered from one to eleven) along with the obligatory local advertisements; these even included one for Ann Jewell Ladies' Hairdressing, showing that many females attended football matches to try to forget what was happening in both our own country and other countries both near and far. Page seven gave full and detailed Air Raid Arrangements, including the news that "Play will be resumed if possible immediately the all clear is received". The back cover listed the fixtures, although only the next two or three months were usually shown

1939/40 after war was declared.

due to the fact that very little planning could take place too far into the future.

The next season that the club actually played any football was 1945/46, and the restrictions on paper were still in full force. This meant that, like many other clubs, single sheet programmes were the order of the day. For 1d, the supporter would receive a pastel coloured programme (again, many colours were used, depending on what was available on the day) detailing the line-ups on the front, with some notes and fixtures on the back. Very little information, but very welcome at a time when people were attempting to piece their lives back together.

With the return of "real" football in 1946/47, Southend United started issuing a true programme once more. Although only four pages, and devoid of any advertising whatsoever, the 2d price tag remained. The inside contained the normal team line-ups, along with both first team and reserve fixtures and the half-time scoreboard. The back had Club Notes and an application form for joining the Supporters' Club. Although the war was over, paper was still in short supply and programmes were again issued on light blue, orange or white paper.

The 1947/48 and 1948/49 seasons followed the same design as that of 1946/47, with the same content spread across the four pages.

It wasn't until the 1949/50 season that things began to chance significantly, although the new design introduced would be used for six full seasons before another redesign took place.

The first major change was the price. After countless years of a 2d programme, the price was raised to 3d. The price rise was introduced to help offset the cost of adding four pages to the programme, effectively doubling its size. The other major change was the redesign of the front cover which, although retaining the "Southend United Football Club Ltd" theme, now carried an advertisement for EkcoVision. The idea of having a multitude of local companies advertising in the programme resumed, although there was no space for the cinemas, The Kursaal or Garon's. Pages two and three carried Club Notes as before, with the centre pages still devoted to the team line-ups, something that had remained unchanged since the first programme. Page six carried fixtures and results for both the first and reserve teams, and page seven was now the home of the Supporters' Club Notes. Finally, the back cover held the half-time scoreboard and the league tables.

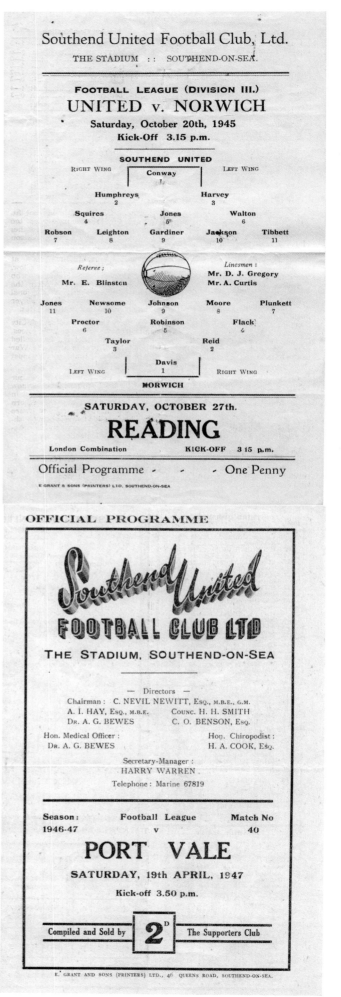

1945/46

1946/47

So, with a new, successful design in place, things remained static with the Southend United programme until another great moment in the clubs' history, the move to Roots Hall, brought about a change in the programme design.

After such a long period of time with no change in the programme design, it was hardly surprising to find that the 1955/56 season didn't see a major shift. The front cover now boasted an aerial view of the new Roots Hall Stadium, but the major difference was that the eight page programme now comprised of one sheet of paper, twenty-two and a half inches wide by eight and a half inches deep,

Above (left to right):
1947/48, 1948/49
Left: 1949/50
Right: 1950/51

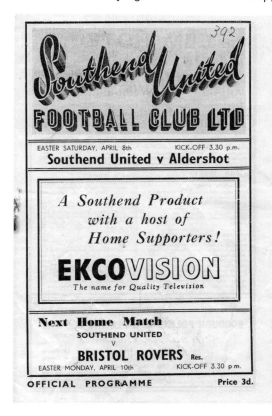
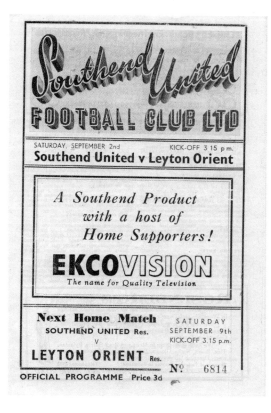

Below (left to right): 1951/52, 1952/53, 1953/54, 1954/55

folded twice to make a standard size programme. How this was handled on a wet and windy day is anyone's guess, and may explain why there are not too many good condition examples of this programme around now.

Opening this programme up, one side contained the standard Club Notes, along with fixtures and Supporters' Club Notes, whilst the reverse contained the team line-ups, half-time scoreboard and league tables. Not a great deviation from

ups would still appear in the centre spread.

The 1956/57 and 1957/58 programmes were identical to the 1955/56, and it wasn't until the 1958/59 season that another change was made, although this was purely cosmetic. Having allowed the supporters to fight with the "ever-expanding programme" for three seasons, the club now cut and stapled the programme, making a standard 16-pager - everything else stayed the same as the previous season.

Left to right: 1955/56, 1956/57, 1957/58, 1958/59, 1959/60

previous efforts, but very nice to see the return of The Kursaal to the advertising, with its "fully licensed lounges, billiards and snooker, winter indoor cricket, badminton and modern ballroom dancing". Incidentally, although the shape of this programme was unusual when unfolded, by refolding it along the correct lines, the team line-

1959/60 saw no change, but in 1960/61 the club made a strange decision to change the ink used in printing the programme to black, thus removing the blue link between the club kit and the club programme. Apart from some minor changes to the layout of the cover, again the programme remained almost completely unaltered.

The 1961/62 season saw the start of a trend that was adopted by many clubs in the early 1960's, that of the truly pocket-sized programme. Measuring only approximately four inches wide by five-and-a-quarter inches high, this style of programme was issued by Notts County, Halifax Town, Bradford Park Avenue, Barnsley, Reading, Crystal Palace, Northampton Town and Swindon Town amongst the opponents of Southend United, as well as the club themselves. With only twenty small-format pages the fill, the club stuck to a tried and tested formula. Page three had details of the match the programme was being issued for (thus causing all programme collectors to have to open the programme to check), page four contained the managers notes and page five carried news from the club secretary. Page seven had opponents pen pictures and page nine carried the league tables for both the first and second teams. A link to the past came in the centre pages, where the team line-ups were, once again, shown. Page twelve showed the seasons fixtures, which continued on page fourteen, and the half-time scoreboard was on page eighteen. It was great to see the full-page advert for The Kursaal in its rightful place on the back cover. The price of the programme was 4d.

The 1962/63 programme contained even less content, with the managers notes being dropped, to be replaced by Supporters' Club Notes and the opponents pen pictures getting moved towards the back of the programme. The 1963/64 and 1964/65 seasons also saw various tinkering being carried out with the contents, including the addition of a Today's Personality section on page six, possibly in an attempt to justify the increase in cost to 6d at the start of the 1964/65 season.

1965/66 was the final season of the small-format programme, and in 1966/67 the club made a return to the "normal" programme, with an issue of 16 pages, five-and-a-half inches wide by eight-and-a-half inches high. The front cover carried a different photograph on each issue, with page three entitled From the General Manager's Office. Pen pictures of the opponents were on page four and then lots of adverts up to the centre pages, which again carried the team line-ups. Pages ten and eleven were variable in content, although usually they had a photograph and the Suppoerters' Club News. Page thirteen gave the seasons fixtures with the league tables on page fourteen. The Kursaal's advert still held pride of place on the back cover.

1960/61

1961/62 (actual size). The programme covers for 1962/63, 1963/64, 1964/65 and 1965/66 are not shown, as they are identical to 1961/62 (except for a change in price).

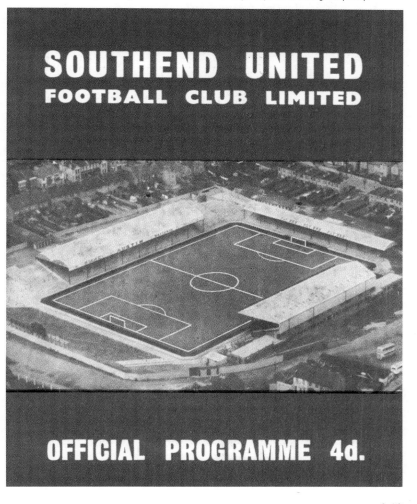

1967/68 saw a very similar issue, with a minor change to the cover, a simpler badge being used along with a change in the way the opponents were named. The 6d price tag was also held steady, but this wouldn't be the case for the 1968/69 season, where major changes were

tors, What The Papers Said and a photograph of a current player. The statistics were enlarged to two pages, with great detail of the league tables, fixtures and goalscorers. The last link to programmes of old was lost with the team line-ups being listed in numerical order, rather than laid

Left to right: 1966/67, 1967/68

afoot.

The 1968/69 season saw the club change just about everything with regards to their programme (apart from The Kursaal advertisement on the back cover). The page size was increased to six-and-a-half inches wide by nine-and-a-quarter inches high, the number of pages was increased to twenty-four and the cover price was increased to one shilling. The cover was predominantly blue, however the content was exclusively black and white. With extensive use of photographs on the inside, this programme was a major advance for Southend United, and the fans certainly couldn't complain about lack of content. The usual Managers Comments (along with a nice photograph) were on page three, with United in Action given a double-spread on pages six and seven. There was space for news on the Youth Section and the Supporters' Club with full pages on Our Visi-

out on a field of play. However, each player of both teams had a small fact listed which gave plenty for the fan to absorb during the half-time interval. All-in-all, the programme was excellent and set the club off on a great adventure, producing programme of increasing standard for a fair few seasons to come.

The 1969/70 programme was very similar in content to the previous season, with a new cover being the only major change.

The 1970/71 season, however, along with a mid-season change of price from one shilling to five new pence, undertook another content make-over. The excellent (for the time) photographic content was increased, and new articles were added, including Whistle Stop! (a biography of the referee), Yesteryear, The Pad, an additional page of statistics for the Eastern Professional

NEWPORT COUNTY
28th APRIL, 1969
KICK-OFF 7.30 p.m.
ONE SHILLING

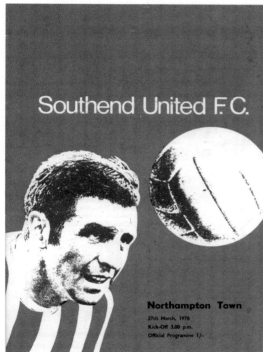

Southend United F.C.

Northampton Town

27th March, 1970
Kick-Off 3.00 p.m.
Official Programme 1/-

couple of reasons. Firstly, it was the first season that the programme changed design part-way through, and secondly, it was the first season that the team line-ups moved from the centre-pages of the Southend United programme.

The season started with a cover design showing a Southend United player in action on a reduced page size from the previous season. The

Official Programme 5p
United v. Chester
Football League Division 4. Kick-Off 7.30 p.m. Monday 22nd February, 1971.

Floodlight Competition and the London Midweek League and a three-page article called Blues Album, which gave an in-depth review of one of the Southend United players.

The only change, apart from the cover design, for the 1971/72 season was that the Blues Album feature was dropped and replaced with biographies of the Visiting Manager and Visiting Captain and a page called 4th Scene, which reviewed the current goings-on in the Fourth Division.

The 1972/73 season was memorable in the history of the Southend United programme for a

SOUTHEND UNITED
v. CREWE ALEXANDRA
Monday, 13th March, 1972
Football League Div. 4. Kick-off 7.30 p.m.
Official Programme 5p

new nine inch high by five inch wide programme retained its twenty-four pages, but the price was raised to seven pence, and the content was again revamped. The print quality was significantly increased, with the photgraphic content being much better than the previous seasons. Contents now included The Rowley Report, Meet The Players, two pages of Action Highlights, Today's Visitors, The Secretary's Review, The Men In Charge Today, First Team Facts and Fixtures (for the first time including the line-ups for all the games played so far during the season), 3rd Division News, Where Are They Now?, In Off The Post (a selection of fans letters), Supporters News and Fixtures. With the team line-ups now on the back page, this was yet another excellent programme, something the club was becoming well-known for producing. When the cover changed in December 1972, the contents remained the same.

The 1973/74 season drew on a lot of the successes of the previous season, although there was a little less reading content and the price was raised to ten pence. The removal of a few regular articles, to be replaced by advertisements and other less interesting articles was the beginning of an era when the Southend United programme became quite a "cheap and nasty" effort, compared with the previous high-standard productions.

The 1974/75 programme sported a nice new cover, which showed off the new club badge, a boot in the shape of the word "United". Inside, a lot of space was given over to articles that would be quick and easy to put together, but didn't offer too much in the way of reading material. A page of United Bingo Results on page four, a page of United Souvenir Shop prices on page five (duffle bags for £1.10) and a page on Forthcoming Matches were interspersed with eight pages of advertisements, although there were still a few pages worth reading, including Grass Roots, Club History and Focus on Youth. However, nothing was to prepare the Southend United supporter for the programme of the following season.

Admittedly, the cost of the 1975/76 programme was reduced to five pence, but that hardly compensated for the dearth of information contained in its minimal eight pages. The previously used glossy paper was replaced by a poor relation, and the typesetting appeared to have been done on a typewriter. The cover, which was sponsored by Southend General Market, was followed by Don Stewart's Grass Roots on page three. The centre pages were given over to the visitors, pages six

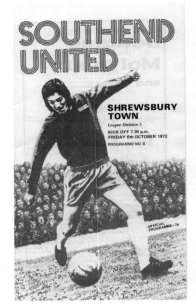

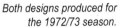
Both designs produced for the 1972/73 season.

and seven contained Southend Facts & Figures and some poorly reproduced photographs, while the team line-ups were on the back cover (page sponsored by Frank Walton Insurance Brokers). This programme, although fulfilling all the requirements of a football programme (team line-ups, minimal reading material), was really the worst that the club had ever produced. Things could only get better for the programme fan from here onwards.

1976/77 saw a return to glossy paper and a cover price of ten pence, along with an increase to twelve pages. The quality of the production was much better, and for the first time since 1966/67,

1973/74

A CENTURY UNITED

a different photograph was shown on the cover of each programme. Dave Smith's notes were on page three, with the Opposition File on page four and Blues' Statistics including the line-ups for all the season's matches on page five. Unfortunately, the double-page centre spread was given over to a advertisement, but with Blues Scene on page eight and Blues in Focus on page nine, there was at least something for the fan to read at half-time.

Above (left to right): 1974/75 , 1975/76

Below (left to right): 1976/77, 1977/78

The 1977/78 programme was very similar in looks to the previous seasons effort, although this time the centre spread was given over to photographs of a previous match.

The 1978/79 programme again changed its shape, this time almost becoming square, with a height of eight inches and a width of six-and-a-half inches. The increase in price to fifteen pence also coincided with an increase to sixteen pages, and the content was much improved. Dave Smith still provided his full page of interesting notes, and with Club Scene, Blues in Action, two pages of Facts

& Figures, The Opposition, Third Division Scene and Supporters' Club News, there was a return to the standards of six or seven years previously.

the season for any player cost £130, whilst just £10 allowed you to sponsor a players match day socks.

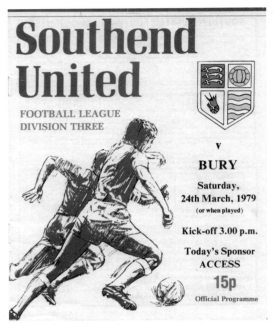

1978/79

A massive increase in pages to twenty-eight in the 1979/80 programme was offset by the fact that sixteen of these pages were provided by Programme Plus, a generic insert used by many clubs at the time. Like the old fashioned Football League Review, which was included in many programmes of the sixties, this full-colour insert contained articles about clubs and players from Britain and around the world. Although adding reading content, it was so general and advertisement filled that most supporters just flicked straight past it.

The actual Southend United content of the 1979/80 programme was good, with Dave Smith still churning out his copious notes, a Club News Desk page, full-page Player Profile and two pages of Statistics. Whether it merited a 100% increase in price to thirty pence was doubtful.

The 1980/81 programme, which saw Southend United win the Fourth Division championship, was a mammoth forty pages, although the price was left unchanged from the previous season. Although Programme Plus now contributed twenty-four pages, there was an increase in Southend United content, including Junior Corner, Spotlight On a current player, a Blues Quiz, a Social & Commercial page and the first ever Sponsor A Player page, which allowed the fans to contribute towards the match day and training kits of the players. Full match day kit sponsorship for

Top to bottom: 1979/80, 1980/81

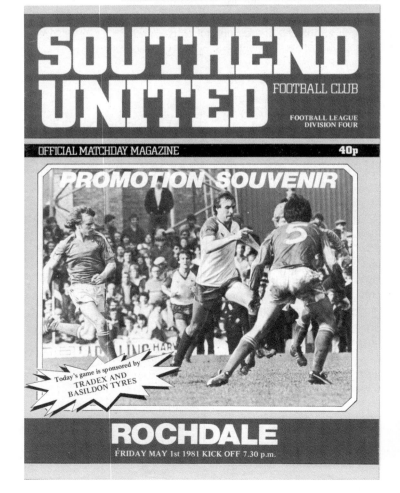

A slimmed-down 1981/82 programme saw the coloured Programme Plus contribution reduced to just eight pages, whilst the Southend United content remained at sixteen pages. Strangely, the back cover was given to Firstline International to advertise their luxury holiday homes in Costa Dorada. Because of this, the team line-ups were moved to page three, although this move was offset by the inclusion of full colour on the first four and last four pages of the programme for the first time in the club's history. Lots of content, including Youth, Reserves and an Introducing page allowing players to answer questions about their likes and dislikes made for a good read during those cold half-time intervals.

1982/83 continued to use the eight page Programme Plus insert, and the programme itself was relatively unchanged, apart from the line-ups being returned to their rightful place, on the back cover. Although swapped around a little, the content of the programme was remarkably similar to the previous season, with the cost rising to thirty-five pence, the equivalent of seven old shillings!

1983/84 saw the return to a smaller format programme, this one measuring just over eight inches high by six inches wide. Although only containing twenty-four pages, the Programme Plus section was dropped, thus providing the supporters with 100% Southend United content. With Programme Editor Terry Smith providing an article for page three, the Manager Talks was relegated to page five, Our Visitors were given page seven whilst Terry Smith was busy again on page nine with his 3rd Division Scene. Three pages of statistics helped to offset the pages of advertisements, and after another Terry Smith

penned page, Around Roots Hall, a half-page Player Profile was shown on page twenty-two. Standard team lines were shown on the back cover.

The 1984/85 programme started as a matt-paper programme, but moved to glossy halfway through the season. The sixteen pages also were devoid of any colour apart from the blue of Southend, although for forty pence, there was a reasonable amount of reading material. With a different action shot on the cover of each programme, the Roots Hall Newsreel started on page three. There were many smaller articles in this programme, taking up a half or a quarter page, which gave it a slightly disjointed look, with the team line-ups returning to the centre pages, along with all the reserve fixtures and tables.

1985/86 kept the same look as the previous season, although the price went up to fifty pence for the first time. There were more larger sized articles this season, with Jane Austen providing a series entitles The Southend United Story, which ran throughout the season. Just to keep the fans on their feet, the team line-ups were once again moved to the back cover.

Not much changed for the 1986/87 season (except the price, which went up to sixty pence), with over seven of the twenty pages being filled with advertisements.

1987/88 again remained very similar in style to the previous season, although it was noticeable that there was a lot more sponsorship and product placement creeping into the programme. This included the beginning of the now famous Roger Buxton column plus a whole page of Pub Talk presented by "Southend's Newest

1981/82

1982/83

United supporter was now beginning to get used to a programme packed with advertising content and devoid of any real reading material; a far cry from the great Southend United programmes of the late 1960's and early 1970's.

The thirty-six page programme of 1990/91 was a little better than the efforts of the previous few seasons, but there was still a prevalence of advertisments which made finding the proper articles a little difficult. With Webb's Words on page three, Boardroom Blues and Most Fashionable Wine Bar and Pub" West One.

With 1988/89 and 1989/90's programmes being the same style again, with just a few extra pages added and ten pence put on the price each season, the Southend

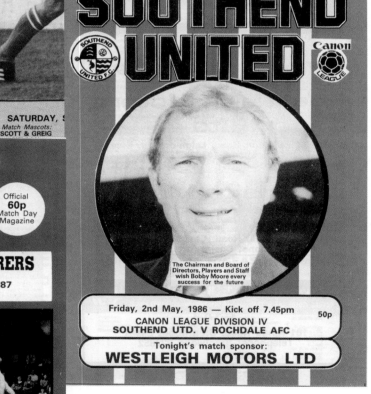

on page nine, Blues and Their Fans on page fourteen, The Memory Game on page seventeen and a Player Profile on pages twenty-eight and twenty-nine, there was plenty of padding within the pages of the first Southend United programme to hit the £1 mark.

With Southend United's elevation to the Second Division for the 1991/92 season, the programme needed to also take that step up, and it did hap-

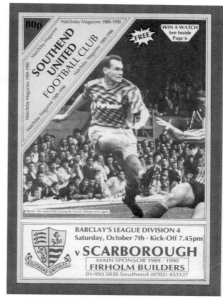

Clockwise from top left:
1987/88, 1988/89, 1989/90,
1990/91, 1991/92

pen, along with a rise in price and increase in page size. Indeed, this became the first of the large style programmes produced by the club, its nine-and-a-half by six-and-a-half inch size remaining almost constant up to the programmes of today. As well as all the standard features expected of a programme, there were many contributed by Southend United supporters, a trend which also continues today. There was even space for a Fan File, which allowed a supporter to answer the questions normally reserved for the players themselves. Also included were articles on Collecting Football Programmes and Blues Bygone Days, a look back at events that had happened on this particular date thirty, twenty and ten years ago.

With the programme price now standing at £1.40, and the club attracting larger attendance now it was in the First Division, it was important to provide more for the fan to digest. This was achieved in the 1992/93 season, with only ten of the thirty-six pages given over to advertising, a lower proportion than in previous seasons, and the introduction of new articles such as In The Wings, One Vision with Nick Alliker, Blues in the Community with Frankie Banks, Around the Ground with physio Alan Raw, Those were The Days with Kevin O'Donnell and The A-2-Z of SUFC by Dave Goody.

The 1993/94 programme was produced along the same lines as the previous year, although there was a rise on the amount of advertising, a full twenty of the forty pages being revenue generators for the club. It was good to see that the club did start using full colour in the Reel Action section, the centre spread of the programme showing action from a previous match.

The 1994/95 programme showed a nice innovation in cover design, with players pictures being displayed like an old-fashioned cigarette card al-

bum. All the standard programme contents were included, and they were there again the following season, 1995/96, although this season's programme showed a lot more use of colour in its forty-four pages.

An almost totally full colour forty-four page programme is what greeted the Southend United fans at the start of the 1996/97 season, and a

Top left to bottom right:
1992/93, 1993/94, 1994/95,
1995/96, 1996/97, 1997/98

As the club had now found a format which achieved both a good level of advertising revenue and a good read for the supporter, it was no surprise to find the 1997/98 programme significantly unchanged from the previous season.

However, its £1.60 price tag was increased to £1.70 for the 1998/99 season. Unfortunately, it also coincided with a reduction in programme

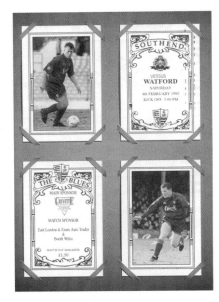
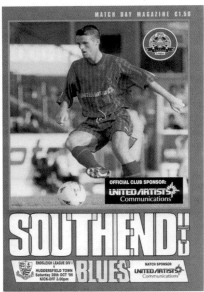
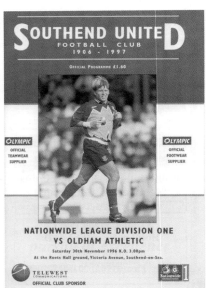

pretty good programme it was too. Although still containing its fair share of advertisements, the articles themselves were more substantial, including a double-page spread on previous encounters with the opponents, a Fitness Feature with physio John Gowens, Blues Moments, Programme Collecting, Safety Matters, Player Focus, Around The Hall, Centre of Excellence and Blues Records.

size to forty pages and an increase in advertisements, as many of the interesting features were dropped or had run their course without being replaced.

The 1999/2000 programme was memorable for being the first Southend United issue to cost £2, whilst its contents were again unremarkable, a mix of standard fare and advertisements.

2000/01 saw the beginnings in the shoots of recovery for the Southend United programme, but it wasn't heped by an abortive attempt to issue an A4 sized programme. "The Longest Pier" was issued for a few matches from the beginning of the season, and although an admirable attempt to do something different, the programme's unwieldy size was not liked by fans and was fairly swiftly dropped. The revamped programme, which reverted back to its size of the previous season had more content of interest to the supporter than the previous season, and the colour and layout was an improvement. Phil Whelan started a trend with his Whelan's Witterings page, something that most captains now continue, whilst the Supporters' Club Trust began its revival with its own section. As befits a club that was trying to regain its past glories of the First Division, the Marketing Department had its own page to try to drum up support from the business community, whilst Rewind looked at the previous few matches. There were plenty of colour photos throughout and Steve Tilson began his contributions with a page called Youth Focus.

A massive sixty-four page issue was produced for the 2001/02 season, and the content was much improved, as was the price, now rising to £2.20. There was just about everything you could wish for within the thick pages, and many different contributors.

A similar programme was produced for the 2002/03 season, with Kevin Maher taking over the Captain's Log page. Unlike the early days, the Kit Sponsors page had now spread to two pages and included both home and away kits. With the internet also becoming more accessible, it was interesting to see that the information on the visitors was much more comprehensive and there was often interviews with fans of the visitors, conducted by email.

2003/04 was now a glossy covered magazine-style issue, with its price set at £2.50. Its sixty-eight pages were packed with reading material as the club began to realise that the rising attendances were buying more programmes and more revenue could be generated from their sale.

The final two programmes of Southend United's first one hundred years, 2004/05 and 2005/06, were high quality, glossy issues that were very fitting for a club that was having one of the most successful spells in its history. Its rise through the divisions was equalled by the programme, which became better, bigger and more readable as the

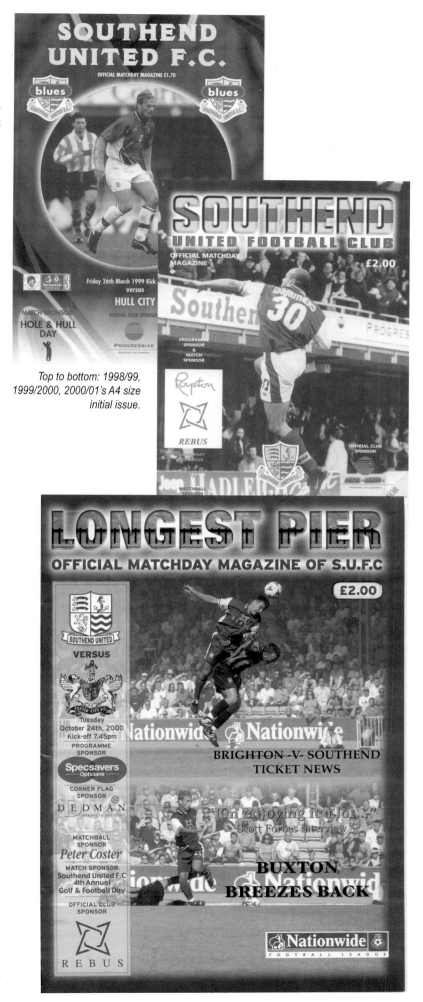

Top to bottom: 1998/99, 1999/2000, 2000/01's A4 size initial issue.

effort required to produce a good programme reduced, thanks to the advent of computers and the internet.

Comparing the original issues from the first twenty years of the clubs' existance and those produced in the final ten years, there are some elements that have been present throughout, whereas some are relatively new. Its fairly certain that in the 1910's the physios thoughts on players injuries would not have been considered fit to include in the official club programme, whilst news that a particularly rough match that had resulted in one player being booked (as reported in a 1926 Southend United programme) would no longer be deemed worthy of inclusion in today's glossy production.

Top to bottom: 2000/01, 2001/02, 2002/03, 2003/04, 2004/05, 2005/06

THE RISE AND FALL OF SOUTHEND INVICTA

The first Southend Invicta home programme, for the visit of Bramley on 9th September 1984

Southend Invicta

Kent Invicta were formed by Paul Feires and were admitted to the Rugby League on 6th April 1983. They played their first game at London Road, Maidstone, a ground they shared with Maidstone United and a greyhound company. The game was against Cardiff City and, in what was a portent for the future, they lost 12-31 before a crowd of 1,815.

The record attendance whilst based in Maidstone was 2,107 against St. Helens on 6th November, 1983, by which time the club was bankrupt and the reins were taken over by Jim Thompson, the chairman of the football club. The last game at their shared home was on 12th May, 1984 against Rochdale Hornets, which they won 32-12 before 412 spectators.

The Kent Invicta team finished the season in a respectable 9th position in Rugby League's 18-team Slalom Lager Division Two, winning 17 and losing 17 of their 34 matches, but problems with ground-sharing and wear of the football pitch resulted in the club having to move. Today the London Road site is an MFI superstore.

Invicta were then approached by Southend United Football Club and became Southend Invicta, sharing the Roots Hall ground with their footballing hosts, although there appeared to be little support from the football club themselves, with only the most fleeting of mentions of the oval-ball game in the football club's home programmes.

The first home game on 9th September 1984 against Bramley attracted a crowd of 371, comprised of a few exiles indulging in their love of the game and a few curious southerners, no doubt wanting to see how a live game compared to the afternoon experience of Grandstand on the telly. Some had even travelled from Maidstone, the previous home of Invicta. Southend lost 14-17 to Bramley, a result the faithful few would get used to over the coming nine months. The team's first win (of four) during the whole season was against Dewsbury on 7th October 1984.

Not only were the rules of the game slightly alien to the residents of south-east Essex, but so was the way the fixture list was compiled. Although there were 20 clubs in Division Two of the Slalom Lager Rugby League Championship, each club only played 28 matches. For the purposes of compiling the fixture list, the clubs were divided into two groups, with ten teams in each. The ten teams in Group One (including Southend Invicta) played each other home and away, as did the teams in Group Two, thus giving each team nine home and nine away matches. Then, the first half of the teams in Group One (again, including Southend Invicta) played the first half of the teams in Group Two home and away, giving each team another five home and five away matches, making a grand total of 28 matches. In truth, by the time most supporters had understood how the fixture list had been devised, they had lost interest in Southend Invicta.

Crowds steadily dwindled and even the Evening Echo soon lost interest. On a foul day in January 1985, a grand total of 86 folk saw Southend Invicta lose 2-27 to Blackpool Borough (another club no longer in existence). But even this crowd was larger than that attending what was to be Southend Invicta's final ever home game. On 26th April 1985, there were 85 fans to witness Southend Invicta lose 16-24 to Huddersfield Barracudas. The match started late and speculation was rife that it wouldn't start at all, that Southend could not even raise a team. Two days later Southend Invicta played their last ever game. Obviously overawed by the sheer size of the crowd (250), Southend Invicta lost to Blackpool Borough 12-14.

In the programme for the match against York on 21st April 1985, the secretary of the Supporters Club, Peter Jones, wrote:

"I only wish at this final stage of the season, I could assure you that Rugby League would defi-

nitely be here at Roots Hall at the beginning of next season. Unfortunately I do not possess the necessary psychic abilities to forecast such an event. Silence on the part of the Southend management, who control the Rugby Club's destiny, about the future of Invicta, is probably the most honest comment they can make about next season. We'll just have to wait and see."

After the Huddersfield game, club director Matt Wheatcroft admitted the club was in an extremely precarious position. He said "there is no commercial reason for us to carry on. The support we receive is abysmal, and the picture at the moment is extremely gloomy. The club needed a big sell when we came here, which it hasn't received, and our hopes haven't been fulfilled. We came to the wrong place at the wrong time."

The local Yellow Advertiser commented wryly "the hackneyed saying that Rugby League is a northern man's game seems to be true."

Southend Invicta were struck from the 1985/86 fixtures by the Rugby League only days before the commencement of the new season because they were considered not to have formed a team. They went into liquidation soon afterwards.

Southend Invicta 1984/85

A CENTURY UNITED

Match Reports

2nd September 1984 - York 46 Southend Invicta 14

The new Southend Invicta team faced a difficult first game at York, a team widely predicted for promotion. So confident was the feeling at York that one of the directors had placed a £5,000 bet on the team gaining promotion (something they duly achieved by finishing third). York also boasted a player who was to go on to bigger things - the great Graham Steadman. Invicta got off to a good start, but found themselves 2-22 down at half time. Amazingly, Invicta hit back early in the second half when Mark Elia intercepted a York pass in his own 25, cooly sprinting 75 yards upfield before arrogantly side-stepping the full back to score under the posts, but they never managed to get back into the game. However, five minutes before the end, Elia struck again. From a tap penalty 15 yards out from the York line, he received a pass on the burst and rounded four players to score under the posts - Cholmondeley again added the goal.

9th September 1984 - Southend Invicta 14 Bramley 17

The first home game! In an end-to-end game Invicta narrowly lost to Bramley in front of a disappointing crowd of 371. Southend battled hard with Frank Feighan scoring two tries and Dave Harding one (he also dropped a goal); Dave Cholmondeley also kicked a goal. The game was marred by injuries to Tony Cooper (broken leg), Alan Bishop and Neil Bishop.

23rd September 1984 - Southend Invicta 13 Wakefield Trinity 22

Despite what was to be a very disappointing season for them, Trinity had a useful side and were always too good for Invicta despite two tries from Mark Elia, two goals from Dave Cholmondeley and a dropped goal from Dave Harding.

30th September 1984 - Huddersfield Barracudas 22 Southend Invicta 14

Before the game had started, one of the Huddersfield cheerleaders lost her skirt, but in true showbiz style carried on to the bitter end! Unfortunately for Invicta, it proved to be a highlight of the match. The Barracudas dominated the first half, scoring three tries. Three minutes before half time Mark Elia intercepted the ball and scored unchallenged under the posts - new kicker Tony Neel adding the conversion. Invicta took the lead 18 minutes into the second half when Frank Feighan touched down, following a fine passing movement involving Adrian Alexander (a recent acquisition from Oldham), Cholmondeley and Elia. Tony Neel added the goal to give Invicta a deserved 18-16 lead. But it was not to be and a Barracuda's try and conversion left Southend still looking for their first victory.

The Huddersfield **BARRACUDAS**
Rugby League Football Club
on **ARENA'84** Huddersfield HD2 2SD

Sunday, September 30th, at 3-30 p.m.

Versus

Southend Invicta

Slalom Lager
RUGBY LEAGUE
SECOND DIVISION
CHAMPIONSHIP

MATCH
PROGRAMME
40P

Programme No.

No 3018

Season 1984/5

7th October 1984 - Southend Invicta 22 Dewsbury 12

This was the match in which Invicta recorded their first victory in front of a crowd of 284. Strangely, Dewsbury only lost six games all season and in finishing in fourth place, gained promotion to Division One of the Slalom Rugby League; the trip down south must have taken its toll on the players! Southend totally dominated in the first half and led 18-2 at the break. Dewsbury came back in the second half, but it was too little too late.

14th October 1984 - Bramley 30 Southend Invicta 8

Invicta found the trip to Bramley difficult to say the least. The coach blew a gasket south of Sheffield on the M1 and the team had to wait for a replacement. They arrived two minutes before the kick off at 3.30pm and the game eventually got underway 15 minutes late. Despite this trauma, Invicta battled well and were only 2-11 down at half time, with Dave Cholmondeley dropping two goals. Despite a valiant effort, Invicta ran out of steam and Bramley added three further tries to finally win 8-30.

21st October 1984 - Swinton 22 Southend Invicta 18

Invicta were total underdogs for this game. Swinton were unbeaten, top of the table and boasted Danny Wilson in their line-up, the father of Ryan Giggs. Invicta had Frank Feighan, Wayne Millington and Adrian Alexander missing through injury and fell behind to an early try and conversion, but Mark Elia's ninth try of the season and Tony Neel's conversion saw them level the score at 6-6, then Tony Neel forced his way beneath the posts and added the conversion to make it 12-12. Swinton then scored again to make it 12-20 at half time. Invicta put up a great performance in the second half with Andy Scanlon outstanding at full back. Ten minutes from time Tony Neel scored his second try and added the conversion to make it 18-22. Swinton hung on but it was a tremendous effort by Invicta against a team who were to be the season's Second Division champions.

28th October 1984 - Southend Invicta 22 Keighley 18

Invicta's second win. No match report available.

4th November 1984 - Bramley 20 Southend Invicta 6 (John Player Trophy - Preliminary Round)

Invicta managed to beat their Bramley jinx and arrived on time for the game. Invicta were on the defensive for much of the first half but tackled well and restricted Bramley to a 0-6 lead at half time. After half time, Invicta gained more possession and finally scored two minutes from time when Mark Elia received the ball just outside the Bramley half and outwitted five Bramley tacklers on a sparkling 50 yard run to the line for his 13th try of the season. Neel converted to make the final score Bramley 20 Invicta 6.

11th November 1984 - Batley 19 Southend Invicta 10

This match was billed as the clash of the tryscorers as Invicta's Mark Elia and Batley's Carl Gibson were joint second in the try list with 13 touchdowns so far. Batley played in the first half with the benefit of the notorious Mount Pleasant slope, but a Chris Wellman try and Dave Cholmondeley conversion put Invicta in front 6-0. Batley rallied, however, and scored two tries to lead 6-12 at half time. In the second half, Invicta failed to capitalise from playing down the slope and Wayne Millington scored Invicta's only points with a well taken try ten minutes from time.

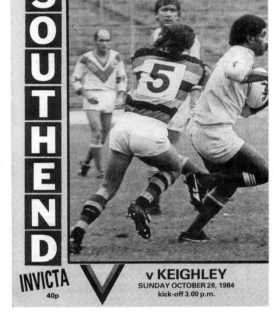

18th November 1984 - Wakefield Trinity 31 Southend Invicta 0

No match report available.

Dave Cholmondeley

9th December 1984 - Doncaster 12 Southend Invicta 4

This should have been Invicta's first away win of the season. Doncaster had lost their previous two games 0-72 (to Dewsbury) and 0-64 (to Whitehaven). Southend started well but two penalty kicks gave Doncaster a 0-4 lead at half time. After the interval Doncaster got an unexpected interception try and conversion to put them 0-10 up. This spurred Invicta on to greater efforts, with Atherton finally scoring a try in the corner. Invicta continued to attack during a furious last ten minutes but couldn't score. Two minutes from time, a Dave Cholmondeley indiscretion gave Doncaster another easy penalty kick to make the final score 4-12.

16th December 1984 - Keighley 26 Southend Invicta 16

Things started badly for Invicta when Keighley scored two early tries to go 0-12 up after only ten minutes. Four minutes before half time Johnston scored a try following good approach work by Wellman and Donnelly, with Alexander selling a couple of outrageous dummies. Two minutes later Mark Elia snapped up a loose ball to score beneath the posts, Tony Neel adding the conversion to put Invicta 16-12 up at the break. During an exciting second half, Keighley took advantage of their limited opportunities to score two further tries to finish 16-26 victors in a tough, thrilling encounter.

23rd December 1984 - Southend Invicta 10 Swinton 28

No match report available.

1st January 1985 - Southend Invicta 14 Fulham 16

This was a match of great significance - the first time a local derby had been played between two professional Rugby League teams in the South for fifty years, when Acton and Willesden (1935 to 1936), Streatham and Mitcham (1935 to 1937) and London Highfield (1933 to 1934) had been in existence. The game started in exciting fashion with John "Dallas" Donnelly punching Fulham's Gourley after only 60 seconds of play. Having led 9-0, Invicta's third win beckoned but Fulham pressure towards the end of the match brought its reward when Rochford broke clear to level the scores and Chris Wilkinson sealed Fulham's victory with a simple conversion.

27th January 1985 - Southend Invicta 2 Blackpool Borough 27

Severe frost and snow had led to the postponement of the games at home to Huddersfield (January 13) and away to Salford (January 20). The lay off didn't help Southend and they were totally outclassed. The lay off and bad weather also affected the attendance - a pathetic crowd of 86 watching.

3rd February 1985 - Whitehaven 22 Southend Invicta 8

This was Mark Elia's last match for Invicta, having been called up for the New Zealand International Training squad. As a team already struggling, losing your best player would always be a problem, and it signaled the beginning of the end for Invicta.

24th February 1985 - Bradford Northern 50 Southend Invicta 18 (Silk Cut Challenge Cup First Round)

Invicta's biggest game of the season. Although by no means the greatest Bradford Northern team ever (they eventually finished mid table in the First Division that season) they had the immortal Ellery Hanley playing at stand off. Southend had been drawn at home but the club's deteriorating financial position had meant an inevitable switch to Odsal. This caused great controversy, with the Supporters Club much perturbed by the decision. Peter Jones, secretary of the Supporters Club, stated: "This move makes a mockery of the Club's supposedly long-term expansionist policy and has done nothing to maintain our credibility with the game's Governing Body and other Clubs in the League." The game should have been played on 10 February but the continuing bad weather had meant the game had been postponed and the freeze meant further postponements on 14, 17 and 19 February. The game was eventually played two weeks after the original date. Invicta certainly didn't disgrace themselves, playing some excellent open rugby they scored three tries through Atherton, Donnelly and man of the match Harding and earned the respect of both the home crowd and the northern press.

3rd March 1985 - Southend Invicta 14 Doncaster 17

As Doncaster hadn't won an away game since October 1983, hopes were high for an Invicta win. However, despite creating several scoring opportunities, Invicta made too many elementary mistakes and eventually lost a keenly fought contest to an effective Doncaster team.

10th March 1985 - Southend Invicta 12 Salford 56

Invicta were totally outclassed by a very strong Salford team containing the likes of John Pendlebury, Mick McTigue, Darren Bloor, Clive Griffiths and Paul Fletcher.

16th March 1985 - Salford 42 Southend Invicta 6

Invicta did slightly better the following Saturday in a game rearranged from 20 January but were still well beaten. Colin Penola scored a try after only 45 seconds and received an alarm clock for his achievement before the

home game against Whitehaven on 24 March! Shortage of players meant that Coach Bill Goodwin had to name himself as substitute, even though he hadn't played for five years. Fortunately he wasn't called upon to play.

17th March 1985 - Mansfield Marksman 18 Southend Invicta 31

Having been heavily defeated by Salford only 24 hours previously, Invicta produced a miraculous performance against Mansfield, cruising to victory. They scored 29 points in the second half - the most points the team had scored since their formation as Kent Invicta in August 1983. This was to be Invicta's only away win of the season.

24th March 1985 - Southend Invicta 2 Whitehaven 22

Whitehaven had started the season well but had slipped to seventh place in the table by the time

Colin Penola

they arrived at Roots Hall for this game. Unfortunately, they had little trouble brushing aside an Invicta team who were beginning to look a sorry sight.

31st March 1985 - Southend Invicta 10 Batley 15

Batley came to Roots Hall having done the double over Dewsbury but had only just beaten bottom of the table Bridgend 14-9. Hopes were therefore high for a home win but Invicta disappointed yet again.

5th April 1985 - Fulham 24 Southend Invicta 17

No match report available.

12th April 1985 - Southend Invicta 14 Mansfield Marksman 12

This match should have been played on 25 November but the delay obviously favoured Invicta as they recorded their first home win for over 5 months and their only double of the season.

14th April 1985 - Dewsbury 46 Southend Invicta 10

Dewsbury had all but secured promotion and it was becoming ever clearer that Southend's future was very much in doubt. Dewsbury won the game at a canter.

21st April 1985 - Southend Invicta 10 York 30

No match report available.

26th April 1985 - Southend Invicta 16 Huddersfield Barracudas 24

There was an eerie silence as supporters entered the ground for Invicta's final ever home game. The match should have kicked off at 8 pm but as the time arrived, not a great deal of activity seemed to be taking place. Some supporters had the horrible feeling that they was about to attend the first professional Rugby League game which would be cancelled due to shortage of players. However the two teams did eventually appear to a cheer from the 85 spectators present. True to form, Invicta battled hard and lost, mainly due to the fact that they made more errors than Huddersfield.

28th April 1985 - Blackpool Borough 14 Southend Invicta 12

Another narrow defeat for Invicta's final ever game.

Player Profiles

A total of 43 players appeared on the Invicta teamsheet for the 1984/85 season. Due to the almost complete lack of interest in the club towards the end of the season, there are no records as to who played in the club's last match, a 12-14 defeat at Blackpool Borough, although end of season statistics published by the Rugby League show the names of a few players having made just one appearance for Invicta. It is assumed, therefore, that these players played in that fateful last match.

Players of which very little is known, who are recorded as having played for Southend Invicta, are Tony Best, Trevor Carson, Dave Cordery, Bill Daley, Les Day, Bernie Doyle, Dave Grainey, Ken Johnston, Tony McCafferty, Glen McGahan, Ian Nicholson and Chris Seldon.

Alexander, Adrian - Former Rugby Union player who signed for Kent Invicta from Oldham. Returned to Oldham and played on loan for Leigh. Signed for Southend Invicta on 27 September 1984.

Anderson, Chris - Made his one and only appearance for Invicta in their final ever game away at Blackpool Borough when he scored a try.

Atherton, Mark - Joined Invicta from Sharks Club, Mackay, Queensland.

Barwood, Adrian - Signed from Bridgend on 30 August 1984.

Bishop, Alan - Uncle of Neil. Signed from Runcorn Highfield on 2 September 1984.

Bishop, Neil - Son of the famous St Helens and Great Britain player, Tommy Bishop. Born on October 14 1962. His brother, Gary, played 16 times for Kent Invicta at scrum half. Nephew of Alan Bishop who also played for Southend Invicta. When Neil was six years old, the Bishop family emigrated to Australia. On his return to England he joined his uncle Alan at Huyton and scored two tries in 5 appearances. He made his debut for Kent Invicta on October 9 1983 against Huddersfield. Scored three tries for Kent Invicta. His first of two tries in a pre-season friendly for Southend Invicta

Neil Bishop

Phil Briscoe

were the first ever Rugby League touchdowns at Roots Hall. Injured early in the season, he made only 3 appearances (one as substitute).

Briscoe, Phil - Born in Liverpool on 8 May 1961. Represented Widnes Schools at all levels up to the age of 18. Also appeared in the successful Widnes Tigers amateur team which won the Lancashire Cup three times and appeared in the BARLA Cup Final. Moved south in 1980 and was introduced to Bill Goodwin (then coaching Peckham ARLFC) by Fulham physio Gordon Pinkey. Played for Peckham for the next three years, helping them to win the Southern Amateur Cup final. Made his debut for Kent Invicta in their home win against Dewsbury on 23 October 1983. Made 16 full appearances as well as 6 appearances as a substitute, scoring 8 goals.

Bruen, Bob - Signed from Runcorn Highfield on 2 September 1984.

Burley, Daryl - An Australian who signed from the Southern Suburbs Club on 28 September 1984 (with Reg McGill). Left club in January 1985.

Cholmondeley, Dave - Former centre at Halifax and Keighley. Joined Invicta on 26 August 1984 in exchange for Ian Van Bellen. A true servant of the club who always gave 100 per cent. Played in every game (30) scoring 4 tries, 21 goals and 7 drop

Dave Cholmondeley

goals. A remarkable achievement given the fact that he was the only Invicta player not based in the south.

Cooper, Tony - Born in Manchester on 23 March 1952. Moved south when he was 11 years old. Attended St Columbus College, St Albans. Studied PE and English for three years at Loughborough College. Joined Wasps RU Club when he was 21 and played for them for six seasons. Represented Hertfordshire and Southern Counties. As captain of Wasps he had trials with Leigh RLFC before Swinton stepped in with an offer. Made over 50 first team appearances with Swinton, all at second row. Lived in the Wirral for 18 months but then moved South, eventually joining Kent Invicta. Lived in Newport, near Cambridge and was a Special Needs teacher.

Tony Cooper

Dean, Martin - Born in Clitheroe on 10 June 1956. Lived for various times in Portsmouth, Lincolnshire, Chelmsford, Blackburn, West Germany and Singapore. His rugby career began at 19 when he began playing for Portsmouth Rugby Union Club as a winger. After moving to college in London, he played for Blackheath RU Club. He then moved to Loughborough College where he joined the Rugby League team and was selected for the 1981 Great Britain University side which toured France - playing at Prop. After leaving Loughborough he moved back North to Blackburn and played for Keighley and Swinton 'A' teams. Injury stopped him playing for two years. In 1983 he moved south again and resumed his playing career with Ealing ARLFC and was recommended to Invicta coach Bill Goodwin at the beginning of the season. He was signed from Ealing RLFC on 2 September 1984.

Donnelly, John - Aka "Dallas". A larger than life character. A big, burly prop who had been signed from the Wests club in Sydney on 8 December 1984. Made three appearances for Australia in the 1975/76 World Cup.

Mark Elia

Elia, Mark - Invicta's "golden boy" and one true superstar. Born in Auckland on Christmas Day 1962, he played for the Premier Grade Club Te Atatu in Auckland. In three seasons he not only broke the club's tryscoring record , but also the Auckland League record. Had also ran the 100 metres in a recorded time of 10.35 seconds. Arrived in England to play cricket for Surrey Second X1 and signed for Kent Invicta. Was their top try scorer with 19 tries in 33 appearances. Continued his great try scoring record with Southend Invicta, scoring 15 tries in 17 appearances. Left Invicta shortly before the Bradford Northern game to join the New Zealand international training squad. It was inevitable that he would be snapped up by a bigger club and he signed for St Helens in November 1985.

Feighan, Frank - Invicta's flying winger. Originally signed from Peckham ARLFC. Made most appearances (34) for Kent Invicta the previous season.

Gillan, David - A New Zealander who made 22 appearances for Invicta (one as substitute) scoring one try.

Grimoldby, Nick - Signed from Peckham ARLFC on 31 August 1984.

Hanney, Ray - Hard tackling loose forward from Victoria, Australia. Signed from Colonials ARLFC on 22 September 1984.

Harding, Dave - Born 29 April 1960 in Birkenhead City, New Zealand. Played for Northcote Tigers in New Zealand. Arrived in England in October 1983 and contacted his ex-Northcote Tigers team mate, Gary Freeman, at Kent Invicta. Started training with Kent Invicta and made his debut

Dave Harding

Frank Feighan

for them against Bramley on 16 October 1983. Made 19 appearances and scored 3 tries for Kent Invicta in the 1983/84 season. Played in several positions for Southend Invicta, appearing at full back, winger, centre, stand off and scrum half, and was voted Player of the Year by the Supporters Club at the end of the season.

London, Steve - Signed from Peckham ARLFC on 2 September 1984.

McGill, Reg - Signed from the Southern Suburbs Club in Australia on 28 September 1984 along with Daryl Burley. Left the club in February 1985 because of his mother's illness.

Millington, Wayne - Born in Hull on 18 December 1959. Younger brother of Hull KR prop, John Millington. Father played for Batley just after the war. On leaving school (David Lister High School) played Rugby Union with Hull and East Riding, making many regular appearances for Yorkshire Under 16s. Then reverted to Rugby League, playing for Hull KR colts and the 'A' team. Went abroad before moving to London where he met Bill Goodwin, who was then coaching Peckham ARLFC. Made his debut for Kent Invicta against Cardiff City, playing at centre. Sent off against Keighley for kicking on 28 October 1984 and served a 6 match suspension starting at Wakefield on 18 November.

Wayne Millington

269

Neel, Tony - Tony Neel (or "Noel" during his time at Kent Invicta and part of his time at Southend) was born in Auckland, New Zealand, on 25 January 1957. His real Christian name, originating from his mother's Samoan side of the family, was Tusiata-fuso. Didn't start playing Rugby League until he was 19, when he joined Premier Grade club, Marist, as a second row. After coming to England he was put in contact with Bill Goodwin and played on one occasion for Peckham ARLFC before making his debut for Kent Invicta as an emergency hooker at Swinton in October 1983. Made four full appearances for Kent Invicta before leaving the club in February 1984 following a dispute with the club's management. Rejoined Peckham and signed for Southend Invicta from Peckham ARLFC on 2 September 1984. Invicta's leading points scorer for the season with 70 points.

Penola, Colin - Born in Mackay, Queensland, on 15 February 1956. His great, great grandparents were from the Soloman Islands. Played for three years with Carlton before coming to England on a working holiday in 1983. Whilst working in Leeds he was put in contact with Carlisle RLFC and appeared four times for them. He was spotted in action by Kent Invicta coach Bill Goodwin, who signed him for Kent Invicta's debut season 1983/84. Made his first full appearance in the game against Batley on 11 September 1983. Kent Invicta's Player of the Season in 1983/84 after making 31 appearances and scoring 5 tries.

Pike, Alan - Signed from Peckham ARLFC on 22 September 1984.

Scanlon, Andy - Signed for Southend Invicta on 19 October 1984 from Keighley. Dewsbury lad who was a product of the famous Shaw Cross Boys Club.

Schaumkell, Kevin - A Maori from New Zealand. Member of the 1982 New Zealand touring side to this country.

Wadworth, Ian - Signed from Peckham ARLFC on 14 October 1984.

Walker, Clive - Signed from Bridgend on 2 September 1984.

Wellman, Chris - Veteran Aussie. Signed for Invicta on 26 September 1984 from Sydney club, Cronulla. This was his second spell in England, having appeared for St. Helens in the early 70s.

Wilkes, Calvin - Very experienced player who had previously been with Leeds, Doncaster, Keighley and Carlisle.

Bill Goodwin (coach) - A Yorkshireman who played professional Rugby League with Doncaster, Featherstone Rovers and Batley. Had lived in the South since the early seventies, playing an active role in Amateur Rugby League in the south playing with Peckham ARLFC in the Southern League. He later became club coach and established Peckham as the Southern League's leading club. Bill also became an Official Grade One Coach and achieved the status of BARLA Southern Regional Coach. In 1983, Bill was appointed Kent Invicta's coach for their inaugural season and achieved seven victories in the first ten games. However he was then sacked by the acting Chairman, Jim Thompson. He was then appointed coach when Invicta moved to Southend.

Bill Goodwin

Ken Johnston

A   CENTURY   UNITED

Team Group Line-Ups

To save cluttering up the look and design of the main pages of this book, it was decided to include the names of the Southend United players from all team group photographs (where known) in this appendix. This also saved valuable space that could be used for more illustrations and text.

If you can help identify any of the unknown team groups, please contact us at sufc@shrimperpublishing.co.uk. Thanks.

Page 9 - Southend Athletic Football Club - Unknown

Page 25 - Southend United 1909/10 - Back Row (l to r): Jerry Thomson, Charlie Cotton, George Molyneux, T. Murray. Middle Row (l to r): Bob Jack (Secretary Manager), George F. Harrod, Ernest W. Emery, James H. Bigden, J. Harrower, Alexander "Sandy" McLellan, Arthur Norris (Trainer). Seated (l to r): Norman L. Brown, Albert F.W. Frost, J. Jepson, Alex "Nutty" King, Edward "Dits" Anderson, Jack Wright, T. Crews.

Page 26 - Southend United 1910/11 - Back Row (l to r): J. Harrower, A. Haggar, Ernest W. Emery, Harry Owen, George Molyneux, George F. Harrod, ??, Toone, ??. Seated (l to r): Norman L. Brown, Albert F.W. Frost, Alex "Nutty" King, Alexander "Sandy" McLellan, ??. Front (l to r): T. Murray, Jerry Thomson.

Page 28 - Southend United players at Cardiff - Back Row (l to r): George Molyneux, ??, Ernest W. Emery. Middle Row (l to r): D. Cairns, ??, Heneage Wileman, ??, ??, Joe Bradshaw, ??. Front Row (l to r): ??, J. Harrower, L.G. Parke, Albert F.W. Frost.

Page 30 - Southend United 1913/14 - Back Row (l to r): Ernest Emery, William Barnes, Fred Robson, Councillor H Ward (Director), Alex Steel, Billy Kebbell, Mr. Oliver Trigg (Director), Ned Liddell, J Byford (Director), Billy Probert, Councillor G Radford (Chairman), Charles Axcell. Front Row (l to r): Kitto (Trainer), Archibald Wilson, Albert Frost, Lionel Louch, Heneage Wileman, Joe Bradshaw, G A Weston (Director).

Page 35 - Southend United 1919/20 - Back Row (l to r): Percy Sands, Jimmy H. Evans. Middle Row (l to r): Arthur Norris (Trainer), George Marshall, Bob Reid, Edward Leahy, G. Walden, Jack Bollington, Ned Liddell (Manager). Seated (l to r): J. Nuttall, Frank Burrill, Heneage Wileman, Lot Jones, Jack Young.

Page 40 - Southend United 1921/22 - Back Row (l to r): Arthur Norris (Trainer), Harry Buddery, ??, Tom Capper, ??, Harry Dobson. Seated (l to r): David Reid, Harry Baldwin, James Logan, ??, ??, Alex Elliott. Front Row (l to r): James Lawson, ??, George Lawrence, Jimmy Evans.

Page 46 - Southend United team that beat Derby County - Back Row (l to r): ??, Billy Moore, Tommy Sayles. Standing (l to r): Bill Cartwright (Trainer), ??, Billy Morris, Fred Jewhurst, ??, Jack Andrews, Jack French, ??. Seated (l to r): Billy Hick, ??.

Page 49 - Southend United 1929/30 - Back Row (l to r): Bill Cartwright (Trainer), Dave Robinson, Billy Moore, Tom McKenna, Tom Brophy, G. Irwin (Assistant Trainer). Second Row (l to r): Ted Birnie (Manager), Tom Dixon, George Falconbridge, Bob Ward, ??, ??, Jack French. Seated (l to r): Joe Johnson, Jack Bailey, ??, ??, Jim Shankly, ??, ??, ??, ??. Front Row (l to r): Fred Barnett, Fred Baron, Mickey Jones, Dickie Donoven, Les Clenshaw.

Page 55 - Southend United 1934/35 - Back Row (l to r): Bill Cartwright (Trainer), Norman Mackay, George Robertson, Billy Moore, Lawrie Kelly, Billy Carr. Seated (l to r): Harry Lane, Harry Johnson, Fred Cheesmur, Jimmy Deacon, Robert Oswald, Joe Wilson.

Page 61 - Southend United 1937/38 - Back Row (l to r): Frank Higgs, Jack Everest, Jimmy Nelson, Johnny Milne, Dave Robinson, George MacKenzie. Second Row (l to r): Cartwright (Trainer), Thomas MacAdam, Bob Jackson, Doug Wright, Keith Hague, Charlie Jones, Billy Dickinson, Harry Footman (Assistant Trainer). Seated (l to r): David Jack (Manager), Sid Bell, Joe Firth, Bert Oswald, George Willshaw, Arthur Harris, Jimmy Deacon, Billy Carr. Front Row (l to r): Len Bolan, Almer Hall, Tudor Martin, Billy Bushby, Harry Lane.

Page 62 - Southend United 1938/39 - Back Row (l to r): Bill Cartwright (Trainer), Billy Forster, Almer Hall, Johnny Milne, George MacKenzie, Ernie Stokes, Tudor Martin, Sid Bell, Harry Footman (Assistant Trainer). Second Row (l to r): David Jack (Secretary-

Manager), Frank Walton, Jack Trainer, H Downey, Jack Broadhurst, Tommy Shallcross, Billy Bushby, Len Bolan, Billy Leighton, Alf Smirk, J Moss (Director). Seated (l to r): G Winkfield (Director), E Grant (Director), Billy Carr, Bob Jackson, Jimmy Nelson, C N Newiit (Chairman), Charlie Jones, Keith Hague, Jimmy Deacon, A I Hay (Director), Councillor H H Smith (Director). Front Row (l to r): Arthur Harris, Bill Muncie, H Scaife, Bert Oswald, Dave Robinson.

Page 70 - Southend United 1946/47 - Back Row (l to r): Ron Humphries, Arthur Harris, Ted Hankey, L Davis, W Middleton, Stan Bell. Second Row (l to r): Harry Warren (Manager), Charles Benson (Director), Harry Walton, Frank Walton, Harry Woodward, Ken Bennett, J Savage, Tommy Linton, J O'Brien, Frank Sheard, Wilf Copping (Trainer), Dave Robinson (Assistant Trainer), Jimmy Hogan (FA Coach). Seated (l to r): Dr. Bewes (Doctor), Alf Smirk, Bob Gibson, Dave Hamilton, V Jones, Neville Hewitt (Chairman), Bob Jackson, Cyril Thompson, Frank Dudley, Tommy Tippett, Major Hays (Vice Chairman). Kneeling (l to r): Albert Sibley, John Gardiner, Harry Lane.

Page 70 - Southend United Leave for Loughborough - (l to r): Harry Warren (Manager), Arthur Harris, Bob Jackson, Alf Smirk, Cyril Thompson, Joe Sibley, Tommy Linton (partly obscured), Ted Hankey, Harry Lane, Stan Montgomery (partly obscured), Wilf Copping, Alf Hay (Director).

Page 71 - The team that took on the Toffees - Back Row (l to r): Harry Warren (Manager), Tommy Linton, Arthur Harris, Ted Hankey, Bob Jackson, Stan Montgomery, Wilf Copping (Trainer). Front Row (l to r): Joe Sibley, Alf Smirk, Cyril Thompson, Ken Bennett, Harry Lane. Missing from the photo is Frank Walton.

Page 75 - Players in training for the Leyton Orient F.A.Cup tie - Players include Frank Sheard, Cyril Grant, "Choppy" Wallbanks, Jack French, Albert Wakefield.

Page 75 - Southend United players' Christmas party 1949 - Back Row includes Frank Sheard, Frank Walton, Jack French, Jimmy McAlinden. Front Row includes Ted Hankey, David Lindsay.

Page 80 - Southend United 1952/53 - Back Row (l to r): John Costello, Jack French, Frank Sheard, Tommy Scannell, Jimmy Lawler, Sandy Anderson. Seated (l to r): Frank Sibley, Albert Wakefield, Jimmy McAlinden, Cyril Grant, Les Stubbs.

Page 84 - Southend United 1954/55 - Back Row (l to r): Jimmy Whyte, Denis Howe, Harry Threadgold, Sandy Anderson, Bill Pavitt, Frank Burns. Front Row (l to r): Joe Sibley, Kevin Baron, Roy Hollis, Jimmy Lawler, Ken Bainbridge.

Page 86 - Southend United 1955/56 - Back Row (l to r): Sandy Anderson, Harry Threadgold, A Phillips, Jackie Bridge. Second Row (l to r): Harry Warren (Manager), H W Cox (Director), Jimmy Lawler, Arthur Williamson, Jimmy Duthie, Jim Duffy, Doug Young, Tony Oakley, Jimmy Stirling, Dave Robinson (Trainer). Seated (l to r): Major A I Hay, Bill Anderson, Joe Sibley, Alderman H H Smith (Chairman), Kevin Baron, Roy Hollis, Denis Howe, Charles Benson, Dr. A Bewes (Doctor). Front Row (l to r): Crichton Lockhart, Frank Burns, Jimmy Whyte, Dickie Dowsett, Jimmy McGuigan.

Page 90 - Southend United in Germany - Unknown

Page 91 - Southend United 1958/59 - Back Row (l to r): Wilf Dixon (Trainer), Peter Knight, George Wright, Jim Ferguson, George O'Hara, Colin Cairns, Roy Dobson, Ray Smith, Jimmy Walker, Lou Costello, Jim Fletcher, R Edmunds, Dave Robinson (Reserve Team Trainer). Middle Row (l to r): Eddie Perry (Manager), Charles Clenshaw (Director), Stan Jefferson, Willie Morrison, John Duffy, Brian Ronson, Sandy Anderson, Arthur Williamson, Harry Threadgold, Jimmy Thomson, Bill Punton, Ralph Walker, Nelson Mitchell (Director), Alderman H. W. Cox (Director). Seated (l to r): A. Hay (Director), Bobby Kellard, Errol Crossan, Kevin Baron, Jimmy Stirling, Alderman H. H. Smith (Chairman), Sammy McCrory, Roy Hollis, Duggie Price, Vivian Ayres, C. O. Benson (Director)

Page 92 - Southend United 1959/60 - Back Row (l to r): Jimmy Stirling, Ron Fogg, Norman Uprichard, Harry Threadgold, Peter Watson, Sandy Anderson, Ray Whale. Middle Row (l to r): Eddie Perry (Manager), Wilf Dixon (Trainer), Alec Stenhouse, Willie Morrison, Ray Smith, Chris O'Neill, Ralph Walker, Terry Kent, Robert Melrose, Matt Dunsmore, Arthur Forrester, Duggie Price, Dave Robinson, Nelson Mitchell. Seated (l to r): Roy Hollis, C. O. Benson, Arthur Williamson, A. I. Hay, Sam McCrory, Alderman H. H. Smith (Chairman), Bud Houghton, Alderman H. W. Cox, John Duffy, S. H. J. Bates, Lou Costello. On Ground (l to r): Bobby Duncan, Bobby Kellard, Vivian Ayres, Bill Squibb.

Page 95 - Southend United 1960/61 - Back Row (l to r): Ray Whale, Bud Houghton, Harry Threadgold, Arthur Williamson, Alan Dicks, Lou Costello. Front Row (l to r): Alec Stenhouse, Peter Corthine, Peter Watson, Duggie Price, Billy Wall.

Page 96 - Southend United 1961/62 - Back Row (l to r): Jim Fryatt, Peter Watson, Arthur Williamson, Peter Goy, Lou Costello, Alan Dicks, Pat Kerrins. Front Row (l to r): Ken Jones, Roy Goulden, Tony Bentley, Peter Corthine, Bobby Kellard, Sandy Anderson, Jimmy Shields.

Page 96 - Southend United in training - (l to r): Peter Watson, Lou Costello, Sandy Anderson, Jimmy Shields, Roy Goulden, Bobby Kellard, Peter Corthine, Tony Bentley, Norman Bleanch, Peter Goy.

Page 99 - Southend United 1962/63 - Back Row (l to r): Norman Lee, Lou Costello, John Tennant, Peter Goy, Harry Threadgold, Jimmy Fryatt, John McKinven. Middle Row (l to r): Jack French (Assistant Trainer), Ray Smith, Ken Jones, Ian McNeill, Sandy Anderson, Ted Fenton (Manager), Ray Brand, Derek Tharme, Palmer, Ernie Shepherd (Trainer/Coach). Seated (l to r): Bobby Kellard, Billy Wall, Frankie Banks, Norman Liggitt, Peter Watson, Pat Donovan, Tony Bentley, Chris Barnard, S. Faulkner.

Page 102 - Southend United 1963/64 - Back Row (l to r): Terry Bradbury, Norman Liggitt, Ray Smith, Peter Goy, Lou Costello, John McKinven, Mike Beesley. Seated (l to r): Ian McNeill, Ken Jones, John Neal, Derek Woodley, Tony Bentley, Peter Watson.

Page 104 - Southend United 1965/66 - Back Row (l to r): Terry Bradbury, Eddie May, Bobby King, Ray Smith, John McKinven, Peter Watson, Keith Hymas, Trevor Langston. Middle Row (l to r): J.R. Bates (Director), Jack French (Assistant Trainer), Chris Barnard, Frank Matthews, Eddie Firmani, Bobby Gillfillan, Ian McKechnie, Ray White, Peter Bullock, Derek Ewing, Alan Shires, Ernie Shepherd (Assistant Manager), Stan Skinner (Director). Seated (l to r): Alvan Williams (Manager), Reg Smith, John Mellish, Andy Smillie, John Neal, Nelson L. Mitchell (Chairman), Alf Hay (Vice Chairman), Malcolm Slater, Derek Woodley, Tony Bentley, Frankie Banks, B.H. Lewis (Director).

Page 106 - Southend United 1966/67 - Back Row (l to r): Eddie May, Richard Haynes, Mel Slack, Trevor Roberts, Bobby Haddrick, Keith Hymas. Middle Row (l to r): Peter Gordon (Trainer), Ernie Shepherd (Assistant Manager), Eddie Firmani, Reg Smith, John Mellish, Frank Matthews, John Baber, Alec Lumsden, Ray Smith, John McKinven, Alan Cheesewright, John Randles (Secretary), Alvan Williams (Manager). Seated (l to r): Andy Smillie, Derek Woodley, Malcolm Slater, Tony Bentley, Nelson L. Mitchell (Chairman), Alderman L.W. Johnson (Director), Graham Birks, Tony Beanland, Colin Flatt.

Page 108 - Southend United 1968/69 - Back Row (l to r): Geoff Hudson (Trainer/coach), Graham Birks, Sammy McMillan, David Stone, John Kurila, Trevor Roberts, Gary Moore, Ian "Chico" Hamilton, Eddie Clayton, Mike Beesley, Ernie Shepherd (Manager). Front Row (l to r): Mel Slack, Dave Chambers, Tony Bentley, Billy Best, Phil Chisnall, John Baber.

Page 108 - The players meet the press - (l to r): John McKinven, Andy Smillie, Billy Best, Phil Chisnall, Eddie Clayton, Mel Slack, John Kurila, David Stone, Sammy McMillan, Graham Birks, Tony Bentley, Lawrie Leslie.

Page 111 - Southend United 1969/70 - Back Row (l to r): John Chambers, John Kurila, Trevor Roberts, Gary Moore, Mike Beesley. Middle Row (l to r): Geoff Hudson (Coach), John McKinven, Sammy McMillan, Graham Birks, Eddie Clayton, Frank Haydock, Ernie Shepherd (Manager). Front Row (l to r): Phil Chisnall, John Baber, Keith Lindsey, Billy Best, Dave Chambers, Tony Bentley.

Page 120 - Southend United 1975/76 - Left to Right: Sean Rafter, Stuart Parker, Peter Silvester, Alan Little, Alan Moody, Steve Dyer, Dave Worthington, Stuart Brace, Dave Cunningham, Ronnie Pountney, Ken Foggo, Terry Nicholl, Andy Ford, Steve Lamb, Tony Hadley, Neil Townsend, Malcolm Webster.

Page 125 - Southend United 1978/79 - Back Row (l to r): Alan Moody, Steve Yates, Mervyn Cawston, Dave Cusack, Graham Horn, Gerry Fell, Tony Hadley, Peter Abbott. Middle Row (l to r): Dave Smith (Manager), Derrick Parker, Micky Laverick, Ronnie Pountney, Graham Franklin, Steve Goodwin, Colin Morris, John Lattimer (Physio). Kneeling (l to r): john Walker, Andy Polycarpou, Phil Dudley, Micky Stead.

Page 127 - Southend United 1979/80 - Back Row (l to r): Dave Smith (Manager), Steve Yates, Peter Abbott, Mick Tuohy, John Lattimer (Physiotherapist). Second Row (l to r): Alan Moody, Tony Hadley, Graham Horn, Gerry Fell, Derrick Parker. Third Row (l to r): Phil Dudley, John Walker, Mervyn Cawston, Dave Cusack, Andy Polycarpou. Front Row (l to r): Colin Morris, Micky Stead, Ronnie Pountney, Anton Otulakowski, Terry Gray.

Page 129 - Southend United 1980/81 - Back Row (l to r): John Walker, Dave Cusack, John Keeley, Paul Caskey, Mervyn Cawston, Mick Tuohy, Anton Otulakowski. Second Row (l to r): Alan Moody, Garry Nelson, Keith Mercer, Tony Hadley, Micky Stead, Andy Polycarpou, Phil Dudley. Seated (l to r): Brian Beckett (Physio), Steve Yates, Derek Spence, Ronnie Pountney,

Dave Smith (Manager), John Watson, Jeff Hull, Terry Gray, Frank Banks (Coach). Front Row (l to r): Alan Hull, Mark Whitmore, Neil Gregory, Glenn Pennyfather, John Whiskin.

Page 131 - Southend United 1981/82 - Back Row (l to r): John Walker, Steve Yates, Derek Spence, Paul Caskey, Dave Cusack, Mervyn Cawston, Garry Nelson, John Keeley, Tony Hadley. Middle Row (l to r): Frank Banks (Trainer), Neil Gregory, Danny Greaves, Glenn Pennyfather, Alan Moody, Micky Stead, Phil Dudley, Ronnie Pountney, Anton Otulakowski, Terry Gray, Keith Mercer, Matt Johnson, Brian Beckett (Physiotherapist). Seated (l to r): Warren May, Mark Rubin (Vice-Chairman), Tony Rubin (Director), Dave Smith (Manager), Frank Walton (Chairman), Fred Bonfield (Director), John N. Woodcock (Director), Paul Dunstan

Page 133 - Southend United 1982/83 - Back Row (l to r): Frank Banks (Coach), John Keeley, Dave Cusack, Mervyn Cawston, Brian Beckett (Physio). Middle Row (l to r): Paul Clark, Steve Yates, Keith Mercer, Garry Nelson, Tony Hadley, John Walker, Micky Stead. Seated (l to r): Danny Greaves, Steve Phillips, Glenn Pennyfather, Dave Smith (Manager), Ronnie Pountney, Phil Dudley, Anton Otulakowski.

Page 136 - Southend United 1983/84 - Back Row (l to r): Roy McDonough, Brian Ferguson, Tony Currie, Gerry Peyton, Mervyn Cawston, John Keeley, Warren May, Greig Shepherd, Steve Yates, Steve Collins. Seated (l to r): Glen Skivington, Paul Dunstan, Steve Phillips, Ronnie Pountney, Paul Clark, Billy Kellock, Glenn Pennyfather, Mick Angus, Micky Stead.

Page 140 - Southend United 1985/86 - Back Row (l to r): Danny O'Shea, Steve Hatter, Jon O'Brien, Jim Stannard, Steve Oliver, Shane Westley, Roy McDonough. Middle Row (l to r): Buster Footman (Physiotherapist), Kevin Lock (Player/Youth Coach), Alan Rogers, John Gymer, Vic Jobson (Chairman), Micky Engwell, John Seaden, Frank Lampard (Player/Coach), Bobby Moore (Manager), Harry Cripps (Coach). Seated (l to r): Barry Silkman, Steve Phillips, Glenn Pennyfather, Richard Cadette, Micky Stead, Warren May, Paul Clark. Front Row (l to r): Terry Pryer, Mark Lowman, Warren Johnson, Paul Newell, Steve Wiggins, Russell Short, Eddie Paterson.

Page 144 - Southend United 1986/87 - Back Row (l to r): Dave Webb (Manager), Dean Neal, Dave Martin, Paul Roberts, Roy McDonough, Paul Clark, Glenn Pennyfather. Middle Row (l to r): Barry Silkman, Derek Hall, Danny O'Shea, Mervyn Cawston, Jim Stannard, Shane Westley, Buster Footman (Physiotherapist), Kevin Lock (Assistant Manager). Seated (l to r): Richard Cadette, Micky Engwell, Steve Wiggins, John Seaden, John Gymer, Kevin Spires, Phil Cavener.

Page 147 - Southend United 1987/88 - Back Row (l to r): Nicky Smith, Danny O'Shea, Eric Steele, Dean Neal, Russell Short, Martin Robinson. Middle Row (l to r): Buster Footman (Physiotherapist), Roy McDonough, Richard Young, Paul Newell, Shane Westley, David Martin, Kevin Lock (Assistant Manager). Seated (l to r): Peter Johnson, Andy Rogers, Martin Ling, Dick Bate (Manager), Paul Clark, Glenn Pennyfather, Derek Hall.

Page 154 - Southend United 1990/91 - Back Row (l to r): Dean Austin, Peter Daley, Paul Clark, Mario Walsh, Ian Benjamin, Andy Edwards, Steve Tilson, Paul Smith. Middle Row (l to r): David Webb (Manager), Kevin Lock (Assistant Manager), Brett Angell, John Cornwell, David Martin, Paul Sansome, Peter Cawley, Spencer Prior, Roy McDonough, Danny Greaves (Youth Team Manager), Alan Raw (Physiotherapist). Seated (l to r): Adam Locke, Iain O'Connell, Jason Cook, Andy Ansah, Chris Powell, Peter Butler, Christian Hyslop.

Page 157 - Southend United 1992/93 - Back Row (l to r): Chris Powell, John Cornwell, Pat Scully, Andy Edwards, Paul Sansome, Danny Sains, Spencer Prior, Andy Sussex, Ian Benjamin. Middle Row (l to r): Alan Raw (Physiotherapist), Steve Tilson, Scott Ashenden, Christian Hyslop, Francisco Cagigao, Simon Royce, Mark Hall, Mel Capelton, Steve Brown, Kevin O'Callaghan, Paul Heffer, Adam Locke, Danny Greaves (Youth Team Manager). Seated (l to r): Keith Jones, Paul Smith, Bob Houghton (Assistant Manager), David Martin, Colin Murphy (Manager), Brett Angell, Andy Ansah.

Page 160 - Southend United 1993/94 - Back Row (l to r): Andy Sussex, Andy Edwards, Michael Gonzague, Brett Angell, Paul Sansome, Simon Royce, Mick Bodley, David Howell, Pat Scully, Graham Bressington. Middle Row (l to r): Brian Stein (Coach), John Gowens (Physiotherapist), Chris Powell, Gary Poole, Steve Tilson, Jamie Southon, Christian Hyslop, Barry Fry (Manager), John Cornwell, Gary Jones, Tommy Mooney, Craig Davidson, Mark Hall, Alan Raw (Physiotherapist), Danny Greaves (Youth Team Manager). Seated (l to r): Neil Rowbury, Andy Ansah, Derek Payne, Keith Jones, Vic Jobson (Chairman), Ricky Otto, Jonathan Hunt, Jae Martin, Adam Locke.

Page 162 - Southend United 1994/95 - Back Row (l to r): Danny Foot, Andy Sussex, Andy Edwards, Keith Dublin, Paul Sansome, John Cornwell, Simon Royce, Domonic Iorfa, Mark Hone, Graham Bressington, Phil Gridelet. Middle Row (l to r): Danny Greaves

(Youth Team Manager), Ijah Anderson, Gary Poole, Steve Tilson, Mick Bodley, Chris Powell, Declan Perkins, Gary Jones, Craig Davidson, Mark Hall, John Gowens (Physiotherapist). Seated (l to r): Andy Ansah, Andy Thomson, Keith Jones, Theo Foley (Assistant Manager), Vic Jobson (Chairman), Peter Taylor (Manager), Ricky Otto, Jonathan Hunt, Jae Martin.

Page 164 - Southend United 1995/96 - Back Row (l to r): Domonic Iorfa, Luke Morrish, Andy Sussex, Paul Sansome, Dave Regis, Simon Royce, Mark Hone, Danny Foot, Leo Roget. Second Row (l to r): Spencer Barham (Assistant Physiotherapist), Danny Greaves (Youth Team Manager), Ijah Anderson, Declan Perkins, Gary Jones, Roger Willis, Phil Gridelet, Steve Tilson, Keith Dublin, John Gowens (Physiotherapist), Mark Warwick. Seated (l to r): Andy Ansah, Andy Thomson, Theo Foley (Assistant Manager), Mick Bodley, Ronnie Whelan (Manager), Julian Hails, Chris Powell. Front Row (l to r): Juniors

Page 168 - Southend United 1996/97 - Back Row (l to r): Keith Dublin, Mark McNally, Andy Sussex, Paul Sansome, Andy Rammell, Simon Royce, Jeroen Boere, Richie Hanlon, Leo Roget. Middle Row (l to r): Peter Johnson (Youth Coach), Peter Trevivian (Coach), Mark Stimson, Andy Harris, Mike Lapper, Phil Gridelet, Steve Tilson, John Gowens (Physiotherapist). Seated (l to r): John Nielsen, Andy Thomson, Theo Foley (Assistant Manager), Mike Marsh, Ronnie Whelan (Manager), Julian Hails, Paul Byrne.

Page 169 - Southend United 1997/98 - Back Row (l to r): Mark Jones, Paul Taylor, Chris Perkins, Simon Royce, Andy Rammell, Tony Henriksen, Jeroen Boere, Nathan Jones, John Nielsen. Middle Row (l to r): Spencer Barham (Assistant Physiotherapist), John Gowens (Physiotherapist), Adrian Clarke, Paul Williams, Andy Harris, Mark Stimson, Phil Leggatt, Peter Johnson (Youth Team Manager). Seated (l to r): Leo Roget, Paul Byrne, Peter Trevivian (Assistant Manager), Alvin Martin (Manager), Mike Marsh, Andy Thomson, Phil Gridelet.

Page 171 - Southend United 1998/99 - Back Row (l to r): Kevin Maher, Chris Perkins, Leo Roget, Tony Henriksen, Martyn Margetson, Simon Coleman, Trevor Fitzpatrick, Keith Dublin. Middle Row (l to r): John Gowens (Physiotherapist), Mark Beard, Rob Newman, Simon Livett, Andy Harris, Mark Stimson, Julian Hails, Spencer Barham (Assistant Physiotherapist). Seated (l to r): Adrian Clarke, David Whyte, Mick Gooding (Assistant Manager), Alvin Martin (Manager), Peter Trevivian (Youth Team Manager), Alex Burns, Nathan Jones.

Page 174 - Southend United 1999/2000 - Back Row (l to r): Chris Perkins, Neil Campbell, Leo Roget, Simon Coleman, Mel Capelton, Stephen Spittle, Martyn Margetson, David Morley, Neil Tolson, Simon Livett, Adam Morrish. Middle Row (l to r): Mick Gooding (Coach), Martyn Booty, Trevor Fitzpatrick, Mark Beard, Kevin Maher, Gordon Connelly, Adrian Clarke, Barry Conlon, David Whyte, Rob Newman, John Threadgold (Kit Man), John Gowens (Physiotherapist). Seated (l to r): Gary Cross, Yemi Abiodun, Scott Houghton, John Main (Chairman), Alan Little (Manager), Nathan Jones, Julian Hails, Neville Roach.

Page 176 - Southend United 2000/01 - Back Row (l to r): Danny Kerrigan, Yemi Abiodun, David McSweeney, David Lee, Scott Forbes, Craig Edwards, Leon Johnson. Middle Row (l to r): Rob Newman (Coach), Trevor Fitzpatrick, Tom McDonald, Phil Whelan, Chris Porter, Mel Capelton, Darryl Flahavan, Dave Morley, Kevin Maher, Danny Webb, John Gowens (Physiotherapist). Seated (l to r): Martyn Booty, Damon Searle, Gary Cross, Ben Abbey, Mick Gooding (Assistant Manager), David Webb (Manager), Russell Williamson, Leon Hunter, Martin Carruthers, Danny Pitts.

Page 184 - Southend United 2004/05 - Back Row (l to r): Spencer Prior, Adam Barrett, Duncan Jupp, Drewe Broughton, Bart Griemink, Darryl Flahavan, Andy Edwards, Mark Bentley, Tes Bramble, Laurie Dudfield. Middle Row (l to r): John Stannard (Physiotherapist), Michael Husbands, Mark Gower, Jim Corbett, Kevin Maher, Wayne Gray, Stuart Williams, Lee Turner (Goalkeeping Coach). Seated (l to r): Nicky Nicolau, Lewis Hunt, Jay Smith, Paul Brush (Assistant Manager), Steve Tilson (Manager), Michael Kightly, Carl Pettefer, Che Wilson.

Page 190 - Southend United 2005/06 - Back Row (l to r): Adam Barrett, Che Wilson, James Lawson, Mitchell Cole, Wayne Gray, Matthew Driver (Sponsor). Middle Row (l to r): John Stannard (Physiotherapist), Duncan Jupp, Andy Edwards, Darryl Flahavan, Bart Griemink, Spencer Prior, Mark Bentley, Lee Turner (Goalkeeping Coach). Seated (l to r): Freddy Eastwood, Jay Smith, Lewis Hunt, Steve Tilson (Manager), Kevin Maher, Paul Brush (Assistant Manager), Luke Guttridge, Carl Pettefer, Mark Gower.

Page 194 - Southend United 2006/07 - Back Row (l to r): Adam Barrett, Simon Francis, Lee Bradbury, Efetebore Sodje, Spencer Prior, Michael Ricketts, James Lawson. Middle Row (l to r): Vanessa Franklin (Masseur), John Stannard (Physiotherapist), Lewis Hunt, Freddy Eastwood, Darryl Flahavan, Mark Gower, Steve Collis, Mitchell Cole, Che Wilson, Ricky Duncan (Youth Manager), Lee Turner (Goalkeeping Coach). Seated (l to r): Steven Hammell, Jay Smith, Steve Tilson (Manager), Kevin Maher, Paul Brush (Assistant Manager), Luke Guttridge, Jamal Campbell-Ryce.

Page 195 - In the dressing room after beating Manchester United - (l to r): Efetebore Sodje, Steve Hammell, Mark Gower, Kevin Maher, Jamal Campbell-Ryce, Simon Francis (on floor), Peter Clarke, Jay Smith, Franck Moussa, James Lawson, Freddy Eastwood.

Bibliography

Bibliography

The authors would like to acknowledge the part, however small, played in the production of A Century United by the following publications. Needless to say all are highly recommended for further reading. The Leicester City "Of Fossils and Foxes" book in particular was our inspiration for this volume.

Southend United- The Official History by Peter Mason and David Goody (Yore Publications 1993)

Of Fossils and Foxes by Dave Smith and Paul Taylor (Polar Publishing 2001)

Press On by Keith Roe (Followers of the Blue Light 2005)

The Football Grounds of England and Wales by Simon Inglis (Collins Willow 1983)

Football League Grounds For A Change by Dave Twydell (Dave Twydell 1991)

A History of Southend by Ian Yearsley (Phillimore 2001)

Potted Shrimps by David Goody and Peter Miles (Yore Publications 1999)

Images of Sport: Southend United Football Club by Peter Miles and David Goody (Tempus 2000)

100 Greats of Southend United by David Goody and Peter Miles (Tempus 2001)

Southend United 50 Classic Matches by Peter Miles and David Goody (Tempus 2005)

Wheel 'Em In –The Official History of Chelmsford City by Steve Garner (Steve Garner 2001)

The Official Centenary History of the Southern League by Leigh Edwards (Paper Plane 1993)

Football League Players Records 1888 to 1939 by Michael Joyce (Soccer Data 2002)

PFA Premier & Football League Players Records by Barry Hugman (Queen Anne Press 2005)

The Breedon Book of Football Managers by Dennis Turner and Alex White (Breedon 1993)

Denied F.C. by Dave Twydell (Yore Publications 2001)

Advanced Subscribers

The following are acknowledged as being Advanced Subscribers to

"A Century United - The Centenary History of Southend United"

and have named their all-time favourite player to be the following...

Gold Subscribers

Matthew Goody	*Jamal Campbell-Ryce*	Sam Goody	*Mark Gower*
Barry John Venus	*Billy Best*	Karen Goody	*Micky Stead*
Leslie V Wright	*Darryl Flahavan*	Cathy Miles	*Kevin Maher*
David Brabbing	*Billy Best*	JJ Shillingford	*Billy Best*
Billy Best	*Gary Moore*	JW Shillingford	*Billy Best*
Phil Cox	*Chris Powell*	Terry Jeffreys	*John McKinven*
Julie and Michael Pearce		Shrimpers Trust	

Subscribers

Phil Laflin	*Frank Dudley*	Phillip Sullivan	*Billy Best*
Trevor Bashford	*Gary Moore*	Alex Chidgey	*Freddy Eastwood*
Duncan Sheekey	*Darryl Flahavan*	David Rossiter	*Freddy Eastwood*
Stuart Thorne	*Freddy Eastwood*	Leo Clarke	*Chris Powell*
Garry N Smith	*Stan Collymore*	Anthony Clarke	*John McGuigan*
Robin Michel	*Stan Collymore*	Lara McSweeney	*Mark Gower*
Kathleen Raines	*Darryl Flahavan*	John Walton	*Chris Powell*
John A Clench	*Tony Bentley*	Robin A Port	*Roy Hollis*
Karl Sharman	*Freddy Eastwood*	Keith, Cheryl	
James Cornwell	*Steve Tilson*	and Lucy Roe	*Mervyn Cawston*
Robin Stott	*Kevin Maher*	John Wallis	*Sam McCrory*
Mr. Mike Davies	*Kevin Maher*	Mark Wallis	*Chris Powell*
Roy Lynne	*Ron Pountney*	Clare Brooks	*Chris Powell*
Francis Potter	*Billy Best*	Derek Dennis	*Billy Best*
Paul Langton	*Stan Collymore*	Dave Baker	*David Crown*
Joe Hayward	*Freddy Eastwood*	Tony Langton	*Billy Best*
Trevor Emery	*Chris Powell*	Ray Chandler	*Frank Dudley*
Jonathan Humphrey	*Chris Powell*	Stephen Paul Wilson	*Billy Best*
John Smith	*Chris Guthrie*	Alec Trott	*Kevin Maher*
Lee Morgan	*David Crown*	Ron MacKenzie	*John McKinven*
Joshua Hayton	*Freddy Eastwood*	Ian Gosney-Davies	*Freddy Eastwood*
Raymond Sorrell	*Tony Bentley*	Paul Smith	*Richard Cadette*
Eddie Hills	*Billy Best*	Lesley Hicks	*Kevin Maher*
Sam Leveridge	*Kevin Maher*	James Falkingham	*Mike Marsh*
Phil Truscott	*Steve Tilson*	Dave Juniper	*Albert Wakefield*
Paul Livermore	*David Crown*	Paul Brice	*Billy Best*
Mr. Stanley E. Cox	*Kevin Maher*	Brian L. Moore	*Ron Pountney*
Steve Toms	*Stan Collymore*	Terry Hall	*Simon Royce*

Paul Edmonds	*Kevin Maher*	Colin Moody	*Paul Clark*
David Blockley	*Freddy Eastwood*	Alan Shuttleworth 1967 - present	*Billy Best*
Daniel Blockley	*Darryl Flahavan*	William Moore	*Darryl Flahavan*
Michael Ossowski	*Shaun Goater*	Peter Amass	*Billy Best*
Iain "Effy" Findlay	*Stan Collymore*	William Girt	*Freddy Eastwood*
Chris Findlay	*Jimmy McAlinden*	Matthew Nash	*Freddy Eastwood*
Jamie Finlinson	*Stan Collymore*	Alex Scott	*David Crown*
Paul Taylor	*Billy Best*	Mike Child	*Simon Royce*
Warren Sadler	*Adam Barrett*	Paul Posnack	*David Crown*
Anna & Warren Sadler	*Adam Barrett*	Mr. D. Doe	*Jimmy McAlinden*
Melvyn Buxton	*Steve Tilson*	Mr. Brian Gee	*Jimmy McAlinden*
Howard Graham	*Stan Collymore*	David Wilson	*Billy Best*
Graham Bridgeman-Clarke	*Stan Collymore*	Herman Munster	*Ron Pountney*
Leslie H Lesser	*Tony Hadley*	Alan Hale	*Mark Gower*
Richard Wordsworth	*Paul Clark*	Alan Cook	*Chris Powell*
Barry John Venus	*Billy Best*	Mark Folwell	*David Crown*
John Smith	*Brett Angell*	Steve Nead	*Billy Best*
Bill Messer	*Peter Watson*	Mark C. Smith	*Kevin Maher*
John J Coyle	*David Crown*	Ed Morgan	*Stan Collymore*
Colin Harris	*Billy Best*	Jonathan Thomas	*Freddy Eastwood*
Lewis Wilson	*Efe Sodje*	K. Adkinson	*Stan Collymore*
David Lillywhite	*Wayne Gray*	Dave Doo	*Steve Tilson*
Peter Coster	*Chris Powell*	Robert Whybrow	*Colin Morris*
Alan Collin	*Stan Collymore*	Billy Whybrow	*Darryl Flahavan*
James Quinn	*Kevin Maher*	Paul Harvey	*Alan Moody*
Paul Hutchinson	*Kevin Maher*	Mark Griffin	*Kevin Maher*
Ray Cracknell	*Harry Threadgold*	Claire Lister	*Andy Ansah*
Matt Eva	*Stan Collymore*	William N. Murphy	*Bill Garner*
Trevor Reynolds	*Steve Tilson*	Johnny Johnson	*Kevin Maher*
Joe Lachter	*Billy Best*	Gary Lockett	*Kevin Maher*
Jack Hardingham	*Jamal Campbell-Ryce*	The Kirk Family	*Kevin Maher*
Joey Hardingham	*Freddy Eastwood*	Daniel Deadman	*Simon Royce*
Edouard Robinson	*Efe Sodje*	Norman Salmon	*Richard Cadette*
Guy Hetherington	*Billy Best*	John Nixon	*Kevin Maher*
Darren Posnack	*Stan Collymore*	Stuart Hall	*Billy Best*
Mark Goodson	*Billy Best*	Odzey Hall	*Adam Barrett*
Daisy Stretton	*Freddy Eastwood*	Mazey Hall	*Freddy Eastwood*
Steven Hurren	*Mervyn Cawston*	Martin G. Browne	*Stan Collymore*
Gary Colbear	*Ron Pountney*	Keith Brace	*Stuart Brace*
Andy Thorne	*Paul Clark*	Geoff Manning	*Ron Pountney*
James Welham	*Freddy Eastwood*	Adrian Houghton	*Harry Threadgold*
Peter John Smith	*Eddie Firmani*	Bryan Woodford	*Billy Best*
Philip Spooner	*Sandy Anderson*	Richard Cunningham	*John McKinven*
Matthew Wells	*Chris Powell*	Michael D. Sayer	*Bill Garner*
Graeme Yetts	*Bill Garner*	Jason Freemantle	*Steve Tilson*
Paul Lowry	*Steve Tilson*	David Whybrow	*Billy Best*
Andrew Matthews	*Steve Tilson*	Jonathan Whybrow	*Peter Butler*
Rob Montier	*Alan Moody*	Alfie & Stanley Jeeves	*Darryl Flahavan*

A CENTURY UNITED

Sam & Jack Purnell	*Freddy Eastwood*	David John Flack	*Harry Lane*
Brian and Victoria Jeeves	*Ron Pountney*	David Mason	*Stan Collymore*
Katey J	*Steve Tilson*	Colin C. White	*Billy Best*
Benjamin Hall	*Freddy Eastwood*	Keith Riley	*Darryl Flahavan*
Simon Pope	*Steve Tilson*	Peter White "Whitey"	*Ron Pountney*
John Michie	*Steve Tilson*	Barbara Tolson	*Jimmy McAlinden*
Bill Knight	*Peter Butler*	Clare Crammond	*Steve Tilson*
Philip Long	*Leo Roget*	Lee and Daniel Venus	*Stan Collymore*
Keith Newquist	*Steve Tilson*	In Memory of Alf Player	*Billy Best*
Edward Norrington	*Jimmy McAlinden*	Terry Churn	*Billy Best*
Steven Norrington	*Chris Powell*	Mick Harvey	*Billy Best*
Charlie Finch	*Billy Best*	Simon Dodd	*Brett Angell*
Ron Bright	*Billy Best*	Steven Heath	*Richard Cadette*
Brian Denton	*Billy Best*	Terry Edwards	*Stan Collymore*
Jo Denton	*Paul Sansome*	Michael Arnold	*Kevin Maher*
Louis Langenberg	*Jamal Campbell-Ryce*	Katie Bale	*Richard Cadette*
Mr. John Harrison	*Billy Best*	Colin Pollard	*Ron Pountney*
Mr. Paul Harrison	*Steve Tilson*	John Simmons	*Peter Taylor*
Terry Colbourn	*Stan Collymore*	Steve Moore	*David Crown*
Neil Poulton	*Stan Collymore*	Allan Rounce	*Stan Collymore*
David Coulson	*Sam McCrory*	David Hancock	*David Crown*
Peter Jennings and		Jack Bond	*Billy Best*
Judi Babbage	*Ron Pountney*	Tim Sims	*Brett Angell*
Martin Croft	*Brett Angell*	Ian Atkins	*David Crown*
Michael Streat	*Stan Collymore*	Kelly Bishop	*Lewis Hunt*
Peter Chatterton	*Adam Barrett*	Alex Haynes	*Freddy Eastwood*
Ian Michael Murray	*Stan Collymore*	Penny Smith	*Freddy Eastwood*
Stephen Askew	*David Crown*	Ross Lister	*Jamal Campbell-Ryce*
Robert Askew	*Brett Angell*	Mike Tuttlebee	*Ron Pountney*
Neil Whitehead	*Kevin Maher*	Roy O'Sullivan	*Billy Best*
Maurice Tomline	*Stan Collymore*	Nicholas Gladwin	*Alan McCormack*
Anne Stevens	*David Crown*	John Hanks	*Eddie Firmani*
Colin and Jock Rutherford	*John McKinven*	Roy Bradley	*Billy Best*
Dean Allum	*Stan Collymore*	Oliver Priestley	*Stan Collymore*
Paul Strutt	*Brett Angell*	Paul Yeomanson	*Chris Powell*
David Fitzgerald	*Chris Powell*	John Freemantle	*Shaun Goater*
Kevin Eaton	*Ian Benjamin*	Richard Priestley	*Kevin Maher*
Mark Barrington Owen	*Ron Pountney*	Mark Taylor	*Keith Jones*
Charlie Woodbridge	*Kevin Maher*	Richard D. Smith	*Stan Collymore*
Phil Hollow	*Bob Jack*	Mike Smith	*Alan Moody*
Alan Watkins	*Billy Best*	Matthew Ridgwell	*Freddy Eastwood*
Elliott Hutchinson-Khupe	*Tony Bentley*	Ashley Durham	*Stan Collymore*
Tara Shepherd	*Tony Bentley*	Bert Ridgwell	*Richard Cadette*
Matt Francis	*Nicky Nicolau*	John & Charlotte Bridge	*Colin Morris*
Jim Simpson	*John McKinven*	Chris Toll	*Alan Moody*
Phil	*Brett Angell*	Tony Rogers	*Ron Pountney*
Paul Strutt	*Paul Sansome*	Mr I.P. Stammers	*Freddy Eastwood*
Bob and David Hill	*Roy Hollis*	Mark Warner	*Peter Butler*

Tom White
Calum Shepherd
Andy Knowles
Adam Brown
Simon Osborne
Greg Dearlove
Mark Edwards
Andy & Paula Leyh
Andy Skinner
David J.L. Warren
Chris Goulbourn
Nigel Rickard
Ken Evans
Paul Wood
Eddie Harding
Ray Sorrell
David Walden
Dave Russell
Nick Hart
Tony Ellis
Lester Pendrey
Brian Colbear
Dave Self
Pete Adcock
Nick Upton
Thomas Higgins
Timothy Higgins
Graham Hart
Bob Lilliman
James Mint
Philip James Rolls
Gary Townsend
James & Thomas
        Maynard
Malcolm Ostermeyer
Alan Nice
William John Hill
Peter Hill

Don Brown
Stephen Hutton
Dave Oram
Derek Lamb
Gordon Grout
Mick McConkey
Matthew Livermore
Daniel Scott
Alex Ball

Chris Powell
Darryl Flahavan
Simon Royce
Darryl Flahavan
Billy Best
Adam Barrett
Stan Collymore
Freddy Eastwood
Stan Collymore
Stan Collymore
Stan Collymore
Billy Best
Steve Tilson
Chico Hamilton
David Crown
Tony Bentley
Ron Pountney
Chris Powell
Richard Cadette
Billy Best
Kevin Maher
Ted Hankey
John McKinven
Billy Best
Adam Barrett
Freddy Eastwood
Freddy Eastwood
Billy Best
Bill Garner
Freddy Eastwood
Bill Garner
Billy Best

Freddy Eastwood
Billy Best
Stan Collymore
David Crown
Billy Best

Mick Mitchell
Dave Mitchell
Alex Jones
Ken Jones
Cleveland Key
Joe Skeels
Mr. Sid Morgan of Hamersley,
                Western Australia
Mr. Graeme Marinkovich of Kingsley,
                Western Australia
Natalie, David, Matthew & Lewis Oxley
Richard, Michelle, Zoë and Emma Smith
Roger Wash
Gary Robinson
John Ringrose
John Barber
Colin Sargant
Stalky
Bob Sills
Brian Worth
Anne Fitzgerald
Mickey Staines
William Davey
Christine Byford
Nigel Groves
Amy & Gina Perryman, and Rhys Thomas
Mike Davis
Ian Smith
Kevin Smith
Dave Alexander
Ian and Elaine Woolner
Basil Butler
Kitty Butler
Peter R. Butler
Rachel Butler
Penny Rolfe
The Farrance Family
Simon Harrison
David Morris
Deane Murray
J.W.D. Brealey
The Stafford Family

The player with the most "all-time favourite player" votes was Billy Best with 43, followed by Stan Collymore with 32, Freddy Eastwood with 26 and Kevin Maher with 20.